READING CUSANUS

**STUDIES IN PHILOSOPHY
AND THE HISTORY OF PHILOSOPHY**

General Editor: Jude P. Dougherty

**Studies in Philosophy
and the History of Philosophy   Volume 37**

Reading Cusanus
Metaphor and Dialectic in a Conjectural Universe

by Clyde Lee Miller

THE CATHOLIC UNIVERSITY OF AMERICA PRESS
Washington, D.C.

Copyright © 2003
The Catholic University of America Press
All rights reserved
Printed in the United States of America

The paper used in this publication meets the minimum requirements of American National Standards for Information Science—Permanence of Paper for Printed Library Materials, ANSI z39.48-1984.
∞

LIBRARY OF CONGRESS CATALOGING-IN-PUBLICATION DATA

Miller, Clyde Lee.
   Reading Cusanus : metaphor and dialectic in a conjectural universe /
by Clyde Lee Miller.
    p. cm. — (Studies in philosophy and the history of philosophy ; v. 37)
Includes bibliographical references (p.) and index.
ISBN 978-0-8132-3212-6 (alk. paper)
   1. Nicholas, of Cusa, Cardinal, 1401–1464. I. Title. II. Series.

B21 .S78 vol. 37
[B765.N54]
100s—dc21
[189'.5]

2001042474

Preface and Acknowledgments

The six chapters of this book present detailed readings of six of Nicholas of Cusa's major theoretical works that span the quarter century after he finished *De docta ignorantia* in 1440. The year 2001 marked the six hundredth anniversary of Nicholas' birth. I hope that these readings make it clear that Nicholas can speak to us still across the centuries.

In the Introduction I relate Nicholas' project to a well-known image from Plato's *Republic* and add some commentary on one of Nicholas' shortest dialogues, *De Deo abscondito*. Throughout I attempt to place Cusanus in the Christian Neoplatonic tradition, especially as embodied in Dionysius, Eriugena, Thierry of Chartres, and Meister Eckhart, since I believe that attempts to read him either as a late Scholastic Aristotelian or a proto-Kantian cannot be supported by the texts. Part of the difficulty for interpreters is that Cusanus draws on the whole previous tradition, while his original proposals anticipate important themes in post-Renaissance thought. He never hesitates to change and adapt what he inherited to his own purposes in any particular work. In any case, Nicholas is his own kind of Neoplatonist with a philosophical sensibility notably different from that of other Renaissance thinkers who were Platonists, such as Pico and Ficino.

This book draws some material from earlier essays I have published, but everything has been reworked for inclusion here. I quote Jasper Hopkins' translations of Nicholas' Latin in Chapters 1 and 4; otherwise, the translations are my own. I consulted both Hopkins' and H. L. Bond's English versions constantly. I used the Latin of the Heidelberg critical edition, except for *De visione Dei*, where I used Hopkins' critical edition.

The debts one accumulates over many years are numerous, so I apologize for omitting many of the mentors, colleagues, and students who have aided me, some in ways they did not and could not know. I thank everyone, but must name a few to whom I owe most. I am grateful to the students and faculty of the Philosophy Department at the State University of New York at Stony Brook and to members of the American Cusanus Society (and to its dauntless president, Morimichi Watanabe). Both groups listened patiently to early versions of several chapters. Karsten Harries introduced me to Cusanus twenty-five years ago and encouraged my earlier translation of Nicholas' *Idiota de mente*. I thank Louis Dupré and Jasper Hopkins for their encouragement and many kindnesses. Larry Bond made painstaking comments on my typescript, but probably failed to make me the intellectual historian he hoped for. I thank him and the other anonymous reviewer for their suggestions and corrections. Klaus Kremer of the Cusanus-Institut in Trier also encouraged me and provided some helpful corrections.

All of us studying Cusanus remain deeply indebted to the translations and interpretations of Hopkins and Bond. The late Ed Cranz and the late Tom McTighe both taught me much about Nicholas (and even more about being a Christian scholar). I hope they approve of what I have done. My former and present students Niall Caldwell, Bruce Milem, David Patton, and especially Aaron Smith made signal contributions at the beginning and the end of this project. My friends Roland Teske, David Burrell, Ed Casey, and John McDermott deserve thanks for their continuing faith in me. Finally, I thank my family for their love and patience. I dedicate this book with love to my wife, Ruth Kisch.

Stony Brook and Port Jefferson, N.Y.

READING CUSANUS

Introduction
God Unknown but Adored
De Deo abscondito (1444)

A convenient way to regard Nicholas of Cusa is to locate him in the history of thought as a transitional figure whose ideas both echo medieval themes and anticipate later ideas. But the historical placement of a thinker, however significant, may well miss the thrust and power of that person's thought.[1] Cusanus was out to do nothing less than "think God." For him thinking God was a heartfelt religious desire as well as an ambitious intellectual project. He wanted to "touch" the Divine beyond our best human conceptual knowledge and rational discourse.[2] His purpose, to quote his own paradoxical slogan or purpose from the letter that closes his masterpiece, *De docta ignorantia*, was to "embrace incomprehensibly incomprehensible things" (*incomprehensibilia incomprehensibiliter amplecterer;* h 263),[3] namely, the infathomable divine Mystery that transcends our limited and finite minds.

But "thinking God" may seem a Promethean, if not a Sisyphean, project. Is this not human self-assertion bordering on pride or arrogance, even if Nicholas always emphasizes that human minds are but finite images of the Divine, dependent on but hardly similar to God? Yet Cusanus never really veers from this path in any of his theoretical writings. Indeed, each dialogue or treatise may be read as employing one or more paradoxical symbols or formulae designed to conduct us dialecti-

---

1. On the other hand, H. Blumenberg's *The Legitimacy of the Modern Age*, trans. R. Wallace (Cambridge, Mass.: MIT Press, 1983), is an exemplary case of historically locating Nicholas and at the same time illuminating his ideas. Even more telling is K. Flasch's *Nikolaus von Kues: Geschichte einer Entwicklung* (Frankfurt am Main: V. Klostermann, 1998). While Cusanus serves Blumenberg's theoretical ends, Flasch is devoted to helping his readers understand how Nicholas' developing ideas are situated in his life and times.

2. Nicholas' earliest sermon, entitled "In principio erat Verbum," emphasizes these same themes at least a decade before *De docta ignorantia*. He writes: "Therefore, this God, so immense, remains unnameable, inexpressible, to the fullest degree unknowable" (*Sermo* 1 h 3). See Flasch, *Nikolaus von Kues*, 21–26.

3. Throughout I refer to paragraphs of the Heidelberg critical edition of Cusanus' works by "h" followed by the paragraph number.

cally to a threshold of direct cognitive access to God. I want to propose two ways to better understand this Cusan project. The first is to frame it philosophically by returning to its roots in Plato. The second is to situate it in Cusanus' own religious terms by looking closely at what Nicholas writes in his brief early dialogue, *De Deo abscondito*.

One of the best known sections of Plato's *Republic* occurs at the end of Book 6 where Socrates proposes to his interlocutors a second image, the image of the divided line, to accompany the first image representing the Good by the sun. The divided line represents a systematic vision of being and knowledge by means of the geometrical image of a line divided proportionally into four segments. Socrates uses the diagrammed image of the line to differentiate all there is and to relate the kinds of being as image and original. The line image also connects this articulation of what there is to four basic human cognitive attitudes and capacities. Two adjacent segments of the divided line (the longer part often depicted at the top of the line) correspond to what Socrates envisions as the realm of being, as opposed to that of becoming. The human cognitive capacities relevant here are *dianoia*, or discursive reason, and *noesis*, or intellectual intuition beyond such reasoning. Discursive reason deals with the things and images of the sensible world, relating them to the Forms, or originals of which they are images. *Noesis* goes beyond this and attempts to think the Forms themselves, their interconnections, and, finally, even the Good itself.[4]

Richard Rorty has suggested that we may understand philosophy in the West as poised between *noesis* and *dianoia*.[5] A good part of what philosophers have always done and still do is to become masters of discursive reasoning. They use understanding or reason to arrange the familiar and relative things of our experience in comprehensive and elegant patterns. Indeed, scholars in every field of the humanities and social sciences present arguments, or at least informed and sophisticated discussions, that attempt to describe and redescribe, to order and think through the items of human experience and their contexts. But in principle, at the level of *dianoia*, everything is contextualized. Everything is open to redescription and alternate conceptualizations. As Nicholas would put it later, our best knowledge that is truthful is conjectural.

Yet there is a tension in the divided line between *dianoia* and *noesis*.

---

4. J. Klein gives a telling exposition of the image of the divided line in *A Commentary on Plato's "Meno"* (Chapel Hill: University of North Carolina Press, 1965), 112–25.

5. Rorty presented these ideas at a conference on the nature of philosophy at Yale University in 1998.

We cannot limit our philosophical efforts merely to discursive reason without betraying a part of our heritage. However much philosophers love to describe and characterize, to categorize and analyze, to reason logically and present the most perspicuous case they can muster, there is another philosophical attitude that Aristotle captured in his well-known remark (following Thales) that philosophy begins in wonder. Another constant effort of thinkers in the West has been to get in contact with the unfamiliar and the ineffable, to point beyond to what resists categorization, even if they cannot easily talk about this or argue back and forth about it. (The irony of using discursive reason to speak about what is beyond it was not lost on Socrates when he refused Glaucon's request in the *Republic* that he characterize the Good.) Yet precisely what lies beyond the relative and conditioned items of our experience—what transcends the discourse of the professors, so to speak—may well be of most urgent concern.

Whether one speaks here of a drive to the absolute and unconditioned, or recognizes this concern as evidence of our natural human desire to know, the fourth segment of the divided line, *noesis*, may stand for a particular moment or juncture in a thinker's efforts. This is the moment when one realizes that, for all *we* do in dealing discursively with the realm of the relative and the finite, in fact many may enter philosophy (and theology) with the hope that *philosophy* will do something to us. *Dianoia*, discursive thinking, dialogue, and philosophical conversation deal with the rather familiar things of ordinary experience, even when they reconstruct or deconstruct their ordinary construals.

But *noesis* thinks beyond such things and attempts to contact the unfamiliar—what transcends normal human experience. It leaves behind the realm of more and less, better and worse, to seek the best, the maximum, or the infinite. If the tone of discursive reason is businesslike and efficient, the tone of thinking beyond such discourse is one of being awestruck, of being a captive of wonder. To understand Nicholas of Cusa, we must not forget this second moment, even in philosophy, where one loses one's grip because one is gripped by something else, something rather different than any or all of the things "dreamed of in our philosophy."

From such a perspective, one can see the genius of Plato. He did justice both to *dianoia*, or discursive thinking, and to *noesis*, the realm of the nondiscursive and nonrepresentational—moreover, his ideas of image and original preserved the connection and tension between them. There is a similar doctrinal contrast among many of his Neoplatonic descendants, so we cannot be surprised to discover that Nicholas of Cusa also systematically connects and contrasts *ratio* (= *dianoia*) and *intellectus* (= *noesis*), contracted finites with the infinite Absolute, the creaturely realm of more and less with that qualitative Maximum, the Creator.

Placing the Cusan project of thinking God in relation to Plato's initiation of philosophical thinking in the West may not rescue Nicholas' pursuit from the charge of arrogant or prideful self-assertion, something of which every working philosopher may sometimes plead guilty. But Nicholas' thought is as Christian as it is Neoplatonist. And that makes it fitting to turn to *De Deo abscondito*,[6] both to see how Nicholas conducts us to the threshold of thinking God and to understand what rescues his efforts, however Promethean, from overstepping the bounds of the all-too-human.

De Deo abscondito opens by setting a humble scene and thereupon discussing a puzzle. A pagan finds a Christian prostrated in prayer and shedding heartfelt tears. Let me propose at once that in this scene both "pagan" and "Christian" may stand for Nicholas and each of us, his readers, however much he may privilege the Christian. In any case, this context of worship must not be overlooked, especially since it leads to a puzzling question that drives the conversation between the two men: How does one adore a God whom one does not know, of whom one is ignorant? "*Quomodo tanto serio adoras quod ignoras?*" (h 1).

The initial interchanges are somewhat clipped, if not curt, but they serve to transform what is an apparent puzzle or paradox into a real conundrum: How can one adore God unless one at least thinks that one knows that God? This is, of course, quite backward for Nicholas. His question is rather this: How can one think one knows the God whom one adores?! His Christian turns the conversation in that direction by opposing what one *thinks* one knows to what one *knows* one does *not* know. It is pure Cusanus *not* to oppose what one thinks one knows to what one knows one knows—but rather to oppose what one thinks one knows to what one knows one does *not* know! Thinking one knows God amounts to claiming knowledge where nothing can be known, at least not by human knowers.[7]

How are we to make this out? To say one knows is to say one grasps

---

6. There are two fine English versions of this work of the early 1440s: J. Hopkins translates it in his *A Miscellany on Nicholas of Cusa* (Minneapolis, Minn.: Banning Press, 1994), 131–37, and H. L. Bond translates it in *Nicholas of Cusa: Selected Spiritual Writings* (New York: Paulist Press, 1997), 209–13. Both translators add helpful notes and brief discussions. For brief commentary, see R. Haubst, *Streifzüge in die cusanische Theologie* (Münster: Aschendorff, 1991), 79–82, 89–95.

7. Cusanus means that we cannot know God's nature at all—*what* God is. Obviously he believes that we can acknowledge cognitively (either on the basis of religious faith or on the basis of reason) *that* God is, that God exists.

the truth. "But truth can only be grasped through itself" (h 3), not in another, says the Christian. When we challenge the meaning of this dark saying, we discover that the truths we think we know about things are not essential to them, matters of their true quiddity, but rather incidental and external differences we discern and name, using *ratio* to organize and parse the world. The paradigm of knowledge at issue and in the background here is nothing less than understanding of essence, a grasp of what something is, its essential truth. It is this of which we are ignorant, and, if we are ignorant of the true essence of every limited creature, a fortiori, the essence of their unlimited Creator—Truth Itself— cannot be known.

Our knowledge of incidental features merely samples our true firstorder human knowledge of finite things when we use "know" in our strongest sense of *true* discursive knowledge. The dialogue's example of the stone or the human being (h 4) never mentions the rest of our opinions and beliefs about the ordinary world. Instead, Cusanus at once turns to a single vulnerable second-order belief. He highlights our illusory conviction that we think we know what cannot be known.

The puzzle and conundrum at the start of the dialogue arise because his pagan has made the mistake of all those who do not appreciate the difference between the two upper segments of Plato's divided line, that is, the difference between discursive thinking and intellectual intuition. They believe that what can be said or known truly in rational discourse exhausts the truth; indeed, they believe finally not in Truth with a capital *T*, so to speak, but in many truths, all beginning with lowercase *t*. The lesson of the divided line is not to collapse *dianoia* and *noesis;* rather, it is to keep them distinct and in tension, in Nicholas' words, so that no truth may exist apart from Truth: *"nam extra veritatem non est veritas"* (for outside of Truth there is no truth; h 3).

This is why Nicholas has the pagan ask: "Is there one truth or many truths?" The Christian's reply is worth careful notice:

There is only one. For there is only one oneness and truth coincides with oneness since it is true that oneness is one. . . . and whoever does not attain truth in oneness can truly know not a thing. And even though a person thinks that he knows truly, he experiences easily that what he thinks he knows can be known more truly. For something visible can be seen more truly than it is seen by you, for it is seen more truly by sharper eyes. Therefore it is not seen by you as it can be seen in truth. . . . But since everything that is known is also known not by that knowledge by which it *can* be known, it is not known in truth but otherwise and in another way—but truth is not known otherwise and in some other way than the way in which truth itself is. Hence a person is out of his head who thinks that he knows something in truth but does not know truth. (h 5, emphasis added; compare Bond, 210, Hopkins, 132–33)

Nicholas' words preserve in a striking fashion the tension between the many truths of discursive reason and the single Truth of *intellectus* (= *noesis*). The many truths are all the things we rightly know that we know—not through that knowledge by which they *can* be known in themselves and essentially, but *"aliter,"* otherwise, that is, partially, and *"in alio,"* in another way, that is, in something that is other or in a merely human way. Yet these humanly cognized aspects of the finite world, however carefully qualified and ordered, are finally not known in their most basic context—where truth and oneness coincide. Discursive reason, of course, is required if we are to discriminate and relate the contents of what we know in giving a rational account. Yet that reason can remain blind to any further or greater context as it gathers and sorts its many "little" truths, while we remain unaware of the one "large" Truth, so to speak.

For Cusanus all that we know truly is situated within the larger horizon of Truth itself. To refer to Plato's divided line once more, *dianoia* (Cusan *ratio*) and its objects are images of and participate in *noesis/intellectus* and its objects. *Intellectus* is not merely *in ratio*, any more than the soul is *in* the body. Rather body is in soul, *ratio* is in *intellectus*, the truths we grasp are in Truth itself. The originals encompass their images just the way that the Truth encompasses the truths, the way the infinite God encompasses finite creatures.[8]

To claim to know the encompassed without acknowledging the divine Encompassing is as foolish for Cusanus as pretending to differentiate between colors without any awareness of what color itself comes to. It is to refuse to move beyond the relative and the conditioned (what Nicholas terms the "contracted") when the human capacity for transcendence already points to the Absolute and the Unconditioned. What I think I know can be known more truly once I press beyond *dianoia/ratio*, for the Cusan conviction is that only in God is the true meaning and oneness of everything to be found.

But to know more truly, to be someone "deemed knowing" (in Bond's felicitous rendering of *"censendus est sciens"*; h 6), is exactly to know one's ignorance while reverencing that transcendent divine Truth. It is to "know that without *that* truth one can grasp nothing" (h 6, emphasis added; Bond, 210; Hopkins, 133). One worships the God who is unspeakable Truth—the absolute, pure, eternal Oneness of Godself that cannot be communicated. This Oneness is not the oneness found in God's works and manifest in number and plurality.

---

8. An alternate way of understanding how God encompasses all other realities is to recall that God has traditionally been identified as "the fullness of being," and then to ask rhetorically "where" other beings are ontologically situated.

All we know is not God; all we conceive is unlike God because God exceeds every other possible and actual thing. Yet God is not nothing, even though nothing itself has the name "no thing." He is not something either, because he is no more some one thing than he is all things. No human definition encompasses him. God transcends both something and nothing because his omnipotence exceeds in power both what exists and what does not exist so that whether something exists or not is ultimately and proximately his doing. Therefore, he is none of the other things that are, but prior to each and all as their Source. *"Et ob hoc non potest potius dici hoc quam illud, cum ab ipso sint omnia"* (For this reason God also cannot be said to be this rather than that, since from him exist all things; h 9; Bond, 211; Hopkins, 134).

At this point it is worth noting how Cusanus has moved from not knowing God to specifying that God is not one among the other kinds of beings designated and known by *ratio*. Now he will take up explicitly how to speak of God. From this point *De Deo abscondito* will examine the question of naming or speaking of God. What is so telling about this dialogue is that in a brief space it weaves together knowing, being, and speaking—the ancient triad of words and thoughts and things that philosophers find inescapable, however much philosophical history in the West has emphasized one or another of the three. In this dialogue all three have an important place, but to reach their full significance we must reflect on what we are doing. What we can know and how we can speak must change once we move beyond the level of discursive reason and our usual understandings of the things that are mere images of what Plato called the Forms. To be an image is not to be an original, and to think or speak of paradigms or exemplars as if they were images is to distort both the reality and the dialectical connectedness of both.

The Christian explains to the pagan that, of course, we can label and engage in discourse about our little truths, about that world filled "with the grandeur of God." It is only the inconceivable divine Grandeur that remains unspeakable. But God is not merely unspeakable. As cause of all that can be spoken, God also is speakable beyond everything else that is. Nor is the Christian caught in the contradiction that God is both effable and ineffable. The reason is that God's simpleness is prior to the discursive thinking and finite beings that are the basis, or *radix*, of the principle of noncontradiction. Discourse about God must elude the limits of ordinary speaking. Therefore, it is not the case that God is either named or not named *and* it is not the case that God is both named and not named. Neither conjunction nor disjunction applies to God's transcendent infinity, for the simple Infinity that surpasses differentiation stands as the one principle prior to every thought that can be formed of or directed toward God.

At this Cusanus' pagan returns to the question of God's being. The Christian's responses parallel those made about naming God. It is not true that God is nothing or that God does not exist, nor is it true both that God does exist and that God does not exist. God is rather the transcendent Source and Origin of all principles of existing and not existing. But because in this case both denial and affirmation are true, the Christian must add that God is source and God is not source. Here we have to notice how important the principle of contradiction remains at the level of discursive reason. Rationality and standard logic and the usual ways in which we think and talk referentially remain inescapable for *dianoia/ratio*. But at the level of *noesis/intellectus* we stand them on their heads, so to speak. As a consequence, saying that God is transcendent Source cannot remain on a par with someone remarking, for instance, that a therapist is a responsive guide.

Our language about transcendence tends to rigidify and misbehave, as it were, because of its proximity to our language about the ordinary world and especially to our ways of talking about the less perceptible and unseen aspects of everyday experience. Talking about God, even using the language of worship, can become another case of using discourse inattentively and automatically, as if God were just one more item in history, culture, and experience. We slip back into the typical thinking and talking that befit *dianoia/ratio* and our finite condition. That is why even our most careful attempts to think and speak God may well betray what can be known, said, and thought about the divine Mystery.

So the Christian proceeds to repeat himself again, this time because the pagan asks whether God is truth. The answer is that God is not truth because God is prior to all truth. Yet God is not other than truth because God is without otherness. God is in fact prior to all we name or conceive as truth in unlimited transcendence. Even to name God "God" is not to say something either true or false, nor is it to say something both true and false—God's simpleness is ontologically prior to all that can or cannot be said and named. Once again the difference between *ratio* and *intellectus* is at work in our thinking and talking. What has happened in the dialogue is that language and thought have run up against what is not limited or finite. Thinking and speaking must resort to paradox and to the refusal either to avow or disavow or to avow and not avow—lest the God to be adored be betrayed and the divine Mystery be obscured by human mystification.

God is named "God," the Christian says, on the basis of a likeness. In fact this likeness or parallel is a kind of proportion suggested by a fanciful etymology. *Deus* ("God"), the Christian alleges, comes from the Greek *theoro* and is thus equivalent to the Latin *video*, or "I see."⁹ Cusanus therefore argues that, as the power of sight is to visible colors, so God is to created things. Because of Aristotle's remarks about vision in the *De anima*, it became a medieval commonplace that we perceive color with a colorless organ that is not itself the object of vision, but is invisible to the eye.¹⁰ For Cusanus, it is the invisible *power* of vision, the capacity to see, not just the physical organ, that is the issue here, just as it is in his parallel exposition in *De quaerendo Deum*.¹¹ In the domain of things visible and colored, vision is not to be found nor is it given the name of any of the colors. In the realm of the colored (and extended), vision thus counts as nothing rather than something. Yet it is through the discriminations made by unnamed and unseen vision that every color seen is named.

In a parallel way, the various created things are made by the unnameable and invisible God. This Cusan parallel has its limitations, of course, because of the fact that, unlike God, vision is named and understood by discursive thought, no less than the colored extended things we perceive. But just as discursive thinking grasps realities unavailable to visual perception, so Cusan *intellectus* touches what *ratio* barely fathoms.

The dialogue ends with the pagan drawing out the parallels between vision and God. God, too, is not to be found or named in the realm of creatures but escapes or transcends every concept affirmed here. Created things are all composite beings and it is to such things that all our names and our language primarily refer. Such things do not derive from themselves but are fashioned by the One prior to all composition and responsible for all composite things being what they are. Within that domain the God who is simpleness and incomposite remains unknown—hidden from the eyes of all the wise of this world.

By the dialogue's end Cusanus' pagan has learned to distinguish the two relevant levels of the divided line.¹² He has come to see how the language, conceptions, and limited realities handled by *dianoia/ratio* be-

---

9. Cusanus uses this same etymology in *De quaerendo Deum* 1 h 19; *De visione Dei* 1 h 6, h 8, h 33; *De li non aliud* 23 h 104.

10. Commentators on *De anima* 2.7.418b26 dispute whether Aristotle meant the pupil or the "eye jelly" behind it.

11. *De quaerendo Deum*, h 19–24. See also J. Hopkins' notes to his translation, in *Miscellany*, 289–92.

12. One important difference from Plato's *Republic* is that Socrates teaches that the philosopher-rulers, at least, will be able to "see" the forms using their capacity for *noesis*; for Nicholas of Cusa intellectual vision of God does not amount to precise conceptual knowledge of divinity.

come words unsayable, thoughts beyond thoughts, and reality unlimited as we attempt to approach through *noesis* the infinite God. This mysterious One is the God who is to be praised and adored.

"Thinking God" may stand as a slogan for the Cusan enterprise. But such thinking is hardly something Nicholas believes we can accomplish once and for all—nor will it deliver precise conceptual knowledge of what God is. This cannot be another project of human cognitive self-assertion attempting to overreach itself. As Nicholas states at the beginning of *De docta ignorantia*, *desiderium naturale* (natural desire) may thrust us forward, but our *iudicium cognatum* (innate judgment) allows us to recognize in what ways we must remain ignorant and turn to adoration. In adoration this dialogue leaves dramatic room for transformation or conversion, for the realization that in *noesis* human knowers are known even more than knowing, that they are encompassed by the very One who escapes both the reach and the grasp of human concepts.

In this way Cusanus' pagan and his Christian may fairly represent not two separate people but the two sorts of ignorance in everyone who attempts to think God. One kind is the straightforward ignorance of what God is—in this respect we are all pagans, as it were. The second sort of ignorance involves the recognition that God cannot be the sort of thing we could possibly know—and this is a Christian insight expressed eloquently many times over the centuries.[13] This is Cusan learned ignorance, the second-order recognition that we cannot know what God is. Part of what makes this knowledge that is ignorance learned, however, is that it preserves the tension between discursive knowledge and some sort of knowledge or vision beyond *ratio*. Learned ignorance is not simply a combination of first- and second-order ignorance.

That we may correctly assume we are all Nicholas' pagan as well as his Christian finds some corroboration at the dialogue's end. When the pagan says, *"Sit igitur deus . . . benedictus"* (Let God therefore be blessed; h 15), are we not returned to the dialogue's beginning? There the pagan

---

13. Augustine gives eloquent expression to our inadequacy in speaking of God in *De doctrina Christiana* 1.6:

> Have we spoken or announced anything worthy of God? Rather I feel that I have done nothing but wish to speak: if I have spoken, I have not said what I wished to say. Whence do I know this except because God is ineffable? If what I said were ineffable, it would not be said. And for this reason God should not be said to be ineffable, for when this is said, something is said. And a contradiction in terms is created, since if that is ineffable which cannot be spoken, then that is not ineffable which can be called ineffable. This contradiction is to be passed over in silence rather than resolved verbally. (*On Christian Doctrine*, trans. D. W. Robertson Jr. [Indianapolis, Ind.: Bobbs-Merrill, 1958], 10–11)

The contradiction or paradox Augustine here lays out may result precisely from conflating *noesis* and *dianoia*, as well as first- and second-order discourse about God.

saw the Christian prostrated in prayer and adoration—the religious wonder at what exceeds reason. In Nicholas the philosophical tension between reason and what lies beyond issues in worship. That is why the pagan's initial question and the Christian's response stand as a Cusan challenge to all who read this dialogue, and perhaps to Christians especially. *"Quaero, quis es?"* (Who *are* you?). *"Christianus sum. . . . Quia ignoro, adoro"* (I am Christian and, because I do not know, I adore; h 1).

1

Envisioning the Whole
De docta ignorantia (1440)

BOOK 1: HUMAN KNOWLEDGE AND GOD

As its title signals, Nicholas of Cusa's *On Learned Ignorance* is distinctive in taking as its theme "ignorance" or *lack* of knowledge of a certain sort. Making knowledge central differentiates Cusanus from his medieval predecessors. Most of them never questioned the belief they inherited from antiquity that independent things outside thought are epistemologically prior and stand as thought's norm and measure. Without denying any of those beliefs, Cusanus turns first to the human mind and its inadequacies, particularly when it comes to knowing God. Human capacities for coming to know even created things are inadequate to our desire to know, our questioning, and our wonderment. As Nicholas puts it, "The exactness of the connections in bodily things and the suitable fitting of known to unknown exceed human reason" (1.1 h 4, my translation).[1]

1A. Knowledge, Measurement, and Learned Ignorance

The early chapters of *De docta ignorantia* raise several points worth emphasizing. One is the way Cusanus frames our acquisition of knowledge after the model of measurement. A second is his framing God as the "absolute Maximum" and using the "coincidence of opposites" to mark

---

1. All translations in this chapter are taken from J. Hopkins, *Nicholas of Cusa on Learned Ignorance*, 2nd ed. (Minneapolis, Minn.: Banning Press, 1985); any modifications are noted *ad loc*. Hopkins' critical appraisal of *De docta ignorantia* forms the "Introduction" to his translation. Bond's recent translation in The Classics of Western Spirituality series is preceded by a discussion focusing on the themes of learned ignorance and the "coincidence of opposites"; see *Nicholas of Cusa*, 19–31. For a striking overview of the whole work, see Flasch, *Nikolaus von Kues*, 44–70, 97–120; for its historical context, see H. L. Bond, "Nicholas of Cusa from Constantinople to 'Learned Ignorance': The Historical Matrix for the Formation of the *De docta ignorantia*," in *Nicholas of Cusa on Christ and the Church*, ed. G. Christianson and T. M. Izbicki (Leiden: Brill, 1996), 135–63.

God's transcendence. The third is his appeal to geometrical illustrations and examples to move our minds through and beyond the realm of the perceptible, the imaginable, and the conceptual. All three are characteristic moves; all embody Cusan assumptions; all build into his procedures a propensity to employ symbols and metaphors in a way that aids dialectical thinking.

A clear illustration of such thinking occurs in 1.3. There Cusanus compares the human intellect's relation to the truth with the relation between a polygon and a circle in which it is inscribed. Even if we were to increase the number of the polygon's sides so that it appears almost circular, the polygon would never become equivalent to the circle unless it was "resolved into an identity with the circle." The human intellect likewise "never comprehends the truth so exactly that it cannot be comprehended infinitely more exactly" (1.3 h 10, my translation).

With this illustration Cusanus is not merely saying that there is always more to be known and understood for human knowers. Rather, the example demonstrates (1) the Cusan ideal of knowledge (the identity of knower and known), (2) the Cusan use of mathematics in directing imagination and thought, and (3) the basic limitation that keeps "ignorance" bound up with human knowledge, namely, our inability to achieve the identity with intelligible truth our minds desire. Recognizing and coping with our limited status is what first of all constitutes our ignorance "learned."[2]

For Cusanus, then, the ideal of truth amounts to an identity of knower and known conceived after the fashion of mathematical exactness. But because we are not divine, our limited minds are not one or identical with the things we attempt to know, since "whatever is not truth cannot measure truth exactly" (1.3 h 10, my translation). Though we can never reach it except in mathematics, we can at best approach the condition of precise truth asymptotically—the way we can imagine that a polygon approaches identity with its circumscribing circle as the number of its sides is continuously increased.

What view of human knowledge is understood here? In knowing we use "the means of comparative relation [*proportio*]" aimed at "the suitable fitting of unknown to known" (1.1 h 3, 4, my translation).[3] The background metaphor is one of quantitative measurement. (See Figure

---

2. On the meaning of "learned ignorance," see Hopkins' *Learned Ignorance*, 2–3; see also various essays in K. Jacobi, ed., *Nikolaus von Kues: Einführung in sein philosophisches Denken* (Munich: Alber, 1979), which hereafter will be cited as K. Jacobi, ed., *Einführung*. Flasch emphasizes that insight into our not-knowing is knowledge and proposes an interpretative translation of *docta ignorantia* as "Nicht-Wissen als Wissen"; see *Nikolaus von Kues*, 97.

3. U. Offermann, *Christus—Wahrheit des Denkens* (Münster: Aschendorff, 1991), 30–32.

FIGURE 1.1 Measurement: The elements and senses of *mensura*

Items to be measured
Units of measure
Doing the measuring
Results or measurements taken

1.1.) Human knowing should be seen as "taking the measure" of what it attempts to know.[4] In coming to know, our minds do the *measuring*, the relating and discriminating required. We fashion or select the *units of measure* and employ them, while the things we attempt to know in such cognitive measuring stand as *the items to be measured*. The knowledge we gain is equivalent to *the measure taken*. This is not to deny, of course, that the things we attempt to know are themselves norms or measures for cognition in the same way the circle "measures" the polygon's approach. They stand as the referents of what we want to know and as limits or ideal norms for the adequacy of the measures we take.[5]

Such measure taking occurs in at least two ways. The first is the direct, or first-order, measuring of something we investigate. Second comes the reflective, or second-order, consideration where one "measures" one's first measuring, so to speak. Here occurs "learned ignorance": the realization that one's best attempts at knowing fall short of that ideal identity where measurer and measured are one. Cusanus' initial strictures on human knowing are directed to this second-order consideration of knowing as measuring. The illustration of the expanding inscribed polygon is calculated to let us understand the general relation of measuring mind (expanding polygon) and item measured (unattained and unattainable circle), and the dialectical movement in our cognitive efforts.

Cusanus looks to mathematics for help because he believes that mathematics is exact and certain since mathematics is the human mind's own construction. He writes as he begins:

all those who make an investigation judge the uncertain proportionally, by means of a comparison with what is taken to be certain. Therefore, every in-

---

4. For contrasting discussions of the idea of *mensura* in Cusanus, see J. Hopkins, *Nicholas of Cusa on Wisdom and Knowledge* (Minneapolis, Minn.: Banning Press, 1996), 44–49; M. Stadler, "Zum Begriff der *mensuratio* bei Cusanus. Ein Beitrag zur Ortung der cusanischen Erkenntnislehre," in *Mensura, Mass, Zahl, Zahlensymbolik im Mittelalter*, 2 vols., ed. A. Zimmermann (New York: de Gruyter, 1983), 1:118–31.

5. Aristotle (*Metaphysics* 10.1.1053a) and Aquinas also appealed to measurement in discussing human cognition. In *De veritate* 1.5, Aquinas explains how God measures creatures and creatures measure human knowledge. We are to understand God as measuring and yet ever beyond human measures when Nicholas "names" God the "Maximum."

quiry is comparative and uses the means of comparative relation.... But since comparative relation indicates an agreement in some one respect and, at the same time, indicates an otherness, it can not be understood independently of number. (1.1 h 2–3)

"Comparative relation" translates the Latin *proportio*. When we use a proportion in mathematics, for instance, A:B::B:D or A:B::C:D, we may discover the last term (D) when we are aware of the relation between the terms, for a three- or four-term proportion indicates "agreement" in the relation, even though the two sets of terms are *different* (Cusanus' "otherness"). But when we apply the term more generally to inquiry, *proportio* may also suggest, given the illustration of the circle and the inscribed polygon, that acquiring knowledge involves the active shaping or proportioning of our measures to better fit what is measured.

This suggestion will mislead us if we assume that in cognition we have independent access to both measure and measured, the way we do when we use a yardstick or a ruler. In everyday situations both measuring tool and item to be measured are separately available to perception and judgment. This is not the case with human knowledge for Cusanus: often our access to what we want to know and measure is only through the cognitive measures we select, even though we can assess such measures independently. The difference or "otherness" between conceptual measure and nonconceptual measured prevents knowledge from being completely adequate to the task. Since this fundamental "otherness" is incorrigible and discloses our limited status, our best efforts as knowers leave more to be done and much to be desired.

1B. Reaching Toward the Unknowable God

Nicholas of Cusa is most concerned with understanding the four central Christian realities: God, the created universe, human beings, and Christ. *De docta ignorantia* devotes an explicit book to three of these, while human beings pervade the whole. Cusanus believes that every cognitive measure we employ will be inadequate in the case of the finite things of our experience. A fortiori, when it comes to knowing the infinite God, the gap that opens so confines our knowledge that it amounts to ignorance. But this is not the ignorance of one who lacks knowledge or of those who are merely thoughtless. Understanding and appreciating our ignorance regarding God involves grasping the reasons for it. Only then do we achieve reflective, educated, that is, explicitly "learned ignorance."

To stress the incommensurability between our cognitive measures and the Divine, Nicholas proposes a regulative principle he believes obvious and never rejects: "It is self-evident that there is no comparative relation [*proportio*] of the infinite to the finite" (1.3 h 9).[6] One way to interpret *De docta ignorantia* (and all his writings about God) is as a series of creative proposals that help us reach toward the God who is ever beyond our grasp.

Cusan learned ignorance recalls Socratic ignorance. Both involve recognizing and acknowledging that one does not know something of great importance.[7] In Plato's dialogues knowledge of virtue or courage or piety was conceived as knowledge of essence or nature (and ultimately of a Form, or *Eidos*) that could be expressed in a definition. Definitional knowledge of essence also forms the background ideal of knowledge for Cusanus. Like Plato's Socrates in the *Meno*, Cusanus viewed mathematical definitions as paradigm cases of knowledge. Because the numbers and figures of mathematics are not subject to change, mathematical definitions exemplify in a paradigmatic way an identity between the definition, say, of a circle or an odd number and any token circle or odd number. Here the cognitive proportioning provides an exact fit, so to speak.

By contrast, in the nonmathematical realm of the natural universe we are limited to finding a proportional fit that is more or less accurate. Furthermore, dealing with the infinite Creator leaves us at a complete impasse because of the in-principle incommensurability already mentioned. No wonder Cusanus points out that language about God must follow suit: "someone who desires to grasp the meaning must elevate his intellect above the import of the words rather than insisting upon the proper significations of words which cannot be properly adapted to such great intellectual mysteries" (1.2 h 8). Such considerations commit Nicholas to a metaphorical use of language and symbols in order to propose less inadequate ways to know God and creatures. To follow Cusan thought is to confront one's inadequacy in knowing God and to be willing to entertain various proposals rather than any final story about how such matters stand. Human minds are not divine and so do not penetrate the true natures of things.

1C. Maximum and Coincidence

In chapter 4 Nicholas sets to work to apply what he has already explained in chapters 1–3 about our cognitive abilities and their limitations to the case of knowing God, whom he terms the "absolute Maximum." This is a way of "naming" God that is connected with what Nicholas already argued about our knowing capacities. We humans

---

6. For a listing of various texts where Cusanus states this principle, see W. Schulze, *Zahl, Proportion, Analogie* (Münster: Aschendorff, 1978), 55–57.

7. T. Van Velthoven, *Gottesschau und menschliche Kreativität* (Leiden: Brill, 1977), 43–47.

Contents

Preface and Acknowledgments	vii
Introduction: God Unknown but Adored: *De Deo abscondito* (1444)	1
1. Envisioning the Whole: *De docta ignorantia* (1440)	12
2. Conjecturing Oneness and Otherness: *De coniecturis* (1442–1443)	68
3. Metaphors for Mind: *Idiota de mente* (1450)	110
4. The Dialectic of Seeing Being Seen Seeing: *De visione Dei* (1453)	147
5. Not Other Than Divine: *De li non aliud* (1461)	180
6. Possibility and Divine Prey: *De venatione sapientiae* (1463)	206
Reprise and Conclusions	241
Bibliography	257
Index	267

come to know in a realm where what we achieve as knowers is always a matter of more or less, *plus aut minus;* we never reach perfection, a most or a maximum. Whether we employ sense perception, imagination, or reason, our measuring fits best the finite realm of created things. Even here we never attain or obtain complete accuracy, never achieve absolute parity between our concepts and judgments and what we seek to know. There always remains inequality, always difference, always otherness between what we attempt and what we grasp. In this way our knowing shares and reflects the ontological status of all the created things it attempts to know.

If such limits mark the ontological status of created things and our capacity to know them, all the more do they come into play with regard to the actual truth of things, that is, the Maximum, their (and our) Creator. God remains disproportionate, too—infinitely removed from what we are obviously designed to know. Precisely *this* is what Nicholas teaches that we should come to know about our ignorance. Yet recognizing and acknowledging our ignorance regarding God is not as far as human knowledge can go. For Cusanus, this very recognition lets us draw closer to divine truth—we are to attain or touch it *incomprehensibiliter*. The puzzle is what such "touching" comes to, for apparently Nicholas is not speaking of some mystical undertaking or special experience, even if he does not exclude them explicitly.[8]

Nicholas proceeds in chapter 4 with expressions that recall St. Anselm's *Proslogion*. Beginning with the absolute Maximum is beginning with something than which there cannot be a greater. But Nicholas is not Anselm; he adds at once that the Maximum is as well that than which there cannot be a *lesser*. The Cusan Maximum is thus at one and the same time the minimum. Why? The Maximum escapes the scale of more and less because it transcends all finites. If greatness and smallness are now equivalent ontologically to both infinite *and* infinitesimal, we have not only left the realm of the quantitative, we have moved to an utterly different sort of reality.[9] Nicholas' own reason lets us see what kind of reality: *"cum sit omne id quod esse potest"* (since it is every thing that can be; 1.4 h 11, my translation). (And it is everything *it* can be, as well, hints the ambiguous Latin.) Where Maximum is minimum the possible is identically the actual. In this way Nicholas prevents anyone from

---

8. As Flasch (*Nikolaus von Kues*, 103) points out, not-knowing hardly leads to skepticism for Cusan thought; rather, it transforms the content of all we claim to know of God, of the world, and of human knowledge.

9. Hopkins comments that Nicholas' point here (that God is beyond all oppositions) overrides any fallacies in his argument; see *Learned Ignorance*, 5–6, and *A Concise Introduction to the Philosophy of Nicholas of Cusa*, 3rd ed. (Minneapolis, Minn.: Banning Press, 1986), 10–11.

thinking that God is merely the highest point on some hierarchical scale of finites, whether possible or actual.

The Cusan God also counts as absolute equality, since God encompasses all possible and actual creatures and penetrates each. Here Nicholas parts company with the usual medieval hierarchies of creatures and their degrees of ontological goodness. Each created thing, however we compare it to other things, is infinitely distant from and infinitely close to the creator—*"a nulla est alia et diversa"* (From nothing is it [the Maximum] other or different; 1.4 h 11, my translation). While we find no precise equality between creatures when we measure them, neither do we find objective degrees of ontological goodness or perfection, except by using norms that reflect our human viewpoint. So Nicholas writes that "all things exist in the best way they are able" (*omnia sunt eo meliori modo quo esse possunt;* 1.5 h 13; 1.1 h 2).[10] Creatures do not constitute higher and lower ontological levels apart from our construals. In Cusan Neoplatonism we have God; we have creatures; but there are no Neoplatonic hypostases as in Plotinus or Proclus, no ontological "in-betweens" easing or mediating the chasm between them. We have returned in Cusan style to the separation, or *chorismos,* of Plato's *Phaedo* and *Republic,* but without Plato's Forms.[11]

Nicholas thus removes from God any literal or metaphorical notion of quantity or commensurability. This in principle blocks our knowing God, given that our knowing is a kind of measuring. God is not measurable; God escapes all humanly constructed proportions. "Maximum" may be a metaphor taken from quantity, but it ends up being equivalent to "absolute"—*ab-solutum,* "absolved" or free from creaturely limits and thus incommensurable. (Nicholas says as much in explaining how quantitative minimum and maximum are alike as superlatives, while opposed as amounts or numbers.) This takes us to Nicholas' dramatic and characteristic way of construing God's absolute transcendence. He affirms that in God the maximum coincides with the minimum. He writes that in the absolute *"maximum est minimum coincidenter"* (h 11), and again, that the absolute stands *"supra omnem oppositionem"* (h 12).

The fact is that the oppositions and contrarieties we take for granted in making sense of our ordinary world simply do not apply here. To say

10. For discussion of why it is appropriate to construe the Latin comparative *meliori* by the superlative in German (and English), see G. von Bredow's essay, "Der Sinn der Formel '*meliori modo quo,*'" in her *Im Gespräch mit Nikolaus von Kues: Gesammelte Aufsätze 1948–1993,* ed. H. Schnarr. (Münster: Aschendorff, 1995), 61–69.

11. For a standard account of the separation of Platonic Forms from sensible things, see R. Kraut, "Introduction to the Study of Plato," in *The Cambridge Companion to Plato,* ed. R. Kraut (Cambridge: Cambridge University Press, 1992), 8, 41, note 34. See also G. Fine, "Separation," *Oxford Studies in Ancient Philosophy* 2 (1984): 31–87.

God is beyond every "not this but that" and every "such but not so" is to pursue the Infinite beyond the reach of rational discourse—*super omnem affirmationem est pariter et negationem* (h 12). But this gives us some insight into what is meant by the coincidence of opposites. It is not that the difference between human affirming and denying is lost or dissolved. It is not that all nays become yeas when humans speak of the Divine or vice versa. The principle of contradiction continues to govern rational thought and discourse, or we would be at a loss in attempting to make sense of the coincidence of opposites. The coincidence of opposites is not some sort of theoretical "black hole," as it were, into which disappears all philosophical and theological human insight.

In these early pages of *De docta ignorantia*, Nicholas is at pains to put it precisely so we get it right. Since God *is* actually all possibles as well as their ontologically unbounded limit, since God is a Maximum that cannot itself be limited or bounded, our discourse about God is going to seem peculiar. In Nicholas' own words,

And [the Maximum] no more *is* than is not all that which is conceived to exist. And it no more *is not* than is all that which is conceived not to exist. But it is this thing in such a way as to be all things and it is all things in such a way as to be no thing. And it is maximally this in such a way as to be it minimally. (1.4 h 12, my translation)

What is remarkable about these sentences is that they state just how God is related to the domain of things that may or may not exist, even though God is beyond that domain. The sentences say this, as best they can, in the language of being *and* of nonbeing, *and* they apply both of those contradictory expressions to God at the same time. They thereby illustrate just what sort of dialectic it is that the coincidence of opposites commits us to in our thinking and our speaking. Nicholas would have us hold oppositions together, insofar as we are able, whether paradoxical and metaphorical contraries like "maximum" and "minimum" or contradictories such as "is" and "is not." God is paradoxically both and neither. Nor can we resolve the paradox. Thus we "touch" *(attingere)* in speaking and thinking such sentences just what God's transcendence may amount to, even though we cannot pretend to penetrate or comprehend all that we are saying.

Nicholas' final observations in this chapter attempt to spell out his point in more reasonable terms. He says that we cannot positively relate the contradictory statements so as to give them the meaning they have in their divine Source, for that Source transcends our understanding. Rather, we assert that the infinite God stands beyond and therefore is without the oppositions we comprehend in our discursive reasoning. "*Cui nihil opponitur*" (to whom nothing is opposed; 1.4 h 12). Speaking negatively, nothing is God's opposite, nothing is differentiated from or opposed to him. God encompasses all things without canceling their differences. The other side of the same point is the fact that, speaking positively, where there are no oppositions everything comes together, as it were, in oneness. God is therefore coincidence of opposites! This marks a high point unique to Cusan metaphysics.[12]

We have also discovered why we may touch or reach God *incomprehensibiliter*, yet cognitively. Our comprehending works, in Nicholas' words, *via rationis*, by way of reason. Reason comprehends by distinguishing and connecting, by affirming and denying, by working through differences and likenesses. But the absolute Maximum is the One to whom nothing is opposed and, unless it can use oppositions, human reason is struck dumb. Exactly so. Language stumbles, as it were, over divine oneness. But Cusanus hopes that we may enter cognitively this transcendent realm, now not comprehending but able to recognize or touch *(attingere)* the One beyond human speech and reason. (His later works will introduce *intellectus*, intellectual vision, at just this juncture.) The first sentence of chapter 6 summarizes: the Maximum is both *incomprehensibiliter intelligibile pariter et innominabiliter nominabile* (h 13). We are to understand the incomprehensible and name the ineffable.

One way to understand the Cusan coincidence of opposites is to notice how it embodies what Dionysius had proposed centuries earlier about speaking of God. Dionysius put it briefly in *Mystical Theology* 1.2.1000B:

What has actually to be said about the Cause of everything is this. Since it is the Cause of all beings, we should posit and ascribe to it all the affirmations we make in regard to beings, and, more appropriately, we should negate all these affirmations, since it surpasses all being. Now we should not conclude that the negations are simply the opposite of the affirmations, but rather that the cause of all is considerably prior to this, beyond privations, beyond every denial, beyond every assertion.[13]

---

12. In "Das Leitwort der 'coincidentia oppositorum'" (in *Streifzüge*, 117–40), Haubst traces the origin of *coincidentia* to Cusanus' studies of Dionysius, Albert the Great and his follower Heymericus de Campo, and Raymond Lull; then he sketches how the doctrine plays out in Nicholas' works. Other important treatments of the theme include K. Flasch, *Die Metaphysik des Einen bei Nikolaus von Kues* (Leiden: Brill, 1973), esp. for the treatment of opposites—contraries and contradictories—and his *Nikolaus von Kues*, 44–70, 103–7, for more recent reflections; J. Stallmach, *Ineinsfall der Gegensätze und Weisheit des Nichtwissens* (Münster: Aschendorff, 1989), and the same author's briefer essay "Der 'Zusammenfall der Gegensätze' und der unendliche Gott" in K. Jacobi, ed., *Einführung*, 56–73. See also Bond's intriguing overview in *Nicholas of Cusa*, 21–36, 335–36.

13. *Pseudo-Dionysius: The Complete Works*, trans. C. Luibheid and P. Rorem (New York: Paulist Press, 1987), 136. What is key here is Dionysius' final sentence. It suggests that

This puts briefly Dionysius' conviction that "negative theology" is not just about negating our affirmations, but also about rejecting as utterly inadequate the interplay of both *sic et non, et affirmatio et negatio*, even as we hold both together in reaching beyond toward the divine.

What is Nicholas doing in *De docta ignorantia* 1.4? To call God maximum is to make what appears to be an affirmation; to call God minimum is to make another affirmation, which, cleverly enough, is opposed to the first, since there cannot be a greater than the maximum and there cannot be a lesser than the minimum. For Cusanus, it follows that, in God, minimum coincides with maximum since both stand outside or beyond the finite realm of more and less. It may be easy enough to map onto Nicholas' moves what the medievals saw as the threefold Dionysian schema of affirmation, negation, and hypernegation, or eminence. Then, in the case of God, Nicholas' coincidence of opposites becomes both sign and symbol that we have left the finite and the contracted and moved to that "other" ontological domain. There we are lost and yet at home, because finally found beyond our deepest hopes.

But almost as if this is moving too quickly, Nicholas reinterprets the maximum and minimum as quantitative symbols, and explains that once you remove the quantity, you simply have equivalent superlatives. We are expected to replace superlatives and comparatives with infinite and finites, no doubt. Don't we have to wonder whether this explanation does not undercut the whole enterprise of showing maximum and minimum coincident? We end up with the conclusion that the maxi-

---

what Eckhart was to later characterize as the *negatio negationis* is not simply a move on the same level as the initial affirmations and their negations. These "hypernegations," as B. McGinn has termed them, the statements that go beyond denying that God is a being like other beings, are also statements about what God-language amounts to (see T. A. Carlson, *Indiscretion* [Chicago: University of Chicago Press, 1999], 160, note 10). D. Turner, in *The Darkness of God: Negativity in Western Mysticism*. (Cambridge: Cambridge University Press, 1995), 19–49, interprets these statements as second-order characterizations of such discourse rather than first-order propositions within the discourse. This is why they turn out to be rather empty as characterizations of God, though this outcome does manifest our ignorance of the Deity.

My own view is that Dionysius uses this third transcendent or supereminent moment both ways: as an attempt to bespeak the beyond, but an attempt that defeats itself and thereby helps us recognize just why previous affirmations and negations were both necessary and inadequate. As M. Sells has put it (*Mystical Languages of Unsaying* [Chicago: University of Chicago Press, 1994], 1–13), we have here a kind of performative "unsaying," an undercutting of both the affirmations and negations that preceded as we continue to speak. We cannot but talk of God and yet we cannot but know that what we say is no truer than its denial and that God eludes both our reach and our grasp. Dionysius reminds us that the third step into further negation is an ironic movement—into the silence that matches our human ignorance or unknowing. This last step recognizes a beyond "considerably prior to this" human business of speaking about God's attributes and then stripping them from God.

mum and the minimum are both ontologically infinite. And if the opposition is removed, the coincidence of course turns out to be identity! If maximum is the same as minimum, both are identically the absolute. The infinite is the infinite. This is true, but trivial, and we seem to have taken a long way around to get back to where we started without much more enlightenment than when we began.

Whatever Nicholas says, if this initial example of coincidence is to be workable, he cannot leave the contracted, metaphorical realm of quantity or the maximum will not be not opposed to the minimum at all. True, in the end, the Maximum is *not* opposed to the minimum at all. That is the right conclusion, but we are supposed to struggle in thought to reach it. The real theoretical point of this chapter is about reaching the coincidence of finite and infinite and the coincidence of actual and possible in God. Making God the maximum, then insisting God must be the minimum, does posit God's greatness and then strip it of all we might imagine or conceptualize as greatness—moves cataphatic and apophatic, indeed. But unless these are *opposing* metaphors, there is nothing special about their coincidence, nor can such a coincidence of opposites count as Dionysian hypernegation. If their dialectical opposition cannot be held together in thought, maximum and minimum cannot help us experience what we need to think through in order to acknowledge our ignorance. Nor can their opposition lead us to recognize the Divine who is opposite without opposition. And these crabbed thoughts and words can hardly let us realize the inadequacy of how we speak of God.

That is why it is perhaps arguable that one should not map onto the opposition of maximum and minimum the moments of Dionysian cataphatic and apophatic theology. If Nicholas dissolves the differences between maximum and minimum he is already working, so to say, at the level of hypernegation. By symbolizing God as maximum/minimum, Nicholas moves the whole business of concurrent affirmation and negation directly to a level of theoretical abstraction already stripped of anything concrete or scriptural, even if maximum/minimum remains a conceptual symbol. The point of the coincidence of opposites that marks Cusan thinking in *De docta ignorantia* 1.4 is not to illustrate the way oppositions between finite contraries in the realm of more and less are enfolded in or unfolded from God. That will be the work of Book 2 of *De docta ignorantia*. Nicholas' focus here is the divine oneness. That is why we must think dialectically such abstruse contradictory oppositions as finite and infinite, actual and possible, being and not being, everything and nothing. How are these coincident and to be thought together in the transcendent One? We can't find out unless the minimum and the maximum are opposed, even if their opposition begins symbolically in the human conceptual realm, only to move beyond it.

Is it fair, then, to say that the coincidence of opposites does represent in Cusan terms the process we find in Dionysius' affirmation, negation, and hypernegation? Yes and no. Nicholas slips by most of the positive concrete, symbolic, and conceptual names for God to be found in such abundance in Dionysius.[14] Hence he need not negate what he has not affirmed. He moves directly to the third moment. Chapter 4 exhibits how we may hold together in thought and language the "maximum" and the "minimum," the "is" and the "is not," the "this thing" and the "all things," the "all things" and the "no thing."

To say both that the coincidence of opposites occurs in God and that God is beyond the coincidence of opposites is to claim these oppositions are simultaneously true of God, even though we cannot fathom their meaning in the One who is Source of all things. This may be why Nicholas must assert *both* that in God opposites coincide *and* that God is beyond the coincidence of opposites. This echoes Dionysian hypernegation in asserting that God is transcendent and by that very assertion exhibiting how all our thought and talk must here "crash and burn." To put it in other words, the coincidence of opposites underlines our human ignorance of the divine transcendence. We have no idea where the negation of negation takes us, let alone of how God *"super omnem affirmationem est pariter et negationem"* and thus *"supra omnem oppositionem est."* The coincidence of opposites thereby demonstrates that discourse about God as God is finally unworkable on the model of discursive reason.

Does Nicholas go beyond Dionysius? I believe he extends the Dionysian proposal that knowing God is finally unknowing, for Nicholas stresses our ignorance as a cognitive achievement, something we learn when we acknowledge and understand its significance. For him, this is sacred ignorance, and thus a gift as much as a feat. His coincidence of opposites is therefore a shorthand reminder of how our thought must operate "incomprehensibly" if we are to do justice in our thinking to the infinite One we seek beyond all our cognitive and linguistic measures.

14. This lets us understand better what is taking place later in *De docta ignorantia* 1.24–26, where Nicholas explicitly takes up the names of God and affirmative and negative theology. These chapters may seem both curious and not quite satisfying, especially if one expects a second-order Cusan theory of how we are to name God. Instead, in those chapters we find two kinds of summary notes about where Dionysius led Cusanus. One kind leads him to examine the various epithets and positive names historically given to the Divine in chapters 24 and 25—he even calls this *theologia affirmativa*. Not surprisingly he invokes the notion of enfolding—how all the names are enfolded in the one ineffable name of God—that will be thematic in his discussion of the created universe in Book 2. Second, in 1.26 Nicholas mentions Dionysius by name and proceeds to recall his teaching about negative theology.

As cognitive conundrum the coincidence of opposites is characteristically Cusan, for in thinking it through we come out in ignorance before the One to whom nothing is opposed—not even us! Holding the opposites together is not a way of collapsing in confusion or floundering in contradiction. Ironically, it is a way of attempting to move beyond the *via rationis*, of attempting to become open in sacred or saving ignorance to that One who, as the *oppositio oppositionum*, stands unopposed to everything and to nothing.[15]

1D. Mathematical Symbols and the Infinite God

Nicholas proceeds to propose what amount to thought experiments to educate us about God's relation to created things. His thought is intriguing just because he employs a range of novel metaphors or symbols for imagining and conceiving less inadequately how things stand on their ultimate divine foundations. In Book 1 of *De docta ignorantia* this is done by an exploration of mathematical symbols for the Divine.[16]

This appeal to mathematical symbols is the most striking and original feature of Book 1. Cusanus has explained our way of knowing as a kind of measuring, an assessing of the proportional fit (and lack of exact fit) between our thought and language and the changing, limited things of the created universe. In 1.11 he restates these limits to motivate turning us to mathematics:

> Now, when we conduct an inquiry on the basis of an image, it is necessary that there be no doubt regarding the image, by means of whose symbolical comparative relation we are investigating what is unknown. The pathway to the uncertain can be only through what is presupposed and certain. But all perceptible things are in a state of continual instability because of the material possibility abounding in them. In our considering of objects, we see that those which are more abstract than perceptible things, namely, mathematicals . . . are very fixed and are very certain to us. (1.11 h 31)

Even though we are attempting to advance toward what is in principle unmeasurable (because unlimited), Cusanus proposes that we work with conceptual tools that are as "fixed and certain" as can be.

---

15. W. Beierwaltes, in "Der verborgene Gott: Cusanus und Dionysius," *Trierer Cusanus Lecture* 4 (Trier: Paulinus Verlag, 1997), gives an overview of the way themes from Dionysius and Proclus make an impact on Nicholas' ideas about God as transcendent, especially in his late work *De li non aliud*. Bond remarks that in relation to Dionysius, Cusanus is "able to use the accomplishments of both the negative and positive ways and at the same time to exceed them." His thought "presumes to see what reason excludes as impossible, such as the notion that the coincidence of being and non-being is necessity itself" (*Nicholas of Cusa*, 33).

16. K. Jacobi, *Die Methode der cusanischen Philosophie* (Munich: Alber, 1969), 212–14, generalizes Cusanus' method here. See also H. Meinhardt, "Exaktheit und Mutmassungscharakter der Erkenntnis," in Jacobi, ed., *Einführung*, 101–20.

In order to use geometrical figures as a way of approaching things divine, Cusanus specifies a three-stage process in chapter 12. The first two stages deal with mathematical figures: first, finite figures, second, their hypothetical infinite extrapolations. The third stage involves a metaphorical application and comparison of what we discover about infinite mathematical figures to the nonmathematical, ontological Infinite, that is, to God.

Cusanus never teaches that infinite numbers are real or countable or that geometric figures—lines or circles or triangles—extended infinitely really exist or are imaginable or fully conceivable.[17] While we can understand a rule for extrapolation without limits, we cannot conceptually grasp any case falling under the rule. Cusanus extrapolates to the hypothetical infinite case by working from features of the finite geometrical figures that approach such an infinite figure asymptotically. We are to explore the possibilities of geometrical figures as an apt symbol of our exploration of the Divine.

For instance, when we imagine increasing the radius of a geometrical circle to infinity, we find that its circumference and tangents will all coincide with its diameter; the difference between straight and curved lines disappears. As Cusanus puts it, "in the maximum [= infinite] line curvature is straightness" (1.13 h 35). At the infinite limit, he believes, the terms "curved" and "straight" lose the definite sense they have in the realm of finite geometric figures. To claim that they "coincide" in the hypothetical infinite line is a metaphorical way of letting us glimpse beyond the finite, of revealing how the mathematical infinite figure is incommensurable with finite figures and the concepts we use to deal with them. This incommensurability affords some clue to the ontological disproportion between finite things and God, "the simple Infinite, which is altogether independent even of all figures" (1.12 h 33).

In proposing that we work from finite toward putatively infinite geometrical figures, Cusanus sets up a movement of imagination and thought. This is a kind of dialectic that approaches the hypothetical infinite figure perspectivally by constructing or imagining larger and larger figures so that it appears that curved and straight lines, for instance, are approaching one another from the viewer's standpoint so that their differences begin to disappear. Then one imagines transcending the largest conceivable finite figure.[18] This leap beyond *(transilire)* the finite does not yield any positive conception of the geometrical infinite. Rather, we turn back to the finite case to deny and exclude characteristics, such as

---

17. Hopkins, *Learned Ignorance*, 9–10.
18. G. Mar first pointed out to me that this exercise involves imagining oneself watching from a given standpoint larger and larger circles being constructed in front of oneself

straight and curved, that can no longer apply. They apparently collapse into identity in the infinite. In moving back and forth in thought we are thus enabled to fashion a kind of conceptual or linguistic space, a rule for what the infinite line or circle must amount to, without ever grasping or seeing exactly how the different finite figures are identically one in the infinite.

The hypothetical infinite figure and its relation to finite figures can thereupon become a metaphor for letting us glimpse the relation of finite beings to their infinite divine Source. In this way the inconceivable infinite line might be thought to stand at the limit or horizon of finite geometrical concepts. Were it actual, Cusanus believes that it *would* be all that a finite line *can* be—namely, straight *and* curved, able to be constructed into triangles or circles or spheres. The relation of this limit notion to finite geometrical figures provides a symbol for God's relation to the universe as its Essence and ultimate Measure.

The dialectical relation between infinite and finite line symbolizes the connection we cannot conceive between God and everything else. Just as human reason must fail when we extrapolate to the limiting case of the mathematical infinite, so we are not to expect some positive grasp of the infinite God. Concepts and language typical of discursive reason fail in the cases of both the mathematical and the ontological infinite, yet we are left the theorem that, just as the infinite line encompasses all lines without differentiation, so the ontological infinite *is* all that can be. If the notion of the mathematical infinite forms the horizon of geometry for Cusanus, the infinite God encompasses the reality of all there is as both "center and circumference" of the created totality.

1E. Dialectical Symbols and Negative Theology

Cusanus' enterprise stands as one kind of traditional "negative" theology. He is setting out a series of proposals for what an infinite being is not and cannot be, almost in spite of his appeal to the fictive mathematical infinite. His dialectical exercises involve our moving from the finite figure, where we have knowledge, to the infinite case, where we point beyond without reaching any positive knowledge. We end up conclud-

---

and then "observing" that their circumferences *appear* to "flatten out" and "approach" a straight line or tangent meeting that circumference. Conceptually, of course, this is impossible within mathematics itself (the realm of discursive reason for Nicholas, where the principle of contradiction holds), since by definition no curved line can become straight nor can a tangent meet a circle, whatever its diameter, at more than one point. Though he believes that mathematics is stable and certain, in this case Cusanus deliberately plays with geometrical appearances in order to illustrate the putative disproportion between ontological infinite and finites and to propose a conjectural way of thinking beyond the finite.

ing, *a pari*, that the case of God is quite beyond our ken. But the kind of thinking required to move beyond finite figure to hypothetical infinite figure models the sort of thinking Cusanus believes most helpful for thinking God: now not just learned, but "sacred" ignorance—an active progress toward the absolute Maximum beyond differentiation. In thinking God we leave aside all the differentiations and possibilities and imperfections of the created world in order to move toward the self-identical simpleness of God's infinity.

Chapter 17 summarizes how this consideration is central to learned ignorance.

> ... by the illustration of an infinite line, the intellect can in sacred ignorance very greatly advance beyond all understanding and toward the unqualifiedly Maximum. For here we have now seen clearly how we can arrive at God through removing the participation of beings. For all beings participate in Being. Therefore, if from all beings participation is removed, there remains the most simple Being itself, which is the Essence of all things. And we see such Being only in the most learned ignorance; for when I remove from my mind all the things which participate in Being, it seems that nothing remains. Hence, the great Dionysius says that our understanding of God draws near to nothing rather than to something. But sacred ignorance teaches me that that which seems to the intellect to be nothing is the incomprehensible Maximum. (h 51)

God is not comparable to the created things to which his maximal Reality stands as measure and essence. They participate in God, yet God is infinitely beyond them all.[19] So "most simple Being itself" is nothing comprehensible to human understanding. Indeed, removing all participating beings leaves exactly nothing for us to understand. Yet this very incomprehensibility is the "sacred ignorance" we are to expect in our attempt to reach beyond the finite. To recognize it is one sign that our dialectical quest using mathematical symbols has arrived at the divine "Essence of all things."

Since the paradigm of human knowing is measuring, and since measuring (understood as relating and discriminating) is displayed most perspicuously in mathematics, it is hardly surprising that Nicholas attempts to capitalize on mathematics in exploring the meaning and constraints of learned ignorance. He also is aware that mathematical exactness is a function of our prescinding from the physical and constructing an ab-

---

19. Nicholas writes in 1.17 (h 50) that considering the infinite line helps us see how "the Maximum is in each thing and in no thing. ... Accordingly, the fact that the Maximum is the measure [*metrum et mensura*] of all things is not other than the fact that the unqualifiedly Maximum exists in itself—i.e., that the Maximum is the Maximum." For commentary on participation in this passage, see M. Thomas, *Die Teilhabegedanke in den Schriften und Predigten des Nikolaus von Kues (1430–1450)* (Münster: Aschendorff, 1996), 45–50.

stract conceptual domain. Given the parallel incommensurability of finite and infinite in mathematics and ontology, Cusan learned ignorance becomes sacred ignorance in that it both limits us and enables us to choose symbols that exhibit our lack of knowledge of God while at the same time we attempt to transcend this lack.

Cusan philosophical theology pursues and accomplishes two goals in its choice of metaphors and symbols. Some metaphors and symbols are employed for *explanatory* purposes; others are used in an *exploratory* fashion to open up alternate perspectives, whether on human beings, or on the cosmos, or on our relation to God. For instance, to see human cognition as "measuring" is to propose an explanatory metaphor to make sense of what happens when we move from common ignorance to common knowledge and then beyond to learned ignorance. Sometimes, of course, Cusan metaphors work both ways. "Mind as measure" *(mens/mensura)* is itself explored in *Idiota de mente,* but here it is employed to explain the mathematical route directing us toward learned ignorance.

In contrast, the hypothetical "connection" (in spite of the lack of *proportio*) between finite and infinite figures and the movement between them are designed to be more than explanatory. They are *exploratory* as well, a scenario for understanding the impasse we face and the meaning of *docta ignorantia* in our attempt to gain knowledge of the infinite God. These Cusan exercises require a constant back-and-forth movement from finite figure and hypothetical infinite figure to divine Infinite. In this way they illustrate the kind of dialectical reasoning or practice implicit in the metaphor of knowing as measuring. At the same time, both geometry and measurement are metaphors ultimately undercut when applied to philosophical theology. God escapes even metaphorical measures because our attempts to transcend human limitations cannot fill out positively what lies beyond.

1F. Language and Negative Theology

Cusanus' assessment of human attempts to name or to describe God reemphasizes the same point.[20] His final chapters in Book 1 acknowledge that the language of faith and worship, for all the guidance it may provide philosophical theology, ultimately is inadequate. Even negative theological language cannot handle the kind of reality he believes God to be.

Language about God runs up against the same barriers as the thought about God that it signifies and expresses. Discursive reason and ordinary language deal with a realm of differentiation and plurality,

---

20. See H. G. Senger, "Die Sprache der Metaphysik," in K. Jacobi, ed., *Einführung,* 74–100, esp. 85ff.; and Flasch, *Nikolaus von Kues,* 107–18.

where one thing is distinct from another, regardless of how they may also be related. What our ordinary thinking and talking does best is to distinguish and to connect such familiar things, giving us categories for differentiating that are finally both inadequate and antithetical to the project of moving toward the Divine. The Cusan God lies beyond such distinctions and *is* everything we discern as separate and distinct in an unlimited oneness without opposition or differentiation. Little wonder that his God can barely be dealt with in language designed for things entirely different than their infinite Source.

Even if we "purify" all the names humans have used for gods and God and interpret them as generously and carefully as we can, what results will not speak the true name of God any more than our conceptions capture God's true nature. Just denying that any of our language characterizes God in the way it characterizes other things is not enough to help us speak truly about God in God's self. At best the denial opens up a kind of uncharted linguistic space in which human language must be transformed (much as Cusanus' hypothetical geometrical infinite figure) to be employed less inadequately.

In chapter 24 Cusanus proposes "Oneness" as the most suitable name for God. Yet he insists immediately that "it is not the case that 'Oneness' is the name of God in the way in which we either name or understand oneness; for just as God transcends all understanding, so a fortiori, [He transcends] every name" (1.24 h 76). We normally term something "one" that is both undivided in itself and distinct from what is other. What should we make, then, of a Oneness ontologically prior to all such distinctions? God's oneness is unlimited simpleness comprising everything actual and possible without differentiation. We must revise "Oneness" to mean "that oneness to which neither otherness nor plurality nor multiplicity is opposed" if we want the word's sense to befit divinity. What exactly we do understand when we make such a revision is problematic. Even Nicholas concludes that "Oneness" is "still infinitely distant from the true Name of the Maximum—[a Name] which is the Maximum" (1.24 h 77).[21]

Since such language cannot bridge the "infinite distance" or incommensurability of finite and infinite, why does Cusanus say he favors "the theology of negation"? He writes that according to negative theology God is "only infinite" and "there is not found in God anything other than infinity" (1.26 h 88).[22] While this casts no positive light on God's

21. The background in Nicholas' Neoplatonic predecessors, especially Plotinus and Proclus, Eriugena, and Thierry of Chartres, is explored in W. Beierwaltes, *Denken des Einen* (Frankfurt am Main: V. Klostermann, 1985). Beierwaltes' study helps determine what kind of "Platonism" one finds in Cusanus.

22. In the cursory references to Dionysius here, Nicholas does not expand on the

nature, it certainly separates divine Reality from that of limited creatures as "infinitely greater than all nameable things" (1.26 h 87). That God is not finite does not condemn us to silence or restrict us to the language of worship. For Cusanus infinity provides some intimation of where we should search and what sort of thought and speech will better help us appreciate what learned ignorance amounts to and why.

Still, the basic premise of *De docta ignorantia* 1 could be read as undercutting Cusan philosophical theology. If finite and infinite are incommensurable, discursive human thought and language gain no purchase when it comes to thinking or bespeaking the infinite God. Nicholas captures and underlines this moment of "ignorance," marking it precisely as knowledge *(docta)*, only to attempt moving beyond it and achieving further learning (now *sacra ignorantia*). "Learned ignorance" is supposed to encapsulate the real depth of religious faith *seeking* understanding. Cusanus thus challenges traditional religious discourse, even the language of worship, lest it become too easy and too habitual, taking comfort in the illusion that our speaking captures God instead of being ourselves comprehensively grasped by God. By working to find a language adequate to the coincidence of opposites, Nicholas also challenges the inveterate tendency of human thought and language to reduce God to one more thing like other things, where we may inadvertently turn faith into idolatry, mystery into everydayness.

In a more philosophical vein, Cusanus is urging that the inadequacies of speculating and speaking about the Divine will appear once we focus on the constraints of finite intelligence and reflect on the differences between the finite and the infinite. Typical discussions of God's attributes are off the mark when they omit this difference—this is why attempts to shape traditional analogical predication to Nicholas' outlook seem so strained.[23] Yet the problem of "naming God" is itself bound up with a tradition that Nicholas cannot shed, even if he wanted to. He works rather to mark its inadequacies by scoring its dependence on discursive reason where a different language and kind of speculation are required.[24]

"negation of the negation." He has already displayed it in practice earlier in *De docta ignorantia* 1. (This gives his final remarks in Book 1 some of the casual tone of many chapters of *The Divine Names*.) More important in chapter 26 is Nicholas' insistence that learned ignorance is identical with the acknowledgment of God's infinity, beyond cataphasis and apophasis.

23. For a typical attempt, see R. Haubst, "Nikolaus von Kues und die analogia entis," in *Streifzüge*, 232–42.

24. Hopkins, *Learned Ignorance*, 14–16. Senger, in "Die Sprache," 86–94, distinguishes three types of speaking in Cusanus: rational, intellectual, and divine. These correspond roughly to discourse about ordinary oppositions, discourse involving the coincidence of opposites, and discourse "beyond" that coincidence.

In a series of trenchant monographs, D. Burrell has addressed the same problem by

De docta ignorantia tries to have it both ways. With the principle of the incommensurability of the finite and the infinite Cusanus rejects any thinking about God appropriate only for the finite realm. Yet anchored in his religious and speculative tradition, he does not hesitate to initiate his own attempt to "comprehend incomprehensibly" something of the unlimited God beyond the coincidence of opposites. His striking proposals about the absolute Maximum and his novel use of mathematics are designed to get us to look again, to see what we can do or say, and finally to realize what is and must be beyond us. His distinctive story may lead us in imagination and thought to the limits of the finite where we may reach toward what he is sure lies beyond. *De docta ignorantia* 1 gives this story its classic and definitive Cusan expression.

BOOK 2: THE WORLD AND LEARNED IGNORANCE

Book 2 of *De docta ignorantia* continues the paradoxical Cusan project of advancing our understanding of learned ignorance. While the first book aimed to ground our intellectual (and religious) orientation to God by working toward a recognition of what we cannot know of the divine Maximum, the second book aims to extend that recognition to another, parallel "maximum": the created universe. Cusanus frames the book with initial and final chapters that refer to the quadrivial arts, the common sources of knowledge about the created universe for his original readers. The difference in the ways Nicholas uses the quadrivium to open and close this second book provides an intriguing initial access for understanding what he is doing.

The opening chapter of Book 2 recalls how the natural realms explored and ordered in arithmetic, geometry, music, and astronomy are calculated to reveal dimensions of the created universe. In this sphere of limited created things we should expect to find no maximum or minimum, but only things comparable as more and less. This was the thesis Nicholas proposed in Book 1 and now restates as follows: "with regard to things which are comparatively greater and lesser we do not come to a maximum in being and possibility" (2.1 h 91).[25] Each of the quadrivial

---

comparing Aquinas with Maimonides and various Muslim thinkers. For a summary, see his "Aquinas and Jewish and Islamic Thinkers," in *The Cambridge Companion to Aquinas*, ed. N. Kretzmann and E. Stump (Cambridge: Cambridge University Press, 1993), 60–84, in particular 75–79. For a fuller account, see his *Knowing the Unknowable God: Ibn Sina, Maimonides, Aquinas* (South Bend, Ind.: University of Notre Dame Press, 1986).

25. In his later *De venatione sapientiae*, c.26 h 79, Cusanus calls this proposition "the rule of learned ignorance." For brief commentary on its ontological basis and epistemic implications, see K. Jacobi, "Ontologie aus dem Geist 'belehrten Nichtwissens,'" in Jacobi, ed., *Einführung*, 33–36.

arts (here arithmetic and geometry are to be understood as applied to the physical world, not as abstract conceptual realms) explores a realm of imperfect, limited things and discovers no exactness, proportion, or harmony in them that could not be made more exact or more perfect.

Nicholas read each member of the quadrivium as mathematical and thus involving the proportional calculation and measuring Nicholas believed paradigmatic for human knowing. Even so, each quadrivial art falls short of finding the exact combinations and proportions in the things God has created. In Book 1 Nicholas asserted that learned ignorance recognized no proportion between finite and infinite. Here he extends our ignorance by noting that the comparison and measurements we make using the quadrivial arts do not take the exact measure even of the finite things we study in the natural universe. We begin Book 2 with a strong reminder that our best means of knowing God's creation fall short: *"ex hoc nos ignorare intelligimus"* (we hereby recognize that we are ignorant; 2.1 h 94).

Yet the final chapter of Book 2 returns to the quadrivial arts with proposals that seem to go in a different direction. Nicholas has completed his discussion of the universe's origin, nature, and correspondences (as contracted or limited maximum) with the absolute Maximum. He now proclaims that "in creating the world, God used arithmetic, geometry, music, and likewise astronomy" (2.13 h 175), producing all things "in number, weight, and measure," as the Vulgate Bible puts it (Wis 11.21). Our recognition of creation's harmony and diversity, of the wondrous order reaching from the elements to the heavens, now turns our minds and hearts to marvel and praise their Creator, who though inaccessible to our minds, will graciously aid us if we seek him.

What motivates this change in the way Cusanus employs the quadrivium? How can he first use it to recall our ignorance regarding the created universe only to claim at the end that the quadrivial arts guided the ultimate Artist's creating? One way to understand the underlying problematic of this second book of *De docta ignorantia* is to realize how it embodies two parallel if opposing claims. First, there is some basis in the limited, contracted things with which we are familiar for moving beyond this realm of more and less toward the Creator (= God can be "known" from things God has made). Second, acknowledging our ignorance entails realizing that we cannot really know *how* God created or *how* God and the universe are related. Indeed, we cannot know precisely or with perfect accuracy the quiddity of any created thing we encounter or experience in the created world.

Where does this leave us? Learned ignorance amounts to "comprehending incomprehensibly" God and the universe, but it does not leave us speechless. Such ignorance involves our proposing alternatives that do some justice to our best knowledge of things without imagining that such alternatives let us grasp what is beyond our competence. For Cusanus, the quadrivium is a kind of normative compendium of human measures and measurements that have proved useful in dealing with the world, however short they fall of "getting it exactly right." When he proposes that God creates in accord with these norms, Nicholas reminds us that we do reach some understanding of the whole of creation that God creates and sustains.

Created things are not silent; Nicholas has them speak at the end of Book 2 in a way that points to God without revealing anything of what God's creating comes to, without revealing how that creating works, and without revealing, finally, anything of what they themselves truly are. This is what they say:

"Of ourselves [we are] nothing, and of our own ability we cannot tell you anything other than nothing. For we do not even know ourselves; rather, God alone—through whose understanding we are that which He wills, commands, and knows to be in us—[has knowledge of us]." (2.13 h 180)

In this way Cusanus attempts to preserve what knowledge we do have of the universe. We are not to jettison the quadrivial arts, yet we should not pretend that we know more than that we are ignorant of what God is and of God's relation to all that is not God. We have to move dialectically as we read Book 2 between the proposals and conjectures Nicholas makes to illuminate our darkness. He does this by drawing parallels between creature and Creator and by constantly reminding us that there is no common measure between limited and unlimited, contracted and absolute, creature and Creator. Book 2 begins by stressing our inadequacy and ignorance in these matters; it ends by capitalizing on the knowledge of creation we do have to seek out the Creator in awe and praise.

2A. Unfolded Images and Their Source

The second chapter of Book 2 raises the question of how we are to frame and understand created things as both many and one.[26] We recognize their diversity and multiplicity; we acknowledge that their source is the divine Oneness, the absolute Maximum; but if we do not understand the divine Being, what can we understand about the creating of things derived from the divine Source? Further, what can we grasp

---

26. For an extended analysis of Book 2, see Offermann, *Christus*, 97–139.

about their natures as "contracted," that is, limited, images of God? Can we conceive their inner ontological structure in a way faithful to their status as creatures?

These questions arise for each particular creature and for the natural universe as a whole. Each thing and the totality or universe of created things stand as derivative and thereby diminished being. Cusanus attributes their being derived or created to God, but he refuses to speculate on the mode of their derivation or to attribute their limited, diminished status either to God or to any positive internal principle they exhibit. Insofar as things exist, they are from the first principle, but that they exhibit "corruptibility, divisibility, imperfection, difference, plurality" (2.2 h 98) is a function of their being contingent.

Cusanus refuses to make creatures composites of the opposites that are his heritage as a Neoplatonic thinker. Creatures are not composites of being and nonbeing, sameness and difference, oneness and otherness, or the like. Rather, Cusanus stresses that in whole and in part creation is a diminished, contingent, contracted way of being one and real and good—a limited image of the Creator. In his words, each being's "oneness exists in plurality, its distinctness in confusion, and its union in discord" (2.2 h 99). This is simply its factual condition, that state of affairs comprising those dependent things that need not exist at all. Again, creation as such cannot be called "both one and many conjunctively. But its oneness exists contingently and with a certain plurality" (2.2 h 100).

What Cusanus is driving at in the various formulations he offers in 2.2 is some way of capturing both the relative perfection and the relative imperfection of the creation and the things it comprises. To be created is to have some sort of ontological center, some density as a being, some oneness or form, even though the precise quiddity or definition of this form or essence remains impenetrable for human minds. As Cusanus says, "derived being is not understandable, because the Being from which [it derives] is not understandable" (2.2 h 100). To be created is to comport oneself ontologically in a dependent condition that entails that one need not be at all. This contingency finds ontological expression when we understand that to be a created thing means to exist imperfectly, to be subject to corruption, division, change, otherness, and plurality. This factual condition and way of being is what Nicholas calls "contracted," or limited, being.[27]

27. These pages revise my earlier understanding and analysis in "Aristotelian *Natura* and Nicholas of Cusa," *Downside Review* 96 (1978): 13–20. For other commentary on 2.1–5, see esp. Jacobi, *Methode*, 267–79, 295–300; Hopkins, *Learned Ignorance*, 16–25, and *Nicholas of Cusa's Metaphysic of Contraction* (Minneapolis, Minn.: Banning Press, 1983), 33–112; and Thomas, *Teilhabegedanke*, 82–91.

Later in chapter 2, Nicholas turns to a striking metaphor to point us toward what he is trying to say:

Who is he, then[,] who can understand how it is that the one, infinite Form is participated in different ways by different created things? For created being cannot be anything other than reflection [*resplendentia*]—not a reflection received positively in some other thing but a reflection which is contingently different. Perhaps [a comparison with an artifact is fitting]: if the artifact depended entirely upon the craftsman's idea and did not have any other being than dependent being, the artifact would exist from the craftsman and would be conserved as a result of his influence—analogously to the image of a face in a mirror (with the proviso that before and after [the appearance of the image] the mirror be nothing in and of itself). (2.2 h 103)

Cusanus uses two metaphors here: the artifact and the mirror image. Both cut the same way, emphasizing the utter dependence and contingency of created things. In the first, the artifact is described so that its dependency is underlined and the initiating and sustaining power of the divine Artisan comes to the fore. Created things have a reality parallel to the reality of ideas in human minds—they have no "other being than dependent being." Of course, God need only take thought to give the artifact or the creature reality. No other tools or preexisting materials are required; creatures are not "received positively in some other thing." Rather, they "exist from the craftsman" and are "conserved as a result of his influence."

The second is a striking image—that of a face's mirror image, but without the mirror. It recalls Nicholas' earlier remark in this chapter: God is no more mixed with the created things that reflect and participate in the divine Essence than is a single face mixed with the multiple images that happen to be reflected in many mirrors at the same time. Here Cusanus emphasizes the mirror image's total dependence on its original, even to the denial of an independent mirror. A further connotation of the two metaphors may be that, when compared to God's absolute reality, creatures are no less ontologically ephemeral than fleeting thoughts to our minds or passing images captured in our mirrors.

Both the craftsman's idea of the artifact and the "mirrorless" mirror image do have some reality of their own, however dependent. Yet Cusanus slants the metaphors to suggest that creatures are better understood as utter contingency, indeed, as so contingent that we do best to take them as brute created givens. He does not hasten to explore their internal structure or expect them to resemble their originating divine Source. And yet for Cusanus each is *resplendentia*—"splendor" or "resplendence"—a word we may translate too prosaically as "reflection." His word underlines the brilliance and beauty of creation in its own right as a limited image or reflection of God, whether or not it resembles its divine Original. *Resplendentia*—that brilliant shining forth that reflects the divine—points to the fact that creatures have their own perfection as limited and contingent expressions and manifestations of God even though they are not comparable or similar in any way.[28]

Nicholas does not attempt to describe or explain directly in literal terms the way creation takes place or the way creature and Creator are connected. Chapter 3 of Book 2 proposes instead that we think God and creatures together using the Cusan quasi-technical couple or metaphor, *complicatio/explicatio* (enfolding/unfolding), that goes back to Boethius and Thierry of Chartres. This metaphor serves as Cusanus' favorite way of "explaining" or at least framing all one–many relationships where a derivative multiplicity can be traced back to a oneness that is its source.[29]

A list quoting Nicholas' lapidary statements and questions about the enfolding/unfolding metaphor in chapter 3 may be useful at this point.

Therefore, God is the enfolding of all things in that all things are in Him; and He is the unfolding of all things in that He is in all things. (h 107)

And, indeed, this [is what it] is for oneness to unfold all things: viz., for it to be present in the plurality. (h 108)

No one understands how God is unfolded through the number of things. (h 110)

How can we understand that the plurality of things is unfolded by virtue of the fact that God is present in nothing? (h 111)

Then you will have to admit that you are thoroughly ignorant of how enfolding and unfolding occur and that you know only that you do not know the manner, even if you know (1) that God is the enfolding and the unfolding of all things, (2) that insofar as He is the enfolding, in Him all things are Himself, and (3) that insofar as He is the unfolding, in all things He is that which they are, just as in an image the reality itself [*veritas*] is present. (h 111)

---

28. In interpreting *resplendentia*, I have tried to combine insights from T. P. McTighe, "*Contingentia* and *Alteritas* in Cusa's Metaphysics," *American Catholic Philosophical Quarterly* 64 (1990): 64, and from Hopkins, *Miscellany*, 11–13, 215. My own view on the deeper disagreement between them is that, for Cusanus, each created thing has its own form and this is the basis for its ontological determinateness or oneness as a contracted image or reflection of and participation in God's infinite oneness. However, "form" is not to be understood as if Cusanus were an Aristotelian, let alone a Thomist—the image–original relation is a more "Platonic" way to interpret form, especially in the realm of becoming.

29. Here Cusanus uses this metaphor in an ontological context; he extends it to philosophy of mind and epistemology in his *Idiota de mente* and to mystical theology in *De visione Dei*. For the historical background, see G. von Bredow, "Complicatio/explicatio," in *Historisches Wörterbuch der Philosophie*, 6 vols., ed. J. Ritter (Basel: Schwabe 1971), 1:1026–28. See also T. P. McTighe, "The Meaning of the Couple 'Complicatio-Explicatio' in the Philosophy of Nicholas of Cusa," *Proceedings of the American Catholic Philosophical Asso-*

In God each created thing and, indeed, the whole universe finds its true and precise essence, but there its truth transcends its contingent, spatiotemporal particularity in the realm of change and matter. In God there is no differentiation between things and God—they all collapse or implode, as it were, into the undifferentiated infinite oneness of the Godhead. *Complicatio*, or enfolding, then, enables us to think and bespeak that moment or aspect of God's relation to creatures that preserves God's transcendence. As enfolded, creatures are to be understood as identically God's infinite oneness without any distinctness or determinateness of their own at all.

Explicatio, or unfolding, even though it is not separate from but complementary to *complicatio*, involves God with creatures as the many varied things we encounter and become familiar with in the world. For Nicholas, God is the unfolding of these things "in that He is in all things." God is not some stuff from which creatures are unfolded; rather, as their Creator he is responsible for their orderly array. The "in all things" here is not intended in any pantheistic sense, for the disproportion between creatures and Creator remains. Rather, it signals God's sustaining presence to everything created and is calculated to capture their continuing dependence on and connection with God.

Cusan grammatical usage is suggestive when he uses the metaphors of enfolding and unfolding. He never suggests that "a many" (even as embraced by "a one") can be the subject of enfolding, whether that one is divine or not. To enfold is not something a plurality is "able to" do. Yet regarding unfolding, one may say indifferently that God unfolds or is the unfolding of things *or* that things unfold or are the unfolding of God. A plurality is "able to" unfold in the metaphorical sense that to recognize unfolding is to recognize plurality. This usage may suggest that we find it easier to grasp unfolding as the locus or nexus of connection between God and the creatures we are familiar with. Indeed, for Cusanus, we have in the metaphor of unfolding a way of recognizing the causal dependence of creation on God and thus of thinking God and limited things together.

Yet both unfolding and enfolding are identical in God. Since this is so, to understand unfolding as the entry to keeping together God and creatures requires that we recall as well the ontological parity of the divine enfolding and unfolding. God and creatures cannot be justly separated or understood in isolation from each other. Yet within the couple

---

ciation 32 (1958): 206–14, and his "Eternity and Time in Boethius: His *Complicatio-Explicatio* Method," in *History of Philosophy in the Making*, ed. L. J. Thro (Washington, D.C.: University Press of America, 1982), 35–62. For a helpful summary of the couple, see Bond, *Nicholas of Cusa*, 336–37.

complicatio-explicatio, we are to emphasize God's transcendence and ontological priority by recalling the creative act that embraces and sustains the unfolding represented by creatures.

At the end of chapter 3 Nicholas uses another metaphor to encapsulate God's presence to unfolded things—as the truth present in an image:

> [It is] as if a face were present in its own image, which depending upon its repeatedness, is a close or distant multiple of the face. (I do not mean according to spatial distance but according to a progressive difference from the real face, since [the image] cannot be repeated in any other way [than with a difference].) [It is as if] the one face—while remaining incomprehensibly above all the senses and every mind—were to appear differently and manifoldly in the different images multiplied from it. (2.3 h 111)

Again Nicholas turns to a visual metaphor, one familiar from our experience of portraiture where we take for granted the difference between a living face and its depictions. Here Cusanus manages to suggest both aspects central to Plato's original notion of an image: its dependence on and its likeness or resemblance to its original.[30] Nicholas contrasts "spatial distance" *(distantia localis)* and "progressive difference" *(distantia gradualis)*, asserting that the second is what he has in mind. But to recognize such a qualitative *distantia gradualis* presupposes that we can have independent access to both creatures and God, just as we do for portraits and the person sitting for them. In no other way could a likeness be judged "close or distant."

But learned ignorance has already blocked independent access to God and any common measure for comparing God and creatures, as Nicholas' parenthetical remark reminds us: "the one face—while remaining *incomprehensibly* above all the senses and every mind." This leaves us with the conclusion that *distantia gradualis*, and, indeed, any metaphorical distance or difference that is a matter of degrees or ranking, can only be measured against other creatures—"the different multiplied images" of the divine "face." And this makes sense, since the whole universe comprises a realm of more and less for Cusanus. Within the whole each being exists "in the way this can best occur.... Wherefore, we infer that every created thing qua created thing is perfect—even if it seems less perfect in comparison with some other [created thing]" (2.2 h 104).

Not surprisingly, Cusanus' analogy with the face and its portraits may suggest we know more than we can. Here seeking outruns knowing, for

---

30. For a nuanced treatment of Plato's view of images, see R. Patterson, *Image and Reality in Plato's Metaphysics* (Indianapolis, Ind.: Hackett, 1985).

learned ignorance means that our only way of discerning the distances of the varied portraits from their putative divine face is by noting their differences from one another. God's truth gets expression in every created unfolding since each creature is a limited reflection, an attenuated oneness, that depends on that unknowable divine enfolding. But such created expressions reveal in their contingency and their limitation merely *that* there is and must be such a Source, not *what* it is like or what it amounts to. However we measure the distance or difference of these Cusan portraits of the Divine, even their dependence finally must conceal and disguise the mystery of God's infinite oneness—and this on Cusanus' own principles!

2B. The Universe as Contracted Maximum

In chapters 4 and 5 Cusanus discusses how taking the universe as contracted maximum lets us see how it parallels God, the absolute Maximum. While God is absolute Oneness and utterly without plurality, the universe is a contracted oneness, a unity-in-plurality. The universe comprises the many things that make it up, enabling them to be seen as a single whole instead of simply as a sheer multitude of diverse items. While Cusanus' explication here raises many unanswered questions, his main theses are straightforward:

> ... we consider the Absolute Maximum to be antecedently in the contracted maximum, so that it is subsequently in all particulars because it is present absolutely in that which is contractedly all things.... And so we can understand the following: (1) how it is that God, who is most simple Oneness and exists in the one universe, is in all things as if subsequently and through the mediation of the universe, and (2) [how it is that as if] through the mediation of the one universe the plurality of things is in God. (2.4 h 116)

The "as if" here is not meant to cast doubt on the ontological reality or priority of the universe as a whole of parts. Rather, it should be taken as qualifying the notion of mediation. Cusanus explicitly rejects the ontological picture or scheme of hypostases, or intermediate levels of being emanating from the first and transmitting reality to what is below, common to the metaphysical systems of Plotinus, Proclus, and even the Muslim thinkers (for the supralunary realm). For Nicholas there is no intermediary reality between God and God's creation.

In this way the universe is, as it were, created concomitantly with the diverse creatures. The latter constitute its plural or multiple character, even as the universe, the whole, is the basis of their being a unity limited to the various sorts of created things. Individual things and the whole they make up are coequal and simultaneous in being, while totally dependent on their divine Source. Yet the universe is correctly styled a "maximum," not an absolute Maximum like the unlimited God, but a contracted or limited maximum, an image of the Absolute, restricted to the manifold beings it embraces and unites. As the absolute Infinite, God is "negatively" unlimited, Cusanus says, in the sense that nothing does or can limit God in any respect.

For Nicholas, the physical universe, this limited maximum, is also paradoxically unlimited, but only "privatively." That is to say, since the universe lacks limits, there is nothing else outside this physical whole that can or could mark its physical limits.[31] Cusanus writes:

> Therefore only the absolutely Maximum is negatively infinite. Hence it alone is whatever there can at all possibly be. But since the universe encompasses all the things which are not God, it cannot be negatively infinite, although it is unbounded and thus privatively infinite. And in this respect it is neither finite nor infinite. (2.1 h 97)

The Cusan universe is thus ontologically limited, but "infinite" or unlimited in extent—"neither finite nor infinite." It is a dynamic and comprehensive one as contrasted with the many that make it up, yet an attenuated or contracted oneness parallel to, and the image of, the divine Oneness who is without opposite because beyond opposition. Or better, God is the One responsible for the "opposition" between the universe and finite beings and the opposition or diversity among the beings themselves.

One of the most difficult chapters to interpret in *De docta ignorantia* is 2.5, entitled (after Anaxagoras) *"Quodlibet in quolibet"* (Each thing in each thing). Cusanus proposes, building on chapter 4, that because God is in every thing, through the mediation, as it were, of the universe *(quasi mediante universo)*, "it is evident that all is in all and each in each" (2.5 h 117). It is plausible enough to understand collectively the sum total of all the individual things in creation as a totality or whole simultaneous with and consisting of them as parts. We may even concede to Nicholas a kind of priority of the whole or universe with regard to the individual parts (for reasons to be discussed presently). But where is the plausibility in the claim that each and every thing is in each and every thing?

Cusanus writes,

> For in each created thing the universe is this created thing; and each thing receives all things in such way that in a given thing all things are, contractedly, this

---

31. See also T. Lai, "Nicholas of Cusa and the Finite Universe," *Journal of the History of Philosophy* 11 (1973): 161–67; Hopkins, *Learned Ignorance*, 17; and E. Brient, "Transitions to a Modern Cosmology: Meister Eckhart and Nicholas of Cusa on the Intensive Infinite," *Journal of the History of Philosophy* 37 (1999): 575–600.

thing. Since each thing is contracted, it is not the case that it can be actually all things; hence, it contracts all things, so that [in it] they are it. (2.5 h 117)

Two points do seem clear. First, Cusanus draws a parallel between God's presence to each thing and the universe's presence to each thing. Because of God's presence to each creature, the creature is a limited or contracted reflection, a dependent image of its divine Origin and Exemplar. Second, he regards the universe's presence to each thing as a unique whole–part relationship. If we construe "all things" *collectively* as comprising the whole or the universe, and "each thing" *distributively* as one of the plurality of actual things, what results is an understandable relation of whole and parts.

What exists are the plural individual things and no one of them can actually be simultaneously all the other individual things, taken distributively, as the actual individuals they are. But each individual thing, understood as part of a simultaneous whole, is a limited or contracted reflection of that collective whole or universe. Just as its formal oneness is an attenuated image of the divine Oneness, so as an individual part or contracted image of the universe or totality of things it is all things, taken collectively—in Nicholas' words, quoted above, "in a given thing all things are, contractedly, this thing." As Nicholas wrote in the previous chapter, "*Contraction* means contraction to [that is, restriction by] something, so as to be this or that. Therefore God, who is one, is in the one universe. But the universe is contractedly in all things" (2.4 h 116).[32]

Contraction may thus be understood as Nicholas' own construal of Platonic *participation*. Here participation, as the relation of originating Oneness to dependent and plural onenesses, can be spelled out in terms of exemplar and dependent image. All things, taken collectively as the universe, are in each and every thing, the constitutive parts of the universe, because each individual thing's oneness is a "contracted" or limited reflection of the oneness of the collective whole *(uni-verse)*, the exemplar. That is why Nicholas writes that "the universe is in each thing in one way, and each thing is in the universe in another way" (2.5 h 118). As a collective whole or unity, the universe is reflected in each thing's oneness (= "is in each thing"). As a constitutive part of the universe, each thing contributes to the whole (= "is in the universe").

How, then, does "the plurality [of things] exist in oneness"? In the Cusan cosmos of more and less, "each thing was not able to be altogether like the other. This, then, caused all things to exist in different degrees" (2.5 h 120). But with all their differences and plurality, "one de-

---

32. Hopkins, in *Metaphysic of Contraction*, 99–101, lists the texts and summarizes the varied senses of *contrahere* and "contraction" for Nicholas.

gree could not exist without another" (h 121). Cusanus' background picture seems to be a constructed or organic whole where each part contributes and is content with its contribution to the whole. And his examples here refer to how walls and roof constitute a house and to how foot and hand and eye contribute to the whole bodily person.

These examples also help us understand how the universe is antecedent to the parts it comprises. Its priority is not temporal but is rather the priority of an ordered whole required for the connections of the parts, even though no one part is required for the whole. Thus the parts or created things that make up the universe are related to one another not merely as a sheer multiplicity whose separateness and diversity are brute matters of fact, but as a plurality that builds up or constitutes a unity. That each thing is itself and not another also means that each is simultaneously related to the rest as diverse parts of a whole, a cosmos or universe. (In the background is the traditional picture of the universe of creatures as hierarchical, a picture Nicholas makes explicit when he comes to Book 3.) As a maximum built up of plural entities, the universe is more than any one of its parts. As a *contracted* maximum, it limits its reflection of the divine Oneness to this existing oneness-in-plurality.

"Contracted" here also connotes a kind of drawing together into a whole or universe—another sense for *"con-tractio"*—of all the many varied individuals created in time and space. Each creature can thus be viewed metaphorically as a drawing together into itself of all the related other things and the universe they constitute together. Each "microcosmic" contracted entity reflects the universe as a whole, a "macrocosmic" oneness of multiple related things. These things are not actually present in any individual, though there is a basis for the metaphor of contraction in each thing's unity and in the totality of its connections with everything else. This implies that the universe is not just a conception or notion of a collectivity whereby we gather things together in thought. In actual fact, in reality, things constitute this ordered, interrelated whole whether we advert to the state of affairs or not.

Individuals, then, are "in the universe" as its constituents or component parts. The universe is "in the individuals" as the sum total of each individual's connections with everything else. As both whole and parts, "each thing is in each thing," because each thing reflects or is an image of the oneness of the whole universe and thus of all the interrelated individuals it comprises as parts.[33]

33. Flasch, in *Nikolaus von Kues*, 101, advises that this is the crucial philosophic insight of Book 2: "Cusanus will zeigen, wie die Welt zu denken sei, nämlich nicht als Konglomerat selbständiger 'Substanzen,' sondern als Präsenz der Allnatur in jedem Einselding und als Insein der Einseldinge im Universum, und die nicht als starre Aufstellung von Dingen im Raum, sondern als Prozess wechselseitiger Durchdringung von Gegensatzpaaren."

TABLE 1.1. Degrees of Contraction in the Universe—*De docta ignorantia* 2.6

1	point	God	absolute oneness
$10 = 10^1$	line	universe 10 categories	first contracted oneness
$100 = 10^2$	surface	genera/species	second contracted oneness
$1{,}000 = 10^3$	physical objects	actual things	third contracted oneness

2C. Envisioning the Whole

The next several chapters of Book 2 attempt to parallel Nicholas' treatment in Book 1 of the absolute Maximum. In them Nicholas proposes some ways in which the universe as a oneness-in-plurality could be considered both one and three—a contracted image of the divine Trinity. In the course of his own proposals he reviews various ideas proposed by earlier Platonists, adopting and adapting some of them to his own ideas. These chapters are particularly notable because he rejects any interposition of a realm of preexisting ideas whether in an intelligence such as the Plotinian Nous or in a "world soul" to mediate between God and the creatures who make up the universe. The essences of things are enfolded in an undifferentiated way in God's absolute Infinity; they are unfolded and differentiated in diverse and plural contracted creatures.

Chapter 6 lays out in a series of parallels the "degrees of contraction" of the universe. Perhaps the parallels Cusanus here envisions can best be captured in tabular form (read Table 1.1 from top to bottom).

For Cusanus, this schematic table is to be understood as charting how God is unfolded through a putative hierarchy of lesser onenesses, each related to the previous (above it in the table) as unfolding to enfolding and as more contracted to less contracted. But the schematic neatness of these "degrees of contraction" is so seriously compromised by Nicholas' insistence on no ontological intermediaries between God and actual creatures that it finally seems little more than a *jeu d'esprit*. Further, his discussion of the relation of universals to particulars qualifies to such an extent his use of the quasi-technical term "contraction" that we may do well to interpret *contractio* both metaphorically and as a term of art.[34]

For Cusanus, individuals or particulars contract universals no less

---

34. H. L. Bond proposed (in a personal communication) that we should understand contraction as Nicholas' way of pointing to how we must rethink creation and indeed the

than species contract genera and genera contract the ten categories. This at worst confuses and at best conflates the relation between more and less inclusive universals with the relation between universals and particulars. The purported parallel does not hold, so long as one says that a species or subspecies is a *contraction* of a genus (since there may be other species of the same genus) *and* that an individual instance is a *contraction* of the species to which it belongs, as do many others. "Contraction" is, strictly speaking, equivocal between the two cases.

After all, genera and species have real existence only in particular instances; otherwise, for Nicholas, they have the reality of objects of thought, "rational entities." Cusanus holds that all individuals or particulars are limited instances of the kind to which they belong—they are not more or less pigs, for instance, but more or less perfect instances of what pigs can be. Now the species "pig" is not more or less part of the genus "animal," nor is it more or less perfectly "animal" than other sorts of animals. For Nicholas the particulars alone are mind-independent and real. Their quiddities or essences—understood as enfolded in God and hence no different from God—are also real—indeed, divinely so.

What we call universals are the results of our taking thought about particulars:

Although universals do not exist as actual apart from particulars, nevertheless they are not mere rational entities. (By comparison, although neither a line nor a surface exists apart from a material object, they are not on this account mere rational entities; *for they exist in material objects, even as universals exist in particulars.*) Nevertheless, by [the process of] abstracting, the intellect makes them exist independently of things. To be sure, the abstraction is a rational entity, since absolute being cannot befit universals. For the altogether absolute universal is God. (2.6 h 125; my emphasis)

Perhaps using contraction to cover such cases that hardly seem parallel is simply a metaphorical extension and application of its central use in comparing God to creatures—as if genera and species had some reality apart from minds the way particulars do.

Another way to organize our understanding of the contracted universe as a reflection of God, who is one and three, is to consider, first,

---

whole relation of God and creatures—emanation without intermediaries. Nicholas spelled out this point a few years later, in 1445–1446, writing in *De dato Patris luminum* 2 h 99:

The Giver of forms does not give something other than Himself; rather, His gift is best and is His own maximal goodness, which is absolute and in every respect maximum. But it cannot be received as it is given, because the receiving of the gift occurs in a descending manner. Therefore, the infinite is received finitely; the universal, singularly; and the absolute, contractedly. But since such a receiving falls short of the truth of the one who is imparting Himself, it turns toward a likeness and an image, so that it is not the truth of the Giver but a likeness of the Giver. (Hopkins translation, *Metaphysic of Contraction*, 118–19) matter or possibility; second, form or soul; and third, spirit or movement (reflecting Father, Son, and Holy Spirit, respectively). But Nicholas asserts that in creating God is responsible as well for the matter or contracted possibility of the universe. He denies that there is a world soul in the sense adopted by the late Platonic commentators on the *Timaeus*. In Book 2, chapters 8 and 9, Nicholas takes pains to assert his own distinctive position:

> God alone is absolute; all other things are contracted. Nor is there a medium between the Absolute and the contracted as those imagined who thought that the world-soul is mind existing subsequently to God but prior to the world's contraction. For only God is "world-soul" and "world-mind"—in a manner whereby "soul" is regarded as something absolute in which all the forms of things exist actually. (2.9 h 150)

2D. A Decentered Universe

In 2.10 Nicholas proceeds to the third element in the universe that reflects the divine Trinity: the nature of the whole viewed as "motion." Nicholas terms the Holy Spirit "union" or "connection." No less is "motion," whether movement or change, responsible for the things brought about by motion, as well as the basis for their being related one to another. In the contracted maximum that is the natural universe, the changes whereby things come to pass or are modified and thus related to other changing things are limited reflections of the loving union in the triune God personified as the Holy Spirit. Motion, then, connects, relates, and unites all changeable, contingent things into a single whole, though qua natural motion, it too is always contracted, a matter of more or less.

Nicholas believes our ignorance becomes learned regarding the universe once we understand the contracted state of creation. We recognize that the differences between created things are such that no two of them are exactly equal and that all the specimens of any type we choose to examine display differences of degree without ever reaching maximum or minimum. When we consider movement, then, we never find a fixed or stable point of reference where things are at rest. (As the minimum of movement, rest has to coincide with maximal motion and thus with God.) It is on metaphysical grounds, then, that Nicholas argues in chapters 11 and 12 to reach some remarkable conclusions about the physical universe and the place of the earth within it.[35]

Traditionally the earth had been seen as the unmoving, fixed, central point of the universe. But since there is nothing created and contracted

---

35. A. Zimmermann, "'Belehrte Unwissenheit' als Ziel der Naturforschung," in Jacobi, ed., *Einführung*, 129–34; Flasch, *Nikolaus von Kues*, 100–101.

that is completely at rest or exactly at a given point, the earth cannot be either fixed or exactly at the center, even if it appears to be nearer the center than the outermost sphere of fixed stars. Nor is the physical center of the universe within the earth. Rather, the universe is without any fixed boundaries, whether center or circumference.

What lies behind Nicholas' break with traditional medieval thought about the physical universe is his philosophical conviction that the limited universe is devoid of exactness as much as of unqualified minima or maxima—be these rest (= minimal motion) or physical extent (fixed center and circumference). He thus modifies (and undercuts) the Ptolemaic world picture because he concludes that none of the spheres is exactly spherical, that the outermost sphere is not a boundary, and that no sphere has a center. He writes:

> For since the center is a point equidistant from the circumference and since there cannot exist a sphere or circle so completely true that a truer one could not be posited, it is obvious that there cannot be posited a center [which is so true and precise] that a still truer and more precise center could not be posited. Precise equidistance to different things cannot be found except in the case of God, because God alone is Infinite Equality. (2.11 h 157)

Because there is only one divine Absolute, because all creatures and the universe comprising them are contracted or limited, because the domain of contracted things is *ontologically* a realm of more or less, Cusanus tips the medieval world picture off balance, not on scientific but on metaphysical grounds. Cusanus peers into the heavens and sees stars in movement, but now they only appear to describe maximal or minimal circles in their motion and this only because we ascribe fixed poles and centers to the spheres whose motions we attempt to measure. Such ascription is what Nicholas calls, in a Cusan term of art, "conjecture." All we are dealing with is conjectural poles and centers, not actual ones. The motions, the distances, and the measurements we make do not capture the actual state of planetary motion beyond our ken.

Finally, the exactness of the universe, its true center and its true circumference, is found nowhere else but in God. As infinite equality God is the sole center and circumference of the universe because God is ontologically "equidistant" from the universe as a whole and its constitutive parts.[36] Here again Nicholas uses a quantitative spatial metaphor, that of equal distance, and transfers it to God, just as he did the metaphor of

---

36. K. Harries, "The Infinite Sphere: Comments on the History of a Metaphor," *Journal of the History of Philosophy* 13 (1975): 5–15. I touch on the same metaphor in connection with Nicholas' late *De ludo globi* in "Nicholas of Cusa's *De ludo globi:* Symbolic Roundness and Eccentric Life Paths," *Acta* 10 (1983): 135–48, esp. 140–41.

size in Book 1 when he proposed that in God maximum and minimum coincide because God is the absolute Maximum.

In fact, the metaphor of God as center and circumference combines both geometry and extension. The geometrical exercises in the middle of Book 1 are calculated to help us think through and understand how God's transcendence means God is beyond our rational capacities of conceptualization. At the same time, they point us in a direction beyond the finite. This present metaphor is also intended to help us break from our normal ways of imagining the universe and its connection with God.

Nicholas in fact proposes some directions to assist us: "Therefore, if with regard to what has now been said you want truly to understand something about the motion of the universe, you must merge the center and the poles, aiding yourself as best you can by your imagination." And a bit later, "Therefore, merge these different imaginative pictures so that the center is the zenith and vice versa. Thereupon you will see—through the intellect, to which only learned ignorance is of help—that the world and its motion and shape cannot be apprehended" (2.11 h 161). Nicholas' Latin for "merge" is *complicare*, the same word he uses for "enfolding" as opposed to "unfolding" in other contexts. Evidently he is urging us to exchange perspectives in imagination as we entertain different standpoints (earth, then antipodes) so that we see how center becomes zenith and vice versa, depending on our viewpoint.[37]

This lets us realize that center and zenith are only fixed or stationary because they appear to be so from a given standpoint. When we merge them in thought we realize no standpoint is more privileged than another and that what we term "center" may just as well be "zenith." This will let us conclude with him that "the world-machine will have its center everywhere and its circumference nowhere, so to speak" (2.12 h 162). Any and every location we pick as center (and none is better than any other) will alter what we take as circumference and what seems to be moving in relation to what is apparently unmoving.

Yet the reason Cusanus adds for concluding that the universe's center is everywhere and its circumference nowhere is more than a matter of perspectives to be exchanged and "merged." He writes, "for God, who is everywhere and nowhere, is its circumference and center" (2.12 h 162). This ontological theorem was earlier justified by the notion that God's transcendence made him equally present to all of creation. Here, how-

---

37. See my longer exposition in "Perception, Conjecture and Dialectic," *American Catholic Philosophical Quarterly* 64 (1990): 35–54, esp. 41–45; also see K. Harries, "Problems of the Infinite: Cusanus and Descartes," *American Catholic Philosophical Quarterly* 64 (1990): 89–110, esp. 91–95; and Hopkins, *Learned Ignorance*, 27–30.

ever, it has a somewhat different force, since it backs up a conclusion about the physical universe, and lets us see from a different perspective how the universe is its own sort of contracted maximum. Moreover, the very imaginative merging or enfolding that Cusanus proposed to let us see how all parts of the physical universe are moved, whether it appears so or not, led us to conclude that its physical center was everywhere and its circumference nowhere. The universe is not bounded or centered physically, even though ordinary thinking might imagine it that way.

Any enfolding of human perspectives or physical locations can remind us of how the whole universe is a contracted oneness, the maximal, if limited, image of the absolute divine Oneness. As absolute, God alone sets ontological boundaries to what God has created. For Cusanus, we are actually thinking toward God in realizing that the shape and motion of the contracted maximum "cannot be apprehended" any more than can its divine ontological Measure.

We find a pattern for such moving toward God in thought when we attempt to merge center and circumference, to think them together. God is Measure or Limit for all things created and in that sense is everywhere we find contracted beings; but God is also nowhere, because as absolute, God is not contracted or "intermingled" (*absque immersione;* h 166) with limited things but transcends them while unfolding them. Yet to attempt to think God's immanence and transcendence, his *undique et nullibi,* together, we have to approach the divine Enfolding and Unfolding in a movement parallel to that of merging zenith and center for the universe. Both will remain beyond our conceptual grasp, but the attempt to think them together in a dialectical way can open us to some insight that will render our ignorance learned.

BOOK 3: JESUS CHRIST—THE MAXIMUM AT ONCE ABSOLUTE AND CONTRACTED

There are four basic realities for Christian thought: God, the universe, human beings, and Jesus Christ. That all four appear in Nicholas of Cusa's *De docta ignorantia* can hardly be surprising, for this deeply Christian masterwork of the fifteenth century advances Cusanus' systematic view of the whole of reality. Book 1 dealt with God, termed by Nicholas the absolute Maximum. Book 2 dealt with the created cosmos or universe, what for Nicholas is the contracted maximum. Human beings are presupposed throughout the first two books, for human knowing and measuring are central to Cusanus' discussion of the first two realities.

The third book takes up human nature explicitly in order to explore the fourth reality, Jesus Christ—the Maximum at once absolute and contracted.[38] Cusanus expounds where being human fits into the whole of reality in the course of explaining the God-man's exemplary reality. In his unique case, Nicholas proposes, we are led to see all that being human can amount to.

The religious import of his subject should not, however, cover up the singular methodology Nicholas lays out so carefully in Book 1 and encapsulates in his title. What we are finally to understand of God, the universe, and Jesus—indeed, even of our selves and our hapless striving to know and understand—will be an understanding in the light-and-darkness of learned ignorance. For "learned ignorance" is more than a striking title or even a reminder of our lack of knowledge. Rather, learned ignorance is *the* way Cusanus proposes that any human being searching for wisdom has some chance of attaining all-too-human an understanding of God, the universe, the human self, and now of Christ Jesus. Learned ignorance builds in the constraints that constitute Cusan method, guiding us along a road to insights never detached from blindness.

Nicholas does not begin Book 3 of *De docta ignorantia* by expounding directly a Christology. He mentions neither the Christian Scriptures nor the teachings of the Fathers nor the dogmatic pronouncements of the early Christian councils such as Nicaea and Chalcedon. They form the backdrop but seldom appear explicitly in the initial chapters. Cusanus returns instead to the central and original concepts he explained and employed in the first two books. He first touches on his teaching about God as the absolute Maximum and infinite Oneness. Then he reviews in more detail his teaching about the universe, the contracted maximum whose oneness consists of the interrelated plurality of created things.

Cusanus capitalizes on the ineluctable connection of absolute and contracted in order to move into the Christian mystery of the Incarnation. He devotes the first chapters of Book 3 to a hypothetical exercise or thought experiment. Perhaps these chapters are better understood as responding to a question: Given what has been taught about absolute

38. The classic commentary on Cusanus' Christology is R. Haubst, *Die Christologie des Nikolaus von Kues* (Freiburg: Herder, 1956). See also his later articles: "Nicolaus von Kues und die heutige Christologie," in *Universitas. Dienst an Wahrheit und Leben*, 2 vols., ed. L. Lenhart (Mainz: Matthias Grünwald, 1960), 1:165–75, and "Die Wege der christologischen manuductio," *Mitteilungen und Forschungsbeiträge der Cusanus-Gesellschaft* 16 (1984): 164–83. (From this point on, I will cite *Mitteilungen und Forschungsbeiträge der Cusanus-Gesellschaft* as *MFCG*.) Shorter summaries are provided by C. Schönborn, "'De docta ignorantia' als christozentrischer Entwurf," in Jacobi, ed., *Einführung*, 138–56; Hopkins, *Learned Ignorance*, 30–42; and Flasch, *Nikolaus von Kues*, 102, 135–42. The notes of H. G. Senger in his German translation and edition of *De docta ignorantia III* (Hamburg: Meiner, 1977) provide essential references to Nicholas' sources and his other works.

and contracted, under what conditions could they appear together in a human individual? They do so appear in each human person, of course, but what would happen were some contracted creature to be united "hypostatically," that is, substantially or "personally," with the divine Absolute? Chapter 4 identifies this hypothetical possibility with what occurred in Jesus Christ, while the remaining chapters of Book 3 (5–12) comment in order on what the other articles of the Christian creed teach about Jesus' life, death, and resurrection and the community he founded.[39]

3A. Rethinking Absolute and Contracted

Why does Nicholas return to what he considers already explained and established in the first two books of *De docta ignorantia*? Book 2 closed with Cusanus imagining creatures responding to questions that asked how or for what purpose they exist. That purpose is to be sought not in creatures themselves but in their "Cause and Reason" (*in ratione et causa;* 2.13 h 180). Yet Book 1 demonstrated how that Cause remains inaccessible unless somehow disclosed to learned ignorance and revealed to faith. And so Cusanus returns to the contracted universe. Now he will entertain a further possibility: a philosophically anomalous revelation in which absolute and contracted meet and are joined in a completely new kind of oneness.

But is another variant of the crucial connection between absolute and contracted a real possibility? What is limited or contracted in the realm of creatures is encompassed by the transcendent Absolute—the Oneness free or "absolved" *(ab-solutum)* from every constraint we might imagine or conceive. Nicholas restates this in the first chapter of Book 3, after pointing out that every contracted thing can be measured as more or less perfect of its kind: "Therefore, there is only one Limit of species, of genera, or of the universe. This limit is the Center, the Circumference, and the Union of all things" (3.1 h 185). This unlimited but limiting limit is God. While we cannot spell out positively what such an Absolute might be in itself, at least we can realize that the contracted things of creation cannot be truly thought for what they are (and what they are not) without thinking them as at once bound up with the infinite God. Infinite and finite may be incommensurable, but they are inextricably bound together in Cusan thought.

39. Offermann's *Christus* provides a book-length commentary on *De docta ignorantia* read from the viewpoint of Book 3 and Nicholas' Christology. He also provides a very useful bibliography of (mostly German) books and articles relevant to Book 3. See also H. L. Bond, "Nicholas of Cusa and the Reconstruction of Christology: The Centrality of Christology in the Coincidence of Opposites," in *Contemporary Reflections on the Medieval Christian Tradition*, ed. G. H. Shriver (Durham, N.C.: Duke University Press, 1974), 81–94.

To understand the connection of Absolute and contracted is to recognize that the Absolute is identical with the contracted, even if the contracted cannot be identical with the Absolute. The Infinite encompasses the finite, but the finite depends entirely on the Infinite. In relation to God, a creature has barely the being of an accident in relation to substance—a mere nothing in comparison to God. To be encompassed by God is thus to be dependently related. For God to encompass is to be causally responsible for and thus present to created things without being thereby correspondingly dependent on them. Because the Absolute encompasses, it is not dependent; because the contracted is dependent, it is encompassed. In other terms: without the divine Exemplar, there can be no created images at all; without images, the Original or Exemplar abides untouched and transcendent.

Because God is all in all and nothing in nothing, God's *complicatio* and *explicatio* surpass the usual categories of oneness and difference. Therefore, God both is and is not creatures. Likewise, God neither is nor is not creatures. Because God is the being or form of creatures, God is not the creatures themselves. And because God is not the creatures themselves, God is their being or form. The both–and of God's identity with and distinction from creatures is thus disclosed as simultaneously a neither–nor where creatures are concerned. Because the opposition of God and creatures entails their connection, the laws of noncontradiction and of excluded middle do not apply. Therefore, *how* God is related to created things must escape our ken.[40]

To complete his task in Book 3, Cusanus must consider the possibility that absolute and contracted are related in yet another way than those already explicated in Books 1 and 2. God is eternal, unchanging, and in principle unchangeable. Finite, contracted things reside in a temporal, changing universe. Since the absolute Creator stays utterly free and infinite, we can expect any variations to occur on the side of the contracted and finite creatures.

The Cusan universe is the totality or whole of such finite things. As a whole or maximum, it is limited in its being though unbounded in its physical extent. Its oneness is realized only in the dynamic, ordered plurality of entities that constitute or make it up. In this way the universe is

---

40. This formulation of God's transcendence and immanence echoes that of Turner, in *Darkness*, 128. See also P. Casarella, "His Name Is Jesus: Negative Theology and Christology in Two Writings of Nicholas of Cusa from 1440," in *Christ and the Church*, 281–307. Casarella, Bond, in "Historical Matrix," 159–63, and Flasch, in *Nikolaus von Kues*, 123–35, remark on the importance for Book 3 of several sermons Nicholas preached at the time of writing *De docta ignorantia:* "Verbum caro factum est," "Nomen eius Jesus," "Intrantes domum," and the well-known "Dies sanctificatus." These sermons are numbers 19–22 in the Heidelberg critical edition.

also a maximum whose contracted oneness is but a reflection or image of the absolutely maximal divine Oneness. In just the same way, each individual being is a contracted oneness, a reflection of the divine Oneness and of the oneness of the universe, the totality of created beings that make up the whole.

But the created universe of change, consisting as it does of individuals who manifest the characteristics of their types and kinds, is not without its own ordered determinate forms and unities. Nicholas returns to his earlier teaching on genera and species (Book 2.6) to explain the contracted maximum as further contracted to a natural kind or species. In Book 2 he had discussed the traditional teaching about genera and species, couching it in his own terms of "degrees of contraction." While the Aristotelian doctrine of the ten categories and of natural kinds apparently rules the sublunary realm for Nicholas, it requires adjustment and modification to fit his more Platonic doctrines of contraction, of image and original, and of the interrelated whole *(quodlibet in quolibet)*.

True enough, Nicholas says that only individuals exist and that each exists as a specimen of a type. Yet he also superimposes on the common doctrine of genera and species his idea that each individual is both a concentration and a reflection—a contracted image—of the ideal possibilities, the "truth" of its type or kind, as well as of the oneness of the universe and its Creator. Yet ideal types or originals do not exist in a separate realm of Forms, but are indistinguishable in God's infinite oneness. And so Nicholas writes that each species is a contraction or constriction of the possibilities of a given genus, while the various genera contract or demarcate the possibilities of the categories and of the universe as a whole. While the universe and every individual in it are contracted images of God, each individual is also an image of its authentic original type. Each is a limited case or a specimen that more or less fulfills the possibilities of its kind. In this way each particular entity reflects the oneness and interconnectedness of each and all created things—the limited maximum oneness that is the universe.

This extension of "contraction" to genera and species means that human measuring of existing individuals and classifying them into kinds should not omit how each specimen of a type is related to others of its own kind as well as to other kinds of things. As a contracted image, each specimen is not only a limiting or restricting *(ein Eingeshränkte)* that draws together in a given individual the possibilities of its kind, but also a concentration *(ein Zusammengezogenes)* or node of connections between itself and all other individuals.[41] In this way each individual's for-

---

41. Here I follow the two German translations of *contractio* and their connotations explained by Offermann, in *Christus*, 106, note 52. Both are required to do justice to all that

mal oneness is both an image of its own kind as one of a type and a reflection of the other instances of oneness to which it is connected. As itself contracted, a thing's very imperfection also reflects and is one with its relatedness to all—*quodlibet in quolibet*.

Cusanus' background assumption here is that human knowing is a kind of measuring or proportioning able to rank individuals as more or less perfect specimens of their types in an ordered universe where the types of substances themselves can be graded in a hierarchical fashion. Nor is he nominalistic in this regard: the ways things are in fact imposes restraints on our ways of construing them. We cannot arbitrarily make the conceptual universe into whatever we please or impose on the rest of the world our own ideal construction, while claiming our concepts will match what God has wrought. Rather, it is our constant awareness that God *has* wrought this universe and each thing in it that enables us to view it sacramentally—*quodlibet in quolibet*—that is, as a whole of connected onenesses, a contracted or limited whole that reflects or is "charged with" God's greatness and maximality.

3B. A Maximum at Once Absolute and Contracted

Given this view of the created universe, Nicholas begins to analyze what would happen were a perfect instance or specimen to actually occur. That is, what would be the implications were there an individual entity who was the perfect fulfillment of its type? Such a hypothetical individual, Nicholas says, would reach the limits of a given species and transcend what is possible for any ordinary instance of that kind. In the Cusan language of maximality, what would ensue is another maximum, but one restricted or contracted to a single specimen of a given type or species.

This hypothetical case of a contracted maximum obviously differs from that other contracted maximum, the Cusan universe.[42] The universe is a totality or maximum contracted to, because constituted by, the multitude of entities that it comprises. This new contracted maximum would be a finite, uniquely perfect individual who would instantiate in actuality every possibility that could be realized in its kind or species. We might spell out the difference as follows. While the universe is a contracted or restricted maximum of all limited things, a created whole of interconnected creatures, such a hypothetical individual would be a sin-

---

Nicholas sees reflected and concentrated, as it were, in actual created things and summarized in his slogan *quodlibet in quolibet*. His is not a Platonism that undervalues the sacramental dimension of limited things, but one that capitalizes on their constraints as so enmeshed with other creatures as to reflect both the whole of creation and their Creator.

42. For a similar summary, see Schönborn, "Christozentrischer Entwurf," 145–46.

gle contraction "at the maximum"—one creature surpassing the usual possibilities and attaining the truth of its nature. Nicholas' Christology, one might say, contrasts "intensive" maximality (the maximum of a limited or contracted type) with "extensive" maximality (the restricted or contracted maximum that is a whole of parts or universe without physical limits).

Such an individual, then, would transcend degrees of more and less and would realize the full potential of its type. As Nicholas puts it, this individual being "would be the means [*via*], form, essence, and truth of all the things which are possible in the species" (3.2 h 191). This language recalls that used to describe a Platonic Form, and thus marks an important difference in a universe where Nicholas finds degrees of more and less even between individuals of a type, since no single entity plumbs the depths or scales the heights theoretically available to its kind.[43] So this putative discovery would be unique. This would not be just another contracted thing, but a contracted nature "at the maximum," so to speak, instantiated in a creature unlike every other.

While such a creature would not be the universe, neither would it be simply God, for God is utterly without contraction. What would make this creature possible as an individual maximum contracted would be its unique union with God, the absolute divine Maximum which is the single source of every contracted reality, maximal or not. God's uniting with this creature would render it an individual at once contracted-and-absolute—and maximal on both counts—an individual marking an exceptional union, a singular case of oneness of God and creature. Its unique maximality would compensate, as it were, for the finitude of the universe's unity-in-plurality and for the imperfect oneness of every other creature by uniting and manifesting God and all created things in one individual whose perfection as creature would equal that found in the rest of creation.

Nicholas writes:

Suppose Maximum Power united to itself this contracted [individual thing] in such way that it could not be more united and the respective natures still be preserved. [And suppose that], as a result, this contracted thing—its contracted nature being preserved (in accordance with which nature it is the contracted and created fullness of its species)—were, on account of a hypostatic union, both

---

43. H. Meinhardt stresses the authentic Platonism of Cusanus' Christology in "Das Geheimnis des Todes und der Auferstehung Jesu Christi nach Cusanus, ineins damit sein Verständnis der Auferstehung der Toten," *MFCG* 23 (1996): 71–82, esp. 72–76. What is particularly helpful is his pointing out, first, how Cusan created things are images of their divine Original and, second, how the notion of a maximum of a given kind of thing corresponds to Platonic Forms, both in Plato and in the later Christian thinkers who placed such Forms in God or God's creative *Verbum*.

God and all things. [In that case,] this admirable union would transcend our entire understanding. (3.2 h 192; Hopkins, p. 129, modified)

The number of times this passage mentions "contracted" surely underlines the necessity of modifying and extending this key Cusan notion that covers created things to fit an entirely new possibility, the God-man.

In the case of Christ there would be a special relation of the absolute Maximum and the contracted maximum of a kind, signaled by the traditional notion of "hypostatic union." How would such a union of Absolute and contracted differ from a "nonhypostatic" union of the two, given that once again the encompassing triune God would be causally responsible for the Incarnation of the divine Word in the historical Jesus Christ? As in the case of all other creatures, so in that of Christ's maximal human nature, God would create and sustain the whole of this finite, dependent, and contingent reality. Yet while remaining maximally human, Jesus' body and soul, his complete human nature, would be united in a unique and unimaginable way with the absolute God so that the "both–and" and "neither–nor" of the ordinary connection between Absolute and contracted would have to be reconceptualized.

Ordinarily the contracted creature is to be understood as dependent on the absolute Creator, while the absolute Creator as such is independent. In the instance of Christ, the Absolute's independence could not be separated from this case of the contracted creature. Expressed in anthropomorphic terms of choice, even should God not have chosen to create ordinary creatures, God would abide in absolute, infinite Oneness. Yet that same eternal God has chosen both to create finite things and, further, is here hypothetically assumed to have chosen to create and assume this single, limited nature so as to remain, as God, inseparable from this one human creature. Although we cannot imagine or conceive positively the union of human and divine in Christ, we would misconceive the Incarnation if we take it to be the same kind of ontological relation that other creatures have with God. Dependence and inseparability have to be construed anew and altogether otherwise so that both the dependence of Christ's human nature *and* its inseparability from the divine Word would be understood as the ultimate ground and reason why Christ's human nature is maximal of its kind.

Put in terms of the coincidence of opposites, no longer would God's enfolding be transcendent beyond even contradictory claims (such as both "is" and "is not" plus neither "is" nor "is not") and thereby immanent, the unfolded divine Encompassing of everything created.[44] Now

---

44. Bond writes insightfully about how to adapt the *coincidentia oppositorum* to Book 3, in *Nicholas of Cusa*, 24–26.

God's transcendent oneness would appear in a new sort of created oneness. This would unite divine and human in a manifestation of the Divine that would transcend but not erase the human because this revelation would occur solely and uniquely *through* the human. This would be a whole new sort of created unfolding *(explicatio)* in a human being that would at once disclose the Divine enfolded *(complicatio)* in Jesus' human life, death, and resurrection. In these early chapters of Book 3, Cusanus is working both hypothetically in terms of his own opposition of absolute and contracted, and yet not entirely hypothetically, just because he is also guided by his faith and the teaching of tradition about the God-man.

This "hypothetical" consideration is spelled out in Cusan philosophical terms that are extended or reinterpreted to express the Christian faith that Jesus is both God and man. Nicholas' point is to acknowledge the full eternal reality of both Jesus' divinity and Jesus' humanity and their oneness in created time and space. What Nicholas usually put in terms of the relation of oneness to the other numbers and the relation of exemplar original to image now must be reinterpreted. If those parallels were to apply, we may imagine Christ would be that number whose relation to oneness did not simply presuppose but entailed oneness. Because he is taken up into the equality of the Trinity's Second Person, Jesus would be and would remain a human image of God that is both truth and image at once. Jesus would be an image of God so utterly transparent as to be opaque, except that faith has us bend the knee before the babe at Bethlehem.

Learned ignorance can count some lessons that Nicholas' initial assumptions already make plain. Clearly we cannot comprehend the *how* of such a union of creature and Creator. Nonetheless, we can specify how and why such a union is not like all the other familiar unions it surpasses. Since God is and is not separated from ordinary created things but is ever beyond all things as enfolding and at once in them all as unfolding, this new union goes beyond such "ordinary" connection between God and other things. This is, besides, no uniting of two previously separate or independently existing things, since no before or after is to be found in God. Moreover, no such maximal creature could exist as the truth or paradigm of its type, unless the divine Nature was united to it. Nor is this of an addition of two physical parts to make a whole or an ontological composition of form with matter, for God cannot be a part in any sense, nor does God inform matter, but encompasses all informed material things and their parts.

Here a contracted maximum (Jesus' human nature) exists only because it is one with the absolute Maximum (his divine nature); otherwise, the human nature would not be maximal as contracted. Yet Jesus' humanity adds nothing to the Absolute. Nor does it lose its identity qua contracted maximum or become absorbed into the Absolute. We cannot think this maximum as God alone, since what is contracted is not erased or obliterated; we cannot think this maximum as creature alone, since what is Absolute loses nothing of its infinite transcendence. Nor is the Incarnation some sort of composite mishmash of maximally contracted and maximally Absolute. We have to conceive this extraordinary case, Nicholas writes, as

(1) in such way God that it is also a creature, (2) in such way a creature that it is also Creator, and (3) Creator and creature without confusion and without composition. Who, then, could be lifted to such a height that in oneness he would conceive diversity and in diversity oneness? (3.2 h 194)

"Ut in unitate diversitatem et in diversitate unitatem concipere"—this could serve as Nicholas' call to the dialectical insights of learned ignorance. Only if we think dialectically—holding both Absolute and contracted in mind as just what they are, diverse, while asserting their union or oneness—can we do justice to this case. Earlier in *De docta ignorantia* the coincidence of opposites (and, indeed, most of the metaphors that are characteristically Cusan) required a similar sort of dialectical thinking. In Book 1 Nicholas proposed a movement from finite to infinite that involved holding together both sides of an opposition or even contradictory judgments in order to realize that God's infinite oneness lies beyond such discourse and thinking. In Book 2 a similar process of considering God as both center and circumference of the universe and of thinking through the *quodlibet in quolibet* required holding together in thought opposed conceptions without distorting or conflating them. Cusan dialectic holds onto both opposing sides without reconciling them or comprehending how they can be made compatible—it is precisely here that one sees *incomprehensibiliter* the divine Oneness that surpasses all contradiction.[45]

---

45. What makes this dialectic (Neo)Platonic (instead of Hegelian, for instance) is that it does not move to some sort of *Aufhebung*, some reconciliation or sublation that transforms yet preserves what was earlier seen as opposed. For a helpful brief differentiation of Hegelian and Cusan dialectic, see W. Beierwaltes, "Identität und Differenz: Zum Prinzip cusanischen Denkens," in *Rheinisch-Westfälische Akademie der Wissenschaften* (Opladen: Westdeutscher Verlag, 1977), 28–31. While Beierwaltes brings Cusanus closer to Hegel, M. de Gandillac underlines their differences in "Nikolaus von Kues zwischen Platon und Hegel," *MFCG* 11 (1975): 21–38. In a private communication, H. L. Bond has proposed that Cusan thinking here should be termed "thinking hypostatically and coincidentally" to underscore how it is peculiar to Cusanus.

3C. Human Nature as Microcosm

Nicholas is not done with his "hypothetical deduction." He next asks which created nature would be best suited for such a remarkable oneness with the divine Absolute. Understanding why this kind of contracted nature is suitable will clarify what it means to say that such a contracted maximum would be an enfolding of all created things. It comes as no surprise that Nicholas picks human nature; what is significant is the thinking that leads him to do so.[46]

Nicholas parallels the contracted nature required for the third maximum with the absolute Maximum. He begins by recalling that the absolute Maximum "is in the most universal way the Being of all things, so that it is not more of one thing than of another" (3.3 h 195). This counts as a gloss on what Cusanus had first written of the divine Maximum in Book 1: "it is a given thing in such way that it is all things; and it is all things in such way that it is no thing; and it is maximally a given thing in such way that it is it minimally" (1.4 h 12).

What sort of contracted entity could be united with such an Absolute? No contracted nature "is a given thing in such way that it is all things." Nor can any creature be "all things in such way that it is no thing." But there can be a created nature "more common to the totality of beings" (3.3 h 195). This would make it, according to Cusanus, "more unitable with the [absolute] Maximum" (3.3 h 195). Two considerations lead Nicholas to this conclusion. One is the order among created natures such that types of things sort hierarchically into higher, lower, and in between on the basis of the capacities some have and others lack. If we find an in-between kind that displays the capacities both of kinds above it and of kinds below it, we have the type of contracted entity we seek, one with common ties to the whole range of creatures based on shared capacities. Human beings traditionally have had just such an intermediate status—a bit below the angels while above other bodily creatures. When divine and human are united in Jesus there is not simply a new manifestation of God: the Incarnation reveals as well all that it can mean to be human.[47]

A second consideration from the side of the absolute Maximum directs us toward such a created nature with capacities in common with all

---

46. See Turner's parallel considerations about Bonaventura's Christology, in *Darkness*, 117–27.

47. Flasch writes (*Nikolaus von Kues*, 102) that for Nicholas, "Die Menschwerdung is kein vereinzeltes, bloss faktisch hinzunehmendes Ereignis; sie offenbart den Sinn der Menschheit."

creatures. Nicholas points out that the Maximum encompasses "one thing in such a way that it does not repel another thing but is all things together" (3.3 h 197). Considered ontologically, God's enfolding and unfolding shows no favoritism but God creates, sustains, and is present to each moment and facet of all creatures in an immediate and equivalent way. This means that an in-between created nature displaying a commonality or "parity" with other created natures parallel to the divine impartiality is most suitable for personal union with the Absolute. As "what is highest of the lower and what is lowest of the higher" natures, such a middle nature "enfolds within itself all natures" (3.3 h 197).

This creaturely enfolding parallels but does not duplicate the way God's infinite oneness and equality enfolds all things. God's enfolding parity or equality is an impartial causal unfolding and sustaining. In the case of human nature, the equality or commonality is metaphorical or virtual because it is a different sort of enfolding/unfolding, namely, a sharing of common powers or capacities distributed across a range of higher and lower natures. For Nicholas this provides, fittingly enough, a contracted creaturely *complicatio* to be united to the Absolute divine *complicatio*. Once again human nature is the obvious candidate since "it enfolds intellectual and sensible nature and encloses [*constringit*] all things within itself, so that the ancients were right in calling it a microcosm, or a small world" (3.3 h 198).

As microcosm human nature reflects and represents the interrelatedness of everything in the created universe. But as a totality of interconnected and contracted unities that universe is also a reflection of the intradivine relations that the Absolute triuneness encompasses. If one sort of parity made human nature an appropriate choice, Nicholas now points to another parity—the divine Equality. He recalls that God's creating finds its source in the Absolute as "Equality-of-being-all-things." And Nicholas named the Second Person of the Trinity, the divine Word, "Equality" in Book 1, just as the Father was called "Oneness" and the Holy Spirit their "Union" or "Connection." The upshot is that, just as in-between human nature was fitting on the side of the creature or contracted, so on the side of the Absolute, human nature would fittingly be assumed by the Son of God, the in-between second person, "the Word in whom all things were created, that is, Equality-of-Being" (3.3 h 200; Hopkins, p. 132, modified).

Such a union of God and human nature could only occur in one historic individual since human nature does not exist as such. Only particular women and men are real. Such an actual human being would not forego contractedness or humanity in union with the divine Absolute, any more than the Absolute would cease to be Absolute. Rather, it is precisely through union with the Absolute that such a human "would be a man in such way that He was also God and would be God in such way that He was also man" (3.3 h 199).

In this hypothetical union of contracted and Absolute learned ignorance gains another perspective on the absolute oneness of God and the contracted oneness of the created universe. They are no longer united simply as Creator and creature, *complicatio et explicatio,* in spite of there being no proportion between infinite and finite. Now they are united in Jesus, the one who is God and man. If discursive reason had to balk at the coincidence of all things in the transcendent God or had problems understanding how God is both center and circumference of an unbounded and decentered universe, the Incarnation represents a further coincident conundrum beyond reason's comprehension. What Nicholas originally ordered as absolute Maximum, contracted maximum, and maximum at once absolute-and-contracted must now be rethought and reordered. Nicholas writes:

... through Him who is the contracted maximum [individual] all things would go forth from the absolute Maximum into contracted being and would return unto the absolute [Maximum] through this same Medium, as through the source of their emanation and the goal of their return. (3.3 h 199; Hopkins, 132, modified)

And again:

Thus, God exists first of all as Creator. Secondly, [He exists as] God-and-man (a created humanity having been supremely assumed into oneness with God); the universal-contraction-of-all-things [that is, the humanity] is, so to speak, "personally" and "hypostatically" united with the Equality-of-being-all-things. Thus in the third place, all things—through most absolute God and by the mediation of the universal contraction, viz., the humanity—go forth into contracted being so that they may be that-which-they-are in the best manner and order possible. (3.3 h 202)

This is precisely to say that the third Maximum should come second, as being the one *through* whom the universe and all it comprises comes to be. For Cusanus no less than for Christians since St. Paul the true order is God, the God-man, and the universe. In this way Cusan dialectical thinking not only leads us to the central mystery of the Christian faith, the Incarnation, it also enables us to rethink the connection between the absolute God and the contracted things of creation. Jesus' human nature, that contracted individual maximum, mediates the creation and return of all that is not divine.[48]

48. Schönborn, in "Christozentrischer Entwurf," 147 and 154, emphasizes this point.

3D. Jesus Christ, the Absolute-and-Contracted Maximum

In chapter 4, Cusanus finally turns explicitly to what Christian faith proclaims: Jesus Christ is the one who is human in such a way as to be divine and divine in such a way as to be human. Jesus is the historic person who is the maximum at once contracted and absolute, the human image who is simultaneously the divine Original. But in having created image and divine Original so united or connected, how does Cusanus ensure that the creeds and conciliar dogmas about Christ remain true? How is the connection between image and original to be rethought in order to avoid Docetism, adoptionism, Arianism, Apollonarianism, Nestorianism, monophysitism, and all the other ancient and modern "isms"? Each of those early attempts to understand the Incarnation pressed a single insight too far or too one-sidedly and ended up undercutting the uniqueness of Jesus Christ. Cusan dialectical thinking may again lead us to the brink even as it hints at a corrective.

Chapter 4 of Book 3 stands as Nicholas' conjecture about the way the divine and human natures of Christ are united in the person of the Word. Nicholas begins by quoting St. Paul's hymn to the cosmic Christ from Colossians. He focuses on the words "all fullness dwells in him" *(in ipso complacuit omnem plenitudinem inhabitare)*, and proceeds to gloss them with his own notion of *complicatio* or enfolding. In Book 2 Nicholas wrote the words he repeats here: "God is in all things in such way that all things are in him." There these words meant that *complicatio* and *explicatio* must be thought together so that God is present to contracted things unfolded in their diversity in the universe just because and insofar as they are at once one in God's absolute, enfolding infinity. God's presence to created things now takes on new significance for those who believe in the Incarnation.

Nicholas indicates this importance by paralleling the way Christ's human nature mediates or enfolds all created things with the way the divine Absolute is the ultimate enfolding. Everything created is enfolded in simple absolute Oneness in the divine Word, God the Son, who is the Equality of being all things. Yet "every creature [exists] in the supreme and most perfect humanity, which completely enfolds all creatable things. Thus, all fullness dwells in Jesus" (3.4 h 204). It is because the divine Word is one with Christ's human nature that this nature is perfect of its kind, at once contracted and maximal. This creaturely nature can therefore stand as an enfolding of all things, mediating their creation and redemption.[49]

---

49. Cf. Offermann, *Christus*, 165–67.

"Because the divine word is one with Christ's human nature"—exactly here is where learned ignorance must pause and attempt some conception of this novel unity. Nicholas points to the way the human sensorium is changed by its relation to the human intellect. Ever since Plato and Aristotle sense knowledge had been acknowledged as a limited sort of cognition shared throughout the animal kingdom. Human beings are anomalous animals, however, for in "the human species, the senses give rise to an animal such that it is so animal that it is also intellect" (3.4 h 205). While intellect transcends the limits of human sense knowledge, it also transforms what sensation and perception, imagination and memory amount to. All the sensory powers and operations are now ordered beyond themselves while retaining their capacities to discern the particular sensory features of the world. Both sensation and intellection are united operatively and substantially in the oneness of the human knower. It is the oneness of the human person or supposit that Nicholas points to when he writes *"contractio sensualis quodammodo in intellectuali natura suppositatur"* (the sensory contracted nature is somehow substantially founded in the nature of the intellect; 3.4 h 205, my translation).[50]

Subsumption or assumption into the intellect's mode of knowing thus transforms the sensory powers to be more than they could be without the intellect. For Cusanus, there is a parallel in the way Jesus' human nature is substantially founded in the divine Word. As Cusanus writes in chapter 5: "[To it] He (the Holy Spirit) so inwardly united the word of God the Father that the Word would be human nature's center of existence" (*verbum dei patris adeo interne adunavit, ut centrum subsistentiae humanae naturae exsisteret;* 3.5 h 211). Indeed, if we take intellection to be the core of what it is to be human, to say Jesus' human nature is the contracted-as-maximum is to say also that his human intellect is maximal. This means that, as such, his human intellect cannot exist "without being intellect in such way that it is also God, who is all in all" (3.4 h 206). While ordinary human intellects can know all things but generally do not, it is a feature of Jesus' perfection as human (based on this nature's foundation in the Divine) that in him human intellection is actually all things. This is another way in which Jesus' human nature functions as mediator for and as enfolding of all of creation.

And there is a further way human beings count as microcosms: in human minds the created universe of hierarchically ordered nonconscious things is brought to awareness. As Cusanus remarks later in chapter 8, ". . . human nature (which is an intermediate nature) is an essential part of the universe; and without human nature not only would the universe

---

50. Senger comments further on the meaning of "suppositatur" in his note *ad loc., De docta ignorantia III,* 117.

[not] be perfect but it would not even be a universe" (h 230). The representative centrality of the human as microcosm thus takes on a further dimension in Jesus' mediation as the center or *medium* at once absolute-and-contracted. The way that the capacities humans share with other creatures are transformed by human intellectual powers embodies one understanding of the way higher and lower realities may be related hierarchically—the lower are not canceled but preserved and transformed in relation to and dependence on the higher. In this same way all creatures, and especially human beings, are transformed in relation to Jesus Christ.[51]

What we have seen in these four chapters is contraction or creatureliness pushed to the limit and, in particular, human possibilities pressed to the maximum. This is the result of Cusanus' attempt to account for the union of the divine and the human in Jesus and for the union of Jesus' humanity with all other finite things. In this novel case of coincidence, the oneness of God and the universe takes on a new reality and meaning, for Jesus as God-and-man is the paradigm of the cosmic position of human beings. For Nicholas, all other creatures are ordered to humanity, the epitome of creation, and human being finds its fulfillment in God. Jesus Christ is thus no mere symbol, but the actual archetype in which Nicholas finds finite and infinite, contracted and absolute, united *incomprehensibiliter*.[52]

Like the many-sided polygon that at the maximum limit apparently

---

51. The conception of hierarchy in the background here was a commonplace of medieval thought. It goes back to Proclus and Pseudo-Dionysius and uses the metaphors of closeness to and distance from the oneness of the first or, alternately, from the lack of oneness of matter. Of course, it was also a dynamic view of proceeding out from the first and at the same time returning (*exitus-reditus*). For an extensive survey of the primary sources (though not Cusanus) and contemporary commentary, see E. P. Mahoney, "Metaphysical Foundations of the Hierarchy of Being According to Some Late-Medieval and Renaissance Philosophers," in *Philosophies of Existence Ancient and Medieval*, ed. P. Morewedge (New York: Fordham University Press, 1982), 165–257. See also M. L. Kuntz and P. G. Kuntz, eds., *Jacob's Ladder and the Tree of Life: Concepts of Hierarchy and the Great Chain of Being* (New York: Peter Lang, 1987).

52. Flasch, *Nikolaus von Kues*, 136–37. Nicholas wrote as follows in "Dies Sanctificatus," his well-known sermon from 1440 (22 h 33):

And it was not possible for universal created nature to be able to be taken to divinity except in human being, which has been constituted in glory and honor a little less than the angels and above all the animals and works of God's hand. And so the human spirit, which enfolds in itself the natures of all things, does not rest in anything created, but seeks beyond itself and does not find satiety except in immortality which is life and eternal wisdom. And because this human being, who ought to be the end of everything, its rest or sabbath, could not be the highest creature who would enfold everything in himself in his perfection unless he were hypostatically God in whom alone there is rest; because he is everything which is sought, it was therefore necessary that God become man so that in this way all things could attain their goal.

merges into identity with its inscribing circle, maximal human nature and maximal human intellection merge into a unity or identity with Jesus' divine nature, a subsistent oneness of being that never cancels or obscures Jesus' humanity.[53] Nicholas' point throughout these chapters is not simply to set out calculated parallels or correspondences between cases of oneness, each one of which is beyond the human mind's grasp. Rather, extending Nicholas' favorite formulations and ideas as far as possible is designed to make our ignorance an achievement based on insight—even if only the reverse insight that the understanding we seek is beyond us. In *De docta ignorantia*, Nicholas teaches that, first, God's infinite oneness and, second, the oneness-in-multiplicity of the universe are beyond our comprehension. We cannot be surprised if the hypostatic oneness of the incarnate God also eludes us, even as we acknowledge its appropriateness.

3E. Exploring the Mysteries: Jesus' Life, Death, and Resurrection

The next five chapters of Book 3 focus on the earthly life of Christ, considering his conception and birth, suffering and death, resurrection and ascension to be judge of the living and the dead. Here Cusanus expounds on the articles of the creed that deal with Christ's existence in time. He proposes explanations about how fittingly these events took place and comments on their significance for other human beings. No doubt Cusanus can be read as following traditional teaching here, but these chapters serve to emphasize that what is unavoidable in Christian belief must be anomalous for philosophic thought. God became flesh and took on human nature in a particular time and place. Jesus Christ was born and lived, suffered and died, as do every woman and man in history. The divine Absolute undertook in Jesus' contracted human nature to live a bodily human life and to die a bodily human death.[54]

For Cusanus, as for the tradition before him, what is philosophically unthinkable turns out to be done in solidarity with the whole human

---

53. Nicholas writes: *"Quasi ut si polygonia circulo inscripta natura foret humana, et circulus divina: si ipsas polygonia maxima esse debet, qua maior esse non potest, nequaquam in finitis angulis per se subsisteret, sed in circularia figura, ita ut non haberet propriam subsistendi figuram etiam intellectualiter ab ipsa circulari et aeterna figura separabilem"* (3.4 h 206). I have given this illustration a more orthodox Chalcedonian interpretation in line with Nicholas' intent. See Hopkins, *Learned Ignorance*, 36–37, for a reading that finds the illustration problematic, and Senger, *De docta ignorantia III*, 116, for a suggestion that links the symbolized perfection of Jesus' humanity to its existence in the divine nature.

54. Offermann, in *Christus*, 167–74, emphasizes the point that the identity of human beings with Christ means we must rethink the meaning of what it is to be human. For instance, Christ's death and rising mark more than the death or end of sin; they also mean the death or end of human death. H. L. Bond in a private communication adds that this identity with Christ "also means 'the death or end' of certain ways of 'thinking' nature, God and the human as well as 'thinking' death and life and even 'thinking' thinking."

race. Because the human nature of Jesus Christ is maximal, Cusanus writes,

> it encompasses the complete possibility of the species, so that it is such equality-of-being with each man that it is united to each man much more closely than is a brother or a very special friend. For the maximality of human nature brings it about that in the case of each man who cleaves to Christ through formed faith Christ is this very man by means of a most perfect union—each's numerical distinctness being preserved. (3.6 h 219)

Because of this union all believers are taken up into Christ just as his human nature is taken up into the divine Word so "that the Word would be the human nature's center of existence" (3.5 h 211). Christ's redemptive death frees not only himself but all those united with him in faith from death to the life of resurrection: ". . . in Him they die; in Him they are made alive again through resurrection; in Him they are united to God and glorified" (3.6 h 219).

That the divine Absolute took on human flesh and spirit in a union we cannot fathom means that Jesus Christ is, in principle, one with the rest of humankind. In Jesus there is available to everyone a union with the divine Absolute we can only acknowledge in faith and trust as closer than any human ties of blood or friendship. But as Christ is a novel and unique reality in the metaphysics of Absolute and contracted, so too are the unique possibilities open to human beings in and through Christ. In interpreting what he terms the "mysteries of faith," Nicholas weaves together the ways of speaking found in the New Testament and in the Church councils with his own philosophical conceptions of Absolute and contracted, truth and image, and of the maximum as contracted to a kind. Often he moves back and forth in his analysis from the technical terms of his philosophic outlook to more traditional biblical, liturgical, and conciliar language that is packed with religious significance. When terms like "union" are employed, Cusanus clearly believes they are not merely metaphorical or merely spiritual; rather, such terms represent the best learned ignorance can offer to penetrate the mysteries of faith.[55]

3F. Christ the Measure

Nicholas of Cusa, no less than other thinkers in the Christian Neoplatonic tradition—Dionysius, Eriugena, the Chartrians, Lull, and Eckhart come to mind—moved freely in employing his more technical, abstruse

---

55. For Cusanus' views on religious faith, see 3.11; cf. also Offermann, *Christus*, 174–80, and J. Hopkins, "Glaube und Vernunft im Denken des Nikolaus von Kues," *Trier Cusanus Lecture* 3 (Trier: Paulinus Verlag, 1996), 17–27.

language to open up the mysteries of faith. While it is true that his attempt to interpret the Incarnation presses his theoretical categories to their limits, it is no less true that the coincidence of opposites and the interrelated couples of his theoretical framework—absolute/contracted, exemplar/image, *complicatio/explicatio*—open up a different slant on the reality of Jesus Christ. If Jesus' human-divine reality has transformed all there is for Christian believers since St. Paul, any theoretical framework for interpreting reality will have to strain to be adequate to the transformation. Book 3 of *De docta ignorantia* demonstrates how Nicholas uses parallels, correspondences, and metaphors as well as his established terms of art to attempt some understanding of his faith in Christ. Learned ignorance once again approaches without completely penetrating what has been revealed to faith.

Book 1 of *De docta ignorantia* used geometrical figures while Book 2 used more metaphysical and hermetic metaphors to enable us to think dialectically and recognize that God and the universe are coincident onenesses of different kinds. Book 3 in fact takes its basic metaphor from the God-man and highlights the historic individual in whom the oneness of God and the oneness of the universe meet and are brought together in the "hypostatic," or personal oneness, of human and divine natures. The dialectical thinking employed to think Absolute and contracted together in this instance has obvious significance for faith seeking understanding and for Christians responding with mind and heart to what God has done in Jesus.

But for the program of learned ignorance and for understanding the Cusan view of the whole, what Cusanus does in Book 3 embodies as well a provisional response to the *aporiai*, the perplexities or difficulties, embodied in the first two parts of *De docta ignorantia*. There Nicholas taught that there is no proportion between infinite and finite, no imaginable or conceivable measure or model that will enable us adequately to conceptualize either the infinite absolute Oneness or its contracted image, the universe, let alone grasp with exactness how they are connected. The rest of his teaching in Books 1 and 2 remains conjectural, a learning always cognizant of its ignorance. The Cusan Christ of Book 3 is also a reminder of the limits of our understanding, as well as the object of Christian faith.

Yet the historic reality of Jesus has a theoretical and systematic role to play in extending our conjectural understanding. Along with his theological and religious significance, the Cusan Christ provides a more adequate, if conjectural, norm and measure for theory and for practice. Christ provides another way to explore the connection between Absolute and contracted even if we come up short. For Nicholas' ontology, then, Jesus is the human image of the absolute One beyond our ken and the paradigm of creaturely connection with the infinite God. Jesus' human nature is available to historical knowledge and to faith in its temporal reality as a disclosure of what God is.

Cusanus teaches us human knowers that our cognitive measures cannot be definitive when we deal with the absolute God, but he believes God's choice is to make one person in human history the manifestation and expression, indeed, the measure, of God's union and connection with everything else. When God decides to give temporal, finite contracted expression to who and what God is, what historically occurs is the human nature, the flesh-and-blood reality of Jesus. Jesus Christ therefore stands as the unique mediating reality that is *the* proportion between finite and Infinite, even if we cannot completely factor the terms of that proportion or simplify its terms into intelligibilities our limited understandings grasp and comprehend with precision.

Even apart from Christ, human nature is itself a *medium* or center possessing or "enfolding" the powers common to all the other natural kinds, a node of unity reflecting the multiplicity of the created universe. As possessing that limited nature in its perfection, the God-man is a contracted maximum and thus normative for what other human beings may become. This human perfection, of course, is due entirely to Jesus' personal oneness with the uncreated Word, a maximal oneness that is both model and norm and goal for the ceaseless striving and passion that characterizes human knowing and loving. Here is no abstract norm or measure, but a concrete person who has taken on bodily existence in time. And though even Jesus Christ may give us no final positive insight into the divine Reality and Infinity as such, faith in him provides a measure for practice and a norm for theory. This is a more secure place from which to conjecture as we explore the realms of both the human and the divine.

2
Conjecturing Oneness and Otherness
De coniecturis (1442–1443)

Between 1440 and 1445 Nicholas of Cusa completed *De coniecturis* (*On Conjectures*), his second major theoretical work. This treatise (framed as a letter to Cardinal Julian) designedly complements and extends the views proposed in *De docta ignorantia*.[1] *De coniecturis* provides an occasion for Cusanus to explore from a rather different standpoint the whole of reality already investigated in *De docta ignorantia*, as well as our human knowledge of it. Once again Nicholas presents a comprehensive vision of the whole—Creator and creation—now envisioned as a universe of oneness-in-otherness.

De docta ignorantia introduced such fundamental Cusan ideas as the coincidence of opposites, learned ignorance, and the incommensurability of finite and infinite. There Nicholas proposed exercises for thinking together "enfolding and unfolding" (*complicatio/explicatio*) and for understanding dialectically the relation of Absolute and contracted. *De coniecturis* extends his insights about God and creation by reworking the dialectical nature of reality and thought in the categories of oneness and otherness. While the divine Oneness transcends our efforts to reach it in discursive thought, we find its contracted reflection in creatures, each of which can be construed as a limited oneness, that is, a oneness-in-otherness.[2]

The ontological condition of creation as limited, contingent, and

---

1. *De coniecturis* does not always work out its ideas in ways its announcement in *De docta ignorantia* might have led readers to anticipate. On the date of *De coniecturis* and its connections with *De docta ignorantia*, see J. Koch's remarks in the Heidelberg critical edition of *De coniecturis*, ix, 218–19. Cf. also the Latin-German edition of *De coniecturis*, ed. and trans. J. Koch and W. Happ (Hamburg: Meiner, 1988), ix–xxi; and J. Koch, *Die ars coniecturalis des Nikolaus von Kues* (Cologne: Westdeutscher Verlag, 1956), 7–12, 31–35. Flasch has underlined the epistolary quality of this work and how it is addressed to a single individual (*Nikolaus von Kues*, 145–46); this may help account for its leisurely pace and somewhat disjointed formal structure when compared to that of *De docta ignorantia*.

2. Cusanus expresses it this way in 2.6 h 98: "Oneness cannot be participated in its exact simpleness. But because no multitude exists without participation in it, [oneness] can

mutable is what Cusanus describes as otherness, *alteritas*. *Alteritas* is not an ontological constituent or intrinsic principle of created things, all of which are attenuated or participating onenesses. Rather oneness-in-otherness marks their ontological status or condition, so to speak, much as does their finiteness or their contingency. This status contrasts with God's utter Oneness, the oneness that all created things share and reflect in varied ways. "Otherness" is thus an abstract term for the contingent plurality and variety of contracted things in the created world. In contrast, the divine Oneness corresponds to the infinite and absolute status of divine reality. God is without otherness.

Although *De coniecturis* is fundamentally religious in tone (and even explicitly Trinitarian near the end of Book 2), Cusanus does not make Christ central to his teaching here, as he did in his book on learned ignorance. This treatise also omits the direct, explicit appeals to earlier authorities found in *De docta ignorantia*. Human beings are central to Nicholas' considerations, both as conjecturing subjects and as a singular part of the creation about which he makes conjectures. The ignorance that was to be rendered learned in the first treatise is now to be trained further as *conjectural* knowledge, for conjectures are all that the human mind can grasp of the truth of things.[3]

1. BOOK 1

Nicholas' second effort to set forth the harmonious order of all things is itself an example of what *coniectura* means.[4] The two books spell out the conjectural nature of human speculation and some of the varied conjectural contents of human knowing. Just as human knowledge and its limits were central to the book on learned ignorance, so the present book makes conjectural knowledge, as well as the dialectic of oneness and otherness, further implications of learned ignorance.[5] At the beginning Nicholas writes to Cardinal Julian to remind him that conjecture cannot be separated from the dialectic of oneness and otherness:

---

be participated not indeed as it is, but in otherness. On account of this, reason itself sees in otherness the participability of oneness." All translations of *De coniecturis* are my own. See also the translation in J. Hopkins, *Metaphysical Speculations*, vol. 2 (Minneapolis, Minn.: Banning Press, 2000), 149–247.

3. This analysis of Book 1 revises and expands my earlier essay, "Nicholas of Cusa's *On Conjectures (De coniecturis)*," in *Nicholas of Cusa: In Search of God and Wisdom*, ed. G. Christianson and T. Izbicki (Leiden: Brill, 1991), 119–40.

4. Cusanus does not come to define and explain *coniectura* until chapter 11 of Book 1. In private correspondence, B. Milem has proposed that Nicholas does this to situate his definition of conjecturing within prior conjectures. This both reflects the character of human knowing and underlines the nonfoundational aspects of conjecturing.

5. Besides Koch's monograph and Flasch's thought-provoking overview (*Nikolaus von*

You have seen that the exactness of truth cannot be attained. The consequence is that every positive human assertion of the truth is a conjecture.... And so the unattainable Oneness of truth is known in conjectural otherness and the conjecture of otherness is itself known in the most simple Oneness of truth. (h 2)

These initial remarks let us see how oneness and otherness must be thought together dialectically. They thereby imply that we must transcend discursive reason and its conjectures, turning to intellectual vision *(intellectus)* to achieve a further sort of thinking or knowing.[6] The emphasis on *intellectus* marks an explicitly new development beyond what Cusanus wrote in *De docta ignorantia*.[7]

1A. Fundamentals

The first chapter announces the basic themes that structure the whole treatise. Cusanus introduces two favorite theses. First, human knowledge is to be understood as an image of and parallel to God's creative knowledge. Second, all of creation is to be understood as issuing from God's oneness into the plurality of created things and at the same time as returning to its single divine Source.[8] Both theses count as foundational assumptions and involve metaphors that provide the broader context and presuppositions for the whole work. Cusanus' extension of the *imago Dei* theme is decisive for his understanding of human knowledge. He applies to the conceptual, constructed universe of human ideas the Christian Neoplatonic vision of procession from and return to the Source that goes back to Plotinus and Proclus.[9] Human beings produce conjectures (concepts and judgments), just as God's knowledge produces created things. In the divine Original or Exemplar our conjectural knowledge finds its source, pattern, and goal. Nicholas writes:

Kues, 143–64), see the following studies and essays directly concerned with *De coniecturis*: S. Oide, "Über die Grundlagen der cusanischen Konjekturenlehre," *MFCG* 8 (1970): 147–78; P. Hirt, "Vom Wesen der konjekturalen Logik bei Nikolaus von Kues," *MFCG* 8 (1970): 179–91; H. Schnarr, *Modi essendi* (Münster: Aschendorff, 1973), 40–67; Meinhardt, "Exaktheit," 101–20; and Haubst, *Streifzüge*, 164–215.

6. Book 1 of *De coniecturis* works out the foundational metaphors of conjectural knowledge and the universe. Book 2 reviews and applies this foundational exploration to some examples of different things we know. Nicholas' "Prologue" suggests that *De coniecturis* is a handbook *(manuductio)* for the cardinal, and uses the medieval commonplace of branch, flower, and fruit to adumbrate the progression of the whole. More detailed outlines of the work can be found in h, xxxii–xxxiii, and in Koch and Happ, xi–xx.

7. Flasch sees Nicholas as adapting Proclus' philosophy here insofar as "er den Intellekt interpretierte als die Herstellung der Besonderheiten des Verstandes, insbesondere als aktiven Ursprung der Widersprüche und Distinktionen. Die neue Analyse des Verhältnisses von *intellectus* und *ratio* dient zugleich als Erklärungsprinzip für die Mängel der bisherigen Philosophie" (*Nikolaus von Kues*, 155).

8. The same themes appear in Nicholas' later *Idiota de mente* 3 h 72–73; see Chapter 3, this book.

9. It can be found as well in St. Augustine, Eriugena, the Chartrians, Lull, and Eckhart; all are influential sources of Nicholas' ideas.

Conjectures should proceed from our mind as the real world does from the infinite divine Reason. For the human mind, the exalted likeness of God, participates in the fruitfulness of creative nature as far as it can. As the image of the all-powerful Form it puts out from itself rational entities [*rationalia*] in the likeness of real entities. So the human mind exists as the form of the conjectural world, just as the divine [Mind is the form] of the real [world]. Therefore, just as that absolute divine Entity is all that which is in whatever is, so too the oneness of the human mind is the being of its conjectures. (1.1 h 5)

Nicholas here conceives God as infinite, all-powerful mind or intellect, the "Form" of the created world, all that is in whatever is real. Our human minds, as images, participate in the divine productivity and creativity, even if what we create as knowers is the realm of conjectural entities, *rationalia*, not real things. The conceptual entities we fashion mentally are no less dependent on us than the entities of the created cosmos are dependent on God. In both cases, this dependence is interpreted as the relation of oneness to otherness. Whatever is other than and distinct from the principle on which it depends becomes real and one by sharing or participating in a limited way in that principle's oneness. In this way it is an image in otherness of that principle's originating oneness. Just as God's infinite oneness is the ultimate "Form" or "Being" of whatever exists, so our mind's limited oneness (as God's image) is the source of our ideas, the dependent beings of the conceptual world.

The active productivity of our knowing thus becomes an entry point for coming to understand conjecturally God's creating and the dependence of created things on their divine Source. We cannot fully understand ourselves, our knowing, its point and purpose, or our relationship to God unless we search reflectively the breadth and depth of our active mental lives. *De coniecturis* 1.1 continues by explaining what we are about as knowers.

Now God does everything for his own sake, so that he is equally intellectual beginning and end of all things. Likewise the unfolding of the world of [human] reason, which proceeds from our enfolding mind, takes place for the sake of that fabricating [mind]. For the more acutely it [the mind] contemplates itself in the world it unfolds, the more richly fruitful does it become in itself. For its goal is the infinite Reason in which it [the mind] will behold itself as it is and which alone is the measure of all reason's [works]. The more deeply we enter our own mind, of which God is the single living Center, the more closely we raise ourselves to becoming like the divine Mind. For this reason out of natural desire we pursue the sciences which perfect us. (h 5)

Here we see how the outflow or unfolding of the conjectural universe is at once its return and enfolding. Knowledge is for the sake of the knower and, while self-knowledge is our proximate goal as we "contemplate" the mental universe we construct as knowers, our ultimate goal is knowledge of God, "infinite Reason," the truth and measure of our mental lives.[10] Nor are these purposes separate. Understanding ourselves as images involves some encounter with the Exemplar, some contact with the ultimate measure of mind. Only in attaining its goal will the human mind "behold itself as it is." The two simultaneous movements marked out here recall Augustine's emphasis on turning within and ascending from there to the beyond.[11] In one movement we progress more deeply into our selves only to discover that God's mind is "the single living Center" of the human mind. At the same time we ascend, in the second movement, from sense perception to reason and beyond to intellectual vision, moving toward the infinite divine Mind beyond. Ultimately the same cognitive activities constitute both movements and let us approximate the divine Mind.[12]

The above passage also employs *complicatio/explicatio* (enfolding/unfolding). This metaphor—really quasi-technical terms of art—was introduced in *De docta ignorantia* to speak of creation and God's relation to the created universe. This is the first time Nicholas formally extends the quasi-technical couple to describe the human mind's relation to what it knows, in accord with his proposal that our knowing activity and its products are parallel to God's creating and the universe that results.[13] In the background, of course, is the familiar Neoplatonic view of a dynamic universe proceeding out from a single source or origin in hierarchical stages while at the same time returning thereto. So Nicholas mentions here almost casually "the unfolding of the world of reason, which proceeds from our enfolding mind" *(rationalis mundi explicatio, a nostra complicante mente progrediens)*.

That the theme of procession and return also explains just how our mental lives are images of God's productive creating exemplifies an important and characteristic facet of Cusanus' views in *De coniecturis*. There is a simultaneity about the various aspects of Nicholas' ideas that fits the temper of this epistolary treatise as a conjectural vision. What Cusanus spells out discursively is fundamentally a single dynamic piece to be grasped all at once. Every fundamental Cusan idea may be presupposed, alluded to, echoed, or explicitly employed to help make sense of any other. Nicholas' conjectural insights encompass concur-

---

10. The final chapter of Book 2 of *De coniecturis* is addressed personally to Cardinal Julian and gives a kind of object lesson in self-knowledge and its goals.
11. Turner, in *Darkness*, 50–101, attends carefully to what Augustine says about interiority and ascent. The classic text in Augustine is found in *De libero arbitrio* 2. Augustine summarizes the movement of the whole book in 2.16.
12. On this process and its goal, see Van Velthoven, *Gottesschau*, 131–96.
13. See the explanation of *complicatio/explicatio* in Chapter 1, this book.

rent and conjunctive themes and elements, the kind of gestalt we expect from any perceived or imagined visual panorama. The striking use of geometrical schemata (*figurae*) throughout this treatise illustrates the same point.

Chapter 1 closes with a transitional passage important for introducing two further themes crucial to *De coniecturis:* the trinitarian or unitrine character of the human mind and the fashioning of mathematics that exhibits its character. Both themes are implicit in the idea that the human mind is an image of the divine Mind, which is both triune and productive. The human mind is said to enfold multitude, magnitude, and composition as a triune principle that "distinguishes, compares, and connects" (h 6). In other words, we construct the whole numbers (multitude), the geometrical figures (magnitude), and the relations within and between "multitude and magnitude" (composition). The metaphors of "unfolding" and "measuring" are spelled out in the mental activities of distinguishing, comparing, and connecting employed in dealing with mathematical objects.[14]

1B. Symbolizing the Whole

1B.1. Counting, the Decad, and the Four Unities

Chapter 2 turns explicitly to mathematics and to counting the series of whole numbers. This chapter is especially important for the whole treatise because it underlines the significance of mathematics for understanding Nicholas' view of the human mind. Beyond this, the chapter prepares us for the way Nicholas uses arithmetic and geometry as conjectural schemata or metaphors for understanding how nonmathematical realities are ordered harmoniously. As he remarks:

> For reason to unfold number and use it in constructing conjectures is nothing else than for reason to employ itself and to fashion everything in the highest natural likeness of itself, just as God, the infinite Mind, communicates being to things in the coeternal Word. (1.2 h 7)

What is the significance of mathematics for understanding human knowledge? For Cusanus, the numbers of arithmetic are neither preex-

---

14. Klein says that "the basic function" of discursive thought "consists indeed in discriminating *and* relating, that is to say, in *counting or numbering.* For in the act of counting we both separate and combine the things we count.... Moreover, whenever we are engaged in counting, we substitute—as a matter of course even if we are not aware of what we are doing—for the varied and always 'unequal' visible things to be counted 'pure' invisible units ... which in no way differ from each other and which constitute the only proper medium of counting" (*Plato's "Meno,"* 117). See Chapter 1 and Chapter 3, this book, on measuring as the basic metaphor or model for knowing in *De docta ignorantia* and *Idiota de mente.*

isting Platonic Forms nor Aristotelian concepts abstracted from numbered things. Rather, the whole numbers are conceptual entities *(entia rationis)* that are humanly constructed images of the mind's own unity, fashioned "in the highest natural likeness of [reason] itself." When we construct or count through the number series we experience one example of what Nicholas means by *explicatio*, unfolding from oneness. In fact, number and geometrical figures are the sole conceptual realities Cusanus says are *not* conjectural. Since they are our own constructions, and since they deal with entities not subject to physical change, mathematical concepts display an exactness and precision not available in other domains of human knowledge.[15]

Cusanus opens the second chapter by observing that only human beings count and employ number as "nothing else than reason unfolded" (h 7). Counting is a paradigmatic activity of discursive reason. The mind's own oneness is mirrored in the first unit, the number 1.[16] When we number or count, our capacities to discriminate and relate are clearly employed. Each succeeding number is a composite unity, a sum of so many further units. The whole number series is constructed by adding the first unit iteratively while keeping each new sum separate as a distinct number or member of the series. Typically learned by rote, counting becomes automatic, but the mind's discriminating and relating are presupposed to make the series of whole numbers intelligible and applicable. In this way Cusan *ratio* measures each member of the series and

---

15. See *De docta ignorantia* 1.11 h 31–32, and Nicholas' later *Trialogus de possest* h 43–44. Hopkins translates the latter passage in *Concise Introduction*, 119–21:

> For regarding mathematical [entities], which proceed from our reason and which we experience to be in us as in their source [*principium*]: they are known by us as our entities and as rational entities; [and they are known] precisely, by our reason's precision, from which they proceed. (In a similar way, real things [*realia*] are known precisely, by the divine [intellect's] precision, from which they proceed into being.) These mathematical [entities] are neither an essence [*quid*] nor a quality [*quale*]; rather, they are notional entities elicited from our reason. But the divine works, which proceed from the divine intellect, remain unknown to us precisely as they are.... So if we rightly consider [the matter, we recognize that] we have no certain knowledge except mathematical knowledge. And this latter is a symbolism for searching into the works of God.

For interpretations of Nicholas' use of mathematics, see Van Velthoven, *Gottesschau*, 131–96; M. de Gandillac, *Nikolaus von Cues* (Düsseldorf: Schwann, 1953), 61–86; and K. Volkmann-Schluck, *Nicolaus Cusanus: Die Philosophie in Übergang vom Mittelalter zur Neuzeit* (Frankfurt: V. Klostermann, 1957), 87–96.

16. Cusanus is surely saying that "number" is part of the nature of things. At least oneness seems both an ontological and epistemological presupposition of his views in *De coniecturis*, given that the Creator is named as divine Oneness and the human mind is named a parallel oneness, fabricating the cognitive domain of conjectures. In spite of what might seem to be similarities, this is still a long way from Kant.

De coniecturis   75

FIGURE 2.1 Four numerical unities in *De coniecturis* 1.3.

```
                                              1
         1   +    2   +    3   +    4   =    10
        10   +   20   +   30   +   40   =   100      4
       100   +  200   +  300   +  400   = 1,000
                         ―――――――――
                             4
```

---

its connection with all the others.[17] That we can speak of the whole series or select certain members from it (for instance, prime numbers) is based on reason's capacity to put together and separate whole and parts.

Further, what human intelligence does with numbers parallels its "measuring" what it knows in other domains. That is to say, the mind discriminates and distinguishes one thing or idea from another. In knowing, the human mind compares and draws parallels between things, between things and concepts, or between concepts alone, "sizing them up," as it were, in assessments and judgments. We also are able to join and put conceptions together as we discover and invent conjectural connections between things or among disparate ideas. For Nicholas, our mathematical concepts are nonconjectural mental concepts that witness best to our productivity as knowers.

Cusanus also stresses the usefulness of mathematical ideas "in constructing conjectures," or symbolic models for understanding what is not mathematical. In chapter 3 he proceeds to put number to work by spelling out four numerical "unities" within the system of whole numbers.[18] These four will be applied conjecturally to the four mental unities or ontological realms that comprise all of reality. The key here is the traditional Pythagorean tetraktys or quaternary: $1 + 2 + 3 + 4 = 10$. In this "first natural" progression Cusanus finds synthesized the whole power of numbers useful for conjecturing. The array of rows and columns in Figure 2.1 may clarify how he uses the import of 4 and 10 in arranging for the four numerical unities.[19]

---

17. In a private communication, H. L. Bond has remarked on the resonances of the word *ratio* because the Latin word can also mean "calculation" or "proportion," exactly the activities paradigmatic for Cusan discursive reason.

18. On the four mathematical unities, see Koch, *Die ars coniecturalis*, 26–28; and Oide, "Grundlagen," 158–60.

19. By repeating the first progression from 10 to 40 and from 100 to 400 we obtain four sums: 1, 10, 100, 1,000—Cusanus' four numerical unities. The first is the number 1, itself the source of the original progression and unique in being neither root nor power of any number but itself. Ten results from the first progression and is the second unity. It is the starting point of the second progression, as well as the square and cube root of 100

For Cusanus, each of the four unities (1, 10, 100, 1,000) represents a stage in the unfolding of 1. Each is the origin and/or sum of the first progression or its repetition. Nicholas then extends the four unities to a corresponding geometrical unfolding: the derivation or progressive construction of line, surface, and solid from the point. Cusanus even asserts that the numbers beyond 1,000 add nothing new! This is because they have little utility for Cusan conjectures in dealing with the three-dimensional created universe or its Creator (whose oneness is beyond dimensionality).

What the human mind unfolds in nonconjectural exactness in deriving the four unities from the number 1 finds conjectural application in the next five chapters and, indeed, the rest of Book 1. In 1.4–8, Nicholas discusses in detail the four metaphysical unities, the hierarchically ordered spheres of being that comprise all there is. To 1, 10, 100, and 1,000 Cusanus sets in correspondence God, intelligence (the angelic realm and that of human *intellectus*), soul (*ratio* and the rest of the human realm), and body (all corporeal things), respectively. Each of the four spheres represents a hierarchical stage of outflow and simultaneous return as well as a domain of reality. Each is created by God, but imagined here as proceeding in order from God's utter oneness. Each participates in and is an image of that infinite Oneness in a more or less restricted or "contracted" fashion.

Just as the numerical unities can be understood as unfolding what is enfolded in the number 1 (and in the human mind's power to count), so the three successive metaphysical domains or unities are intended to be understood as unfolding what is enfolded in the infinite oneness of God's intellect. As measured by the divine Mind, each of the metaphysical unities manifests a level of truth and certitude. Since human minds share through intellectual intuition, reason, and sensation in the domains of intelligence, soul, and body, there is a mode of human knowing and of human mental or verbal expression corresponding to each of the three unities after the first.[20]

Examining what Nicholas says about the first unity, God, makes it clear that the divine Unity is not something we can grasp the way we conceive the number 1. Suppose numerical oneness is understood as prior to and enfolding "all manyness, diversity, otherness, opposition, inequality, division, and everything else that accompanies manyness"

---

and 1,000. One hundred, the third unity, is the sum of the second progression and starting point of the third, as well as the square of 10. The fourth unity is 1,000, the sum of the third progression and the cube of 10.

20. On the metaphysical unities, see Koch, *Die ars coniecturalis*, 18–19; Oide, "Grundlagen," 161–62; and h III, note 11, 193–94.

(1.5 h 17). Then it may provide a conjectural image, however limited, of the infinite divine Oneness, of that utterly absolute Simpleness that is no more simple than not, no more one than not.

Nicholas writes:

> Therefore, that is not the truest conjecture about the First, which allows for an affirmation to which negation is opposed or which prefers negation as though it were truer than affirmation. Although it seems truer that God exists as no one of all the things that can be conceived or spoken of than as any one of them, nonetheless the negation to which affirmation is opposed does not reach exactness. Therefore there is a more absolute concept of truth, at once disjunctive and conjunctive, which discards both opposites. (1.5 h 21)

Though presupposed by every question we might pose, the divine Oneness remains beyond speaking because every question we might formulate about God remains ill-formed (*inepta;* 1.5 h 20). Whether we affirm or deny something of God, we fall short of the One who in unspeakable simpleness is prior to all oppositions, whether between things, thoughts, or words.[21]

The difficulty, as Cusanus sees it, is that we approach all four unities from the standpoint of human reason. What we must remember is that each unity in the hierarchy stands to the one above as more contracted and to the one below as less contracted or limited in its oneness. This means that we cannot expect the normal ways in which discursive reason thinks and speaks to match the higher unity of the realm of intelligence or the lower unity of the realm of body. Only in the realm of soul are our minds and tongues naturally at home. Cusanus stresses that we must adapt our thought and speech to the kind of unity we are dealing with: *"secundum illius regionis regulas loqui necesse est"* (one must speak in accord with the rules of that region; 1.8 h 35). Once we do this, we are able to use examples from any of the lower domains to enable us to conjecture about the higher spheres.

Neoplatonic metaphysical hierarchies may be readily viewed as projections of the capacities and functions of human knowing, metaphoric extrapolations or parallels that are constructed and employed to order systematically all there is.[22] In the present case Cusanus never hesitates to match the ontological domains of intelligence, soul, and body with the "parallel" human knowing capacities: intellect, reason, and sense. *De*

---

21. This passage echoes Nicholas' ideas on the coincidence of opposites in *De docta ignorantia*.

22. This is the first way Flasch sees Cusanus changing the Proclean background of the four unities; the other two involve (1) Nicholas understanding reason by way of intellect and thus (2) making intellect both the source of the reason's principle of contradiction and the sphere where contradictions coincide (*Nikolaus von Kues*, 153–59).

coniecturis makes it clear that mind and reality are coprimordial in Cusan thought. He also conceptualizes the various human knowing powers as issuing or "unfolding" from the unitary power of mind.[23] The point of the parallel here is to clarify the dynamic interconnectedness of the ontological domains in proceeding from and returning to God's infinite oneness. At the end of chapter 4 Cusanus stresses how all four unities must be thought together, because all coinhabit each, as it were:

> Now everything in God is God, in intelligence [everything] is intelligence, in soul [everything] is soul, in body [everything] is body. This is nothing else than for mind to embrace everything either in a divine way or in the way of intelligence or in the way of soul or in the way of body. . . . Therefore, just as intelligence is not entirely divine or absolute, so the rational soul does not completely depart from sharing in Divinity—in order that the mind may distinguish and equally connect everything: in a wondrous reciprocal progression the divine absolute Unity descends step by step into intelligence and reason, and the contracted sensible [unity] mounts through reason into intelligence. (1.4 h 15–16)

1B.2. Figure P: Participation in a Universe of Oneness and Otherness

In Book 1, chapter 9, and again in chapters 12 and 13, Cusanus proposes further geometrical diagrams as conjectural aids to understanding the whole of reality as "a wondrous reciprocal progression" of oneness and otherness. He calls the first *"Figura Paradigmatica,"* or P, and uses it to represent and symbolize how oneness is shared by otherness as one moves from the highest to the lowest reality. The diagram of Figure P in Figure 2.2 represents what Cusanus describes, with additions to designate how the four numerical and metaphysical unities can be integrated with his representation of oneness-in-otherness.[24]

Depicted as two overlapping triangles in the diagram, Figure P in fact is to be imagined as consisting of two interpenetrating cones or "pyramids of light and darkness." They symbolize the way otherness participates in oneness in every reality but God. The divine infinite Oneness is represented as the base of the pyramid of light. Utter otherness or nothingness *(nihil)* is pictured as the base of the pyramid of darkness. Cu-

---

23. *De coniecturis* 2.16 h 157–67; *Idiota de mente* 11 h 141; Oide, "Grundlagen," 150–53. Flasch tags this correspondence of divine and human minds Nicholas' "Parallelismusformel," noting that this gives the mind a higher status from the start than it had at the beginning of *De docta ignorantia* (*Nikolaus von Kues*, 148–49).

24. In the manuscript of *De coniecturis* extant in Kues, Figure P is slightly colored to distinguish lighter (oneness) from darker (otherness) regions. For interpretation of Figure P, see Koch, *Die ars coniecturalis*, 28–30; Oide, "Grundlagen," 162–67; and h III, note 22, 204–5. The diagram of P follows h III, 46; cf. Oide's figures 5, 6, 7, 163–65. See also Haubst, in *Streifzüge*, 164–68, 171–73, who cautions readers not to think the diagram captures either God or nothing, but only the realm between.

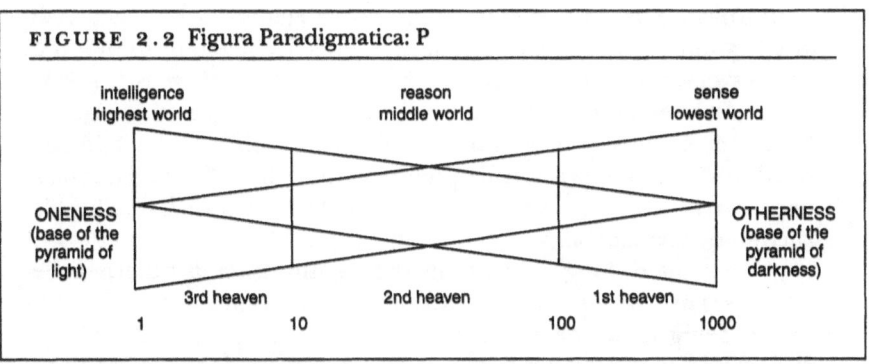

FIGURE 2.2 Figura Paradigmatica: P

sanus uses the phrase *quasi basis* to remind us that neither God nor *nihil* can be pictured with created things. The infinite Oneness transcends all that shares its oneness in otherness, while to be nothing is precisely to be lacking any share in oneness at all. In between are to be found all created things—in this way Nicholas has schematized the dynamic realm of creaturely becoming.

The point of Figure P is that to have any reality at all outside of God's infinite oneness is to share that Oneness as more or less limited by otherness. The threefold partition of the overlapping pyramids from left to right represents the three ontological unities that issue from God's oneness, here designated as worlds *(mundi)* or heavens *(caeli)*. These three domains are correlated with the three lesser arithmetical unities after the number 1 and with the hierarchy of human knowing capacities. Moving from left to right in the diagram represents the procession from more light, perfection, and oneness to more darkness, imperfection, and otherness, all in orderly gradation. Among creatures we find no highest degree of oneness or lowest degree of otherness; nowhere in creation is there one without the other.

Cusanus also reminds us not to view the diagram too analytically or only statically—in fact, returning to the first principle is best conceived as identically processing from it—because the pyramids interpenetrate. He writes in the next chapter:

Note the following most attentively. For oneness to proceed into otherness is at the same time for otherness to return into oneness. Attend to this very carefully if you want to see intellectually oneness in otherness. . . . Grasp the fact that in simple intellectual vision procession is joined with return—if you are taking pains to reach those secret matters beyond discursive reason that separate procession from return. They are more truly attained only by intellect enfolding opposites into one. (1.10 h 53)

But what are the opposites we are to hold together dialectically as we move beyond discursive reason toward intellective vision or intuition of what lies beyond them? Cusanus defines oneness *(unitas)* as "undividableness in itself and separation from anything else," pointing out that what befits oneness is "a certain undividableness, distinctness, and connectedness" (1.10 h 44). But he prefers to describe otherness *(alteritas)* using a series of synonyms he sees as opposed to oneness: divisibility, destructibility, changeability, compositeness, plurality. If the oneness of any given created thing points to its self-identity, then its otherness describes its status as something finite and created, contracted and contingent. In being itself one and contracted, each thing that is not God is distinct from, that is, "other than," every other created thing. God's oneness is shared or participated in by everything else in different ways, not in the way that oneness exists in itself. The term "otherness" is thus an abstract way of characterizing this state of affairs for the plurality of finite creatures.[25]

1C. Defining Conjecture

Cusan *coniectura* must not be confused or conflated with what is ordinarily meant by *conjecture* today, even in academic discourse. By "conjecture" we often mean a guess or hunch—some provisional belief or thesis to be investigated or checked against (usually empirical) evidence. Much less is Cusan conjecture a scientific hypothesis whose content is quantifiable and to be verified or falsified by experimental procedures.[26] Cusanus' conjectures are provisional in the sense that their content only partially captures the nature of the things they are about. In fact, Nicholas considers "true" conjectures only, and he believes that even these can be revised to be more faithful to the truth of the things we know.[27] The correct sense of conjecturing or conjectural knowledge therefore does not parallel what we mean today by a surmise or a suggestion. Rather, in the theoretical realm, Cusan conjectures are proposals that Nicholas believes are true as far as they go, even if they never capture the nature of things exactly. Much of his theoretical writing is

25. McTighe, *"Contingentia* and *Alteritas";* Hopkins, *Miscellany,* 3–38, esp. 31, 33–34. Both authors go beyond Koch's treatment of *alteritas* in *Die ars coniecturalis,* 19–21. For further treatment of *alteritas,* see K. Bormann, "Zur Lehre des Nikolaus von Kues von der 'Andersheit' und deren Quellen," *MFCG* 10 (1973): 130–37; and M. Thomas, "Zur Ursprung der Andersheit (Alteritas)," *MFCG* 22 (1995): 55–67. For a fuller treatment of the general theme, see Beierwaltes, "Identität und Differenz."

26. Nicholas' fourth *Idiota* dialogue, *De staticis experimentis,* however, shows him using conjecturing in a more empirical way—on the road to "modern" science.

27. In the final chapter of *De coniecturis* (2.17 h 183), Nicholas points to some general norms that will measure mistaken moral norms; this suggests that, indeed, conjectures may be either true or false.

designed to propose conjectures, often paradoxical and metaphorical, to aid us in our quest to understand God and God's connection with everything else.

The passage where Nicholas "defines" *coniectura* in chapter 11 is worth careful analysis.[28] He writes, addressing Cardinal Julian Caesarini,

> You see now that the positive assertions of the wise are conjectures. For when you look with your clear eyes, Father, upon the face of the supreme pontiff, our most holy lord Pope Eugene IV, before you, you conceive a positive assertion about it which you affirm as exact in terms of the eye. But when you turn to the root from which sense discrimination issues—to reason, I mean—you understand that the sense of sight participates in that power of discrimination in the otherness contracted to a sense organ. For this reason you see the defect of a fall from exactness because you gaze upon his face, not as it is, but in an otherness corresponding to the angle of your eyes, which is different from that of all the eyes of living creatures. *A conjecture, therefore, is a positive assertion which participates in the truth as it is, but in otherness.* (1.11 h 57, emphasis added)

In discussing this example Nicholas clearly does not separate perception from discrimination and articulation in thought and language. In his words, one "conceives a positive assertion" about what one looks at. His implicit assumption is that language and thought do not distort what we perceive, however much our cultural and linguistic practices, not to mention our memories and personal histories, shape what we pick out and identify within the visual field. So Cardinal Julian has no real problem finding the pope's face in that group of male clerics. Cusanus says explicitly that reason and sensation operate inseparably in our perceptual experience. Our eyes take in what is visible from their angle of vision but in conjunction with reason's discriminating power.

There is no doubt that Cusanus believed that perception is paradigmatically perception *of* something independently visible or audible or tangible.[29] To term perceptual judgments "conjectural," then, does not make them merely the product of fanciful guess or subjective whim or insufficient evidence, whatever their limitations. No less than his medieval predecessors, Cusanus took for granted that human perception both contacted and partially captured the independent world of nature and culture. Thus he is *not* opposing perceptual conjecture to perceptual knowledge.

In the example of Julian looking at the pope, Nicholas points out why

---

28. With minor changes, this analysis follows what I proposed in "Perception, Conjecture and Dialectic," 36–38.

29. Nicholas later writes in *De beryllo* 32, for instance, that "fire has truer being in its sensible substance than in our intellect where it exists in a confused concept without its natural truth. So with all things" (h 57). Later in the same passage he speaks of the "sensible qualities" of fire, "which we sense in it."

the resulting perceptual judgment is conjectural or inexact. There is a twofold otherness *(alteritas)* that conditions and limits all sensory perception. What this amounts to is that perception occurs between extended or bodily things. The first result is that what perception can discriminate in a particular visual field is limited to what organic eyes can see, the otherness Nicholas describes as "organic limitation" *(alteritas organice contracta)*. The second outcome is that human eyes, no less than human bodies, have but one location at a time, and thus but one standpoint or viewpoint. The cardinal does not see all of the pope's face but only the profile visible from where he looks. This limitation Nicholas terms "the otherness corresponding to your angle of vision" *(alteritas secundum angulum tui oculi)*; it implies that bodily perception is always and necessarily perspectival.

This limiting otherness, Nicholas remarks, is something we can recognize ourselves upon reflection *(dum autem . . . te convertis)*. This implies that even as we make perceptual judgments we are at least implicitly aware of their limitations. Yet his subsequent definition of *coniectura* makes it clear that perception delivers valid knowledge. In his Neoplatonic language, such perceptual assertions as "There's the pope!" will "participate in truth as it is," but in a recognizably limited way, that is, "in otherness." What we see will never be identical with all that could be seen of a given visible thing.[30]

There are other sources of otherness besides the bodiliness of the perceiver that limit our perceptual knowledge. One is the fact that the objects of perception are also limited and contracted: the otherness of the perceived object. So perceptual judgments about the pope's face must be conjectural because anything extended cannot show all that can be seen of itself at a particular time to another viewer who is also embodied. Otherness, or limitation due to bodily estate, is not limited to the viewer but ingredient in the viewed as well. As Nicholas wrote in *De docta ignorantia*, "All perceptible things are in a state of continual instability because of the material possibility abounding in them" (1.11 h 31). This does not mean that our conjectural perceptual judgments are false or invalid, simply that they are not exact or perfectly complete. In perceiving we are not transparent to ourselves, and the things we perceive are hardly pellucid, either.[31]

---

30. Nicholas thus writes in *Complementum theologicum 11*, "the visible, as it is visible, is not attained exactly by any eye." For a different analysis of *De coniecturis* 1.11, see E. Fräntzki, *Nikolaus von Kues und das Problem der absolute Subjecktivität* (Meisenheim am Glan: A. Hein, 1972), 104–6. For overviews of Cusanus' epistemology, see Van Velthoven, *Gottesschau;* K. Kremer, "Erkennen bei Nikolaus von Kues. Apriorismus-Assimilation-Abstraktion," *MFCG* 13 (1978): 23–57; and Hopkins, *Wisdom and Knowledge*.

31. More on these points is explained in the next chapter of the book on the *Idiota de mente*.

Another source of otherness in perception is that due to the *alteritas* of the mental and linguistic signs, images, and symbols we employ in thinking and talking about what we perceive. Mental and linguistic signs are different from both our mental capacities and the things we perceive. In his later *Compendium* Nicholas wrote about this difference as follows:

> Moreover, it cannot be denied that by nature a thing exists before it can be known. Therefore, neither sense nor imagination nor intellect attains its way of being, since the latter precedes them all. But all the things that are attained by whatever mode of knowing signify only that prior way of being. And hence they are not the thing itself, but its likenesses, images [*species*], or signs. Therefore there is no knowledge of the way of being, even though it is most certainly seen that there is such a way of being. (c.1 h 1)[32]

Nicholas thus provides another reason why perceptual judgments are conjectural. The very terms in which they are couched are inexact, incomplete, and perspectival, for they reflect the broader history and interests of the perceiver and the perceiver's linguistic community.[33]

Given all the constraints under which human perception operates, it is not hard to understand why Nicholas would judge perceptual knowledge to be limited, partial, and approximative—characterized by otherness. Perhaps it is more difficult to see why he believes that perceptual judgments "participate in the truth as it is." The fundamental reason returns us to the basic assumptions Nicholas laid out in the first chapter of *De coniecturis*. He is convinced that our status as images of the divine Mind's oneness will secure the cognitive validity of what we know, however imperfect and approximate our conjectural knowledge. The conjectural assertions that issue from the human power of judgment "participate in Truth as it is" because the human mind is the image of the Divine where all things are known as they are in their identity with God's infinite oneness.

Nicholas of Cusa calls our knowledge "conjectural" to contrast it with God's knowledge. For him, God's knowledge is both aperspectival and omniperspectival, totally complete and utterly exact, a coincidence of knower and known in infinite Oneness. We approach this ideal in seeing our present knowledge as conjectural and in recognizing its otherness. Doing so places us already beyond the limits of conjectural knowl-

---

32. Hopkins' note on this passage (*Wisdom and Knowledge*, 512) is illuminating:

> Epistemologically speaking, Nicholas is not a direct realist but is a critical representative realist. He affirms (1) that the human mind knows of the *existence* of material objects, (2) that it knows many things about these objects, while knowing nothing *precisely* about them, and (3) that although the mind does not know the objects as they are *in themselves*, it does know the *objects themselves* through their mental representations

33. *Idiota de mente* 2 is a further source for Cusan ideas about language. See Chapter 3, this book.

edge and at least partially in touch with the ideal of knowledge as the complete identity of knower and known. If the ideal is realized only in God's knowledge, we remain faithful to it by recognizing our own knowledge as conjectural. Our conceptions and assertions about God and about everything God creates remain partial, limited, perspectival, approximate.

1D. Knowledge and Otherness

Nicholas' explicit teaching about conjectures and conjecturing is thus situated firmly within his view of the finite universe as a created domain where each thing reflects or participates in the oneness of the infinite God but in a limited or contracted way, that is, in a condition of otherness. Human knowledge is no different, even though human knowers pursue knowledge of the Divine. Because there is no ontological proportion between infinite and finite for human beings, we can neither discover nor construct any conceptual measure to bridge the gap. As Cusanus stated in the "Prologue" to *De coniecturis,* "Therefore, since our actual knowledge cannot be related to that highest, humanly unattainable knowledge in any respect, the uncertain falling away of our weak knowing powers from the purity of truth reduces our assertions of the truth to conjectures" (h 2).

Conjectural knowing and its conceptual results underline the thesis that we never grasp Divinity with conceptual precision. As human knowers, both what we know about God and how we know it are irremediably and irretrievably limited by our ontological distance from God—by our condition of otherness. This finite or contracted condition prevents our adequately grasping God's oneness. Cusanus concludes: "the consequence is that every positive human assertion of the truth is a conjecture" ("Prologue," h 2).[34]

This conclusion may seem to undercut the initial *imago Dei* thesis on which *De coniecturis* hinges, as well as underscoring how that and everything else Cusanus proposes in Book 1 is a matter of conjecturing.[35]

---

34. Bond has underscored the importance of "positive" in this definition of conjecture. E. Wyller proposed in discussion with J. Stallmach (*MFCG* 11 [1975]: 121) that the word "positive" lets us understand the much debated relationship between *De docta ignorantia* and *De coniecturis.* While the former work stressed what we do not know and thus has a somewhat negative emphasis, *De coniecturis* is the further "positive" moment founded on that ignorance and therefore conjectural: "Eben weil dies alles positive gedacht ist, muss es konjectural verstanden werden."

35. I make more of this general point in "Nicholas of Cusa and Philosophic Knowledge," *Proceedings of the American Catholic Philosophical Association* 54 (1980): 155–63, and in "Irony and the History of Philosophy," *Poetics Today* 4 (1983): 465–78. One conviction that runs throughout Nicholas' works is that there is a connection between God and creatures, even if the parallels and correspondences that we construct, such as that between divine Mind and human mind, are conjectural.

While he believes that mathematical knowledge is exact and nonconjectural, its application to the relationship between God and creatures and to the order of created things is explicitly termed conjecturing. The employment of the decad and of geometry is an apt way to articulate for rational thought and imagination the varied aspects of a complex vision of the totality of things and their Creator. All the parts of *De coniecturis* that deal with or touch on God can exemplify the art and secret of conjecturing, for the burden of the treatise, especially in Book 1, is to expound the Cusan recognition of the disproportion between God's oneness and the otherness of everything else, without ever denying their connectedness.

But conjectural knowledge includes even more. All our conceptual, discursive knowledge about God and God's universe—about all that is real and independent of our knowing activity—counts as conjectural. This would include both the organized knowledge of the human and natural sciences, as well as the common generalizations of everyday knowledge based on our cultural experiences. The contents of both perceptual and conceptual knowing remain conjectural—they are always inexact approximations to the truth of what things are.

Chapter 11 of Book 1 makes it clear just why the content of human knowledge apart from mathematics is conjectural. For Nicholas, the only knowledge that is not conjectural is the knowing activity causally responsible for the reality of what is known. Therefore, all God's knowledge is exactly and precisely true; but apart from mathematics, no human knowledge is. Nicholas writes:

You see that you can understand no intelligible as it is [in itself], once you admit that your intellect is a reality other than the intelligible itself. For only that intelligible is understood as it is in its proper intellect from which its being stems; in every other [intellect it is understood] in an other way. So nothing is attained as it is, except in its proper truth, through which it exists. Therefore only in the divine Intellect through which every being exists is the truth of every thing attained as it is. In other intellects [truth is attained] in other ways and differently. (1.11 h 55)

The first sentence of this passage ("your intellect is a reality other than the intelligible itself") refers to the separation between the knowing mind and created knowable things. The distance between our minds and what we know is due to the finite status of both knower and known. Each is obviously not the other, but in a more fundamental sense each is not the Creator, even though each shares in God's infinite oneness in a limited way. Each created thing is but a contracted instance of its Exemplar or true essence. Hence neither human mind nor knowable things can perfectly fulfill their own natures. In its paradigmatic truth every created essence is identical with God's oneness. Every creature's existence in the universe of space and time and change is thus limited and deficient—the state of affairs Cusanus terms "otherness." Given this ontological condition on both sides, it is no wonder that the content of human knowledge remains inexact, approximate, and conjectural.

This passage thus underscores two fundamental separations that are at the same time, and significantly, connections: one between the human mind and knowable things, the other between the human mind and the divine Mind. If we turn to the second separation, we realize that, unlike God, we do not penetrate to the exact essence or nature of things as knowers, for we do not create the things we know but only the conceptual measures whereby we approximate them in thought. A thing's essence or truth can only be comprehended exactly in the mind that produces or creates it; only there does the divine Mind fashion the limits and the intelligibility of a created thing. For Nicholas of Cusa, human beings at best approach this active creating when they construct the concepts of mathematics whose meaning and reality depend on human reason. But only in the divine Mind is the true measure of created things as knowable originally set and so fully and exactly taken. All other minds understand what God creates not as those realities truly are, but conjecturally, that is, in otherness. Yet such knowledge does participate in or share the truth because all other minds are images of the divine Mind—connected to, yet not identical with, their divine Source or with the other things about which they conjecture.

1E. *Conjectural Ordering of Otherness*

By including otherness in his description of conjecture, Cusanus is working to free our speculative imaginations to employ whatever metaphors or constructed schemes we need. In his own case here, Nicholas uses the decad and the tetrad and the geometrical diagrams based on them to display the world of contraction and participation in a fitting order for us to grasp. In *De conjecturis* Cusanus is particularly taken with the quaternary or tetraktys, the ancient Pythagorean assignment of a symbolic meaning to the first four whole numbers summed as 10 and representing the basic principles of all there is. In this thinking, the whole nature of number is contained in the decad and the decad is complete at four. This arithmology was kept alive in the Neoplatonic traditions of which Cusanus was aware.[36] He proposes (and later repeats) a generalization about any participation that combines fourness and one-

---

36. See, for a representative instance, the work attributed to Iamblichus, *The Theology of Arithmetic*, trans. R. Waterfield (Grand Rapids, Mich.: Phanes Press, 1988).

ness toward the end of chapter 11: "For each thing that can be participated, since it is not participated except in otherness, will of necessity be participated in fourness" (1.11 h 58).[37] This cryptic sentence takes on more sense in chapters 12 and 13.

Chapter 12 proceeds to play with the notion of the universe's participation in its divine Source by envisioning three concentric circles to represent "three worlds" *(tres mundi)*. If God is taken to be the center point, then each of the circles represents the intelligible, rational, and corporeal realms already depicted in the Figure P of chapter 9 (see Figure 2.2).[38] The point essential to the chapter is that it represents an alternate combination and depiction of 4 and 10. There is a fourfold progression from the single center (represented by 1) to the three circumferences (representing 10, 100, and 1,000, respectively), as well as the iteration of the tetraktys within each (1 + 2 + 3 + 4; and so on).

Chapter 13 expands on the favored combination of 4 and 10 to construct another conjectural geometric diagram to symbolize the whole created universe. Cusanus names this *"Figura U"* (see Figure 2.3). A more complicated diagram of circles within circles, it is based on the fourfold arithmetic progression, 1 + 3 + 9 + 27. This adds up to 40, the product of 4 and 10. Within a single large circle that represents the universe are drawn three smaller circles (1 + 3) to represent higher, middle, and lower domains or regions *(regiones, mundi)*. Within each of the three circles are again drawn three yet smaller circles (+ 9) to symbolize the higher, middle, and lower orders *(ordines)* within each region. Finally, three more circles are drawn within the circles of the orders (+ 27) to represent higher, middle, and lower ranks *(chori)* therein.

In this way the universe, each region in it, each order of each region, and each rank of each order employs quaternity in a correspondingly parallel way. There is a single source that is participated in by three participants ranked in descent from less to more contracted or limited: "what is found in the universe is also found in each region [*mundo*] and in each of its orders, but in a different way that is more absolute or contracted" (1.13 h 67). In this way the metaphysical unities already set out as central to Cusanus' vision of the whole are found once again in this

---

37. "For there only does the oneness that cannot be participated coincide with what can be participated, in such wise, namely, that only in fourfold [*quaternaria*] otherness does each differently participating thing seek to attain the oneness that cannot otherwise be participated" (1.11 h 59). Chapter 11 ends with a diagram derived from the Pythagorean tetraktys, represented as ten contiguous circles in triangular form. While Cusanus' point is not arithmological here, he does not hesitate to use the familiar symbolic triangle of ten circles to represent how otherness participates in the oneness that cannot be participated.

38. Oide, in "Grundlagen," 168, 174, presents two diagrams integrating the three circles with Figure P.

more complicated schema. Such geometrical diagrams dramatically and unambiguously extend what Cusanus explained about the meaning of conjectural proposals from the ordinary perceptual situation he used in chapter 11 to the broadest conceptual frameworks we can employ.

2. BOOK 2

Cusanus opens Book 2 by explaining to Cardinal Julian that this book will illustrate in practice the art of conjecturing. He begins, however, with some general considerations (*generalium notitiarum praeambulares enodationes;* h 70) designed to augment the cardinal's (and our) expertise in using conjectures. He reminds us yet again that in the effort to experience *veri notitiam* we have to employ conjecturing because all precision escapes us.

2A. *Principles Recalled*

The second book of *De coniecturis* thereupon opens with three chapters of generalizations. The first chapter recalls the sort of universe we are investigating, a created cosmos characterized by diversity and otherness. What keeps this realm from being chaotic and enables our investigation to make sense of things is the fact that diversity is never mere otherness or sheer multiplicity. Rather, Nicholas believes that this diverse universe is ordered most generally as one of degrees, of more and less, of, to use Cusanus' own expression, *excedens et excessum*.

But degrees of what? More and less of what? The opening sentence of chapter 1 is fundamental for understanding the ontological framework within which conjecturing is both appropriate and inescapable: *"Omnia autem participatione unius id sunt quod sunt"* (Now, all things are what they are by participation in the One; 2.1 h 71). What keeps our investigations on track is our effort to discover and capture in diversity what keeps our universe truly a cosmos—namely, the image, reflection, or "shining forth" of fundamental (and ultimately divine) Oneness. We are to look for what is the same in diversity and what is one in otherness. This is a universe, an integral whole of parts, because it participates in oneness.

Then Cusanus refers us again to the geometrical Figures P and U of Book 1 (see Figures 2.2 and 2.3) for help in mapping the different kinds of things within a given domain. Any created participation in oneness descends through two intermediate stages of more or less oneness in otherness until a final fourth stage of otherness is reached. Alternately, any multiplicity is ordered from the absolutely necessary through the consequentially necessary and the contingent or actual to the merely

FIGURE 2.3 Figure U

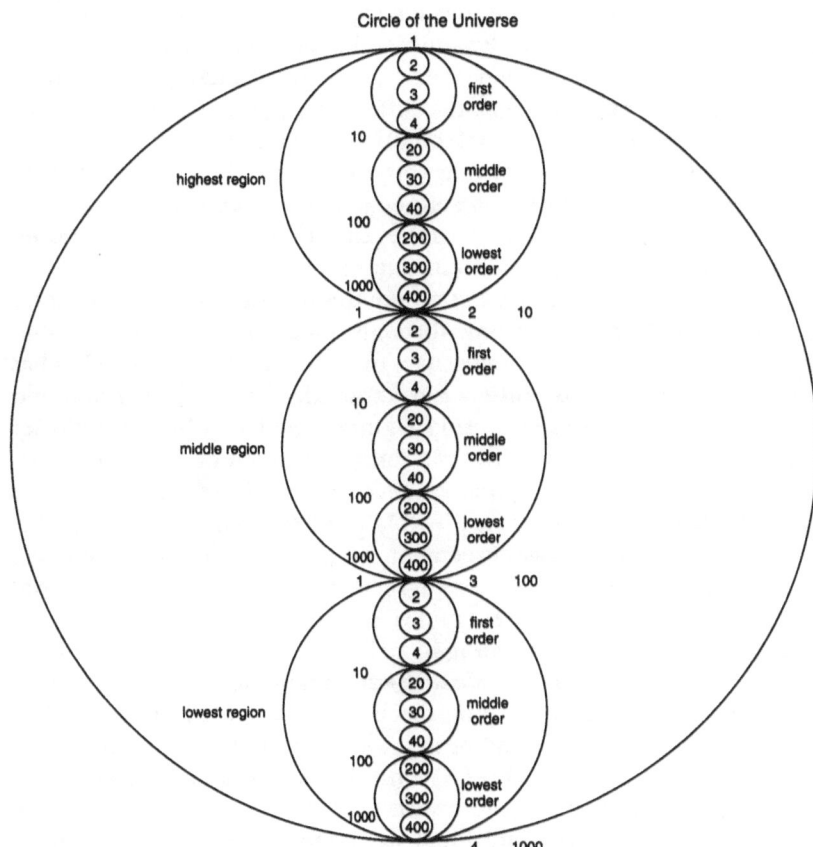

possible. This fourfold scheme corresponds to the way 1, 2, 3, and 4 (summed as the decad) epitomized the universe of number and symbolized metaphysical reality in Book 1.

Cusanus now recalls the kinds of conjecturing human beings do as knowers who employ sense, reason, and intellectual vision in the search for truth. His correlative assumption is that what we come to know of the world will correspond to the variety of our cognitive capacities—another fourfold scheme of oneness/otherness ordered from more to less oneness. Whether it is types of vision, degrees of precision, or kinds of enfolding and unfolding, Cusanus uses the panoply of our cognitive powers, but especially *ratio*, to help us understand conjecturing. It may be that our knowing powers stand as both paradigm and metaphor for what Cusanus means by participation and by stages of relative oneness and otherness. Or it may be that his Figure P is the paradigm for any sort of participation in a dynamic realm of becoming. In any case, Nicholas' paradigms for oneness and otherness, sameness and diversity reflect what we experience as the difference between what our senses and reason capture in ordinary cognition. Starting from the contrast of reasoning (oneness) and sensing (otherness), he then construes intellectual vision or intuition as a refinement of the unities we ordinarily achieve with *ratio* and reinterprets the partial unities of reason as otherness when measured against intellectual vision.[39]

Chapters 2 and 3 of Book 2 continue this line of thinking. In chapter 2 Cusanus reminds us that only through using our cognitive capacities can we grasp conjecturally some share of the truth of the things God has created. The way reason orders our knowledge in the quadrivium and trivium can also be ordered using Figures P and U. Chapter 3 glosses otherness and oneness as difference and agreement or harmony, *differentia et concordantia*. Noting that *concordantia* and *differentia* are inversely related, Cusanus returns to the fourfold progression depicted in the Figures P and U to show how agreement can be unfolded into difference. This makes it clear that the more agreement things manifest to reason, the less diversity will be present and vice versa.

Nicholas continues by locating in an imaginative variant of the Figure U each sensible thing's *concordantiae*—as something in the universe, as something generic, as something specific, and as something individual. Each sensible thing has a kind of *unio* with everything else when it is understood most universally. Every such thing also has both generic and specific connections that unite it with (and differentiate it from) other things. And even among individual specimens of the same type, there are aspects that agree and that differ. Cusanus uses the example of Cardinal Julian himself. What "julianizes" in Julian as individual is also what "humanizes" in humans, "animalizes" in animals, and "universizes" in the universe—each of these points of concord are at the same time differentiated in his particular case. If we measure the progression of *concordantia* from more to less for any given sensible thing, we conclude that every existing thing both agrees with and differs from everything else.

This somewhat fanciful picture tends to conflate in a misleading way individuals and universals, particulars and generals. As ever in Platonic

---

39. This focus on our knowing powers is repeated and extended in the conjectures about human beings in 2.14–17.

thought, there is a tendency to undervalue the individual in favor of the universal, to privilege the type over actual specimens. Yet Cusanus closes this chapter with remarks about contraction[40] that remind us that his Platonism is his very own, that all onenesses besides the first and ultimate (the infinite God) are *contracted* onenesses. Specific, generic, and universal characteristics are instantiated by these bodily, attenuated images of formal realities. (The formal realities do not exist as such outside of human thought, though all forms are identically real in the divine Oneness.) *Contractio* may be no less metaphorical than the projected fourfold progression from more to less *concordantia*, but here Cusanus underlines the fact that the created universe is made up of individuals that contract or restrict or delimit, each in its own way, the more general types to which they belong.

Contractio also calls attention to the problem of just how individuals are related to universals in Cusanus' Neoplatonism.[41] As in *De docta ignorantia*, the fourfold progression of agreement into difference apparently amalgamates types and instances. Nicholas thus appears to give genera and species an ontological status beyond the conceptual. Here Nicholas' speculative schema cannot differentiate properly the sorts of contents he places in it. What remains true throughout Nicholas' works is that whatever is contracted by a sensible individual is there enfolded and unfolded in an individually varied way. Precisely by being this unique individual, each existing thing rings its own changes on the specific, generic, and universal characteristics it shares.

2B. Elements across Domains

Cusanus' doctrine of elements in chapter 4 illustrates in another context how things are in harmony or agreement because they share different sorts of oneness-in-diversity. He sees oneness as elemental in each realm. Given appropriate allowances for the kind of domain or "region," he defines an element as "the oneness of each region absorbed in its own continuous otherness so that it is not able to subsist in itself, strictly speaking, on account of the smallness of its actuality or oneness" (2.4 h 90).

Behind this definition stands Cusanus' general rule that we never

---

40. Bond gives a helpful summary overview of contraction in general, and also in relation to universals and particulars. See his remarks in *Nicholas of Cusa*, 337–38.

41. The Cusan *locus classicus* on the relation of particulars and universals is *De docta ignorantia* 2.6 h 124–26. See Hopkins' remarks on that passage in his *Learned Ignorance*, 25–26. Hopkins rightly indicates that Cusanus' ideas there cannot be separated from his doctrine of contraction and of *"quodlibet in quolibet."* The case is no different in the present passage.

reach an actual maximum or minimum, only something more or less.[42] As a consequence, we cannot discover what is elemental in any realm in its pure state. Nor are we able to reduce or somehow decompose what is composed of elements *(elementatum)* into the actual elements that make it up. Our analysis cannot reach that far and, besides, each of the pure elements is without the power to subsist on its own.

This treatment of elements transfers (and transforms) Aristotle's definition of element by placing it within the Cusan framework of oneness and otherness. Aristotle says in *Metaphysics* Delta: "Common to all the senses [of 'element'] is this: an element of each thing is a primary constituent of it" (5.3.1014b15–16). His initial definition reads: "the first constituent of which a thing is composed and which is indivisible in kind into other kinds" (5.3.1014a26–27). Nicholas understands element as any "othered" oneness unable to exist by itself because of its smallness as one or actual. Aristotle points out as well that we call an element anything one and small, simple and indivisible. He illustrates the point with the example (which Cusanus repeats) of letters, syllables, and words.

At this point Nicholas proposes another schema to help us understand various realms as at once elemental and composite. Not surprisingly, this schema parallels and almost replicates his other schemata of oneness and otherness throughout *De coniecturis*. We are to take the intellectual realm as simpler and more unified than the rational, the rational as simpler than the realm of sense, recalling always that above them all stands utterly simple Divinity—Oneness bare, as it were.

Read from left to right, Table 2.1 puts in visual form what Cusanus says (h 90). For each example, he stresses again that what seems elemental oneness from the perspective of sense is obviously composite to reason and equally what reason takes as elemental is composite from the perspective of intellect.

Cusanus turns next to the four elements of ancient and medieval science: earth, air, fire, and water. Reason, he says, interprets them as mutually flowing into one another in a circular way. Cusanus urges us to imagine them as geometrical points since both points and elements cannot be analyzed into anything more simple and cannot exist by themselves. Clearly three elements will not serve to constitute a solid body any more than three points make up a geometrical solid—it requires four. In fact, in the case of both stereometric and physical bodies, points are inseparable from lines, lines from planes or surfaces, and surfaces

---

42. This general rule applies to the ontological condition of things and, as a consequence, to the inexact conjectural knowledge we are able to gain of them. Announced in *De docta ignorantia* 1.3 h 9, it is repeated in *De coniecturis* 1.10 h 46 and 49.

TABLE 2.1

Divine	Intellectual	Rational	Sensible
(transcendent Oneness)	root number	square number	cube number
		four elements	compounds
	point	line	surface
	letters	syllables	words

from solids or bodies—not one can exist by itself in nature. Just so, Cusanus conjectures, are the four elements inseparably connected, while the complex physical things can be resolved in principle into a simple solid body constituted by the four elements. The case is parallel to that of reducing all quadrilaterals into triangles in geometrical analysis.

We are to imagine six lines drawn from the four point elements so that the four triangular surfaces of the first tetrahedron or pyramid result. This is a geometrical representation of the basic constitution of anything composed of elements in the physical world—something *imperfectissimum* because it is continually subject to flux and change. Moreover, since any one element may dominate in a given physical thing, we may conjecture that it unites the others and envision any one of the four points of the pyramid as its actual apex. In a stereometric model of a pyramid, it would depend on which point element was rotated to become the dominant apex of the pyramid. Or we might likewise imagine the compound *(elementatum)* as a cone with whichever element enfolds or dominates the others in a given case as the apex. Cusanus writes: "The oneness of one element is the actuality of the others and in this way something composed of elements and proper to each element arises" (2.4 h 94).

Here Cusanus continues the medieval tradition that the four elements themselves occur as composite since none could exist on its own.[43] Cusanus restricts himself to ordinary earthy, airy, fiery, and wa-

---

43. For instance, we read in an *opusculum* attributed to Thomas Aquinas (*De mixtione elementorum*, in *Thomas Aquinas: Selected Philosophical Writings*, trans. T. McDermott [Oxford: Oxford University Press, 1993], 120) that

> we have to find some other way of maintaining the reality of compounds: one which doesn't involve total destruction of the elements but lets them exist somehow in the compound. Observe then that the behavioral properties of elements do oppose one another, and can exist more or less. From such opposed properties existing more or less we can construct an intermediate property that retains a taste of what each extreme is like: gray, e.g., intermediate between black and white, and tepid, intermediate between hot and cold. So then, when the extreme properties of elements have been damped down, there remains an intermediate property characteristic of the

tery phenomena. In such cases, fire constrains the other three elements in a more lucid and united way, earth in a grosser and darker mode. In between stand air and water, with the former closer to the lighter fire and the latter to the denser earth. For Nicholas, then, what are commonly known as the four elements are in reality four compounds or composite bodies composed of all four elements in which one of the four is primary or dominant.

In his later *Idiota de staticis experimentis* (h 177–80) Cusanus has the orator ask how by using the balance we can test the commonplace that no pure element can be observed. The layman replies at length for each of the four elements. His "experimental" strategy is the same for each. (He ingeniously uses the effects of the sun on plants to represent fire; in a passage just before he had discussed detecting the various weights of fire from the varying speeds of rising flames [h 176].) On using the balance, one finds that the weights of different samples of what we ordinarily designate earth, air, and water vary.[44] Along with confirming physical phenomena (what we would call changes of physical state), this variation shows that the proportions of the four elements in the samples vary and that they are in fact compounds, not samples of pure elements *(elementata, non elementa)*.

2C. Elements and Compounds

Chapter 5 uses the Figure U to show how each element exists *in elementato*, in something made up of elements. Here again we find the fourfold progression from oneness to otherness illustrated for the elements. If the dominant element in any compound is envisioned as the largest circle in Figure U, the other three are enfolded in the dominant element in a fourfold progression corresponding to the next three large circles. Were we to chart the *explicatio*, we would find the other three elements unfolding the dominant element again and again through the forty circles—through the universal, generic, specific, and most specific levels. In this way, Cusanus imagines, "the cube of three is the unfolding of the specific oneness of each element" (h 95).

---

compound, differing in each compound because of different proportions of the component elements.

Aquinas is speaking of compounds that may retain few or none of the typical characteristics of earth, air, fire, and water. What is significant in the Thomist passage for understanding Cusanus is the parallel emphasis on intermediate states and properties, as well as their being a matter of "more or less."

44. For Cusanus, although air and water and fire have weight *(pondus)*, they do not have heaviness *(gravitas)*. See *Idiota de staticis experimentis* h 172, as well as the passage referred to in the text, and Hopkins' notes on these passages, in *Wisdom and Knowledge*, 336, 340–48, 510.

Next Cusanus reminds us that there can be individual compounds without number because there is no limit to the individuals unfolding the capacity or possibility of each species, any more than there is a limit to the numbers we might count as unfoldings of 1. Rather, each individual composite or compound stands as one limit of the progression of the elements into otherness and the starting point of their return through intermediate stages to the oneness that is the most universal element. At this point Nicholas is moving back and forth from "element" meaning any sort of oneness that exists in otherness to "element" referring to the four elements of earth, air, fire, and water.

This is possible because the scheme of oneness proceeding into fourfold otherness and returning can be transposed across domains. In any area of analysis or investigation, the narrowest species or kind limits or contracts the more and most generic, as well as the universal, oneness or element to its own domain. From there it is envisioned as returning to its source: universal oneness. This also is an application of one of the more intriguing aspects of Cusanus' doctrine of unfolding and enfolding. It turns out that all unfolded unities are also enfoldings. Any place the *explicatio* halts or is imagined or conceived as halting, so to speak, is also and thereby a *complicatio*, whether we are speaking of numbers or of the papal power (as in the letter to R. Sanchez).[45] This is precisely how the three lesser onenesses of any fourfold unfolding are images of the original enfolded oneness: each fold or node, while it is an unfolding, is at once an enfolding, a oneness-in-otherness, that reflects the sourcing oneness of the first.

What is the upshot? Cusanus writes at the end of c.5:

> ... no knowledge reaches the exact composition of the elements, since it is impossible for two things to share equally the nature of the elements. Nor can the relationship of the difference between one thing and a second be known in any way. Therefore, since knowledge does not reach the mathematical point, knowledge of the levels of the elements takes place with ignorance, so that the ignorance is less in more confused and general knowledge, but there is greater defect in assumptions about more individual cases. (2.5 h 97)

Learned ignorance and conjecture come together when we attempt to investigate and understand the natural world. What Cusanus says about elements and compounds is simply one instance of these themes.

---

45. Writing about the sharing of papal power to Rodrigo Sanchez, Nicholas says, "Wherefore, the power of the first and supreme one [Peter] contains in its plenitude every power of all others. Thus there is no power except one, that of the first, which is shared variously in a diversity of prelates, by none, however, maximally. As such it is imparticipable." The translation is that of T. Izbicki in the Appendix to his paper, "The Church in the Light of Learned Ignorance," *Medieval Philosophy and Theology* 3 (1993): 186–214; the quote is from 210.

Chapter 6 applies the notion of participation to the fourfold "othering" of elemental oneness across domains. As Nicholas concludes halfway through this chapter, *"Habet igitur omnis ars sua elementa"* (Every art, then, has its own elements; 2.6 h 102). He returns to earth, air, fire, and water as paradigmatic of a more general point, namely, that there are elemental unities to be harmonized in each region or domain investigated conjecturally. He writes:

> But when you propose to enter into the particularity of elements, use rules that can correspond to the [different] regions. For just as in the sensible world you may conjecture that earth, air, fire, and water are the sensible elements, so in rational nature make conceptual elements fit for reason, that reason may be firelike, airlike, waterlike, and earthlike, and so that each sort of reason shares the oneness of reason in such elements fit for reason. Indeed, in this way make symbolic concepts about the intellectual region with elements fit for intellect. And to be able to construct your conjectures, fashion the elements as four unities like 1, 10, 100, 1,000, for the onenesses of the elements of 1 itself must differ. (2.6 h 103; see also 2.9 h 117.9–21)

Yet the point of conjecturing such fourfold participation goes beyond the order it lends to any created domain. This chapter ends bespeaking the joy of attaining "the Oneness of infinite Truth in the variety of true intelligibles" and embracing with intellectual joy "all things in the Truth that alone one loves" (h 105). While *De coniecturis* may be read as an exploration of how conjecturing can help our minds order the creation, Cusanus never forgets that what ultimately "shines forth" and is reflected both in the ordering and the ordered elements is "the Oneness of infinite Truth" (h 105).

2D. Tetrad, Hexad, and Heptad: Conjecturing the Natural World

Chapters 1–6 of Book 2 employ 4 and fourness or quaternity as the numbers that best organize our understanding of unfolding and enfolding in the created world. The sum of the first four whole numbers, after all, is 10 and since the time of Pythagoras, the decad was a number both sacred and paradigmatic. Chapter 7 is entitled "About 6, 7 and 10" and in it Nicholas explains how these numbers may be the basis for further conjecturing in exploring certain phenomena in the created world.[46]

This constant use of numbers and geometrical diagrams or schemata throughout *De coniecturis* is worth remarking. Here we find Cusanus adapting the numerology or arithmology of the Neoplatonic and neo-

---

46. See on these points V. Hösle, "Platonism and Anti-Platonism in Nicholas of Cusa's Philosophy of Mathematics," *Graduate Faculty Philosophy Journal* 13 (1990): 79–112, in particular 83, 89–90.

Pythagorean traditions to his art of conjecturing.[47] Numerology refers to the metaphysical as well as to the symbolic use of mathematics to explain the principles that lie behind the qualitative phenomena that thinkers in these traditions were trying to account for. Mathematics was thus taken to be the paradigm on which the physical world is modeled. Mathematics provided the closest images humans could find of the highest divine realities, much superior to those images we might garner from the physical cosmos.

Cusanus clearly believes mathematical objects in their simplicity and unity are in our mind as unexplicated or enfolded truths. His favorite examples of reason unfolding the numbers from 1 and the geometrical figures from the point suggest that mathematics gets articulated in increasingly differentiated expressions as it proceeds from the human mind no less than the world does as it proceeds from its Creator. But Cusanus differs from some of his Platonic predecessors in that they believed mathematical objects preexist and are independent of the human mind—that they are something we discover. But mathematical ideas are not innate or independent for Cusanus; rather they are *entia rationis*, beings of reason. He taught that the mind fashions them from its own resources no less than God fashions the world. As ever, Cusanus trades on the traditions he inherits here, even as he changes them in his favorite directions.[48]

Four is the number of creation. The tetrad or quaternium works best at helping us understand the cosmos conjecturally as a harmony or ordered domain of intelligibility and beauty. This use of quaternity is contrasted with 3, the triad, as the number of the uncreated, the Creator. More divine than 4 with its double middle, the 3 is kept separate for trinitarian and unitrine considerations. But the physical world is a tetrahedric unfolding of the point into the compounds of the four elements; physical things have this fourfold fundamental structure that reaches its term in the 10 (or 10^2 or 10^3). It was thus only fitting that 10 (the sum of 1, 2, 3, and 4) be the number immediately following the square of 3.[49]

Chapter 7 thus provides another way of framing the tetradic structure of created unfoldings. The 6 is taken to depict conjecturally the dynamic outflow from the divine Oneness and the return thereto of the

---

47. See D. J. O'Meara, *Pythagoras Revived* (Oxford: Clarendon Press, 1987), for the history from Hellenistic times to Proclus.
48. Ibid., 97–103.
49. "On the Tetrad," in *Theology of Arithmetic*, 55–63, presents the many features of the physical universe that are fourfold. Nicholas does not use five or fivefold in these chapters.

four "unities" of Book 1. The stages of one, intellect, reason, and sense are now to be seen as a complete "circulation," so that descent from the divine Oneness and ascent to it are simultaneous. This gives a total of six stages of outflow and return *(effluxus et refluxus)*. Cusanus diagrams them as the points of a hexagon circumscribed within a circle in the first diagram of this chapter.

In arithmology, the 6 or *senarium* had long been seen as a perfect number.[50] It was the sum of its "aliquot parts": $6/6 + 6/3 + 6/2 = 6$. Because of the perfection of the 6, God saw fit to create the world in six days. Six thereby became the number of God's works, no less than four was the number of the cosmos once created. This may be why Nicholas writes:

> With intellectual ingenuity, therefore, connect the ascent to the descent so you may conjecture more truly. Conceive then the perfect circulation with this understanding of the number 6, so you will be able to intuit how the measure of perpetuity exists ascribed to the number 6.... (2.7 h 107).

Nicholas then turns to the heptad or 7, "which goes out from the 6 as do time and succession from what is perpetual" (2.7 h 108). He uses it as the basis of conjectures about the living things that we experience as subject to generation and destruction. If the 6 provides us a conjectural schema for the Neoplatonic ontology of *exitus* and *reditus*, the number 7 enables us to organize conjecturally many cosmic phenomena associated with birth and death, growth and development.[51]

For this diagram Cusanus draws the capital letter N and arranges four points along each vertical stroke and two above the diagonal connecting them (for a total of ten stages). His example is that of the seven stages in the generation of one tree from another: seed, sprout, sapling, tree, branch, twig, fruit/seed. Now, the second seed in this progression begins a numerically separate tree, so the progression is best conceived conjecturally as first seven and then ten stages. There are seven from the first seed to the second seed or offspring, ten from the first seed to the second full-fledged tree (adding again sprout, sapling, tree to the seven stages in the developmental progression mentioned above). Thus when an individual specimen dies the species is continued and preserved in

---

50. "On the Hexad," in *Theology of Arithmetic*, 75–85, where we read on 75: "The hexad is the first perfect number; for it is counted by its own parts, as containing a sixth, a third, and a half. When squared it includes itself, for $6 \times 6 = 36$; when cubed, it no longer maintains itself as a square, for $6 \times 36 = 216$, which includes 6, but not 36."

51. "On the Heptad," in *Theology of Arithmetic*, 87–99, says (87): "We see seven things—body, distance, shape, size, color, movement, and rest. There are seven movements—up, down, forward, backward, right, left, and circular. Plato composed the soul out of seven numbers. Everything is fond of sevens. There are seven vowels and seven alterations of voice. There are seven ages, as Hippocrates says."

the offspring. Cusanus ends by proposing not only that we use this progression to understand the natural cycles of the perceptible world, but also that we transpose the seven and employ it symbolically to explore the rational and intellectual domains of thought.[52]

Whether he speaks of elements or employs numbers or geometrical figures in this section of *De coniecturis*, Nicholas never fails to stress that these are exercises in the art of conjecturing. He is fashioning the conjectural concepts and schemata that will enable us the better to understand and organize our study of the created world. While mathematics, because of its clarity and exactness, is especially useful in our explorations, what we measure with it can be employed itself to measure and explore further. In the case of elements, for instance, the very phenomena he studies themselves become symbolic guides to help us better understand the fourfold egress from and regress to God of all creatures. What may begin as conjectural exploration becomes conjectural construction—the phenomena discovered or measured conjecturally then become measures of further phenomena.

One telling example of this occurs in chapter 9 of Book 2. There Nicholas employs the hierarchy of the four elements (from fire to earth) to help him structure our understanding of the four "ways of being." He writes:

In progressing into conjecturable objects conjectural oneness has four elements, namely, subtlety, coarseness, and two intermediate elements. For in extreme subtlety conjecturing proceeds upward, *as if it were fire*, and intuits the mode of being of things in some absolute oneness or necessity. But by proceeding coarsely, and *as if it were earth*, conjecturing fashions a shadowy mode of being in possibility. Indeed, it produces two other modes of being, one of which approaches absolute necessity. And this is the mode without which a true thing cannot be understood and indeed is the mode of second necessity, [necessity] of implication. For when the truth of humanity is said to exist of necessity, from this there follows necessarily those conditions without which it cannot exist. The second [intermediate] mode of being arises closer to possibility but above it, while below the mode already mentioned. It has less of necessity and much of possibility so that it is indeed an actual mode of being. (2.9 h 117, emphasis added)

Since number provides a basic metaphor for understanding the universe in its fourfold and decadic character, the four elements can also be used in this way to construe symbolically the progression from necessity through actuality to possibility.[53] This progression, in turn, characterizes the kinds of existence encountered in each of the four unities of

---

52. On the association of seven and ten, see "On the Heptad," 89.
53. Cusanus also mentions the modes of necessity and possibility in *De docta ignorantia* 2.7 h 129–31, and in *Idiota de mente* 7 h 107 and 9 h 125. The fourfold distinction comes from Thierry of Chartres.

the universe. And one "sees that the four modes of being are to be reduced to the number 10, which is the whole of number" (2.9 h 119).

2E. Variety and Difference in Things

From chapter 8 until the end of *De coniecturis* 2, Cusanus explores what conjecturing will uncover through the various levels of the so-called great chain of being, though not exactly in the traditional order. He begins in chapter 8 by explaining how the principle that finite things are matters of more and less has implications for every individual specimen of any type. For Nicholas, it is not just that each individual creature never fulfills all the possibilities of its kind; each also differs from every other individual of the same type. On whatever basis they are compared, they never turn up exactly equal or the same. Where things are composites or result from interacting causes, they may turn out to be more or less of the dominant composite: male/female, actual/potential, nature/nurture. Behind this stands what Cusanus has already said about the way in which otherness participates dynamically in oneness.

Such variation and difference occur perceptibly in the realm of corporeal things, and Nicholas extrapolates from there to the rational and intellectual spheres. In having its own sort of oneness, each domain of otherness varies its participation in the ultimate divine Oneness. This can be read at the level of genera and species, yet Nicholas insists that concrete individuals are also different. There is variety at the level of the individual existent within whatever one counts as a particular item. That is why he continues to use Figures P and U. They map onto *any* scale of differentiation and within types across individuals. Cusan participation is identically Cusan "contraction," and contraction is always a matter of more or less.[54]

Chapters 9–13 work out these general ideas in more detail. Whether he considers modes of being (9), things composed of body and soul (10), living things (11), nature and art (12), or angelic intelligences (13), Cusanus' focus is on likeness and difference (= oneness and otherness, again). There is no agreement or similarity without difference;

---

54. In 2.9 Nicholas points out the individual differences among those who do the conjecturing:

> From these considerations you may conjecture sufficiently what I intend and, if you wish, you may conceive in a kind of general art the difference among both conjectures and conjecturers. For just as some conjectures based on sensation are confused, others based on reason are truthlike, others based on intellect are true, so indeed those making conjecture differ: some discourse in the confusion of the sense realm, others reason from premises, others are devoted to intellectual matters freed from such constraints. (h 117)

likewise, there is no difference without likeness. Thus in chapter 10 Nicholas repeats his thesis that likeness and difference in created things are matters of more and less. He remarks that our minds cannot reach precision in measuring either differences or likenesses or their combinations. Comparisons fall short of exactness when we attempt to say to what degree things are alike or not. The reason is that both the likeness and the difference we discern differ in comparable cases by a difference we cannot measure. Thus in speaking of different souls or spirits, Cusanus says: "Therefore the exactness of the comparably proportioned difference cannot be attained. And so one spirit agrees with another spirit by a befitting difference" (2.10 h 122).

What sort of thinking is this? What Cusanus does throughout *De coniecturis* is to propose numerical and geometrical schemata and diagrams as ways of exercising and exemplifying what he means by conjectures and conjecturing, both as a kind of thinking and as intelligible content to be gained about the worlds of perceptible nature and of thought. But this art of conjecturing is more than a series of fascinating, if sometimes fanciful, exercises and proposals. There is a dialectical movement back and forth, as it were, from a given proposal or diagram and what it initially captures or orders for our thinking to other domains where it may apply, then a return back to the original conjecture.

As it turns out, this is the best way for our thinking to match the dynamism of the Cusan universe. In his vision of the whole, each created thing and the totality of creation are related as different proportions or ratios of the oneness and otherness *(unitas et alteritas)* that are the basis in *De coniecturis* of the interconnectedness of everything from God to the four elements. We can only do the parallel applications and examples of the art of conjecturing justice when we refuse to take them as so many fanciful proposals or as simply a late medieval Neoplatonic resystematization. Their real power and originality only appear if we understand conjecturing in Cusan terms. Conjecturing is the human effort to capture the divine truth things share but in a dynamic otherness at once their own and connected to, because reflecting, God's infinite oneness.

2F. Conjecturing the Human
2F.1. Microcosm

Throughout *De coniecturis*, the paradigm image of God is none other than human nature itself. With a closing set of conjectural proposals Cusanus' final chapters in Book 2 turn back to what it is to be human, and especially to the multiple knowing powers of human beings. He begins chapter 14 by proposing the use of the Figure U, even though the details he sets out about the panoply of human powers and their relative dominance in various people do not form an exact or tight fit with that figure. What is more important in this exposition is the tracing of human sensation and imagination to reason and intellection. Nicholas' own poetic description is to be noted:

> Wondrous is this work of God, in whom step by step the power of discriminating is borne upward from the center of the senses into the highest intellectual nature. [It proceeds] through stages and some organic channels, where the links of the very subtle bodily spirit are filled with light and simplified because of the dominance of the soul's power, until it is extended into the organ of the rational power. After that it arrives in the highest stage of the intellectual power, as if sailing down a stream into an unbounded sea. . . . (2.14 h 142)

The image of sailing begins already in the first sentence in the Latin (*"supervehitur," "rivulos"*) and is completed in the dramatic simile (*"quasi per rivum in mare interminum"*). This simile contrasts the unboundedness of the sea with the limitations of a stream to underline the difference between what sensation can manage and all that intellect is open to. This openness implies that there is nothing knowable closed off to humankind. Each human being is truly *capax omnium*, "because it [human nature] conjectures that it reaches all things either by sense or by reason or by intellect" (2.14 h 143). Moreover, since the phrase *mare interminum* had been long used by medieval authors as an image of God's infinite being, it here serves a twofold purpose.[55] It recalls, first, Nicholas' thesis that only via intellect can we manage to touch the Divine. Second, the image provides some transition to Cusanus' next rather dramatic remarks about each human person being a "human god."

Nicholas writes:

> For man is God, but not in the absolute way [that God is God], because he is man: so he is a human god. Man is also the world, but not in the contracted way [that the world is] all things, because he is man. Therefore man is a microcosm or human world. The region of humanity, therefore, embraces God and the whole world in its human power. So man can be a human god and, as god, in a human way he can be a human angel, human beast, human lion or bear, or whatever else. For within the power of humanity all things exist in their own way. In humanity therefore all things are unfolded in a human way, just as in the universe [they are unfolded] in a universal way, because [in humanity] a human world exists. Finally all things are enfolded in it in a human way because [in humanity] a human god exists. For humanity is oneness which is also infinity, contracted in a human way. (2.14 h 143–44)

---

55. Cusanus may have read the phrase in Thomas Aquinas, though it goes back to St. John Damascene, *De fide orthodoxa* 1.9.

This celebrated passage presents the motif of man the microcosm in a rather different context than that of Book 3 of *De docta ignorantia*.[56] There Cusanus employed it as part of a thought experiment to find the creature best able and most appropriate for union with God in a hypostatic union. Here the notion of microcosm is reinterpreted using Nicholas' own favorite metaphors of unfolding/enfolding and contraction. Indeed, these metaphors recall his exploration of the created universe in Book 2 of *De docta ignorantia* and his use there of the slogan attributed to Anaxagoras, *"Quodlibet est in quolibet"* (Every thing is in each thing). For while this passage in *De conjecturis* celebrates human nature as indeed God's *mirabile opificium*, it does so by working out for the human sphere just what "quodlibet in quolibet" amounts to. In fact, man is a microcosm just because human nature is not divine nature as such nor the universe of creatures as such.[57] Rather, any human being has the capacity in principle to "embrace God and the whole world." What it means to be human is to be able to encompass all that is knowable through sense, reason, and intellectual vision.

Nicholas' next metaphor interprets human nature as constituting the center of a circle. As the circumference is generated from the center, so from our knowing capacities we can generate a conceptual world and in so doing discover ourselves by reaching out to embrace all things in knowledge. This is godlike because knowing has no limit and because its goal is none other than itself. This creating is *humanly* godlike because human knowledge does not create the world outside the human mind by its knowing activities, even though knowing activity fashions conceptual frameworks and fills them out with ordered and related content. In accomplishing this the knowing activities change the one who knows. "One does not go outside himself, when he creates, but reaches himself when he unfolds his power. Nor does he bring about anything new, but finds that all the things that he creates by unfolding were in that power" (2.14 h 144).

---

56. But Nicholas does refer to human being as *deus occasionatus* in *De docta ignorantia* 2.2 h 104, adding, "For the Infinite Form is received only finitely, so that every created thing is, as it were, a finite infinity or a created god, so that it exists in the way in which this can best occur." Students of the Renaissance can hardly read this passage of *De coniecturis* without recalling Pico's famous *Oration on the Dignity of Man* and the importance of the status of human beings for such Italian Renaissance thinkers as Ficino. See C. Trinkaus, *In Our Image and Likeness: Humanity and Divinity in Italian Humanist Thought*, 2 vols. (London: Constable, 1970), and his later essay, "Marsilio Ficino and the Ideal of Human Autonomy," in *Marsilio Ficino e il ritorno di Platone: Studi e documenti*, 2 vols., ed. G. Garfignini (Florence: L. S. Olschki, 1986), 1:197–210.

57. See W. Dupré, "Der Mensch als Mikrokosmos im Denken des Nikolaus von Kues," *MFCG* 13 (1978): 68–87, esp. 72–74.

Cusanus ends chapter 14 with one of the relatively rare references to the Trinity in *De coniecturis*. He aligns God's oneness, equality, and connection with creative divine ruling, ordering, and conserving in order to parallel how human beings employ knowledge. He first mentions imagination/memory; here we create, order, and preserve sense images. This contracted "imaging" of the Divine happens as well in our use of reason and intellection, and in doing this we learn to understand and govern ourselves so that we may approach our own true end: *deiformitas*.[58]

2F.2. Knowing the Soul/Self

Chapter 16 is a lengthy discourse on the human soul and particularly on human cognition as consisting of the characteristic powers and activities that belong to and disclose the nature of the soul. This chapter is also a recapitulation of the main conjectural themes that structure the whole of *De conjecturis*. Nicholas discusses the knowing powers of the human self by weaving into his explanation once more the parallel between the divine Mind and the human mind, the correspondences between the fourfold ontological hierarchy and the four knowing powers of human beings. He brings in the familiar dialectical opposition and connection of oneness and otherness through levels or steps of greater or lesser contraction in the universe and the mind. Once again he employs *complicatio* and *explicatio:* the dynamic outflow and emanation from simpler unities to their dependent images that is at once and identically the return of dependent otherness to independent or absolute Oneness.

In this chapter the long-standing motif of human being as microcosm announced in 2.14 gets filled out in distinctively Cusan terms. Nicholas is continuing in his own way the earlier pre-Christian and Christian Neoplatonic tradition in which ontology recapitulates, as it were, mentality. Once we uncover the mental activities and capacities we possess as knowers and what each capacity reveals of reality, we may extrapolate from these disclosures to the nature of reality. That is why the lower three rungs of the conjectural ladder of reality (intelligence, reason,

---

58. Later, in 2.14 h 174, Nicholas again connects the intellect with Trinitarian *deiformitas:* "Therefore, the more you participate intellectually in absolute equality, in which are oneness and connection, the more 'deiform' you are." See also the final chapter of *De coniecturis* 2 h 182. In chapter 15 Nicholas proposes some conjectural remarks about the differences and likenesses among actual human beings, employing the *figura universi*. He first suggests how they may be ordered in terms of their cognitive proclivities and then their religious concerns. Then Nicholas draws on what earlier writers such as Albert the Great, Aristotle, and Ptolemy had said about how actual differences in people's temperaments are affected by climate, locale, and time of life. He then arranges these incidental differences according to the three main circles in the Figure U. K. Bormann has termed chapter 15 an exercise in "geographic ethnography," in "'Übereinstimmung und Verschiedenheit der Menschen' (*De Coni.* II,15)," *MFCG* 13 (1978): 88–104.

body) conveniently mirror, even as they transcend, our capacities of intellectual intuition, discursive reason, sensation as imagination. Lest this schema appear too static, we are reminded that what has been created independently of our knowledge is itself also the product of mind in action—that divine Mind that eternally orders, governs, and preserves in being the whole finite universe as its image, a universe constantly struggling to return to the God who fashioned and made it.

Here again Cusanus parallels the dynamic interdependence of our own knowing activities that operate as one (even though they are many) with the relation of the infinite divine Oneness to the otherness of the created cosmos. Indeed, both are coprimordial paradigms for the connections in any instance of absolute and contracted, infinite and finite. Because this chapter's focus is the human soul (viewed mainly as cognitive), Nicholas writes:

> The unity of intellect descends into the otherness of reason, the unity of reason into the otherness of imagination, the unity of imagination into the otherness of sense. Therefore, enfold the ascent with the descent using intellectual intuition so that you may grasp it. For it is not the intent of intellect to become the senses but to become perfect intellect in actuality. Yet because it cannot otherwise be constituted in actuality, it becomes the senses so that by this means it thus can proceed from potentiality into actuality. In this way the intellect returns again to itself by a complete circular reversion.[59] (2.16 h 159)

Because these are conjectures about human knowing capacities, not about the conjectural content of knowledge, Cusanus turns to the objects of those capacities only to clarify the differences and connections between them. Even so, it is the knowing activities that he describes, not what they capture.[60] Moreover, this application of the simultaneity and

---

59. The "complete circular reversion" recalls *Liber de causis* 14.124ff. (see *The Book of Causes*, trans. D. J. Brand [Niagara, N.Y.: Niagara University Press, 1981], 27); it ultimately goes back to *epistrophe* in Proclus. See propositions 31–39 from *The Elements of Theology*, 2nd ed., trans. E. R. Dodds (Oxford: Oxford University Press, 1963), 35–43. Proclus writes in proposition 33: "*All that proceeds from any principle and reverts upon it has a cyclic activity.* . . . Thus all things proceed in a circuit, from their causes to their causes again."

60. Nicholas writes,

> Notice, too, that as you have heard that the intellect for the sake of its own perfection descends and returns to itself by a complete reversion, so should you conceive sense. For sense proceeds upward to intellect for the sake of the perfection of sensate life. . . . Now because the perfection of the intellect is to actually understand—for its capacity to understand is perfected when it moves into its activity—hence the intellect is its own fecundity when of itself it makes intelligible what proceeds into the intellect. For the descent of the intellect into sensible images is their ascent from limiting conditions into less restricted [*absolutiores*] simplicities. Therefore the more deeply [intellect] puts itself into them, the more those images are absorbed into its light, so that in the end intelligible otherness is resolved into intellect's oneness and comes to rest as in its goal. And so the oneness of the intellect becomes more perfect, the more it proceeds from potency into act. (*De coniecturis* 2.16 h 161)

interdependence of the Neoplatonic *exitus-reditus* scheme to the jointly operating powers of the human mind can finally only be thought dialectically. For Nicholas, again, *exitus* is one with *reditus*, *complicatio* with *explicatio*, *unitas* with *alteritas*. If we separate them too rigidly in thought we will not do justice to their dynamic oneness in reality.

Because of the "distance" from intellectual intuition to bodily nature, Nicholas interprets the work of discursive reason and sensation plus imagination as mediating the extremes. In his words, "Oneness is not reached except by mediating otherness.... Nor is otherness reached through itself for the same reason, and so otherness is not reached except by mediating oneness" (2.16 h 162). Here he applies to our cognitive functioning the earlier principle that opposite extremes are mediated at least twice, since no direct connection is possible between unequal opposites and there can be no exact midpoint between them.[61] Cusanus writes:

> Therefore, the intellect, which is the oneness of reason, is joined to the body by the mediation of that very reason. For bodily nature cannot share the intellectual except in otherness, and since [body] is farthest away from [intellect], it requires mediating stages. So bodily nature shares the intellectual nature in the otherness of the light of reason through organic and sensible mediation. Now the sensible ascends through corporeal organs to reason itself, which adheres to the most delicate and subtle corporeal spirit of the brain. The otherness received in reason, however, is taken up into the intellect free from every organ by the mediation of the oneness of reason that is the otherness of intellect. And because this ascent of reason is the descent of intellect, on this account the unimpeded [*absolutus*] intellect when it hunts in the otherness of reason embraces truths as raised high above the phantasms. (2.16 h 166)[62]

What is remarkable about this passage is the subtle way it manages to portray our knowing powers in their operative oneness and the awareness it manifests of how human sensation, imagination, and reasoning are distinctively human just because of their unifying source in intellective vision or intuition. While humans cannot reach such unifying intel-

---

61. Cf. *De coniecturis* 1.4 h 13: "No precise midpoint falls between diverse and opposed unities, the simple [number] and the solid [number, for example], but at least two are obviously required, one of which is closer to the simple, as the root [number], and the other to the solid, as the square [number]."

62. Cf. what Nicholas writes about the otherness of our knowing powers:

> I think we must conjecture in this way regarding the power of intellect and the light of reason. For reason is the otherness of intellectual oneness and, unless [intellect's] power is strong, it will often be absorbed in the otherness of reason so that it takes opinion for true understanding. In this way, too, the otherness of the phantasms often absorbs reason so that a person often judges that what he imagines has been shown by reason. So too the otherness of sensation sometimes absorbs the oneness of imagination so that what one attains by sensing he judges to be the thing he imagines. (2.16 h 165)

lectual vision the way angels without sensate powers might, they nonetheless transform ordinary animal sensation and imagination or memory by their ability to rework and transfigure the sensible, using symbol and metaphor and pressing beyond the limits of ordinary rational discourse.

But Nicholas remains true to the goal of knowing God and the self, to the sought-for *deiformitas* alluded to in 2.14. Whatever the human intellect, the ultimate oneness of the human mind, may accomplish beyond discursive reason, it can achieve that only as otherness and therefore through the infinite divine Oneness. As intellectual, we humans are the otherness for God's oneness.[63] If human being is something marvelous to behold, part of the marvel includes how human intelligence is itself sustained and transformed by the divine Intellect, its Source and transcendent Goal.

> For since all otherness cannot be attained except in oneness, the [human] intellect that is otherness cannot intuit itself as it is except in the most divine Oneness, for it is not the utterly absolute divine Intellect, but human. For the intellect cannot reach itself or anything intelligible as it is, except in that Truth that is the infinite Oneness of everything nor can it intuit that infinite Oneness except in intellectual otherness. . . . And this is the highest perfection of the intellect: it continuously ascends, through the theophany descending into it, to some approximate likeness of the divine and infinite Oneness, which is the infinite Life and Truth and Repose of the intellect. (2.16 h 167)

De coniecturis 2 concludes with an appeal to Cardinal Julian in chapter 17 to use what has been explored of the human self to gain self-knowledge. Self-knowledge here, however, is knowledge about any and every human self, knowledge about human nature and its possibilities. It does not refer to Cardinal Julian's biography or even to his moral character. Still less is such self-knowledge a matter of his psychological history, nor does it involve assessing the adequacy and extent of his own knowledge or education. Instead *docta ignorantia* makes its appearance in another way: Julian is reminded to recognize contraction and otherness, even as he acknowledges and seeks oneness.

First, Cusanus exhorts his patron to recall that his own human nature stands as an individual contraction or limitation of the possibilities of the human species. Each individual person stands as otherness to the oneness of human nature. And *humanitas* is itself otherness when measured against the absolute divine Oneness, an otherness that inescapably participates in *divinitas*, even if the divine Oneness in itself remains uncontracted and unparticipated. Next, Nicholas bids Julian to entertain a

---

63. See J. Stallmach, "Geist als Einheit und Andersheit," *MFCG* 11 (1975): 86–116, in particular 90–100 and 108–13.

"visible example." Suppose he were to picture Divinity as light, then all created things would be color. For color is the otherness of light, that is, the contracted otherness that reflects and participates in light, but is not itself light. Returning to his Figure U, Cusanus proposes that Julian make the largest circle that of color and the other circles a progression of three colored regions each with nine distinct stages. Moving from highest to lowest between and within regions is moving from colors bathed in light to those shrouded in darkness.[64]

There is a corresponding way to envisage the Figure U again, this time with a slight but significant change. Suppose again that Divinity is light. But this time take color to stand for humanity—the largest circle. Let the other three circles and all the smaller circles symbolize the visible universe and all colored things. The gain in "self-knowledge" will be twofold. The first comes when Julian places himself among created things and compares his nature to other natures as part of the visible universe and to other human beings in the *regio humanitatis*. The second corresponds to the fact that humanity is itself microcosmic and embraces the whole (that is why the colored whole can stand for humanity). The fittingly correspondent cognitive powers of human beings mean that human conjecturing measures the visible universe. Even as humans dwell within creation they transcend it—they are color and colored.

As a microcosm of the whole, as the color that is the otherness of divine Light, human nature reflects in a limited way that divine Oneness. Especially human intellectuality participates in the divine Oneness or light—something Nicholas here urges Julian to recognize as a divine gift: *"ut te scias superno dono intelligentiam habere"* (so that you many know that you possess intelligence as a gift from above; 2.17 h 174). But this gift of participating through intellect in the divine Oneness is even more. In Christian belief divine Oneness is at once Threeness, Unity is Trinity. In this final chapter about self-knowledge Nicholas returns to his conviction that in God's true self, God's oneness is identically threefold: Oneness plus Equality plus mutually indwelling Connection or Love. Invoking the Trinity places an emphasis on the unitrine mutual indwelling and particularly on the fact that the Third Person within the Godhead is Connection: the subsistent Love between Father and Word. The more we share intellectually that triune life, the more deiform we become.[65]

This leads to further self-knowledge, here interpreted as insight into

---

64. The use of color and light and especially perceptual seeing continues in the *opuscula* Nicholas wrote just after *De coniecturis*. See my Introduction, this book, for *De Deo abscondito* h 14; cf. also *De quaerendo Deum*, passim.

65. This turn to the unitrine after the many discussions of quaternity and fourfold participation throughout *De coniecturis* underlines the difference between God's own dynamic

how human nature is "unitrine" and thereby *dei similitudo*, the likeness of God. Nicholas bids Julian recognize that each human being is a contracted reflection—in a human way—of the divine Equality and Connection in Oneness. Every human being exists by virtue of his or her own oneness, is rightly or justly ordered by virtue of equality, and stands as an interrelated whole by virtue of connection. Even though human nature is a complex of parts, oneness becomes manifest in every person's life through the interrelatedness of the parts—their right order and connection. It is Connection or Love in which the Oneness and Equality of the Trinity dwell, so the final pages of *De coniecturis* focus on *connexio* or love, a traditional Christian theme Nicholas has not emphasized until this point.

"For love unites the one who loves with what is lovable" (*unit enim amor amentem cum amabili*; 2.17 h 181). Nicholas takes up the traditional Augustinian triad of *amor, amans,* and *amabile* as parallel to *connexio, unitas,* and *aequalitas,* explaining how what is lovable is whatever is equitably ordered to oneness both in heaven and on earth. He thus provides Julian with a norm for choosing and loving: "From yourself, then, you can see the deiform choices" (2.17 h 182). When it comes to loving God, we must realize that God is love. This means that to love God is identical with being loved by God, so that the difference between *amare* and *amari* falls aside. In any case, all our efforts to love God fall short of the divine Love that is the Trinity itself.

As for loving others, Cusanus reminds Julian that what is rightly or justly ordered itself comprises oneness and connection. As an example, he invokes the golden rule: *"quod tibi vis fieri, alteri fac"* (what you wish done to you, that do to another; 2.17 h 183). *Aequalitas,* construed as equitable order to oneness, thus embraces all of moral virtue and provides the standard for choosing and loving. Our choices and our friendships—what and whom we love—are what finally let us manifest in attenuated and fractured form that divine Oneness that is at the center of Nicholas' concerns throughout *De coniecturis*. In this way it is fitting that the lengthy epistolary treatise closes, as it opens, by referring to the friendship and affection between its author and the friend and patron to whom he addressed it.

---

oneness versus the oneness-in-otherness of created things in the realm of becoming and change. It is also worth remarking how Cusanus sees us sharing God's unitrine life *intellectually*, with that power of intellectual intuition which is simpler and more unified than our other cognitive powers and activities. The Trinity is thus not a Threeness "participating" Oneness, but a Oneness that is identically Threeness. As one *and* three God is imparticipable for Nicholas. Creatures participate, so theirs is always a oneness-in-otherness.

3

Metaphors for Mind
Idiota de mente (1450)

In 1450 Nicholas of Cusa completed his three *Idiota* dialogues: one on wisdom in two parts, one on mind in fifteen chapters, and one on experiments with the balance as an undivided piece. All three dialogues feature as the principal interlocutor an *idiota*, an unlearned or unlettered layman, who instructs his betters by answering their questions. The *Idiota de mente* adds to the orator of the other two dialogues a learned philosopher to participate in a discussion about the meaning of *mens*, the life of human intelligence and knowledge that is an image of the mind of God.[1] The Neoplatonic ontology of *De docta ignorantia* and *De coniecturis*, where God and creation are framed as absolute Original and contracted image and as originating Oneness and originated oneness-in-otherness, respectively, are not forgotten. Rather, the same framework is reapplied to understand the human *mens* as the image of God's mind.

Cusanus here articulates his own view of mind and human knowledge by employing several metaphors to explore and explain just how our cognition may be seen as an image of God's knowing. By deliberately using the metaphors of *assimilatio* and *mensuratio*, Nicholas puts a new emphasis on the active and creative features of adult cognition. He does this without ever losing sight of the fact that, as knowers, we are directed first of all to the perceptible world and the items of which it is composed. How we understand and construe that world as adults never captures what the world amounts to exactly and precisely—for Nicholas, this means that human knowledge is always conjectural.

Conjectural knowledge is incomplete and perspectival, but not necessarily false or mistaken. Nor does such knowledge result simply from the mind's imposing ideas on a world that is inaccessible or unintelligible to us. Indeed, Nicholas' metaphors for the harmonious union of soul and

---

1. This chapter revises much of the "Introduction" to my translation of this dialogue: *Nicholas de Cusa. "Idiota de mente": "The Layman: About Mind."* (New York: Abaris Books,

body in *Idiota de mente* are a reminder that the human mind inhabits and belongs in the corporeal world as well as in the conceptual realm. For him, the physical universe and our minds are created by God no less than the world of ideas is produced by our minds. Nicholas believes that the destiny of human knowers and, indeed, of the whole of creation, lies beyond the realm of bodiliness and change. One way we may come to understand and appreciate this destiny is by exploring the human mind, its activities, and where they may lead us. Though brief and suggestive more than definitive, *Idiota de mente* stands as Nicholas' invitation to reflect more deeply in order to find the goal, nature, and significance of human knowing. *"Tunc motu suae vitae intellectivae in se descriptum reperit quod quaerit"* (then through the activity of its own intellectual life [the mind] finds described in itself what it is seeking; c.5 h 85).

1. THE DIALOGUE FORM AND ITS IMPORT

As a literary form the dialogue was well known to medieval thinkers and writers. Their earlier masters, Augustine, Eriugena, and Anselm, had all employed it effectively before the High Middle Ages. When the Scholasticism of the universities came to dominate philosophy and theology, most thinkers abandoned the dialogue form in order to write commentaries on Aristotle or Peter Lombard or the Bible, or to publish their own speculations in the form of disputed or quodlibetal questions. The *commentarium* and the *quaestio* reflected the methods of instruction and disputation used in the universities. Along with the *summae*, these became the standard literary forms for speculative thought and theoretical ideas. Nicholas' return to the dialogue form in the 1440s may well signal how the forms of discourse favored by the Scholastic thinkers became unsuitable for the conjectural and suggestive character of his own ideas.[2]

The *Idiota* dialogues recall St. Augustine's and St. Anselm's dialogues, but with a particular twist. Both earlier writers often characterized their interlocutors as "master" and "disciple," and left little doubt as to whom the master represented and who would dominate the conversation. Nicholas of Cusa reverses this pattern in the *Idiota* dialogues, making the humble layman the *magister* and the principal speaker. By portraying

---

1979), 17–35; it also corrects my earlier essay, "Metaphor and Simile in Nicholas of Cusa's *Idiota de mente*," *Acta* 8 (1981): 47–59. All translations in this chapter are my own. For a detailed exposition of *Idiota de mente* and its importance, see Flasch, *Nikolaus von Kues*, 271–317.

2. Cusanus wrote his first dialogue, *De Deo abscondito*, in 1444; see my Introduction, this book. From that time until his death, dialogues with two or more interlocutors were the literary form he favored for his shorter speculative writings. Still, he never completely abandoned the treatise, and a plethora of his sermons is extant as well.

a Roman orator and an Aristotelian philosopher as the ones in need of instruction, and the uneducated *idiota* as their peer, even their master, Nicholas recalls the Socrates of Plato's dialogues and the wisdom the Christian Scriptures attributed to the humble.[3] This reversal of roles makes the layman a paradigmatic embodiment of the learned ignorance *(docta ignorantia)* Cusanus prized so highly.

This is not to say that the philosopher and the orator do not speak for Cusanus, too. His own education and learning are revealed in the philosopher's questions and his constant references to authorities. Nicholas was also acquainted with the Italian humanists' revival of classical learning. So the Roman orator, the third speaker in the *Idiota de mente*, is emblematic of the enthusiasm then current in Italy for classical antiquity and learning, even though his words are those of Christian piety.[4]

Giving the unlettered layman the role of teacher manifests Nicholas' awareness of the criticism from many quarters directed at abstruse Scholastic speculation and detailed argument. He was well acquainted with the writings of the fourteenth-century mystics and with popular religious movements and groups such as the Brethren of the Common Life. Cusanus sympathized with their emphasis on personal religious experience and lay spirituality as opposed to the theology of the universities and the teaching of official religious institutions dominated by clerics or monks. They promoted the study of the Bible and stressed the need for a return to simple Christian living by lettered and unlettered believers alike.

3. The dialogue was also a favorite literary form of the Renaissance humanists. In the chapter entitled "Humanism," in *The Cambridge History of Renaissance Philosophy*, ed. E. Kessler, C. B. Schmitt, and Q. Skinner (Cambridge: Cambridge University Press, 1988), 125, P. O. Kristeller summarizes its advantages:

> The dialogue, usually patterned after the model of Cicero rather than of Plato, offered the advantage of presenting more than one opinion or viewpoint on the same subject without seeming to take a definitive stand (although the author's true opinion may often be inferred from his preface, from the composition of the dialogue itself or from his other writings). The dialogue also gave a personal and almost dramatic vivacity to the problems discussed. On the other hand, it provided a literary excuse for avoiding tight argument and precise terminology that had characterized the philosophical literature of the ancient Greeks and of the medieval scholastics.

See also D. Marsh, *The Quattrocentro Dialogue: Classical Tradition and Humanist Innovation* (Cambridge, Mass.: Harvard University Press, 1980), though Marsh does not treat Cusanus' dialogues.

4. In *Idiota de sapientia* the orator's initial attitude is noticeably different from his final replies to the *idiota*. His opinion of the latter changes completely, as does his notion of authentic wisdom and where it may be found. This changed attitude remains clear in the orator's questions and comments in *Idiota de mente*. The philosopher does not so obviously change in the course of this conversation, though he learns to respect the layman and treats him as an equal and an expert by the end of the dialogue.

In *Idiota de mente* Cusanus transposes these themes to the domain of philosophy and theology.[5] The unlettered spoon carver is counterposed in the dialogue to a philosopher, dryly presented by Cusanus as one of the most important thinkers of the day.[6] Because the layman embodies the learned ignorance that Nicholas believed was the key to wisdom, the layman's responses to the philosopher and the orator are rarely either simple or matters of common sense, despite his outward appearance and homely examples. Unschooled in the traditional texts and authorities, the layman reflects on his craft and the other crafts of his day to find examples and striking analogies for his proposals concerning the human mind. This wealth of everyday examples once more evokes the Socrates of Plato's dialogues, while the layman's "conjectures" about the mind demonstrate that the *idiota* is easily the superior of his interlocutors. What he says about mind and human knowledge is based on his own experience and reflection, a refreshing contrast to the bookish learning based on authorities of the universities.

The opening scene of this dialogue dramatizes the relationship between the three interlocutors. The narrated introduction stands in contrast to the way earlier medieval dialogues, commentaries, and disputed or quodlibetal questions opened. The usual order of medieval schooling is inverted: we see the learned come to the unlettered craftsman to be taught. Here the philosopher is led by the orator-humanist to the layman to find the significance of human intelligence. The usual order of studies was to proceed from the liberal arts and philosophy to theology. The "mechanical arts" were ranked below them all.

Cusanus thus brings philosophy and eloquence home to wisdom or learned ignorance.[7] This ignorance is symbolized by the inconspicuous, humble workshop where all three men sit on equal stools and hear from the *idiota* how each human mind is a reflection or living image of the divine Mind. Cusanus bypasses humanist and philosophical learning and the authority based on books to reflect on human intelligence, or *mens*, by using the resources and capacities that themselves constitute the life

---

5. See de Gandillac, *Nikolaus von Cues*, 58–60; Hopkins, *Wisdom and Knowledge*, 11–12.

6. Chapter 1 h 51: *"philosophum omnium, qui nunc vitam agunt, praecipuum."* The questions and concerns of the philosopher show Nicholas' awareness of the discussions and debates between the various Aristotelian and Platonist thinkers in the Italy of his day. *The Cambridge History of Renaissance Philosophy* weaves these discussions together in chapters on natural philosophy, ethics, metaphysics, and psychology, while B. Copenhaver and C. Schmitt devote separate chapters to Aristotelianism and Platonism in *Renaissance Philosophy* (Oxford: Oxford University Press, 1992), 60–195.

7. See Hopkins, in *Wisdom and Knowledge*, 3–16, for a sketch of the Cusan idea of wisdom and its predecessors. See also Flasch, in *Nikolaus von Kues*, 251–69, and 312, where he remarks how the layman's comments on language in *Idiota de mente* 2 may well signal the end of centuries of argument about universals, concepts, and reality.

of the mind. The contrast between the layman's reflective appropriation of his own mental life and the philosopher's continuous reliance on and reference to authorities could hardly be more obvious.[8]

After this opening it is not surprising to find the philosopher constantly referring to the views of others in his questions and anxious to refer what the layman says to the ideas of Boethius or Pythagoras or Philo. The philosopher insists that the orator not interrupt the discussion with his eloquence, yet his own questions seem more concerned with connecting the layman's ideas with the proper authority than really reflecting on them. Cusanus nonetheless makes use of the philosopher's learning even as he gently mocks it. In chapter 8, for instance, the orator turns to the philosopher and requests that he expound "the accepted opinions" (*aliquid accepti;* h 112) about sensation and the arterial spirits.

Beyond reversing the roles of student and master, Cusanus has his *idiota* call attention to the difference in how he and the philosopher learn by pointing up the latter's fears, his reading, and his appeal to authorities. As they begin, for instance, the philosopher apologizes because he usually "brings texts into the discussion" and asks how the other person interprets them. "But since you are unlearned," he continues, "I do not know how to encourage you to speak" (c.1 h 55). The layman's reply is direct in calling attention to the fears that may block inquiry:

> For while I admit I am an unlearned layman, I am not afraid to answer anything; learned philosophers and men who possess a reputation for knowledge rightly fear a mistake and so deliberate at length. So if you say plainly what you want from me, you will get it directly. (c.1 h 55)

Later the philosopher hesitates to admit that the craft of carving spoons is an image of the divine Craftsman's creating. The layman replies with a tart reference to the philosopher's reading: "Since the idea is obvious, I wonder if you ever read any philosopher who was unaware of it" (c.2 h 60). Mocking the philosopher about his reading does gain his acquiescence, but it also emphasizes how some kinds of learning may leave certain students without much understanding and too much concern for reputation.

In chapter 6, the philosopher remarks, "You seem much the Pythagorean—they hold that all things stem from number" (h 88). The layman rejects this attempt to classify him, rejoining: "I don't know whether I am a Pythagorean or something else. But I do know that no one's authority directs me, even if it attempts to move me" (h 88). Later, when the philosopher asks for technical terms for the various capacities

---

8. Flasch, *Nicholas von Kues,* 270–71.

of mind the layman has just explained, the latter's response is blunt: "Since I'm a layman, I don't pay much attention to words" (c.8 h 111).[9] Near the end of their discussion the philosopher refers to doctrines attributed to Plato and Aristotle. Before he responds, the layman says again, "I do not know the writings" (c.14 h 152). None of the layman's replies undercut Cusanus' obvious learning and cognizance of his predecessors, but they illustrate his rejection of slavish following of authorities and of quibbling over terms. If we are to become more aware of the limits of our knowledge concerning the mind, we have to cast aside certain trappings and pretenses of learning.

Cusanus' *idiota* embodies all the attitudes he believed were essential for inquiry into the significance of *mens*. He lacks education or clerical status; he lacks the authority of a university degree or of humanist study of the classics. He speaks in private conversation from a workshop stool in a back alley, not in public as a lecturer in a university or as a preacher in a cathedral. In this way his character and the opening setting of *Idiota de mente* dramatize the import of recognizing one's ignorance in undertaking an inquiry into human cognition. Cusan doctrine in this dialogue is itself a *coniectura*, a set of "conjectural" proposals designed to help us reflect on and capture in part the nature of mind, often through metaphors and *figurae*.

Nicholas also signals the difference from earlier Scholastic teaching by using the term *mens* rather than *intellectus* for the title of the dialogue. A more inclusive term than "intellect," "mind" recaptures Augustine's and Bonaventure's emphasis on active interiority and self-awareness. The medieval Scholastics had employed the doublet *intellectus et mens* as well as *intellectus* alone to refer to human intelligence, but the layman uses "mind" alone.[10] In the first chapter Cusanus recalls the traditional etymology that derived *mens* from *mensurare*, "to measure." This etymology stands behind Nicholas' general, if somewhat cryptic, preliminary de-

---

9. Having the layman reject disputes about words does not prevent Cusanus—in the next sentence—from placing the word *disciplina* on the layman's lips as a synonym for *ratio*. Nicholas' own learning and attention to words are manifested by his choosing the very word used since Boethius to cover the whole regime of university teaching and learning that began with the seven liberal arts. Hopkins translates *disciplina* or *doctrina* as "abstract learning = abstract knowledge"; see *Wisdom and Knowledge*, 504, notes 78–80, for his exposition of this and related terminology in *Idiota de mente*. In private correspondence H. L. Bond has pointed out that *disciplina* can also be a way toward *sapientia*.

10. On the use of the doublet by the Scholastics, see M. D. Chenu, *Toward Understanding St. Thomas*, trans. A. M. Landry and D. Hughes (Chicago: Henry Regnery, 1964), 101–2. Flasch has urged that *mens* not be understood anachronistically as post-Hegelian *"Geist,"* underlining how the sense of mind here takes over what was said about intellect in *De coniecturis*, only to extend it further by making *mens* amount to substantial activity, not simply a faculty or capacity such as *intellectus* in Aquinas; cf. *Nikolaus von Kues*, 149–50, 275–77.

scription: mind is that "from which comes the limit and measure of all things" (c.1 h 57).

2. THE HUMAN MIND AS *IMAGO DEI*

While this dialogue breaks with earlier Scholastic teaching about human cognition, its viewpoint also differs from later secular and post-Renaissance interpretations of human cognition.[11] This is primarily because the traditional biblical theme of *imago Dei* is central to Nicholas' doctrine. The *Idiota de mente* is based on a corollary to the Judeo-Christian belief that human beings are created in God's image and likeness, that is, that our minds are images of the divine Mind.[12] Nicholas does not begin from traditional Scholastic questions about mind and knowledge, or from the experience of human knowing, though by the end of the dialogue he has discussed both. What comes first and remains primary throughout is the assumption that the divine Mind is the paradigm of all mental life. This is the reason why Cusanus cannot count simply as a straightforward epistemological realist in the medieval Aristotelian fashion, nor as a proto-Kantian anticipating post-Cartesian views. Any understanding of his views of human cognition is predicated

---

11. As G. Santinello has indicated, the structure of *Idiota de mente* follows loosely that of Aristotle's *De anima* or Aquinas' treatment of the soul's nature, powers, and creation in the *Summa theologiae* 1.75–93. The first five chapters of this dialogue take up the question of the nature of *mens*, chapters 6–10 treat most of the various cognitive powers of human beings, while the final chapters (11–15) treat the creation and immortality of *mens*. See Santinello's "Einleitung" to the Latin-German edition of *Idiota de mente*, ed. R. Steiger (Hamburg: Meiner, 1995), ix–xxviii. Nicholas himself frames the dialogue by raising questions about the immortality of mind in the first chapter and settling the question in the final chapter. (Some might say that his initial description of mind as *ex se* living substance and *ex officio* the body's soul "settles" that question to start with!) For a comprehensive treatment of Nicholas' ideas on immortality, see K. Kremer, "Philosophische Überlegungen des Cusanus zur Unsterblichkeit der menschlichen Geistseele," *MFCG* 23 (1996): 21–70, esp. 21–34.

In any case, Nicholas never hesitates to have his interlocutors diverge to make comments or to consider other topics or to introduce comparisons and illustrations taken from the "mechanical arts," the crafts and technology of his time, in order to emphasize the active power and productivity of mind. This emphasis has led many interpreters to see his view of mind as anticipating Kantian and post-Kantian ideas about human knowledge. Cusanus, however, is neither an Aristotelian Scholastic nor a Kantian in his view of mind and knowledge, for he proposes his own way of balancing Aristotelian and Platonic emphases in the ideas his layman expounds. Albert the Great, Eckhart, and Dietrich of Freiburg were especially influential predecessors for Nicholas' ideas about mind as intellect in this dialogue.

12. Augustine and afterward Aquinas used the way human knowing and loving are related to interpret the relations between the three divine persons within the Trinity. See, for Augustine, *De Trinitate*, Bk.9 ff.; for Aquinas, *Summa theologiae* 1.27–43. Both assumed as well that the human mind is an image of the divine Mind. What is distinctively Cusan is the focus on mind as a creative and productive parallel to and image of the creative divine Mind.

upon our grasping his conjectures about divine knowledge, the connection between divine Exemplar and human image, and, in particular, the way in which as active knowers we are likened or "assimilated" further to the divine Exemplar.

This is not simply exploring the somewhat familiar by the totally unknown (though ultimately Cusanus might say this, too), because certain features of God's mind are known from the tradition of faith and earlier "negative theology."[13] Both provided guidelines for speaking about God, however much they caution that we are on safer ground by maintaining a constant awareness that we have no grasp of the divine Reality we are speaking about. Even though Cusanus is still committed to the principle that there is no proportion between the infinite and the finite, his thought often works as if the finite images do provide leads to the infinite Original. His tone in *Idiota de mente*, no less than in *De coniecturis*, is thus more positive than that in *De docta ignorantia*. He takes up themes about human mind as image of absolute Mind from *De coniecturis* that enable us to appreciate what a wondrous thing our active mental life is.[14]

In any case, God's mental life is incomprehensibly both infinite creative Power and triune Simplicity or Oneness. Cusanus stresses God's profound oneness and capitalizes on the productive or creative character of God's knowing. The divine Mind is the eternal and infinite Art/Artisan, the One who creates our universe and stands as Exemplar for all human making and artistry.[15] As image of the Divine, the human mind will reflect this creative power in its own productive activity.

For God to have created other things as separate from God is thereby to have brought them into being. The order of created things for Cusanus is God's knowledge "unfolded" *(explicata)*. Understood as they are in God, creatures are nothing else but God's own oneness. Nicholas terms them "enfolded" *(complicata)* in the divine Oneness, where their true forms and natural names are identical with God's mind. The created world is thus the "unfolding" *(explicatio)* of the divine Mind's "enfolding" *(complicatio)*, and creatures manifest and reflect God's unitary knowing in temporal multiplicity and otherness.[16]

The importance of the Divine as starting point and paradigm in Cu-

---

13. For discussion of Nicholas' use of negative theology, see Chapter 1, this book, and Hopkins, *Concise Introduction*, 15–27. De Gandillac, in *Nikolaus von Cues*, 267–315, rightly stresses Cusanus' relation to Pseudo-Dionysius' negative theology.

14. *De coniecturis* 1.1 h 5–6, 1.4 h 12; the second passage simply speaks of *mens ipsa*, though it most likely refers to the divine Mind. See Flasch, *Nikolaus von Kues*, 153.

15. Chapter 2 opens by recalling how all human crafts are images of God's creating. The theme is recurrent in the whole dialogue.

16. On *complicatio/explicatio*, see Chapters 1 and 2, this book. What is unique to *Idiota de mente* is the Cusan claim that images are differentiated from unfoldings.

sanus' doctrine of mind is emphasized in chapter 3. There the philosopher asks the layman an ambiguous question: "What do you mean by mind itself?" In response, the layman elaborates a series of antitheses that both contrasts and parallels the human image and the divine Original. God's creating is one with his taking thought; indeed, both are identical with God's infinite being. Our taking thought is but one of the many kinds of limited human activity. Yet the human mind's activities mirror the active creating and ordered "enfolding and unfolding" that Nicholas attributes to the divine Mind. We only understand human cognition correctly when we recognize it *as image*. We must "see through" it, as it were, to the divine Mind that measures it. All the contrasting parallels the layman proposes here make it clear that his initial definition of mind as "the limit and measure of all things" applies best to God's mind.[17] Yet Cusanus is convinced that God has shared his creative noetic power with limited human knowers. Our minds are not simply what they appear to be; they must also be understood in relation to the divine Mind on which they depend.

The layman begins his lengthy response as follows:

> You know how the divine Simplicity enfolds all things. Mind is the image of this enfolding Simplicity. If, then, you called this divine Simplicity infinite Mind, it will be the exemplar of our mind. If you called the divine Mind the totality of the truth of things, you will call our mind the totality of the assimilation of things, so that it may be a totality of ideas [*notionum*]. In the divine Mind conception is the production of things; in our mind conception is the knowledge [*notio*] of things. If the divine Mind is absolute Being, then its conception is the creation of beings; and conception in the human mind is the assimilation of beings. (c.3 h 72)

The nature of the human mind is thus described, as in *De coniecturis*, using the quasi-technical terms Nicholas had applied in *De docta ignorantia* 2.3 to the relation between the utterly simple divine Oneness and created beings. The mind, as God's image, is also an enfolding simplicity.[18] If God's enfolding reality encompasses the true natures of all that is real, the human mind has the capacity to enfold or encompass the ideas of all that it knows. God's conceiving creates or produces things, and they stand as unfoldings. Our conceiving produces knowledge: the human

---

17. Hopkins, in *Wisdom and Knowledge*, 48–49, stresses the difference between God's constitutive measuring and our assimilative measuring, so to speak, and aptly refers to the layman's comment in c.9: "Wood and stones indeed have a fixed measure and limits outside our minds, but these [limits] come from the uncreated mind, from which every limit in things descends" (h 117).

18. For elaboration of this theme and further references to Cusanus' writings and the scholarly literature, see S. Dangelmayr, *Gotteserkenntnis und Gottesbegriff in den philosophischen Schriften des Nikolaus von Kues* (Meisenheim: Hain, 1969), 96–102.

mind unfolds concepts as likenesses *(assimilationes)* of the things God created.

The layman continues:

> What suits the divine Mind as infinite Truth suits our mind as its close image. If all things are in the divine Mind as in their exact and proper Truth, all things are in our mind as in the image or likeness of their proper Truth, that is, as known [*notionaliter*]; for knowledge takes place by likeness. All things are in God, but there as exemplars of things. All things are in our mind, but there as likenesses of things. (c.3 h 72–73)

Nicholas' parallel stresses one important difference between our minds and God's mind, but not another. God's mind produces other beings, ours produces only ideas or assimilations of beings. But this contrast should not lead us to forget the crucial difference: "the divine Mind as infinite Truth" is an undifferentiated *oneness*, while the "likenesses of things" in human minds make up a *manyness*, a multiplicity of ideas. God encompasses the exact natures of things but in the divine Mind those natures' exactnesses cannot be differentiated from the infinite divine Nature. Our mind's enfolding oneness, on the other hand, is undifferentiated oneness only as unitary source or power to know. Once a person begins to have ideas or knowledge, the human mind becomes at best an encompassing totality, that is, it enfolds and unfolds a multiplicity of ideas. Their oneness may be that of systematic whole in content, but these ideas also have oneness because they depend on the single finite source, the mind that is doing the knowing and using the ideas.

Nicholas' layman concludes with a further image taken from portrait painting:[19]

> Just as God is the absolute Being who is the enfolding of all things, so our mind is the image of that infinite Being and enfolds all images, even as the first portrait [*imago*] of an unknown king is the exemplar of all the other portraits that can be depicted in accord with it. For the knowledge or face of God does not descend except in mental nature whose object is truth. It only descends further through mind, so that mind may be the image of God and the exemplar of all the images of God after it. Therefore, insofar as all things that are after simple mind participate in mind, so far also they participate in the image of God, so that mind may be of itself the image of God and all things after mind [may be images] only through mind. (c.3 h 73)

The reference to portraiture recalls once more the lessons of learned ignorance: God remains unknown. Nicholas assumes, for reasons that become clear in chapter 4, that created minds stand prior to everything

---

19. M. Stadler analyzes the image in this text in *Rekonstruktion einer Philosophie der Ungegenständlichkeit* (Munich: Fink, 1983), 70–71.

else in the created universe as God's unique image—the paradigm "portrait of the unknown king." All other created things are ontologically posterior to or come "after" *(post)* mind and are images of God only by being known *(per mentem)*.

In chapter 4, the layman explains this special status of created minds. While it is true that beings without mind are also created, the layman proposes that such creatures are best termed *unfoldings (explicationes)*. Just as numbers unfold the one, and time unfolds eternity, so the plurality of other creatures unfolds the divine Enfolding. But minds are *images* rather than *unfoldings*, because they involve a certain kind of equality with the divine Enfolding. "For equality is the image of oneness," Nicholas writes, "for from oneness taken once arises equality." And again: "I mean that mind is the simplest image of the divine Mind amid all the images of the divine Enfolding. Mind is thus the first image of the divine Enfolding which enfolds in its simplicity and power every image of enfolding" (c.4 h 74).[20]

What stands behind this striking proposal is Cusanus' view of the Trinity, where the Second Person is conceived as equality, the paradigm image of infinite Oneness that does not add plurality—in the words of St. Paul, "the image of the invisible God" (Col 1.15). Since everything is created through the divine Word or equality, and since the Second Person of the Trinity became incarnate in Jesus Christ, and since all human beings are sharers in his "sonship," all who have minds share in his divine Equality as well.[21] In the present case, Nicholas writes, "As God is the Enfolding of enfoldings, so mind, which is God's image, is the image of the Enfolding of enfoldings" (c.4 h 74). Without being images equal to the divine Word, human minds share or participate in the inner life of the Trinity as lesser images and enfoldings. (Table 3.1 summarizes the parallels and highlights the differences between the divine Mind and human minds.)

If God's relation to what he knows and creates can be described in terms of *complicatio/explicatio* ("enfolding/unfolding"), the same terms provide some clue to the way conceptual realities are related to the human mind, understood as God's image. As enfolded in God, creatures

---

20. See chapter 9 where the layman says, "It is very worthwhile to pay careful attention to enfoldings and their unfoldings—and especially to how enfoldings are images of the enfolding of infinite Simplicity. They are not its unfoldings but images.... Mind is the first image of the enfolding of infinite Simplicity..." (c.9 h 122). K. Flasch finds the doctrine influencing Cusanus' position on the human mind as image in Dietrich of Freiburg; see his *"Procedere ut Imago:* Das Hervorgehen des Intellekts aus seinem göttlichen Grund bei Meister Dietrich, Meister Eckhart und Berthold von Moosburg," in *Abendländische Mystik im Mittelalter,* ed. K. Ruh (Stuttgart: Metzlersche Verlagsbuchhandlung, 1986), 125–34.

21. Nicholas himself speaks of believers as "transformed into the image of Christ" in *De docta ignorantia* 3.11 h 253.

TABLE 3.1 Assimilation and Measuring in *Idiota de mente*

	Original (exemplar)	*Image* (imago)
Original	God's mind	Created world
Image	Human mind	Conceptual world

Basic principles:
- Originals *measure* images.
- Images *are like* or *become like* (*"assimilate"*) originals.

Applications:
- God's mind measures the created world and the human mind.
- The human mind measures the conceptual world.
- The created world measures the conceptual world (especially as the latter is derived from perception). The created world and the human mind are images of God's mind.
- The conceptual world is an image of the human mind and the created world; it is an image of images.

Anomaly:
- The conceptual world is not merely likened to the created world.
- Because the human mind measures the conceptual world, the latter, in being an image of the human mind, also measures the created world.

This table extends W. Happ's table in his "introduction" to *de coniecturis* (Hamburg, 1971), XII.

---

are nothing distinct from God's oneness. As enfolded in human knowledge, all knowable things are first of all the mind's unitary capacity to measure and liken *(assimilare)* itself to whatever it knows. As unfolded from God, all created things except angels are beings encountered in the space and time of our universe. As unfolded by, from, and within the human mind, all humanly known things are the conceptual realities *(entia rationis)*, the ideas that make up the more or less organized knowledge we acquire through experience and study.

3. HUMAN MINDS AS DYNAMIC AND PRODUCTIVE IMAGES OF THE CREATOR

Nicholas uses the parallel between our minds and God's mind to stress the unitary and unifying character of our knowing, as well as its active and creative power. The fundamental or root metaphor governing *Idiota de mente* is that our minds are images of the creative divine Mind.[22]

22. In private communication, K. Kremer has proposed that *"imago/assimilatio"* might be considered as the medieval "transcendental of all transcendentals," though not includ-

But this is not the sole metaphor Nicholas uses as he proceeds. Indeed, one way to understand how Nicholas orders the whole dialogue is to recognize how the other images and illustrations the *idiota* employs both explain and explore the basic character and functions of *mens*. Three instances of such metaphors emphasize how human mental activity, as an authentic image of its divine Exemplar, reflects God's productivity in creating all that is not divine.

3.1. Naming and Language

The first of these metaphors compares the human mind's productive activity to the divine Artisan's creative production. To do this the layman parallels language and thought with art or craft in chapter 2. He explains: "Every finite art comes from the infinite Art. In this way the infinite Art must be the Paradigm of all the arts, their beginning, middle, and end, their rule, measure, truth, exactness, and perfection" (c.2 h 61). Human knowing and naming are images of the divine Art and no less productive of the human arts.

In discussing the relation between the conventional and the natural names of things, the layman and the philosopher agree that we know things in the world in a way that parallels our naming of them. The knowledge we acquire and the language we employ are both cases of what human art or skill can produce. The notion of the Creator as a divine craftsman and of human craft or art as imitating it goes back at least as far as Plato's *Timaeus* and the Hebrew Scriptures. It is given a Christian baptism in the patristic writers, Eriugena, and the medieval thinkers of Chartres and their successors. Cusanus characteristically stresses the creative and productive character of our knowing. While this fact has tempted interpreters to identify Cusan epistemology with some of Kant's theses, he is arguably not a Kantian (nor a typical medieval Aristotelian) on matters of human knowledge. His own emphasis here seems to rework Aristotle's differentiation of speculative, practical, and poetic knowledge so that speculative knowledge is no less actively productive than our knowledge in the arts, crafts, and other spheres of practice.

---

ed with the usual five medieval "transcendentals" (being, one, true, good, beautiful), and thus not metaphorical at all. While I concur that likenesses and correspondences and parallels are characteristic of and ingredient in all medieval speculative thought, the fact that Nicholas sees our minds as images of the divine Mind must remain metaphorical since the divine Mind remains "an unknown king" and created mind its "first close portrait." As so often in Nicholas, "image" means dependence but not likeness, particularly when the Exemplar is infinite. What the divine Oneness, Goodness, Truth, and Beauty amount to in Nicholas is finally only available to metaphorical, dialectical thinking and intellectual vision beyond ordinary literal discursive and conceptual reasoning.

The layman makes this proposal more telling by turning to his own craft of carving spoons. He picks up a wooden spoon and explains that it is part of the constructed, sociocultural world. The spoon does not imitate nature slavishly, but is the product of human fashioning, human craft. The layman's craft aims "rather to perfect natural shapes than to imitate them, and in this regard is more like the infinite Art" (c.2 h 62). As a skilled craftsman, the *idiota* possesses in mind and imagination the shape or form of a spoon. This mental model or blueprint guides his carving of the wood until he sees a proper fit or proportion between the mental model and the palpable wooden likeness. The single model of what a spoon is, its "spoonness" or paradigmatic form as a spoon *(coclearitas)*, is reflected more or less perfectly by the different spoons in his workshop or in any kitchen, for "the truth and exactness of 'spoonness' [*coclearitatis*] ... cannot be multiplied and communicated" (c.2 h 63). What is involved in the craft of carving spoons—fashioning them to approach more or less perfectly one's mental model—is no less true of human language and naming.

Following what he read in Thierry of Chartres, Nicholas points out that the natural name of something is connected or united with its natural form.[23] Until the carver has produced the appropriate shape, his product cannot be called a spoon. But using the word *spoon* is a parallel kind of conventional activity that approaches the natural name no less inexactly than the carved spoon approaches the perfect mental model of *coclearitas*. In this way the relation of using language to reality is parallel to the relation of productive knowing to reality: both are special cases of the relation of *ars* to its creations.

Human concepts are not precise but conjectural in that they do not capture the exact or true forms of anything we know, except in mathematics. Human language is likewise inexact. Our thought and language, both products of the activity of *ratio*, reflect only imperfectly the true form and the "natural" name of whatever we know. These true forms and natural names do not subsist in any Platonic realm for Cusanus; they are identically one with the simpleness of God's infinite "form" and with the ineffability of the divine Word. All naming and thinking point ultimately to the divine Infinity; all human arts are derived from the infinite Art.

The layman recapitulates this view at the beginning of chapter 3:

23. Thierry of Chartres, *Lectiones in Boethii librum De trinitate* II, 52–53, in *Commentaries on Boethius by Thierry of Chartres and His School*, ed. N. M. Häring (Toronto: Pontifical Institute of Mediaeval Studies, 1971), 171–72. As will become clear, Nicholas chooses a polished wooden spoon because it can also be a mirror.

Enfold naming and being named into a coincidence by the highest intellect and everything will be clear. For God is the exactness of every thing whatsoever. If, then, exact knowledge were possessed about a single thing, knowledge of all things would necessarily be possessed. In this way if the exact name of a single thing were known, then the names of all things would also be known, because there is no precision outside God. Therefore, whoever reached a single exactness would reach God, who is the truth of all that can be known. (h 69)

And a few remarks later, he adds:

I maintain that were I to know the exact name of one work of God, I would not be ignorant of all the names of all God's works and whatever could be known. And since the Word of God is the exactness of every name that can be named, it is plain that only in the Word can any and every thing be known. (h 70)

What this summary (and allusion to the saying attributed to Hermes Trismegistus) makes clear is that our creation of language and knowledge finds its standard and measure in God's creative divine Word.[24] This is the way Nicholas combines both the Platonic and Aristotelian views to which he and the philosopher refer. Naming and thinking are creative arts that fashion whole new human worlds. When we think and speak we do not simply reproduce the natural world that is independent of thought and culture. Rather, the language and concepts we produce themselves constitute a "universe" of discourse and thought that manifest how both our thinking and our speaking are an image of God's creating. This is quite different from medieval Aristotelian doctrines and an utterly different thought world from what would follow Descartes.

3.2. Seed, Living Law, Diamond Point

Just as creatures do not exist as distinct entities in their own right in God's enfolding Oneness, so in the human mind's enfolding oneness (identical with *intellectus* and the activity of making judgments) there are, to begin with, no explicit innate ideas or a priori concepts. Concepts must be produced by our mind just as all creatures must be produced and sustained by God. Chapter 5 of *Idiota de mente* proposes a series of three metaphors that stress how our activity as knowers is a created image of God's productive knowledge.

In chapter 5 Nicholas first insists that what gets *unfolded* into the various liberal arts and sciences—the contents of cognition—is contained in seedlike fashion in the human mind's enfolding power or capacity. As

---

24. See K. Apel, "Die Idee der Sprache bei Nicolaus von Cues," *Archiv für Begriffsgeschichte* 1 (1955): 200–221; D. Duclow, "The Analogy of the Word: Nicholas of Cusa's Theory of Language," *Bijdragen* 38 (1977): 282–99; J. Hennigfeld, *Geschichte der Sprachphilosophie. Antike und Mittelalter* (New York: de Gruyter, 1994), 292–315; and Flasch, *Nikolaus von Kues*, 308–12.

the layman says, "... the mind is a kind of *divine seed* which by its power enfolds conceptually the exemplars of all things" (h 81, emphasis added). What is enfolded proves its fecundity in the varied activities of the mind (intellection, reasoning, imagination, and sensation) that unfold and construct the conceptual world of thought and reason.

In proceeding to stress our active discriminating as we make judgments, the layman describes how mind or intellect actively controls ("mind informs, enlightens, and perfects reasoning"; h 84) the processes of discursive reason. In the same way, we use reason to discern and differentiate the deliverances of sense and imagination. This active capacity to make judgments about everything is another result of being God's image. As the layman says,

> When the Exemplar of everything is manifest in mind as truth in its image, mind possesses the measure to which it refers and in accord with which it judges things outside mind. Just so, if a *written law* were alive, it would read in itself which judgments should be passed. Therefore, mind is a living description of the eternal and infinite Wisdom. . . . Understand, however, that this description is a reflection [*resplendentiam*] of the Exemplar of all things just as truth shines forth [*resplendet*] in its image. Just as if the forms of all things were reflected in the finest indivisible *point of a diamond* that was alive, it would find by looking within itself the likenesses of all things and through them could construct notions of everything. (c.5 h 85, emphasis added)

This passage first compares the mind's enfolding power and unfolding activities to a "written law" that is alive. More than merely legislating, the human mind is itself a living code or normative law or measure for cognitive judgment because any mind can refer to the divine Source that "shines forth" in itself, the human image. This human image is nothing else than the "living description of the eternal and infinite Wisdom."[25] The visual metaphor implicit in *resplendentia*—that of reflected brilliance—leads Cusanus to propose a second image, that of the living diamond. The mind's enfolding and unfolding is similar to the concentrated play of light and color that the refracting and reflecting surfaces and angles of a diamond capture. Both images may lead us to see what Cusanus means by proposing that our power of judgment enfolds or comprises all things.

These images may be seen as Nicholas' gloss on the common Aristotelian notion that the human mind is *capax omnium*, open to every-

---

25. G. von Bredow, "Der Geist als lebendiges Bild Gottes (Mens viva dei imago)," *MFCG* 13 (1978): 58–67. In another paper ("Der Punkt als Symbol," *MFCG* 12 [1977]: 103–15), von Bredow interprets the image of the living point of the diamond that collects and reflects sunlight as parallel to the mind's active imaging of its divine Source. She also connects the image with the *apex mentis* in Bonaventura and the spark of the soul in Eckhart. Both essays have been collected in *Im Gespräch*, 99–110, 85–98.

thing knowable.[26] As the philosopher comments, "the sharper and finer its [the diamond point's] angle, the more clearly do all things shine forth [*resplendent*] in it" (h 86). Both legal systems and jewels are products of human *ars*, so they provide apt images of the "enfolding" power of human knowledge as productive. The mind unfolds/produces a multitude of judgments and conceptual constructions from what is enfolded in the unitary simplicity of its natural power as God's image. Both of these images are used to extend and explain how we are God's images in our knowing. Because we are cognitively active and productive, we "enfold" in capacity and "unfold" in activity a conceptual universe.

3.3. Self-Portrait

Toward the end of *Idiota de mente* (c.13) the layman invokes again the art of portraiture, in this instance, self-portraiture, to help us understand further the active and productive character of the human mind.[27] Self-portraits had become more common in Nicholas' time and were fascinating to early Renaissance painters and to those familiar with their work. What such a portrait image captured of the original and what it disclosed about the painter's mind and character had to fascinate an age long accustomed to expect the world of nature and culture both to be all that it is and yet to be more, to point beyond itself. Cusanus' layman proposes that God is related to our minds the way a painter is to his self-portrait, that human minds are a kind of revelation or disclosure of the creative mind of God.

> You know that our mind is a certain power that possesses the image of the divine Art already mentioned. So all things present most truly in the absolute Art are present truly in our mind as its image. Hence mind is created by the Creator's Art, as if that Art wished to create itself, but since the infinite Art cannot be replicated, thereupon its image arose. It is as if a painter wished to paint himself and because he could not be replicated, by painting his own portrait his image would then appear. (c.13 h 148)

Nicholas presses this metaphor further, proposing that there is a difference between a static image or self-portrait and a dynamic one. He imagines the dynamic self-portrait able to become more and more like

---

26. Aquinas (*Summa theologiae* 1.88.1.c) uses the Aristotelian differentiation of "agent intellect" and "possible intellect" to make this point: *"Intellectus possibilis est quo est omnia fieri, intellectus agens quo est omnia facere"* (The possible intellect is that by which [the mind] can become all things, while the agent intellect is that by which [the mind] can produce all things [intelligible]).

27. See also the comments above on the exemplar portrait of the "unknown king" (*Idiota de mente* 3 h 73) as a figure of the unique nature of mind as an image of God. Nicholas' *De visione Dei* makes such a portrait (probably of Jesus' face) the central metaphor of the whole treatise.

its original by its own activity, even if the original remains finally unattainable. In his own words,

> It is as if a painter were to make two self-portraits, one of which, though lifeless, appeared more like him, while the other, though less like him, was alive and of a sort that could always make itself more conformed once its object roused it to act. No one doubts the second portrait is more perfect as imitating the art of the painter. (c.13 h 149)

Nicholas shifts the parallel here so that the created portrait's likeness lies not in how it *looks*, but in how it *acts* because it is alive and can imitate God's creative production. Rather than being self-portraits who reveal God's appearance or inaccessible nature, we are self-portraits whose mental activities reflect more and more closely the divine Painter's *ars*, his productive activity.[28] The layman then characterizes the human mind as *"perfecta artis imago"* (c.13 h 149) in its essential capacity to produce and create. Our minds are "living images of the divine Art" (c.13 h 149). Human minds thus become progressively more like their divine Original by taking thought and by actively producing *entia rationis*, the realm of concepts and judgment. Their nature as living images involves the exercise of their knowing powers as they measure and "assimilate" what they know.

4. COGNITIVE MEASURING AND LIKENING *(MENSURATIO ET ASSIMILATIO)*

How are we to understand better what the mind's cognitive power and activity amount to? Two metaphors for mental activity dominate Cusanus' explanation in *Idiota de mente*, the metaphors of measuring *(mensuratio)* and of likening/assimilating *(assimilatio)*. The layman initially "defined" mind as that "from which comes the limit [*terminus*] and measure [*mensura*] of all things" (c.1 h 57). While this description may better apply to the divine Mind, we may expect it to encompass human mind as well. Measuring and assimilating are both key metaphors for understanding the Cusan view of human knowledge.

As knowers we *measure* the things we know and we also are *assimilated*

---

28. In a similar vein Cusanus wrote later to Nicholas Albergati:

If a painter paints a visible image of himself, it remains as it was made. But if there were a painter of the sort able to make an invisible, intellectual image depicting his intellectual art, certainly that image of his art, were it a perfect image of intellectual and living art, would be able to make itself clearer and more like [its original], since it would conform itself to its maker. ("Epistola ad Nicolaum Albergati," #8, in *Das Vermächtnis des Niholaus von Kues*, ed. G. von Bredow, *Cusanus-Texte IV-3* [Heidelberg: Winter, 1955], 28) or *likened* to the objects of knowledge. Human knowing involves both *mensuratio* and *assimilatio*, the first supposedly from the same root as *mens* and the second reemphasizing the connection between image and original. *Assimilatio* extends the notion of being an image "horizontally" as well as "vertically," so to speak. The human mind likens itself to the Divine in the very process of becoming like or assimilating itself to all that it knows. We may be images of God in producing conceptual knowledge, but the concepts themselves are also images of things known (and of the knowing mind). The active *likening to* characteristic of what we know thus stands in tension with the complementary metaphor: we *measure* what we know. The conceptual tools we employ for interpreting cognitive experience are matters of our own measuring and constructing.[29]

4.1. Active Assimilating

Both the Latin noun *assimilatio* ("resemblance," "a likening," "a making like or similar") and the verb *assimilare* ("to resemble," "to become or make like to")[30] recall a Scholastic dictum Cusanus is fond of citing: "For knowledge takes place by likeness" (h 72). Our everyday meanings in English for *assimilation* make sense here, too. One digests, as it were, what one comes to know, making it part of oneself. In cognition one also becomes assimilated to the previously unknown or foreign, making oneself like what was alien. Still, the ideas of cultural and digestive absorption extend rather than settle the crucial epistemological issue raised by Nicholas' use of *assimilatio*: whether the things known or our knowing minds provide measures for the content and validity of knowledge. Is the content of our knowledge derived from what is outside the mind or is it the result of the linguistic and conceptual measures we construct and employ for dealing with reality?

If knowing is mostly creative or productive, it may well be similar to God's creating, but we are hard put to understand how it is also a likeness of extramental things. If things outside mind cause and measure decisively what we know, we may see why our knowledge is an assimilating or likening to things, but then we should wonder why and how our knowledge is an image of God's creative and productive knowing. *Assimilatio* reminds us of the importance of referents outside cognition to test its content and validity. But what, then, of the mind as a measure? If the two metaphors can cut different ways, they jeopardize not just the neat-

---

29. See the remarks below Figure 3.1 earlier in this chapter. I discuss this matter in different contexts in my earlier essays: "Philosophic Knowledge," and "A Road Not Taken: Nicholas of Cusa and Today's Intellectual World," *Proceedings of the American Catholic Philosophical Association* 57 (1983): 68–77.

30. *Mittellateinisches Wörterbuch* (Munich: Beck, 1959), 1077–78.

ness, but the consistency of the Cusan picture of our minds "unfolding" a conceptual universe just as God's mind produces the actual universe.

Ever since Ernst Cassirer's studies, Cusan interpreters have insisted that Nicholas' view of *mens* marks a definitive break with earlier views of cognition as passive and merely reproductive.[31] Without oversimplifying the passivity of *intelligere* in Aquinas or of intuitive knowledge in Scotus and Ockham, we may nonetheless recognize that the earlier Aristotelian Schoolmen stressed the import of natural things as the causes and measures of perceptual and conceptual knowledge.[32] Aquinas' remark in his *De veritate* puts it succinctly. "They [extramental things] can by their very nature bring about a true apprehension of themselves in the human intellect, which, as is said in the *Metaphysics*, is measured by things" (1.8.r).[33]

Cusanus inherited a conceptual framework and a technical vocabulary for dealing with human cognition that embodies this medieval Aristotelian interpretation. In that view, the content of knowledge is caused by extramental things in perception. What we understand is supposed to correspond to the formal or intelligible aspects of things in the world. As regards what is grasped and understood, there is an identity in intelligibility between the mind and the thing. The mind achieves truth only when it judges that the intellect is thus "in conformity" with the thing.

Against this background, it is hardly astounding that the Cusan account of perception suggests that perceptible things measure mental *assimilatio* and that they cause sense perception. Nicholas agrees with the Aristotelian view that the mind has no innate ideas forgotten at birth (in the sense of Plato's *Meno* and *Phaedo*). His doctrine of *mens* requires that

---

31. E. Cassirer, *Das Erkenntnisproblem in der Philosophie und Wissenschaft der neueren Zeit* (Berlin: B. Cassirer, 1906), 52–77; also his *The Individual and the Cosmos in Renaissance Philosophy*, trans. M. Domandi (Oxford: Blackwell, 1963), 7–58. See the whole of "Nikolaus von Kues in der Geschichte des Erkenntnisproblems" (=*MFCG* 11). Mainz: Matthias-Grünewald, 1975. Other essential studies on this problem are Van Velthoven, *Gottesschau;* Kremer, "Erkennen bei Nikolaus von Kues"; and Hopkins, *Wisdom and Knowledge*. Hopkins gives a brief summary of his views in "Glaube und Vernunft," 5–10, in order to demonstrate the inner consistency of Nicholas' views on human knowledge. Kremer's most recent interpretation is to be found in "Das kognitive und affektive Apriori bei der Erfassung des Sittlichen," *MFCG* 26 (2000): 101–38, followed by discussion, 138–44.

32. The way cognitive passivity in these thinkers is often portrayed is no doubt simply mistaken. For *intelligere* as active in Aquinas, see B. Lonergan, *Verbum: Word and Idea in Aquinas*, ed. D. B. Burrell (South Bend, Ind.: University of Notre Dame Press, 1967). On intellectual intuitive knowledge in Scotus, see A. Wolter, *The Philosophical Theology of John Duns Scotus*, ed. M. M. Adams (Ithaca, N.Y.: Cornell University Press, 1990), 98–122. On intellectual intuition in Ockham, see M. M. Adams, *William Ockham*, 2 vols. (South Bend, Ind.: University of Notre Dame Press, 1987), 1:495–550.

33. The passage referred to in Aristotle's *Metaphysics* (10.1.1053a) says that knowledge and perception "are measured rather than measure other things." Earlier in *De veritate* Aquinas remarks, "truth in the intellect is measured by things themselves" (1.5.r).

the whole of mental life be stimulated or awakened by direct experience of the perceptible world, at least at the beginning of mental life. As he writes in chapter 5, "But at the beginning our mental life is like someone asleep until it is roused to activity by wonder at its contact with sensible things" (h 85). Both the technical language Cusanus inherits for these matters and the lack of detailed analysis of the question in *Idiota de mente* can leave the careful reader puzzled about whether and how our minds or the things outside them measure the content and validity of cognitive assimilation.

Chapter 7 of *Idiota de mente* gives the most complete and differentiated statement of what *assimilatio* means for sense, imagination, reason, and *intellectus*. Two distinct lines of thought need differentiating here. First, Nicholas focuses on the knowing activities the human mind performs: sensing, imagining, reasoning (including conceiving and judging), and intellectual intuiting. Second, his layman turns to the things we know and relates the traditional distinction found in Boethius of the three kinds of form studied in physics, mathematics, and theology to the various capacities and activities of mind and to the various sorts of possible and necessary being.[34] This calls our attention to the Cusan belief in an order of being independent of our knowing, an assumption Cusanus never questions here or elsewhere.[35]

Yet when he turns to relate knowing to being, Cusanus insists that, as active and self-moving, *mens* directs and accomplishes all our knowing, from sensation to intuitive vision of God. The single term, *mens*, lets Cusanus emphasize that our minds are operative unities, that sensing, imagining, reasoning, and intellective vision are hierarchically ordered in a dynamic way. Sense, imagination, and reason are directed and integrated by their encompassing unitary source: *mens* or *intellectus* understood as our power of judgment. What takes place in human knowing is the joint operation of as many capacities as are required to know a given

---

34. In *De docta ignorantia* 2.7 h 129–31, Cusanus expounds the same four categories of necessary and possible being: absolute necessity (God), necessity of connection (mathematics), determinate possibility (created corporeal things), and absolute possibility ("matter"). One might construct a fanciful Cusan "divided line" (cf. Plato's *Republic* 6.509–11) by correlating these four types of being with intellectual intuition, reasoning without sensation, perception plus reasoning based on perception, and what Cusanus calls *"adulterinam rationem,"* which understands what actually exists as possibly existing. See also footnote 41 in this chapter.

35. Cf. c.6 (h 93), where the philosopher asks, "Does not the plurality of things exist apart from the consideration of our mind?" The layman responds, "Yes, but it depends on the eternal Mind." Again in c.9 the layman remarks, this time in the context of mathematics: "Outside the mind only solid bodies actually exist. Thus the measure and limit of everything stems from mind. Wood and stones indeed have a fixed measure and limits beyond our minds, but these come from the uncreated Mind, from which every limit in things descends" (h 117). See also *De docta ignorantia* 2.3 h 110.

form or cognoscible object. Mental *assimilatio* is therefore no passive mirroring of the perceptible and intelligible features of those realities that are independent of mind.

Part of the difficulty in interpreting chapter 7 is that Cusanus' account mixes several different kinds of analysis. In part he gives us a rudimentary *physiology* of sense perception based on the sense organs, the "nerves," and the arterial spirits that are supposed to mediate between what the physical organs encounter and the conscious mind. In part, this physiological story is correlated with a rather loose *causal account* in terms of objects and knowing activities at four levels: (1) perceptible bodies and their *species*, (2) images in the imagination, (3) concepts *(notiones)* and reasoning processes, and (4) intellectual intuition. And through both of these stories there runs both a quasi-*phenomenological* description of the contents of awareness (physical things, mathematical objects, the mind itself and its activities, even God—all things we know to some degree), whether particular or universal. Finally, Cusanus intersperses some *epistemic* remarks about the conjectural nature and truth of the knowledge our minds achieve.

Nicholas' exposition in chapter 7 does work with examples to spell out what *assimilatio* means. First of all, human knowers are not restricted solely to sense perception or solely to imagination, even when they are dealing with those present or absent perceptible things—artifacts or items in nature—likely to be encountered in the ordinary human world. For instance, it is the discriminating power of thinking (*mens* as *ratio*, or discursive reason) that enables human beings to make sense of the confusing deliverances of sense or the conflated images in memory and imagination. As Nicholas writes in chapter 7 about imagination,

> Imagining functions in the absence of sensible things as would a sense without power to discriminate between sensible things. When sensible things are not present it conforms itself to things in a confused way and without discriminating one condition from another. But functioning within thinking imagination conforms itself to things while discriminating one condition from another. (h 100)

Here Nicholas' comparisons and his examples provide added illumination. The layman compares the mind's active engagement in perceptual assimilating—in particular, its active employment of the arterial spirits[36] that transmit the sensible *species* or impressions to the mind—to the way a craftsman, sculptor, or artist uses wax or clay to form an impression of something's external shape in order to work from that like-

---

36. The layman has the philosopher expound the common teaching of the *physici* (medical doctors in this context) regarding the arterial spirits in c.8 h 112–15. The ideas originate with Galen, but Nicholas' text is closest verbally to John of Salisbury's *De septem septenis* 4 (*Patrologia Latina* 199, 951–54).

ness. Even such external likenesses are captured and reproduced at the behest of mind. As the layman remarks, "No shapes [*configurationes*], whether in sculpture or painting or construction, can be made without mind; but it is mind that sets limits to everything" (h 100). In the latter case we find reason determining what goes into the concept of something to be fabricated; in acting in or upon the world it is easy to see how the mind is the measure of what eventuates. But this needs to be combined with what knowers encounter in perceptual experience that is not up to them.

The layman proceeds to extend the analogy: "If the wax were conceived as informed by a mind, the mind existing inside it would form [*configurare*] the wax to every shape presented to it, just as now the mind of the craftsman tries to do from the outside. Similarly for clay and every pliable material" (c.7 h 101). The assimilations of sense perception thus result in part from the reason's active directing and interpreting the deliverances of the senses and the arterial spirits; they are not mere passive impressions of the colors, sounds, and textures of the things perceived. Cusanus modifies the language of "conforming" *(conformare)* and "configuration" *(configuratio)* so that our minds may be seen as encompassing and guiding the bodily arterial spirits that transmit the sense impressions from perceptible things, as well as making them available for reason and conceptualization. Throughout this exposition mind functions mostly as *ratio*, or discursive reason, in differentiating and connecting perceptions and images and in forming concepts based on those discriminations.

The resulting perceptual knowledge of the physical world (embodied and made systematic in the mechanical and technical arts, and in the conceptions of empirical science and logic) will remain conjectural. The reason is that *mens* is dealing not with the true forms of things (those are ultimately identical with God's oneness), but with their material embodiments. In Nicholas' words, "the notions that are attained through the assimilations of reason are uncertain, because they are in accord with the images of forms rather than their true [originals]" (c.7 h 102).

The layman has not finished comparing reason's mental assimilating to the use of wax and clay by craftsmen and artists. Speaking a bit later of assimilating or conforming to mathematical forms, he says:

And in this [mathematical] assimilating the mind acts as if flexibility (freed from the flexibility of wax, clay, metal, and every pliable material) were alive with the mind's own life, so that by itself it could liken itself [*assimilare*] to all [mathematical] figures [*figuras*] as they subsist in themselves and not in matter. For thus mind would discern that the notions of all [such] things exist in the power of its own living flexibility, that is, in itself, because it can conform itself to all things. (c.7 h 104)

Extending *assimilatio* from material things to abstract mathematical forms thus requires that Nicholas stretch and extend the metaphor of pliable materials informed by mind to become a metaphor for both intelligence and intelligible—flexibility or pliability itself beyond changing and limiting material conditions. Pivoting on itself, as it were, the mind employs its own living versatility "to liken itself to all [mathematical] figures as they subsist in themselves and not in matter" (c.7 h 104). In this realm the objects to be known are themselves abstract and immaterial, and thus of the same nature as reason itself. Here our minds construct the mathematical sciences whose rational, abstract concepts are precise and certain because they deal with what does not change.[37]

Examining critically such passages in *Idiota de mente* leads to two conclusions. First of all, Cusanus clearly admires the human mind's capacity to understand a range and variety of intelligible things that have little in common except the mind's grasp of what is knowable about them. He is committed to finding vivid metaphors to give some concrete sense of the mind's power and versatility. Second, in chapter 7 the basic metaphor of *assimilatio* underscores the self-directing and self-activating features of discursive reason in concert with the various sensory cognitive powers, but it does not finally settle the question of whether it is the human mind or the things independent of mind that measure human knowledge. Because *assimilatio*, or mental assimilation, covers such a range of human cognitive experiences, and because adult knowers make second-order judgments about how accurately they have "assimilated" what there is to be known,[38] his account in chapter 7 is not decisive. For further light on this question, we need to turn to the other Cusan metaphor for cognition, that of measure.

4.2. Measuring

In chapter 9 of *Idiota de mente* the philosopher asks, "How can the mind make itself a measure equal to such varied things?" The layman proposes the following answer:

---

37. Cusanus continues to extend mental *assimilatio* in chapter 7 until it approaches the divine object of theological knowledge and that unitary intellectual vision of the whole "insofar as all things are one and one all" (h 105). This intuitive, intellectual vision is the fulfillment of the mind's fundamental character as God's image, for here the divine Original "shines forth" (*relucet*) in the human mind. Nonetheless, through most of c.7 mind is understood primarily as *ratio*, or discursive reason, not as *intellectus*. For a helpful summary of the chapter, see Hopkins, *Wisdom and Knowledge*, 474–75, note 201.

38. For instance, the last sentence in the passage quoted above from chapter 7 (h

In the way an "absolute" face would make itself the measure of all faces. For when you attend to the fact that the mind is a certain absolute measure that cannot be greater or smaller since it is not restricted to quantity, and when you attend to the fact that this measure is alive so that it measures by itself (as if a living compass were to measure by itself), then you grasp how it makes itself into a concept, measure, or exemplar so that it attains itself in everything. (h 123-24)

What stands out in this passage is that Cusanus touches on all the requirements for measurement as something the mind actively accomplishes.[39]

As the philosopher recognizes, the "varied things" (all the diverse cognoscible features in the natural world and in human thought and culture) are what the mind is to measure. Mind itself does the actual measuring and "makes itself a measure" or norm in taking the measure of each item across the range of things it knows. Mind is the active source both of its conceptual norms ("it makes itself into a concept, measure, or exemplar") and of the activity of measuring ("[it] measures by itself"). What results is all the knowledge that human beings gain from everyday experience and from the various organized domains of knowledge, the natural and human sciences.

In the end, Cusanus wants to combine the metaphors of *assimilatio* and *mensuratio* in accounting for what provides the cognitive norms or criteria for human knowledge. That is to say, we become like the items we know that are mind-independent *and* we fashion the conceptual and judgmental tools whereby we take their measure in grasping them as knowers. The tension between *assimilatio* and *mensuratio* is to be retained just because, as knowers, we are God's *images*. We do not create but must recognize a domain that is independent of knowledge because we recognize the results of God's creating. We create the interpretive measures whereby we know things, but the full intelligibility of each thing is identified ultimately with the unknowable Oneness of God. This Oneness stands as an ideal limit we acknowledge in recognizing the limitations or conjectural character of our knowledge of that thing's essence or nature.

---

104), or the layman's earlier comment about all concepts based on perceptual knowledge in the same chapter (h 102): "all such concepts are conjectures rather than truths."

39. As explained in chapter 1, measurement presupposes (1) something to be measured, (2) a criterion or normative measure embodying standard units, (3) the actual use of the measure—measuring itself, and (4) the results of measuring or measurements taken. H. L. Bond has pointed out in private correspondence that these requirements do not amount to a definition of "measure." Nicholas' remarks in the passage quoted and his succinct statement early in *Idiota de mente* 1 h 57 about mind as a source of limit setting ("that from which comes the limit and measure of all things") suggest that "measure" for the *idiota* means "to measure," that is, to set or determine fixed limits (though not necessarily quantitative) for something, either in reality (as God's mind does) or in conception and judgment (as human minds do). See the quotes in footnote 35 above.

Two metaphors mentioned in the same passage from chapter 9 lend some confirmation to this interpretation. The layman remarks that the mind becomes a measure adequate to the variety of what it knows "in the way an 'absolute' face would make itself the measure of all faces." This cryptic metaphor makes more sense when compared to a similar metaphor in Cusanus' later treatise on mystical theology, *De visione Dei*. Chapter 6 of *De visione Dei* makes it clear that "absolute" in this context means "unrestricted" or "free from" every limitation. In the context of that work, the face of God we yearn to see is "absolute" or unlimited as opposed to the limited or "contracted" faces we usually see. To understand better how this applies to the mind, we might paraphrase a later passage from *De visione Dei* by substituting "face/mind" where Nicholas originally wrote "face":

> ... my face/mind is a true face/mind because you who are Truth have given it to me. My face/mind is also an image because it is not truth itself but the image of absolute Truth. Therefore, I enfold in my conception the truth and image of my face/mind; and I see that in it the image coincides with the facial/mental truth, so that insofar as it is an image [my face/mind] is true. (c.15 h 68; Hopkins' Latin edition, 196)

As the exemplar of all faces/minds, the divine invisible Face/Mind is ontologically prior to and normative for all the limited and thus visible faces/minds that are its images. The visible faces/minds we see find their truth in the invisible divine Face/Mind we do not see.

The remark in *Idiota de mente* 9 thus means that the human mind is itself a kind of "absolute" measure as the image of the divine Mind.[40] The mind is not a quantitative measure and not restricted to what is measurably more or less in quantitative terms. Unlike the usual quantitative norms or units of measure we employ in ordinary measuring, the human mind can use conceptual measures that fit or are equal to the different kinds of things humans want to know. Our conceptual and judgmental measures are "assimilative," so to speak, and this active likening to what we know occurs because we construct measures appropriate if not wholly adequate to the particular domain we are investigating. As relatively unrestricted, our minds may be conformed or likened to whatever is knowable in whatever way it can be grasped. The human mind can thereupon order, define, and measure the knowables it thereby understands. As the absolute Face is the measure of all the contracted faces that are its images, so our minds measure all the conceptual realities or beings of reason that reflect its oneness.

Cusanus' metaphor of the absolute Face measuring all its limited im-

---

40. Cf. Flasch, *Nikolaus von Kues*, 293–95.

ages cuts in a different direction than did the earlier metaphor of the copies of the self-portrait. Before, Nicholas' point was that a living copy might not appear similar but could come to approximate its original because it could act in ways that would take it toward its exemplar. Now his idea is rather that, because the mind is an image, it is similar to its divine Exemplar in its work of measuring just because it shares some of the unrestricted or absolute features of God. More precisely, it is not restricted to knowing only the "how much" or quantitative aspects of things, but can shape its conceptual measures to capture to some extent the "what sort" or qualitative characteristics and thus approximate the true essences of things.

Yet quantitative measuring remains at the basis of the metaphor here. Just as the choice of a numerical unit of measure is a matter of arbitrary convention and, to that extent, obviously a human construction and a human interpretation, so the use of a particular interpretive framework or set of concepts in the qualitative measuring of other sorts of knowables is a matter of human creating and fashioning. If we recognize something mind-independent that we want to know, we must also recognize that it is up to us to construct and employ the appropriate cognitive measures if we are to take its measure.

Cusanus confirms this point with the second metaphor he proposes in the passage from chapter 9, that of "the living compass that measures by itself" (h 124). As the philosopher remarks in response, since the compass (or caliper) is of no set size (the way a straight-edge rule is, for instance), it can be extended or contracted to fit any given size. This metaphor illuminates the mind's active capacity to accommodate itself to whatever it seeks to know. A compass adapts to *and* takes the measure of the things one uses it to deal with; the human mind does no less.[41]

In spite of the evidence of these metaphors, many readers have seen in this dialogue hints (and more) of what Kant was later to develop in his *Critique of Pure Reason*. But little or nothing in the Cusan account of knowledge corresponds in an obvious way to the forms of sensibility, the categories of understanding, and the transcendental unity of apperception—all central to Kant's view of human knowledge.[42] While it may be

---

41. As the layman adds directly,

> For [mind] conforms itself to possibility so that it may measure everything as possible. [It conforms itself] in this way to absolute necessity so that it may measure all things as one and simply, just as God does, to the necessity of connection so that it may measure all things in their proper being, and to determinate possibility so that it may measure all things just as they exist. Mind also measures symbolically in the manner of comparisons, as [for instance] when it employs number and geometrical figures and transposes itself into the likeness of such things. (h 125)

42. Hopkins provides a convincing, detailed rejection of many Kantian readings of

true that Cusanus mentions medieval Aristotelian ideas about abstraction and universals, he does not expand on them or integrate them very well with what he says about the mind as measure. Perhaps in such passages he is better understood to be making use of ideas that he inherits without fully expounding them in his own terms. Cusanus' chief difference from Aristotle and medieval Scholastics such as Aquinas can be seen in his remarks about mathematical concepts, especially in chapters 5–9.[43] Moreover, his repeated emphasis on the conjectural character of everyday and scientific knowledge of the world of culture and nature stands in contrast to standard readings of what medieval Aristotelians say about knowledge of material things.

The upshot is that both extramental objects and the human mind are measures of the assimilating that is human knowing. That is to say, we become like the nonmental things we know *and* we fashion the conceptual and judgmental measures whereby we take them into ourselves as known. The quiddities, or full intelligibilities, of material things provide a kind of ideal limit that our minds acknowledge in recognizing the inadequacy of the ideas we do have about them. Besides this ideal limit on our quidditative knowledge, mind-independent things provide a measure for our assimilation. The reason is that, first, we recognize that they exist and are what our knowledge is about, and, second, we return to them again and again to assess the adequacy of our concepts and interpretations for dealing with them. Deprived of these outside measures, our knowledge loses any reference beyond the mind and we would have no standard for revising or improving our cognitive measures as more or less adequate to what we are attempting to understand.

The text of *Idiota de mente,* just as the other Cusan writings about human knowledge, cannot be forced onto earlier or later templates so that Nicholas will stand as an instance of late medieval realism or of Renaissance proto-Kantianism.[44] On the one hand, Cusanus stresses the spon-

---

Nicholas in *Wisdom and Knowledge,* 16–75, but a less plausible assignment of Nicholas on epistemic matters to the varied group of medieval Aristotelians.

43. K. Kremer has also argued, in ""Das kognitive und affektive Apriori," 101–11 and 115–16, that for Nicholas our active power of judgment is not empty. Rather, certain prior ethical conceptions are also present for human knowers. Kremer points to the value judgments the philosopher mentions in *Idiota de mente* c.4 h 78: "For we clearly experience a spirit speaking in our mind and judging this good, that just, this true, and reproaching us if we turn aside from the just." Kremer proposes that the good, the just, and the true are conceptions we possess by nature but only use in judgment once we encounter through perception the world around us, pointing to Plato's *Phaedo* as an earlier parallel. One must appreciate the careful and instructive way in which Kremer appeals to this text and parallel texts in Nicholas' sermons. Nonetheless, I take the passage quoted as the philosopher simply giving examples of the sort of judging that proceeds from mind as a way of reaffirming what the layman has just asserted about the *vis iudiciaria.*

44. K. Flasch finds innate in Cusan *mens* certain root concepts *(Stammbegriffe)* or lead-

taneous activity of the knowing mind as a unitary source of the conceptual "universe"—but this is a response to his reflections on the divine creative Mind. On the other hand, he characterizes our knowledge as assimilative, originating in perception and imagination. His language about knowing as measuring seemingly has it both ways: we are measured by the things we know *and* we construct the concepts and frameworks whereby we measure them, however inadequately or "conjecturally." If there are situations we meet as knowers that challenge us to adjust to what we perceive, examine, and experience, there are also situations in which we must adjust our ideas and concepts and metaphors so they will be coherent and internally consistent with one another.

There is a further dimension to the cognitive life of each individual mind that tends to get passed over both by Nicholas and his commentators. This is the difference between the cognitive experience of children and adults, especially of educated adults. Adult knowledge of the arts and sciences is often more abstract and systematic. Adult knowers can employ and construct conceptual frameworks that are more complicated than the concrete images and concepts of children and not so directly and obviously related to the everyday world of perceptual experience. Even if it remains true throughout our lifetimes, Nicholas' remarks about our having no innate concepts and about human knowledge originating in sense perception may well fit the experience of younger knowers better than that of educated adults, sophisticated theorists, or even the interlocutors in this dialogue. That is why his idea that we construct the conjectural conceptions and frameworks whereby we take the measure of things fits better his remarks about the liberal arts, theology, and mathematics, as well as all that he proposes in this dialogue about the mind's nature and functioning. He thinks and writes about cogni-

---

ing ideas *(Leitideen)* or first determinations *(Erstbestimmungen)* on the basis of which we make judgments, even though Nicholas denies any full-blown innate ideas in some simple-minded Platonic fashion (see *Nikolaus von Kues*, 295–306). For Flasch, these conceptions and their opposites—not unlike mind and its conceptual universe—are also examples of *complicatio/explicatio:* the point and magnitude, the one and multitude, the now and time, rest and motion, simplicity and composition, identity and diversity, equality and inequality, connection and disjunction (see *Idiota de mente* c.4 h 74–75). He stresses with Nicholas the paradigmatic character of created mind as image, indeed, the image of the enfolding of enfoldings. Each of these conceptual oppositions manifests as enfolded what the mind must also be to reflect its divine Original. His focus is clearly on the parallel between the divine Mind and human mind as creative sources of the real and conceptual universes, respectively. (Flasch warns explicitly that this is not Kantian and that it cannot solve the problems of later philosophical controversies.) Still, the textual evidence that such concepts are a priori possessions of mind, even as enfolded, is hardly decisive. Nicholas' layman may simply be illustrating the mind's active "unfolding" and using these particular oppositions because they were *loci communes* that go back to Plato's *Parmenides* and *Sophist* and, in the Neoplatonic tradition, to Proclus' commentary on Plato's *Parmenides* and his *Platonic Theology*, not to mention to Thierry of Chartres.

tion within a philosophical and theological outlook that is partly inherited from his Neoplatonic forebears and is partly his own original contrivance. Little wonder that his "conjectures" about human knowledge will hardly satisfy anyone who attempts to make him either a Kantian or a medieval Aristotelian.

5. EMBODIED MIND, ENSOULED BODY

Cusanus' use of metaphors and examples to explain and explore his account of human mind as an image of God's mind is striking and original. He also refuses to overlook that one difference between divine and human reality over which thinkers in the Platonic traditions have often seemed to stumble—when they simply did not look the other way. What is that difference? Human beings and human minds are bodily. One obvious reason why the human mind might be limited as mind is based on its embodiment, its restriction to a given body, to this flesh and these bones. Moreover, the total cognitive biography and conscious experience of a person marks the relation between her body and her mind as uniquely hers.

5.1. Mind as Ensouling Body

Cusanus teaches that there is a fit or harmony between mind and body such that mind functions as soul in animating or being the life principle of the human body, even though it can subsist without a body. As early as chapter 1 the layman summarizes this view:

For mind is one thing when it subsists in itself, another when embodied. Subsisting in itself mind is either Infinite or the image of the infinite. I admit, however, that of the minds that are the image of the Infinite—since they are not the greatest, not absolute or infinite when they subsist in themselves—some [of them] can animate the human body. Then I concede that the same [minds] are souls by reason of their function. (c.1 h 57)

As Cusanus later has his layman declare, "Undoubtedly our mind was placed by God in this body for its own perfection" (c.4 h 77). He is convinced that without bodies human minds could never achieve knowledge, let alone come to their full stature. We require sense perceptions to awaken mental life at its inception, for at birth we are endowed with capacities, not with innate concepts.[45] Cusanus' layman asserts as well that the *mens* does not exist before the body. Its priority is one of nature,

---

45. As Cusanus states this, "Therefore the mind must possess from God all that without which it could not reach its perfection. One should not think, then, that concepts were created together with the soul and it lost them once in the body. But one should believe that the soul needs the body so that the power created along with it can proceed to act" (c.5 h 77).

not in time. In chapter 5 he proposes the following compendium about the nature of *mens:*

> Mind is a living substance that we experience internally speaking and judging in us. It is more likened to infinite Substance and absolute Form than any other of all those spiritual powers we experience interiorly. Its function in this body is to give the body life and because of this it is called "soul/life principle" [*anima*]. Therefore mind is substantial form or a power enfolding everything in itself in its own way, both enfolding the life-giving power through which it animates the body by giving it vegetative and sensitive life and enfolding the reasoning power as well as the intellectual and intelligible powers. (c.5 h 80)

Cusanus combines without attempting to reconcile both the Aristotelian ("substantial form") and Platonic ("living substance") traditions in such descriptions of the mind as substance also functioning as soul or substantial form. Yet his emphasis is decidedly that of Christian Neoplatonism, for it is as living substance that *mens* is "more likened to infinite Substance and absolute Form."

Cusanus' ideas about soul or mind are given particular Christian emphasis in chapter 12 when the layman uses two striking analogies for human mortality to stress that each individual has his or her own soul/mind. He first insists that created souls are many, as are created minds—there is no one world-soul embracing individual souls as its expressions and no single "agent intellect" whereby individual minds know what they know. The reason is that any human soul/mind's connection with its body results in a body uniquely proportioned to itself. Yet even when their corresponding bodies perish, the plurality of soul/minds perdures even if we who survive have no means of counting such a plurality.

> It is as if someone heard an extremely loud shout that a great army of men raised but did not know that an army had shouted. It is clear that each man's shout is different and distinct in the shout that he hears, but the hearer has no idea of the number [of men shouting]. So he judges that it is one voice since he has no way of grasping the number.
> Or again, if many candles are burning in one room and the room is illuminated by all of them, the light of each candle remains distinct from the light of any other. We experience this when they are carried out one by one, for the light is diminished as each one takes its illumination with it when it is removed. Suppose, then, that the candles burning in a room are extinguished but the light remains and that someone enters the illuminated room. Even though the person sees the brightness of the room, he cannot grasp the difference and distinctness of the lights at all. Indeed, he could not know that many lights were there, unless he had knowledge that the lights of the extinguished candles were there. Even if he realized this, namely, that a plurality was there, still he could never distinguish by number one light from another. (h 143–44)

What is of particular interest here is that the illustration of candles in a room goes back to *The Divine Names* of Pseudo-Dionysius (2.4, 641a-b).[46] In *The Divine Names* the one light from the many candles is used to draw attention to the transcendent oneness-in-distinctness of the divine Trinity. One could speculate that what ties the Dionysian source and the Cusan variation together is that both are concerned with "number." Separated human souls are distinct (just as are the divine persons of the Trinity) but in a nonmaterial way beyond our usual grasp of the separate bodily things we can count and even beyond the mind's conceptual discriminations of distinction in multitude. What Nicholas keeps from his source is the suggestion that the illumination in both cases is as much that of the divine Mind as of its created images.[47]

5.2. Creating Embodied Minds

The question of mind's work or function as soul leads to what is an apparently secondary but recurrent question about *mens* that evokes some fascinating Cusan similes and analogies, namely, how does God create mind/soul and body and put them together? Cusanus' vivid images are his attempts to respond to that question. They may well express his wonder that mind and body are together at all and his astonishment that the flesh-and-blood that thinks can truly be the image of God. In fact his layman's proposals may well count first as metaphorical explanations of the relation between mind/soul and body and its requirements, not just as conjectural pictures of how God puts the two together.

In chapter 5 the layman turns again to his craft of carving spoons to explain "the way mind was created" (h 86). He compares putting mind and body together to making a spoon so polished that it is also a mirror. Once the carefully chosen wood has been carved into the shape of a spoon, it is polished until its surfaces reflect the way a mirror does. In this illustration, the wooden spoon stands for the human body, its mirror surfaces for the mind. Because a spoon has several differently shaped surfaces, different parts of it can function as convex, concave, cylindrical, and flat mirrors. The layman continues by commenting on the relation between mirror/mind and spoon/body:

Therefore, the form of the mirror had no temporal existence before the spoon's, but for the completion of the spoon I added it [the mirror form] to the initial form of the spoon to perfect it so that now the mirror form might include in itself the form of the spoon. The form of the mirror is also independent of the spoon's. For it is not essential to a mirror that it be a spoon. Therefore, if the

---

46. For an English translation, see Pseudo-Dionysius, *Complete Works*, 61-62.
47. The Heidelberg critical edition of *Idiota de mente* (196) notes that Nicholas wrote *"tote in totis"* in the margin of his copy of Eriugena's *Periphyseon*, where Eriugena cites the same passage in Pseudo-Dionysius.

proportions were destroyed without which the form of a spoon could not exist, for instance, if the handle were cut off, it would cease being a spoon. But the mirror form would not cease to exist for this reason. (c.5 h 87)

The lesson of this analogy is that God adds mind "as a living mirror" to body, to that fittingly proportioned matter "in which being ensouled [*animalitas*] might shine forth in a more perfect manner" (c.5 h 87). And just as the mirror remains when the spoon is broken, so mind or soul persists once the body perishes. Two points are worth particular note. First, the mirror form or soul "includes" or contains "in itself" the spoon form or body. Cusanus believes that the immaterial encompasses the corporeal. The words stating that the mirror form includes that of the spoon *(in se contineat)* recall the Neoplatonic view that soul embraces body, not vice versa.

Second, the analogy makes it clear that the spoon has its own form and so does the mirror. Neither requires the other to be what it is. If carried to its logical conclusion, the analogy would suggest that body and soul are independent formal realities that can be harmonized but need not be together. This implicit emphasis on the relative independence of body and soul not only preserves the latter's ontological priority and immortality but recalls Cusanus' Platonic and Neoplatonic heritage. For Nicholas, the harmony with the body that the mind achieves in functioning as soul is dependent upon appropriate or suitable corporeal proportions. In chapter 6, returning again to the mirror-spoon but shifting the emphasis, the layman says:

And proportion is the place of form; for without the proportion that is fit and suitable for a form the form cannot shine forth. As I said, when the proportion fit for a spoon is destroyed, its form cannot stay since it has no place. For proportion is like the aptitude of a mirror surface to reflect an image: without the proper surface the image ceases. (c.5 h 92)

Considering this last remark provokes the reader to realize that, even if the human soul or mind has the priority in being, it cannot "shine forth" as God's image without the body. As ensouled, body is thus the image of mind even as mind is image of God.

In chapter 13 the layman is asked again how the mind is "infused by [God's] creating." He responds with an object lesson. Suspending a glass between his forefinger and thumb, he strikes it so that it vibrates and makes a sound. The sound continues until the glass shatters. The layman explains that it was the force of striking the glass that caused the vibration, the sound, and the shattering. Then he proposes that his hearers imagine the force as continuing even after the glass has broken and the vibration and sound have ceased. Such a force or power would be comparable to the human mind or soul that animates the body.

But if that force, because it did not depend on the glass, were not to cease on account of it [breaking] but were to subsist without the glass, you would have an example of how that force is created in us which brings about [bodily] movement and harmony and how it ceases to cause that [harmony] once the proportions are broken even though it will not cease to exist because of that. (c.13 h 50)

Just as the force did not depend on the glass it caused to vibrate, so the "soul-force" or mind does not depend on the body it harmonized with itself but continues to exist once death overtakes the body and the harmony is broken.

In a final brief remark the layman compares the relation of mind and body to lute playing and lute:

[It is] just as if I were to present you the art of lute playing in a lute given you. Since the art does not depend on the lute you were given (even though it is given to you in the lute), if the lute has been broken the art of playing it is not destroyed thereby, even if no lute fit for you can be found in the world. (c.13 h 150)

Once again the mind is parallel to the art or skill of playing the instrument, while the lute or instrument itself stands for the body.

Cusanus' layman thus adds a point to the vibrating force and sounding glass of the previous example. Just as a musician's art and instrument are united in the playing, so the destruction of the instrument does not mean a loss of the expertise or learned capacity to play it well. But why does the layman add the qualification, "even if no lute fit for you can be found"? Cusanus is aware of how particular instruments become special to particular musicians, but he may also want to suggest that souls are fit for particular bodies and thus become differentiated and individuated through bodily life. Neither reincarnation nor prior existence is part of what it is to be a human mind and soul.

All three analogies—the mirror-spoon, the vibrating glass, and the musician's art and instrument—are calculated to explain as much the relationship between mind and body as to provide images for how God puts the two together. As so frequently in *Idiota de mente*, Cusanus chooses examples from human artisanry and craft—where *homo faber* might provide some glimpse of both our mind's creative and productive direction and some image of the divine Creator. Each of the similes gives us some sense of the astonishment any Platonist, even a Christian, has to feel at the realization that such disparate realities as mind and matter should be united in human beings. Moreover, each of these apt comparisons brings out in its particular way how the relation between mind and body is one of harmony and due proportion. While the human mind may be prior by nature, as actually existing, it is affected, differentiated, and conditioned because it is designed to be embodied. The whole dialogue shows how human knowledge occurs as bodily, that is, as modified by sensation, perception, and imagination within the physical world of nature and culture—however much all of these activities give evidence of the active direction of mind.

6. THE PATTERN OF FIGURAE IN *IDIOTA DE MENTE* AS A WHOLE

Table 3.1 afforded a schematic view of the way the Cusan ontology of divine Original and created image provides a clue to the Cusan doctrine of mind and human knowledge. If this stands as the core of the theoretical teaching of this dialogue, the other main doctrines in *Idiota de mente* are expounded in metaphorical terms and illustrated by similes or analogies often drawn from fifteenth-century artisanry. The connections between these metaphors and analogies can be seen more clearly when they are interpreted as working at three different levels, as pictured in Table 3.2.

At a first fundamental level is the regulative source metaphor that human minds are images of God's mind. The connection and contrast between image and original set the explanatory limits for Cusanus' teaching in this dialogue. At a second or intermediate level we find the *imago Dei* motif articulated by several important metaphors. First comes the notion of knowing as the creative unfolding of the conceptual universe actively produced by the human mind. Next, since *mens* and *mensuratio* are associated, our minds take the measure of what we know in conceptual and linguistic terms. We differ from the divine Mind, Nicholas teaches, because our knowing is also assimilatio. In pursuing careers as knowers who are images of the divine we become likened to the things we know. Finally, we are minds in bodies, harmonious if astounding "fits" of mind to matter. Creating, producing, unfolding, being likened to, measuring, being a body's fitting match—all of these are the second-level metaphors Cusanus employs. These metaphors capture something of what mental life and mental activities amount to, and they provide Cusan conjectures for exploring and explaining, interpreting and characterizing *mens*.

Table 3.2 illustrates how Cusanus draws on a third level of similes and analogies from the life of his time to extend, illustrate, and exemplify the doctrines about cognition already interpreted in metaphorical terms. These analogies and examples are impressive for their aptness and novelty, as well as for their reflection of the creative artisanry and technical inventiveness of the early Renaissance world. More intriguing, perhaps, is that their aptness in *Idiota de mente* is based on the fact that the metaphors at the first and second level control and order them. Per-

TABLE 3.2 Three Levels of Metaphor in *Idiota de mente*

1. Basic metaphor for mens	2. Metaphors for mind's basic functions	3. Analogies illustrating these functions
Human minds are images of the divine Mind	a. Mind is creative: it fashions the conceptual world	Language/spoon carving (c.2) Seed, living law, living diamond (c.5) Self-portrait (c.13)
	b. Mind assimilates *and* measures	"Absolute" face (c.9) Living compass (c.9) Pliable materials (c.7)
	c. Harmony of mind and body	Army's shout; candles' light Mirror-spoon (c.5) Vibrating glass (c.13) Lute playing (c.13)

haps these third-level analogies could be omitted or exchanged for others. In this way they are pleasing if dispensable additions.

But the second-level metaphors, no less than the basic or root metaphor of image and original, are utterly integral to what Cusanus does in *Idiota de mente*. He could not proceed nor could we make sense of his analysis without them. Moreover, they show us how Cusan practice in this dialogue is itself an instance of his teaching about the active and creative nature of human cognition. Nicholas' images and likenesses provide the best evidence of how our knowledge is both assimilative and mensurative, for they attempt to capture something of what we experience as knowers, but in the metaphorical terms that Nicholas judges or "measures" as most apt for what he is attempting to explain. One is again hard put to interpret the teaching of this dialogue as either

Scholastic Aristotelian realism or proto-Kantian speculation. What we end up with is neither definitive and obvious, nor closed to revision or improvement. Creative human judgment stands ready to consider further metaphors or conceptual schemes and to assess their relative adequacy in disclosing what cognition comes to—both as complex activity and as conceptual outcome. "Conjecturing about mind" in a thoughtful and reflective fashion always will be a learning that reveals the depth and breadth of our ignorance.

In one way, then, this dialogue turns on the fundamental idea that the human mind is an image of God's mind and that, as images of God's creating, we actively mediate as knowers between God and the finite, knowable realities that are independent of mind. Our power of judgment, in likening itself to extramental things, takes their measure. In another way, the fact that our knowledge always remains "conjectural" lets us recall the distance between the created image and the divine Original. Nicholas' well-known dictum from *De docta ignorantia* 1.3 becomes most striking in this context: "It is self-evident that there is no proportion of the Infinite to the finite" (h 9). This caveat qualifies even the foundational metaphor of image and original on which this work is based, as well as any putative security we might be tempted to find in the rather optimistic and positive account of Cusan conjectural judgment. The nature of the human mind may well remain as inaccessible as the mind of God. No account of *mens* is either definitive or finished.

Idiota de mente thus reminds us of the deep and ineradicable metaphorical foundations of every philosophical interpretation of mind and knowledge. Asked by the philosopher as their conversation begins whether he has some *coniectura* (conjectural proposal) about the nature of mind, the layman responds: "I think that no one is or has been a complete human being who did not frame at least some sort of concept about mind" (h 57). In this dialogue Nicholas of Cusa exploits the metaphorical realm to enrich our understanding of mind human and divine, and in doing so lets us realize the power of human conjecturing and what the working of the human mind can accomplish.

4
The Dialectic of Seeing Being Seen Seeing
De visione Dei (1453)

Each of Cusanus' speculative works may be fairly interpreted as proposing symbols or metaphors for understanding—in learned ignorance—both God and the relation between God and creatures. Once we think through these metaphors we find ourselves involved in a dialectical process of reflection. Such dialectical thinking parallels or even mirrors in human thought and reflection the fact that the relationship between God and all else cannot be understood in any *simpliste* or one-dimensional way. Ultimately, as I have already pointed out, Cusanus teaches that we cannot think God at all, so disproportionate is divine Infinity to the finite things of the created universe from which we take our cognitive measures. Yet belief in God inevitably leads to conjectural attempts to fathom the unfathomable, however dialectical the process and metaphorical the results. No single work Nicholas composed can better exemplify this process and its impressive outcomes than his 1453 treatise on mystical theology, *De visione Dei*.[1]

Celebrated for its prayerful reflection about God as the object of mystical theology and mystical vision, *De visione Dei* is unique in Christian mystical literature for proposing a painting or icon (probably of Christ's face) as symbolic of "the vision of God."[2] Cusanus uses an "omnivoyant"

---

1. Recent German scholarship on this Cusan treatise is well represented in "Das Sehen Gottes nach Nikolaus von Kues" (=*MFCG* 18), Trier: Paulinus, 1989, a whole issue devoted to *De visione Dei*. J. Hopkins' *Nicholas of Cusa's Dialectical Mysticism*, 2nd ed. (Minneapolis, Minn.: Banning Press, 1988) provides a text, translation, and much other valuable material for understanding *De visione Dei*. H. L. Bond provides thoughtful comments on the work in *Nicholas of Cusa*, 43–55. See also Flasch, *Nikolaus von Kues*, 383–443, for intriguing comments about the relation of this work to Nicholas' *De pace fidei* and his other writings of 1453. Besides my debts to these scholars, this chapter corrects and extends my three earlier essays about *De visione Dei*: "Nicholas of Cusa's *The Vision of God*," in *An Introduction to the Medieval Mystics of Europe*, ed. P. Szarmach (Albany: State University of New York Press, 1984), 293–312; "The Icon and the Wall: *Visio* and *Ratio* in Nicholas of Cusa's *De visione Dei*," *Proceedings of the American Catholic Philosophical Association* 64 (1990): 86–98; and "God's Presence: Some Cusan Proposals," in *Christ and the Church*, 241–49.

2. See R. Haubst, "Nachwort der Herausgebers," *MFCG* 18 (1989): 68, and the photo

painting or icon in part to illustrate the dialectical relation between God and human beings, since on both sides there is seeing and being seen. Familiar themes from Nicholas' earlier speculative thought such as "learned ignorance" and the "coincidence of opposites" take on particular importance for interpreting both sides of the vision of God as Nicholas proceeds.

In the "Preface" Nicholas explains how one might use the painting as a symbol or icon of what it means to see God. Nicholas then writes several chapters stressing God's "seeing" before turning attention to God as "seen" in chapters 6 and 7. He returns again to God's seeing in chapter 8 and part of chapter 9, and proposes a second metaphor, that of the wall encircling paradise, beyond which alone God may be seen. With his focus now on the object of mystical seeing, Nicholas turns to more abstruse considerations designed to have us confront the kind of reality this God must be. He elaborates these considerations in chapters 10 through 18. The final seven chapters recall the consoling place of Jesus as mediator of vision and union with God.

De visione Dei, then, does not recount mystical experiences or propose exercises for those who seek mystical vision of or union with God. Rather, its aim is contemplative and thus its focus is the infinite God, the goal of contemplative and even mystical vision, and the sort of not-seeing that alone can "see" such a God.[3] Most of the treatise is teaching cast in the form of personal prayer. The prayer form lets Cusanus acknowledge the priority of God's reality and grace for everyone who seeks to see the face of God.

1. THE ICON

Nicholas sent his treatise about mystical theology to the Benedictine monks at Tegernsee—something they had long requested.[4] With the manuscript he sent what he called an "icon of God," probably a portrait of Jesus, probably as typically represented on Veronica's veil. In this

---

of such a painting (taken from one of the cornices in a cloister at St. Nikolaus Hospital in Kues) that is the frontispiece to that volume.

3. On mystical theology in Cusanus, see L. Dupré, "The Mystical Theology of Cusanus's *De visione Dei*," in *Christ and the Church*, 205–20. On the meaning of "mystical theology" in Cusanus, see A. M. Haas, *Deum mistice videre . . . in caligine coincidencie: zum Verhältnis Nikolaus von Kues zur Mystik* (Basel: Helbing und Lichtenhahn, 1989); and Hopkins, *Dialectical Mysticism*, 15–31.

4. For Nicholas' relationship with this monastery, see M. Schmidt, "Nikolaus von Kues im Gespräch mit den Tegernseer Mönchen über Wesen und Sinn der Mystik," *MFCG* 18 (1989): 25–49, and esp. E. Vansteenberghe, *Autour de la docte ignorance. Une controverse sur la théologie mystique au XVe siècle. Beiträge zur Geschichte der Philosophie und Theologie des Mittelalters* 14 (Münster: Aschendorff, 1915).

painting Christ's face was so portrayed that the painted eyes seemed to look directly into every viewer's eyes at the same time, no matter where any viewer stood or moved, and no matter how many people viewed the icon at that particular time. The portrait of Christ's face was to be an object lesson symbolizing *visio Dei*—both God's vision of us and our vision of God.

This portrait serves as the central, crucial metaphor or symbol to which Nicholas returns again and again through the treatise to explain God's connection with finite things. He begins with a presupposition (in fact, a rule) for interpreting the painting as a symbol of the vision of God. He says: *"Nihil posse apparere circa visum eiconae dei, quin verius sit in vero visu dei"* (Whatever is *apparent* with regard to the icon-of-God's sight is *truer* with regard to God's true sight; c.1 h 6).[5] Then Cusanus moves directly to God's own seeing and comments on the priority and perfection of divine "vision."

But it is worthwhile to pause and consider in detail the painting or icon itself. It is designed as an object lesson, an exercise in visual thinking. To appreciate where this symbol is supposed to lead us, we need to look carefully at what the painted appearances come to. We are looking at a painting. This means that what we apparently see and experience when we look into the painted eyes of Jesus is not really occurring. In fact, the face portrayed is not looking at or seeing anyone. The portrait does not really meet the gaze of those viewing it or draw their eyes to its. The depicted eyes merely *seem* to follow the onlooker's eyes as she or he moves from one side to another for a different view. Indeed, the viewer's gaze measures the looking of the one depicted in the painting and the look from the painting takes place only in dependence on the viewer.[6] Once we reflect on the experience we realize that this apparent face-to-face encounter is a perceptual illusion.

But what does the illusion amount to? For Nicholas' contemporaries, this sort of look from a painting became an invitation to the viewer to enter the world created by the perspectively ordered relationships of the painting.[7] The glance from the depicted face gave the viewer an im-

---

5. I follow Hopkins' edition and translation (cf. footnote 1) throughout; modifications of his translation are noted in the text.

6. Cf. K. Flasch, "Der Mensch als Mass Gottes," in *Gott Heute: Fünfzehn Beiträge zur Gottesfrage*, ed. N. Kutschki (Mainz: Matthias-Grünewald, 1967), 20–30. For further analysis of the exercise described in Cusanus' "Preface," see M. de Certeau, "The Gaze—Nicholas of Cusa," *Diacritics* 17 (1987): 2–38.

7. For the context in the history of art, see A. Stock, "Die Rolle der 'icona Dei' in der Spekulation *De visione Dei*," *MFCG* 18 (1989): 50–62. See also N. Herold, "Bild der Wahrheit—Wahrheit des Bildes: Zur Deutung des Blicks aus dem Bild in der Cusanische Schrift *De visione dei*," in *Wahrheit und Begründung*, ed. V. Gerhardt and N. Herold (Würzburg: Konigshausen and Neumann, 1985), 71–98. Both essays cite A. Neumeyer, *Der Blick*

pression of spatial continuity and temporal simultaneity familiar from encounters with other people. As a result, the viewer could move into the world portrayed in the painting and take that world into her own. Because the painted eyes look into mine, the usual boundaries between what is depicted and what is outside the painting are loosened and tend to disappear as gazes connect in my experience of the painting. The situation is experienced as "metastable" in that one moves back and forth between the habitual beliefs that result from seeing eyes looking into one's own eyes and the realization that this eye contact is illusory.

Once this dialectic is set up between visual perception *(visio)* and discursive thought *(ratio),* we can see that the icon's look mediates and connects two levels of reality, that of the viewer and that of the one portrayed as looking from the painting. Even more, the experience of the painted figure's gaze effectively puts in question our ordinary convictions about the validity and priority of our reality as viewers or onlookers. The encounter with the painted face tends to privilege what is portrayed. The glance from the painted eyes opens a window to a further reality that we can enter, experience, and understand as not separated or isolated from the rest of our world. All of these points, of course, could be made about any portrait whose eyes were rendered so as to encounter the viewer's eyes. Indeed, Nicholas mentions several such paintings in his "Preface." Whenever the eyes of a portrait rendered in perspective are painted to look out of the picture plane, they appear to be all-seeing, just as in the case of the icon Nicholas sent to the Benedictine monks.

Given that this view of perspectival painting was current in Nicholas' time, it is clear why he would use the painting of Jesus' all-seeing face, a "Veronica," as a means of access to another reality and as an introduction to mystical theology. A "Veronica" portrayed the suffering Jesus; it would lead a believer to sympathize and identify with Christ's suffering. The dialectic already described between the painting's and the viewer's reality could be used to parallel symbolically the dialectical connection between God's reality and the reality of creatures.

If the look from any painted image is to mediate between the viewer and what the painting portrays, it is most appropriate that it be an image of Christ's look that invites us to look further, for Christ *is* the image of the Father. As Nicholas puts it: "Therefore in You, O Jesus, who are the son of man, I see, through the kindness of your grace, the Son of

---

aus dem Bild (Berlin: Gebr. Mann, 1964). More may be found in C. Olds, "Aspect and Perspective in Renaissance Thought: Nicholas of Cusa and Jan Van Eyck," in *Christ and the Church,* 251–64.

God; and in You, the Son of God, I see the Father" (c.20 h 89). As a portrayal of the human Christ the painting is twice removed from the divine seeing and being seen it is supposed to symbolize. Dealing with the image of an image, one whose "seeing" depends on a visual illusion, may emphasize how far we stand from God's own seeing. (The structure of the exercise itself thus recalls Nicholas' warning: attributing sight to God is itself illusory if such attribution claims to say anything about *what* God is.)

Understood against his Neoplatonic heritage, Cusanus' use of a painted image is even more intriguing. In that tradition images are taken to be manifestations, even reflections, of what lies beyond them, their originals or exemplars. To be an image is to be different and separate from one's exemplar, to be precisely *not* the original, but at the same time to be bound up with and dependent on the original as its image or deficient likeness. Using the portrait of Jesus' face underlines the dialectic implicit in our recognition of images as images and thereupon extends it as symbolic of our situation before the God who sees us striving to see God.

What have we discovered, then, about the "vision" of Jesus portrayed in this icon? Jesus' look appears never to fail; it seems to precede any viewer's sight and to be all-seeing, taking in everyone who views it simultaneously. Recalling Cusanus' rule, we understand that what is merely portrayed and thereby symbolized in the painting is in fact all the more so in reality: we are preceded and embraced by Christ's seeing us. Through this apparently mutual glance we encounter and are united with Jesus. We share the same time and space in imagination, drawn into what we see portrayed before us. Thus the image enables our moving through it to the reality of Christ so that we identify with his sufferings even as we understand that his look is one of care and love for us.

2. THE REALITY OF GOD'S SEEING

Such appearances are quite useful because they may help us recognize and appreciate the truth about God's vision of and presence to us. *In seeing we are seen*—this mutual relatedness is what the icon's appearances symbolize. God's "vision" is without any of the limitations we recognize in the various sorts of creaturely seeing. The vision portrayed in the painting symbolizes God's all-seeing, omniscient sight. But while the painting merely appears all-seeing, God's sight actually takes in all there is. The painted eyes just seem to exceed the capacities of human eyesight, but God's "seeing" actually is unlimited. God's vision touches each limited thing and remains inexhaustible. Perfect in every respect, God's sight encompasses every conceivable kind of seeing in unrestricted or absolute Vision.

God's vision is ontologically first, creating, sustaining, and anticipating even our desire to see God, let alone its fulfillment. As a look of care and love, God's is a provident vision, never abandoning or betraying what it creates and enables in nature and in grace. This way of using the icon as a symbol of God's vision and providence fits the expectations of Christian piety and orthodoxy and keeps God's presence familiar and consoling.

Yet Nicholas is constantly aware of God's radical otherness. Early in the treatise he is careful to assert that God's having vision is not really different from God's being—that infinite Mystery beyond our ken. Indeed, if we think about what "*absolute* vision" should mean, it is clear that God's sight is not seeing at all in any way that will be intelligible to us.[8] As Nicholas puts it, "God, insofar as He is true Uncontracted Sight, is not sight that is *less* than the intellect can conceive abstract sight to be; rather He is incomparably more perfect Sight" (c.1 h 7). Does this not render what was apparently comforting and familiar suddenly more remote and mysterious than ever? Nicholas is asserting, to paraphrase Anselm's proposal centuries earlier, that God's vision is a vision than which no greater vision can be conceived.

Obviously a believer wants to assert that God watches over us. At the same time no believer wants to assert that God has vision in any anthropomorphic way. Are we "stuck," as it were, with assertions that take us in different directions but not much closer to understanding how to conceive what Nicholas is doing here? In moving from the icon to lessons about God's sight of us we must note the very points our experience of the icon's seeing is supposed to teach.

Nicholas focuses particularly on our experience of looking into the icon's depicted eyes as an experience where, at the same time, it apparently looks into ours. He proposes that God's seeing and God's being seen are identical.

---

8. Cusanus writes in chapter 2:

But Sight that is free from all contractedness—as being the most adequate Measure, and the most true Exemplar, of all acts of seeing—encompasses at one and the same time each and every mode of seeing. For without absolute Sight there cannot be contracted sight. But absolute Sight encompasses all modes of seeing—encompasses all modes in such way that it encompasses each mode. And it remains altogether free from all variation. For in absolute Sight every contracted mode of seeing is present uncontractedly. (h 8)

On God's seeing or vision, see Hopkins, *Dialectical Mysticism*, 17–19; and W. Beierwaltes, "Visio Absoluta: Reflexion als Grundzug des göttlichen Prinzips bei Nicolaus Cusanus," *Sitzungsberichte der Heidelberger Akademie der Wissenschaften* (1978): 5–33.

O Lord, when you look upon me with an eye of graciousness, what is Your seeing, other than Your being seen by me? In seeing me, You who are *deus absconditus* give Yourself to be seen by me. No one can see You except insofar as You grant that You be seen. To see You is not other than that You see the one who sees You. (c.5 h 15)

This passage helps us realize why Nicholas' title, *De visione Dei*, has to be exactly ambivalent. It *must* mean both God's vision of us and our vision of God because God seen is identically God seeing. The reason for Nicholas is clear. For God to be seen by anyone is nothing else than for God to see that person seeing. And so the icon of Jesus is a perfect object lesson for our consideration. To look into the icon's eyes is to experience being seen looking by those painted eyes, if only in appearance. Yet there is a crucial difference in the parallel: I can see the depicted eyes, even though no real eyes are present. I cannot see the divine face or vision, even though God's reality is present and "sees" me. The dialectic of presence and absence, of seeing and not seeing that I experienced with the icon is turned inside out so that in the case of the icon what seemed present but was really absent, namely, its seeing, in the case of God seems absent but is really present.

The important parallel in the icon and what it symbolizes is the experienced simultaneous connection of different levels of reality.[9] Whereas the encounter with the icon's gaze in fact depends on the viewer, the encounter with the Divine is first of all enabled by God. To experience God's unseen presence is at one and the same time to be sustained by the divine presence-in-absence. In my creaturely status I have separate reality as a contracted image of God only through my connection with my divine Source. As Nicholas puts it, "You who are the absolute Being of all things are present to each as if You had no concern about anything else" (c.4 h 10, my translation).

Nicholas expresses all this in terms of seeing, even though God's seeing is nothing but God's being, even though God is invisible, and even though mystical sight of God transcends any experience we might identify as seeing. In God the distinction between seeing and being seen collapses. This differentiation is taken from human sight and perception and applied to the particular case of our looking at the icon or portrayal of Jesus. Were we able to see God the way we see the icon, then we could grasp Nicholas' conclusion about the connection between human vision and divine vision: for us to see God would be identically for us to be seen by God. In Nicholas' most precise terms, this identity and connection becomes even clearer when restated thus: God sees in *our* seeing God the very Godhead. Any sighting of God we do is one with God's be-

---

9. Cf. Herold, "Bild der Wahrheit," 76–79.

ing seen and is exactly God's own seeing of God's self.[10] What is telling about Nicholas' version of seeing God is not what vision discerns or what practices one must follow in order to gain the correct standpoint for such seeing. Rather, it is the way he joins God's vision and our vision. For us to see God is likewise for us to be seen by God. Within our seeing, God is both subject and object of our purported vision of God.

Nicholas effectively uses the icon and his reflections on the ambivalent meaning of the phrase "vision of God" to call attention to the mystical or divine elements in all our experience. God's ontological priority—his antecedent gaze, as it were—is identically his Presence to my reality—to my seeking and "looking," even as I finally learn that encountering God is not an experience of anything visible.[11] Opening up that connection with God as the core of God's presence to us is what reflection on God's seeing and our seeing can do, just as reflection on the icon provided an entry to the meaning of God seeing and seen.

3. SEEING THE FACE OF GOD

Cusanus takes another approach when he turns next to focus on *what* we see, not just on the actual visual encounter or seeing.[12] Looking at the icon we see Christ's face; *a pari*, any vision of God should disclose the divine Face. We might adapt to what is seen Cusanus' earlier rule of interpretation for seeing itself. Now the rule should read as follows: Whatever *seems* true about the icon we see will in fact *be* truer regarding the face of God.

When we look at the painting, we see a face depicted as well as its gaze. No less we seek to "see" the face of God. The face Nicholas sent the monks was a portrayal of Jesus, the one the Bible terms "the image of God [the Father]" (2 Cor 4.4). Nicholas proposes we reflect on the face of God to which the icon points, since in the Neoplatonic tradition what we learn of the image should lead us to the truth of its original. The connection between image and original provides another lead to

---

10. In "Visio Absoluta," 22, Beierwaltes expresses it thus: "Das absolute Sehen also ist das Ersehen des Endlich-Seienden, zugleich aber auch die Ermöglichung, dass dieses selbst von sich her sieht und so das absolute Sehen vom ihm, dem Endlichen, gesehen wird; der unendliche Blick des absoluten Sehens geht so mit dem endlichen Blick zusammen." See also Beierwaltes' later *Visio Facialis—Sehen ins Angesicht* (Munich: Verlag der Bayerischen Akademie der Wissenschaften, 1988), 18–19; and de Certeau, "The Gaze," 16.

11. A remark from de Certeau, in "The Gaze," 30, is thus apropos for more than the look depicted in the icon: "Eyes do not lead to the gaze. It is the gaze that may find eyes."

12. G. Stachel has noted this switch of perspectives in "Schweigen vor Gott: Bermerkungen zur mystischen Theologie der Schrift *De visione Dei*," *MFCG* 14 (1980): 167–81.

seeing God's face, for it is precisely originals that are responsible for the reality of their dependent images. To experience something present *as image* is at once and thereby to "see" its seemingly absent exemplar whose presence is required to keep the image all that it is.

God's face is the Exemplar or Original, not for Jesus' visage alone, but for all created things that depend on God as images. If we were to imagine sighting God's face, Nicholas writes, what we should see there would be our own faces, but in their original guise:

O Lord, I apprehend that Your Face precedes every formable face and is the Exemplar and Truth of all faces—and that all faces are images of Your Face, which cannot be contracted and cannot be participated in. Therefore, every face that can look upon Your Face sees nothing that is *other* than itself or *different* from itself, because it sees its own Truth. (c.6 h 19)

In this way my vision of God's face provides me the sight of my own face—here a symbol of the truth of my own being. To see God's face is to view the original, eternal Reality of my own face, not its created image with which I am more familiar, for in the Godhead I am not distinct from the divine Oneness.[13] I see myself in God because I receive from God that which I am—I see "nothing that is *other* than or *different* from" myself. And that is identically God's self!

Yet Nicholas cautions us not to become fixated on the idea of God actually having a face:

Who could conceive of this unique, most true and adequate Exemplar of all faces?—the Exemplar of each and every face and, yet, so perfectly the Exemplar of each that, as it were, it is not the Exemplar of any other. He would have to pass beyond all the forms and figures of all formable faces. . . . Therefore, as regards whoever sets out to see Your Face: as long as he conceives of something, he is far removed from Your Face. For every concept of face is less than Your Face, O Lord. (c.6 h 21)

Viewing the icon set up a precarious connection between two kinds of reality via the meeting of real and depicted eyes. This connection was symbolic of the one paralleled in the imagined identity of God seeing

---

13. Beierwaltes, in *Visio Facialis*, 20–21, writes:

Der creative Blick des absoluten Angesichts, aus sich selbst herausgehend und dadurch Anderes, als er selbst ist, konstituierend oder formend, ist im Vergleich zur Abschattung [*umbra*] des ihm Eigenen zur endlichen, bildhaften "contractio" des Absoluten die Seins-begrundende "*Wahrheit* und das unangemessenste *Mass* aller Angesichete" (chapt. 6). . . . In der Absoluten seine eigene Wahrheit zu sehen, ist dem Menschen nur deshalb "gegeben," weil die absolute Wahrheit als der sich selbst durchsichtige Grund das Gegründete in ihm selbst sieht und es so zu einem "Sehenden" macht.

A briefer version of this essay may be found in "Visio Facialis: Sehen ins Angesicht," *MFCG* 18 (1989): 91–118.

God's very Self in being seen by us. Now that same connection is revealed again in imagined face-to-face encounter of image with original. Yet we are instructed to discard the face, just as earlier we came to recognize that the icon's eyes were illusory and came to realize as well that we had to transcend human seeing—so that what is left is the connection between us and God. The reason God is present or "seen" in ordinary experience is that God's Truth is not other or different than we are.

4. SELF-POSSESSION AS POSSESSING GOD

Nicholas' point here may become clear if we contrast an earlier text in the same tradition. In the *Proslogion* of St. Anselm, many chapters after his celebrated proof showing that God exists (and, indeed, so truly exists that he cannot even be thought not to do so), Anselm prays almost plaintively:

O supreme and inaccessible Light, O complete and blessed Truth, how distant You are from me, who am so near for You! How far removed You are from my sight though I am present to Yours! You are everywhere present as a whole; and yet, I do not see You. In You I move, and in You I exist; and yet, I cannot approach You. You are within me and round about me; and yet, I do not experience You. (*Proslogion*, c.16)[14]

Anselm's eloquent prayer raises the question whether his classic formula for God—that than which nothing greater can be thought—and his elegant proof that God must exist might not have removed God even further from human experience.

At best Cusanus nods toward the traditional medieval arguments for God's existence. Instead he uses symbols, here the icon, to explore a view of divinity that will keep God visible and ingredient in human experience and still transcendent or divine. No passage in *De visione Dei* shows this more tellingly than one that includes a prayer not unlike that of Anselm:

He who sees You has all things, for no one sees You except him who has You. No one can approach unto You, because You are unapproachable. Therefore, no one will apprehend You unless You give Yourself to him. How will I have You, O Lord?—I who am not worthy to appear in Your presence. How will my prayer reach You who are altogether unapproachable? How will I entreat You? For what is more absurd than to ask that You, who are all in all, give Yourself to me? How will You give Yourself to me unless You likewise give to me the sky and the earth

---

14. Translation from J. Hopkins, *A New, Interpretive Translation of St. Anselm's "Monologion" and "Proslogion"* (Minneapolis, Minn.: Banning Press, 1986), 245–47.

and everything in them? Indeed, how will You give Yourself to me unless You also give me to myself? And while I am quietly reflecting in this manner, You, O Lord, answer me in my heart with the words: "Be your own and I will be yours." (c.7 h 26)

This response may not be quite what we expect. Why does Nicholas not have God answer, "You be mine and I will be yours"? Would not traditional Christian piety lead us to believe that, if God leads us to commit ourselves and actually choose to belong to God, then God will be ours as well? Why would Nicholas have God seemingly turn us back toward ourselves and our own limited resources?[15] The reason parallels what has already been said about seeing God and about the face of God. Whether symbolized as seen or seeing, God is one with our imagined vision of God. If our faces symbolize created images of God, they require the presence of their divine Exemplar to be what they are. In chapter 9, Nicholas says,

If, then, Your essence penetrates all things, then so too does Your sight, which is Your essence. Therefore, just as none of all existing things can escape from its own being, so neither can it [escape] from Your essence, which gives to all things their essential being. Consequently, not from Your sight either. (h 37, Hopkins translation modified)

In a parallel fashion, the choice to be myself is at once the choice to belong to the God who permeates and sustains who and what I am by nature and to respond to God's grace. I cannot choose my true self— whose ultimate Reality and Truth I recognized, as it were, in God's face—even to fulfill its possibilities as created image unless I am bound up intimately with my divine Exemplar. To be myself is *eo ipso* not "to escape" or flee from God's essence. God's essence, God's "sight," is present to me and to every creature in such a way that it is through God that we are ourselves both in nature and in grace.[16]

Possessing God, then, does not mean losing ourselves. Rather, it is only in possessing ourselves that we find God. As Nicholas puts it,

You have placed within my freedom my being my own if I will to. Hence, unless I am my own You are not mine. For [otherwise] You would be coercing my freedom, since You can be mine only if I too am mine. And because You have placed this matter within my freedom, You do not coerce me; rather You await my choosing to be my own. (c.7 h 27)

---

15. On this passage and its broader context in Cusanus, see K. Kremer, "Gottes Vorsehung und die Menschliche Freiheit ('Sis tu tuus, et Ego ero tuus')," *MFCG* 18 (1989): 227–52, esp. 243–44.

16. See Beierwaltes' remarks on Dürer's self-portrait as the Christ, portrayed with an "all-seeing" gaze, in *Visio Facialis*, 52–56.

This opens up for us a further insight into the way in which God can be present to us or "seen" when we respond to what we have already come to know about the divine vision or presence. God's vision is not something alongside our longed-for vision of God. God does not see us as we see other creatures or as they see us—using ordinary sense perception. God's presence is not something alongside our own presence in the world, as if God were present to us as we are present to one another or as the furniture in this room is present to us. Nor is the vision of God or God's presence to us a function merely of some conscious state of ours—whether memory, imagination, or attention, even prayer or ritual. And God does not become or remain present to us as do absent friends or enemies or those we have known who have died. God's vision works otherwise.

All these familiar kinds of presence and vision involve the limits of both parties to the relationship. God could see us or be present to us also in any of these human ways, but they are not fundamental to our connection with God or to the vision of God (in either sense). For the limits on how the things we know can see or be present to one another are precisely a function of their finitude, their "otherness" and distinctness, one from another. God's presence, God's vision is unique, for unlike our own case God's distinctness is *not* distinct from or other than created things themselves. God's difference has to be thought dialectically as at once God's identity with every other thing. Just so, God's presence has to be construed as a kind of absence; just so, God's face reflects our faces; just so, God's "vision" enables our seeing God in our being seen by God.

To choose myself can therefore mean to affirm this connection with the God who paradoxically seems absent. God is unseen and invisible, yet present and seen in a way that does not force but invites me to advance toward my true self and full self-possession. In that self-possession I can be secure that God is mine as well. Not some quid pro quo that I initiate and secure through my own efforts, the presence of God enables and sustains me, precedes and invites me both by nature and by grace.

5. *VISIO* AND *RATIO*

What Nicholas teaches in the early chapters of *De visione Dei* also provides a further lesson, a *manuductio* through the inner demands of *visio* and *ratio*, of human seeing and human thinking. His purpose is to guide us from and through the palpable images of God's presence and "vision" to the intangible reality of God's infinite oneness. Only beyond this point is the object of religious contemplation and mystical vision to be found, beyond the demands and limits of *ratio*, or discursive reason, where *intellectus*, or vision, holds sway.[17]

Nicholas' remark in chapter 6 (quoted above) deserves repetition: "as regards whoever sets out to see Your Face: *as long as he conceives of something*, he is far removed from your face" (h 21, emphasis added). This limitation means we cannot "see God" as an object of rational thought, let alone of normal visual perception. We have used *ratio* to move beyond ordinary *visio* in reflecting on the lessons of the icon. Now we discover that what discursive reason itself "sees" in fact makes known nothing about the divine Face we seek. *Ratio* is mistaken in any hope that mental (or even mystical) sight or insight will eventuate in some rational or conceptual grasp of what God is. We are to move completely beyond conceptual "seeing."

Nicholas summarizes our situation while leading us further:

In all faces the Face of faces is seen in a veiled and symbolic manner. But it is not seen in an unveiled manner as long as the seeker does not enter, above all faces, into a certain secret and hidden silence wherein there is no knowledge or concept of a face. For this obscuring mist, haze, darkness, or ignorance into which the one seeking Your Face enters when he passes beyond all knowledge and conception is that beneath which Your Face can be found only in a veiled manner. Yet the obscuring mist reveals that Your Face is there, above everything beveiling. (6 h 22)

In visual terms the face of God is unveiled or to be seen only where perceptual or rational or intellectual vision cannot occur—in "darkness or ignorance." What human *visio* and *ratio* see or discern merely veils the face of God. The traditional scriptural and Dionysian images of mist and haze and darkness all support Nicholas' point that seeing God's face is not *visio* in any obvious or usual sense. To see God in the fashion of mystical vision is to see that we do not see by *reason* what God is like at all. We must pass "beyond all knowledge and conception," that is, "above everything beveiling." Human revealing conceals the divine. God is revealed in what we count as concealing: darkness and ignorance.

Cusanus has thus employed discursive reason to discriminate a series of meanings for vision. We seek to see God's face in the icon only to "see" ourselves in our divine Original. Once we "see through" both painting and human image, we "see" in darkness that we do *not* see the

---

17. For the ascent from *ratio* to *intellectus*, see K. Yamaki, "Die 'manuductio' von der 'ratio' zur Intuition in *De visione Dei*," *MFCG* 18 (1989): 276–95. Nicholas moves from perceptual seeing to rational "seeing" (thinking) to "intellectual" seeing or vision beyond reason. See also B. H. Helander, *Die visio intellectualis als Erkenntnisweg und -ziel bei Nikolaus Cusanus* (Stockholm: Almqvist & Wiksell, 1988).

divine Face concealed from us and revealed only beyond verbal and conceptual understanding. We move dialectically between discursive thinking and various kinds of sight or insight to discover that our seeing God is hardly *visio* at all.

Why does human vision of God occur only in silence and darkness? Because God's face is seen only symbolically in the icon and in other faces. In fact, we have already noted that the icon symbolizes the simultaneity and inseparability of God's seeing and God's being seen. God's seeing and being seen are at once *in* and *beyond* creatures. Our attempt to hold together in thought that "in" and "beyond" must lead us to the point where ordinary thinking and discourse are frustrated and must be left behind. The silence and darkness stand for this stage in our advance toward seeing God through *intellectus*.

To help us understand reason's impasse, Cusanus turns in chapter 9 to the traditional categories of motion and rest. God is present to both things in motion and things at rest, but God remains free of the limitations entailed by these categories. What is the upshot?

Therefore, You are stationary and You advance, and likewise You are neither stationary nor do You advance. This very point is illustrated for me by this painted face.... If, while I am moving, someone else who is looking at the face remains stationary, then the [face's] gaze does not desert him either but remains stationary with him. However, a Face that is free from these conditions cannot properly be characterized as stationary and as moved; for [such a Face] exists beyond all rest and motion, in the most simple and most absolute Infinity. Indeed, motion and rest and opposition and whatever can be spoken of or conceived are subsequent to this Infinity. (c.9 h 37)

To understand that God is causally responsible for motion and rest as we know them and that God is not just one more thing at rest and in motion leads us at least to paradox, at most to contradiction. For it thereby becomes true to say that God moves and does not move, as well as false to say that God moves and does not move. While God sustains creaturely movement and rest ("neither motion nor rest exists apart from You"; h 37), God is not changeable but remains infinite and apart. When we "describe" God's connection with created things, contradictory judgments become simultaneously valid. The truth of both of these opposed conjunctions (each one of which asserts a contradiction) must be confronted and acknowledged as corresponding to God's reality, even if and just because they baffle ordinary thought and talk. Silence and darkness are symbolic correlates of our mute and blind attempts to see the invisible and unspeakable God.

Cusanus' own words deserve citing at this point:

Hence, I experience the necessity for me to enter into obscuring mist and to admit the coincidence of opposites, beyond all capacity of reason, and to seek truth where impossibility appears. And when—beyond that [rational capacity] and beyond every most lofty intellectual ascent as well—I come to that which is unknown to every intellect and which every intellect judges to be very far removed from the truth, *there* You are present, my God, You who are Absolute Necessity. And the darker and more impossible that obscuring haze of impossibility is known to be, the more truly the Necessity shines forth and the less veiledly it draws near and is present. (h 38)[18]

Here Cusanus joins the experience of darkness, the frustration of *visio*, with that of bafflement or impossibility, the frustration of *ratio*. Both should lead to that learned ignorance that is human knowledge of God, for learned ignorance is the outcome of a search that culminates in accepting and acknowledging what discursive reason finds unreasonable: the *impossibilitas caliginosa*, or true presence, of God signaled by such contradictory statements. What is impossible to us, "beyond all capacity of reason," provides some access for human *intellectus*, intellectual intuition, to the God who cannot be otherwise, whose Infinity must encompass even as it transcends all that *ratio* encounters as impossible.

6. THE WALL OF PARADISE

Both *visio* and *ratio* have come to an impasse as human means of seeing God. At the end of chapter 9 Nicholas proposes another symbol to complement that of the icon. Using imagery that evokes the story of the expulsion from Eden in Genesis 3, he describes God as dwelling in Paradise, walled round by the coincidence of opposites. The wall that blocks our way to seeing is symbolic of the constraints on every sort of human vision.[19] Nicholas writes:

And I have found the abode wherein You dwell unveiledly—an abode surrounded by the coincidence of contradictories. And [this coincidence] is the wall of Paradise, wherein You dwell. The gate of this wall is guarded by a most lofty rational spirit; unless this spirit is vanquished the entrance will not be accessible.

---

18. On the coincidence of opposites, see Chapters 1 and 2, this book. Flasch, in *Nikolaus von Kues*, 439–43, explains how *De visione Dei* extends Nicholas' ideas on this topic.

19. On the symbolism of the wall, see R. Haubst, "Die erkenntnistheoretische und mystische Bedeutung der 'Mauer der Koinzidenz,'" *MFCG* 18 (1989): 167–95; and D. F. Duclow, "Anselm's Proslogion and Nicholas of Cusa's Wall of Paradise," *Downside Review* 100 (1982): 22–30. Historical sources for the wall symbolism are taken up in W. Haug, "Die Mauer des Paradieses. Zur mystica theologia des Nicolaus Cusanus in *De visione Dei*," *Theologische Zeitschrift* 45 (1989): 216–30; P. Casarella, "Neues zu den Quellen der cusanischen Mauersymbolik," *MFCG* 19 (1991): 273–86; and K. Reinhardt, "Islamische Wurzeln der cusanischen Mauersymbolik? Die 'Mauer des Paradieses' im *Liber scalae Mahometi*," *MFCG* 19 (1991): 287–91.

Therefore, on the *other* side of the coincidence of contradictories You can be seen—but not at all on this side. (c.9 h 39)

What is impossible for human *ratio*—direct vision or seeing God—is thus imagined as the wall erected and defended by the limits of human reason itself. This "most lofty rational spirit" *(spiritus altissimus rationis)* relies on the principle of contradiction presupposed for all humanly intelligible discourse. But precisely this principle must be overcome to attain the object of mystical theology in another kind of *visio* beyond the wall, beyond *ratio* itself.

The Cusan image of the wall of Paradise is intriguing, for it encourages us to remember that walls not only separate and keep things on either side distinct. Walls also demarcate the limits or boundaries of what is thus kept apart. Where Genesis told of an angel with a flaming sword assigned to bar any return to Eden, Cusanus has human reason itself guarding the gate to seeing God. The domain of discursive reason, of meaningful human discourse, is here imagined as bounded by what is contradictory. This sort of discourse and the rational vision or insight to which it leads cannot apply to "seeing God." The next several chapters of *De visione Dei* recall the paradoxical lessons gained in taking the icon as symbolic of God seeing and seen. Cusanus refers constantly to the wall as he proposes various ways of attempting to "think through" the coincidence of opposites to move beyond the wall to seeing God.

The oppositions we make and the distinctions we draw between seeing and being seen are matters of *ratio*. In reflecting on the icon, we discovered that these distinctions do not apply to God. In God's simpleness there are no such contrasts or oppositions, just utter oneness. Cusanus imagines that he stands "at the door of the coincidence of opposites" (c.10 h 41; Hopkins 163). He notes further that our distinctions between past and future do not fit the eternal "now" where before and after do not apply but are the same. He writes: "But the wall is the coincidence where *later* coincides with *earlier*, where *end* coincides with *beginning*, where *alpha* and *omega* are the same" (c.10 h 44). And again, "And so to one who approaches unto You, *now* and *then* appear in coincidence in the wall which surrounds the place where You dwell. For *now* and *then* coincide in the circle of the wall of Paradise. But You, my God, who are Absolute Eternity, exist and speak beyond *now* and *then*" (c.10 h 44).

The coincidence of opposites at the imagined wall symbolizes for reason the fact that God's reality is not at all like that of the realities of ordinary experience. The differences we discern among finite things are also reflected in the distinctions we draw in thought and speech. The principle of contradiction governs our thought and language because we grasp determinate finite things as alike and different. Here opposites do not coincide. But the God who is the infinite Source of finite things is both ontologically other than and ontologically prior to those things —and not in the way they differ from or precede one another. In this case opposites appear to coincide. To begin to understand this requires dialectical thinking—a holding together of oppositions that forces us to constantly exchange perspectives as we attempt to grasp to some extent how God is both other than and yet one with created things. The wall where opposites coincide thus forces us to recognize that the principles of identity and contradiction get undercut as our discourse stumbles and stammers before God's unlimited oneness.

In chapters 11 and 12 of *De visione Dei* Cusanus uses position in relation to the wall to distinguish three stages of the mystical quest to see God. These stages illustrate precisely what human *ratio* can and cannot do. Cusanus introduces once more the quasi-technical concepts of "enfolding" and "unfolding" he had first employed in *De docta ignorantia* to capture the connection between God and creatures. In that work he taught that created things "unfold" God's oneness in their multiplicity and otherness, while God's creative power "enfolds" them all as identical with the divine Simpleness.[20] It is clear that *ratio* can understand things enfolded in God as different from things unfolded in creation, an opposition that reflects the distance and difference between created things and divine Reality. At this *first stage* we are outside the wall in ordinary light.

To differentiate things and God is not sufficient, however. The point is that we must also think them together since they are not separate the way one created thing is separate from another. While not God, creatures are only fully understood for all they are in connection with and in dependence on their unfolding Source. This brings us to the *second stage,* at the wall itself. Sometimes Nicholas places us in imagination with Christ at the door or threshold of the entrance in the wall—in his words, at "the door of Your Word and Concept [*ratio*]" (c.11 h 47; cf. h 43). Here we encounter the barrier of the coincidence of opposites— confusion and darkness for ordinary *ratio*. For here unfolding and enfolding are identical; they coincide. At best we can attempt to think both together and to acknowledge that in God creating and being created are one and identical.

Cusanus provides some leads at this point:

And when at one and the same time I go in and out through the door of Your Word and Concept, I find most sweet nourishment. When I find You to be a

---

20. See the comments on Book 2 of *De docta ignorantia* in Chapter 1, this book.

power that unfolds, I go out. When I find You to be a power that both enfolds and unfolds, I both go in and go out. From creatures I go in unto You, who are Creator—go in from the effects unto the Cause. I go out from You, who are Creator—go out from the Cause unto the effects. I both go in and go out when I see that going out is going in and that, likewise, going in is going out.... For creation's going out from You is creation's going in unto You; and unfolding is enfolding. (c.11 h 47)

Cusanus places the *third stage* beyond this wall (the second stage) where we must acknowledge the identity of what ordinary reason finds contradictory. Beyond the wall and within the garden both unfolding and enfolding fall away as either distinct or identical. Nicholas points to the utter transcendence of infinite Oneness, that silent Presence beyond and "free from whatever can be spoken of or thought of" (c.11 h 47).

Chapter 12 reiterates the three stages using both vision and creation as examples to epitomize Cusanus' teaching. The chapter's title underlines the paradoxical nature of what he proposes: "Where the Invisible Is Seen, the Uncreated Is Created" (h 48). There is the uncomplicated sense in which these expressions may mean that God is "visible" in what he creates but invisible in God's self. Likewise, God is uncreated but Creator of other things. Yet Nicholas presses further. He argues that God is both seer and seen in his absolute vision: identically the one who sees, the visible object seen, and the seeing all at once. "In all sight You are seen by every perceiver. You who are invisible, who are free from [*absolutus*] everything visible, and who are superexalted unto infinity are seen in everything visible and in every act of seeing" (h 48).

Regarding creation, God is both created and uncreated: identically the one who creates, the "creatable," and the creating.[21] We are on this side of the wall when we think of the Creator creating, at the wall when we conceive of the Creator as creatable (since everything possible is actual in God). Because we cannot think such distinctions as identical, we have not yet entered the garden beyond the wall of human comprehension. We "only begin to behold ... unveiledly and to enter unto the source of delights" when we recognize God as absolutely and infinitely above all that can be spoken or named, "not creator but infinitely more than creator" (c.12 h 51). Yet even this third stage does not amount to mystical vision but only to our recognizing in awe that God's infinity is transcendent and unknowable to us.

21. Cusanus points out that it seems that being created cannot possibly be the same as being Creator, for *ratio* rightly differentiates the derived from the Underived, and "this would seemingly be to affirm that something exists before it exists." But Nicholas is moving us beyond *ratio* to *intellectus*, that is, to a vision of coincidence in which to say God is created *and* Creator is equivalent to saying that God is everything in every thing and yet nothing of any of them, a formula going back to Dionysius. See K. Kremer, "Gott—in allem alles, in nichts nichts," *MFCG* 17 (1986): 188–219.

Chapter 13 is the center chapter of the twenty-five chapters in *De visione Dei*. Here the movement of the first half of the treatise (and of *ratio*) culminates at what Cusanus imagines as beyond the wall, in the garden where opposites coincide: God's infinity.[22] Here one does not know *what* one sees, only *that* God is not visible or knowable or speakable in any way familiar outside. All names and concepts end at the wall surrounding "the garden of Paradise." The reason is that their senses or meanings cannot apply to a domain where the principle of contradiction is no longer valid and where the divine Reality toward which thought is directed is humanly inconceivable. Divine Infinity is "not approachable, not comprehensible, not nameable, not manifold, and not visible" (c.13 h 52). God thus resides beyond human grasp if not beyond human reach—only in that beyond can we somehow contact or see "God."

But how will he attain unto You, who are the End at which he aims, if he is supposed to ascend beyond [every] end? Does not he who ascends beyond ends enter into what is indeterminate and confused and so, with respect to the intellect, into ignorance and darkness, which are characteristic of intellectual confusion? Therefore, the intellect must become ignorant and must be situated in a shadow if it wishes to see You. But how, my God, is the intellect in ignorance? Is it not with respect to learned ignorance? Therefore, O God, You who are Infinity cannot be approached except by him whose intellect is ignorance—i.e., whose intellect knows that it is ignorant of You. (c.13 h 53)

This is Cusanus' application of "learned ignorance" to the realm of mystical theology. Such "ignorance" amounts to the acquired realization that we do not and cannot see or understand what God is. But our ignorance has also learned that in the darkness beyond *ratio* one's intellect sees (blindly, as it were!) that God transcends the objects of ordinary human seeing and knowing. Darkness or ignorance is the human side of seeking to see God. It is in learning to accept these dialectical limits or constraints on our intellectual condition that we may meet the incomprehensible divine Infinity.

The Cusan schema of stages—outside the wall, at the wall or its entrance, and inside the wall beyond the coincidence of opposites—maps the human quest for mystical vision. That God's infinity is seen to be beyond the limits of *ratio* helps us learn to acknowledge how contrariety confounds human reason and to confront our ignorance of God's nature. Only when discursive reason is set aside can God's gift of "vision" occur, a vision that cannot be conceptualized or verbalized. Later in the treatise Nicholas explains why this is so:

---

22. See W. Beierwaltes, "Deus Oppositio Oppositorum (Nicolaus Cusanus *De visione Dei* XIII)," *Salzburger Jahrbuch für Philosophie* 8 (1964): 175–85.

For the wall is the limit of the power of every intellect, although the eye looks beyond the wall into Paradise. But that which the eye sees, it can neither speak of nor understand. For it is the eye's secret love and hidden treasure, which, having been found, remains hidden. For it is found on the inner side of the wall of the coincidence of the hidden and the manifest. (c.17 h 78)

At this point it seems that Cusanus has brought human vision and reason as far as they can go. Now he turns and uses the very oppositions on which reason's distinctions and connections are founded to exhibit another kind of object—altogether different from those our natures are best fitted to see and understand. To do this he has to employ not so much straightforward discursive reason as dialectical reason. The icon and the wall are symbols that extend our ordinary notions of thinking and seeing in directions calculated to help us deal with God. Indeed, they are themselves preparations for the dialectical thinking of chapters 13 to 16 of *De visione Dei*. Now Cusanus turns to word-play and paradoxical expressions to show how to turn the mind's own conceptions to work as part of the quest for God.

7. THINKING GOD'S INFINITY

The wall around the garden represented the bounds of human reason because it marked symbolically the separation between the finite and the Infinite. If God is incomprehensible just because divine Reality is infinite, God stands as an end or goal unattainable by finite reason or any limited means. Cusanus plays with the ambiguity of the Latin word *finis* in its dual sense of end as goal and end as limit. (Of course, the English "finite" and "infinite" both have *finis* at their root as well.) If the goal of the mystical quest is God, the paradox arises that God is *finis infinitus* (= *finis sine fine*), an end "without an end," a goal that is infinite, a limit that is not limited. As absolute, God is without limit or restriction of any sort. *Ab-solutus* is a synonym for *in-finitus* in Nicholas' vocabulary at this point. This means that God has no goal or end outside God's self. Even in creating other things, God's "goal" is the divine Essence that is identical with God as absolute End. Nothing limits God, yet as ultimate End of all else God sets the limits for all other things *(omnia finiens)*.

Clearly, discursive reason cannot make much sense of an unlimited limit or an end without an end. Cusanus calls our attention to *finis infinitus* precisely to stress the quandary in which human thought finds itself. This paradox seems irresolvable when we attempt to think the infinite God whom we must acknowledge as ultimate Goal, Limit, and Measure of things finite. Indeed, it cannot be resolved straightforwardly, in the ways we can sometimes parse or sort out the oxymorons of ordinary language and typical human experience. Instead, Cusanus will provide an indirect way of confronting and acknowledging the unresolved oppositions reason reaches in the quest for God. If we think dialectically we can position God vis-à-vis creatures and employ productively the very oppositions and contradictions that plague us at the limit of discursive reason. This move will never give us positive insight or a conceptual grasp of the divine Essence in itself. But it does enable us to change perspective and to attempt to think beyond the usual rules of discourse, so to speak, so that we do more justice in our thought to uniqueness of the relation between God and creatures. In the end, we may move to *intellectus*, the intellectual vision that touches God's unlimited oneness.

Nicholas writes: "The oppositeness of opposites is oppositeness without oppositeness, just as the End of finite things is an End without an end" (c.13 h 55, Hopkins). He thus identifies the infinite God with this "oppositeness of opposites." What he is doing is attempting to help us to think God's transcendence *and* God's immanence together, starting from the fact that the ordinary things of our experience are separate and distinct, that their qualities and properties are often opposed or mutually exclusive contraries or contradictories. His designation of God as the Oppositeness of such opposites is supposed to move us from the fact that created things and their features are opposed to what is ontologically responsible for there being such oppositions or oppositeness at all. God is distinct from opposites or contraries, but only in a way that establishes the reality of their being opposed or contrary. In this sense God is the Oppositeness of opposites. But at the same time God's oppositeness is "without oppositeness" just because God's distinctiveness stands in infinity beyond categorical opposites no less than God's being an End places God beyond all ordinary ends or limits. God's oppositeness in fact encompasses or enfolds all opposites in God's self as nothing other than God and encompasses or unfolds all opposites in creation by constituting them what they are.

Here Nicholas has left behind visible and imaginable symbols to remain within the oxymorons of paradoxical language: *finis finitorum sine fine* and *oppositio oppositorum sine oppositione*. The incongruities in the linguistic expressions he employs are designed to liberate our thinking and talking from their usual discursive competence in dealing with the finite things of normal human experience. Paradoxical language has us join at least two contrary cognitive perspectives. We are to think together *both* the way finite opposites are opposed *and* the transcendent Oppositeness that is "opposed" to those opposites, not as they are to one another, but in such a way as to be ontologically responsible for that initial opposition. What keeps the divine *oppositio* itself free from otherness or opposition is precisely its infinity. In Nicholas' words, "Absolute Infinity includes and encompasses all things" (c.13 h 56).

It is of course possible to read Nicholas' subsequent remarks about God's infinity as simply declaring, insofar as human thought and expression are able, the status of all things when they are enfolded in God—their status as identical with the transcendent Fullness of Being. But the real challenge comes in thinking together finite things as created and their unlimited divine Source and Measure. Cusanus is stretching language here to help us understand how God's infinity cannot be named, measured, quantified, or compared with anything finite. All this is involved in divine Transcendence.

Yet Cusanus next proposes that we are not understanding divine Transcendence appropriately if we do not recognize and acknowledge that God's incomparability means that God is also *measure* and *equality* of all else. This equality is unique and exact, because it does not admit of degrees of more or less. God's infinite equality "is not more nearly equal to one thing than to another but is equal to one thing in such way that it is equal to all—and is equal to all in such way that it is equal to none" (c.13 h 57).[23] It is precisely as transcendent infinity that the divine Equality measures all things ("equal to all") without contraction or limitation to their finite measurements ("not more nearly equal to one thing than to another" = "equal to none").

Chapter 14 takes up explicitly the challenge of attempting to think through and articulate how God encompasses or enfolds all things. Nicholas begins with a series of denials about *alteritas*, "otherness." First, nothing in God is other than God, that is, what is enfolded in God is identical with God's infinity. Next, there is no otherness in God whatsoever, even though God is distinct from the creatures that depend on God. Third, what we conceptualize as "otherness" does not exist in itself. Otherness is nothing positive, ontologically speaking. It is merely our attempt to formulate in abstract cognitive terms our recognition that one finite thing is *not* a second finite thing and thus is "other than" the second.[24]

But what accounts for the general state of affairs we recognize among finite entities, namely, their difference and separateness from one another? In fact, Cusanus does not answer that question, but takes multiplicity as a brute fact about creation. Here Cusanus merely reminds us that, while finite things are connected with and related to the divine In-

23. Cf. the remarks in Chapter 3, this book, about equality as "naming" the second person of the Trinity.
24. Recall Cusanus' thematic use of "otherness" in *De coniecturis* (Chapter 2, this book) and in *De li non aliud* (Chapter 5, this book).

finity which encompasses all that is real, they stand as encompassed, not as encompassing. Only the absolutely infinite being of God, God's uncontracted being, is related to finite beings as the absolute Form of being is connected to the contracted forms of creatures.

Nicholas pursues a quasi-Aristotelian analogy to spell out the meaning of this relationship. He cites the Aristotelian Scholastics' dictum about the substantial form that constitutes a thing's essential nature: *"Forma dat esse"* (Form gives being; c.14 h 63). The relationship of God to creatures, then, is similar to that of Socrates' one nature or essence or form to the multiple forms of the organic parts of Socrates: his head, his hands, and so on. The idea is that the simple oneness of Socratic form encompasses all the formed parts and thus makes them Socrates' head and hands, not someone else's. Yet neither head nor hands encompass the whole of Socrates' nature or form or essential being; rather, the parts are encompassed and given their own subordinate formal character by the nature or essential form. One part is not another part because no one of them is the substantial form of Socrates as a whole.

Aristotle saw the essential form of a whole being as the ordering principle of the formed parts or organs of a natural substance. The parts' structure and organization and activities were manifestations of the form that made that substance the kind of thing it was and that gave it power to become a mature specimen of its type. All the varied organs and organic systems were subordinate to the ordering power of substantial form or nature. The latter constituted them an organized and unified whole. Now all this happened, of course, within the confines of a single limited being or substance. But it may give an inkling of why Cusanus calls the infinite God the unlimited Limit or Measure of all things and the utterly unified Power that enfolds everything in omnipotence. Within the whole that is the created universe, creation (the divine Encompassing) results in the empowering of the limited beings as real in their own right through their own forms, but as ever connected to God, the Form of forms, apart from whom they have no being at all.

In chapter 15 Nicholas returns to the icon, for it was in the icon's gaze that he found this treatise's basic metaphor for connecting two levels of reality. The abstruse considerations of the preceding chapters may well have kept the connection between God and creatures somewhat obscure. Recalling that the all-seeing portrait can apparently look on any viewer whomsoever, Nicholas sees in this an image of God's infinity, at least in the sense that the painted eyes are unlimited in being able to gaze (apparently) upon everyone who concurrently views the icon.

While this reminds Nicholas first of all of the way Aristotelian matter is open to any form, he is quick to distinguish the "unlimited" possibilities of matter to be determined by form in finite substances from the infinite possibilities that are actual in God's infinite oneness. Aristotelian "prime matter," after all, is open to determination by only one finite form at a time, while in God all possibilities are simultaneously actual, not limited to the successive possibilities of contracted (because created) prime matter. Nicholas' prayer here acknowledges that in God actuality and possibility are absolute, free from all limitation or contraction: "Therefore, in You my God absolute possibility-to-be and absolute actual being are only You my Infinite God" (c.15 h 66).

Cusanus then explains how the icon might mislead a viewer into comparing God to formable prime matter. Such a mistake rests on the misconception that the gaze of the icon is dependent on the viewer's looking, as if the viewer were giving "form" or determination to the "matter," namely, the icon's apparent capacity to see. The view of perception Cusanus was familiar with understood sight to be engaged by actual colors within the perceptual field. It was the colored objects whose visible forms, or *species*, determined what the viewer could see. In a parallel way, the viewers of the icon determine whose actual eyes it would apparently contact. But in fact this is "inside out" when it comes to seeing God—it is God's causative seeing that determines or bestows being on the person who seeks to see God.

It is as if God's face were a mirror, which provides not a reflection of the usual face I see when I now look in an ordinary mirror, but that perfect original of my face I could recognize though never anticipate. The reason for this is that what I see when I see God's face is the Paradigm or Original of every face and every form. Cusanus metaphorically terms God's face "a living Mirror-of-eternity" (*speculum aeternitatis vivum*), "the Form of forms." He continues:

When someone looks into this Mirror, he sees his own form in the Form of forms, which the Mirror is.[25] And he judges the form seen in the Mirror to be the image of his own form, because such would be the case with regard to a polished material mirror. However, the contrary thereof is true, because in the Mirror of eternity that which he sees is not an image but is the Truth, of which the beholder is the image. (c.15 h 67)

Cusanus proceeds to offer another visual metaphor to explain just how the icon lets us understand God's real priority as exemplar even though the icon's sight seems to be dependent on our look. The real priority that is ours with the painted icon is only apparent when it comes to understanding our relationship to God. In this way the icon's gaze

---

25. Notice that this use of mirror imagery has a different point than the use of such imagery in *De docta ignorantia* 2.2 and in *Idiota de mente* 5. See the comments in Chapters 1 and 3, this book.

seems to shadow our own looking and to change as we change, as if God were but our shadow. Yet in fact it is God's reality that is really solid *(veritas)* and ours that is but shadow. Or to put it in dynamic terms perhaps more adequate to what is really the case, God is shadow in such a way that God is Truth and image in such a way that God is Exemplar.

Nicholas is proposing that we have to hold together in thought that our human faces are really created faces *and* are at once images of the face of God, absolute Truth. Indeed, the human face is only authentically a created face because it is the image of the Creator. *"Quantum imago intantum verum"* (My face is true insofar as it is an image), Nicholas writes (c.15 h 69). If this idea makes sense, we may advance to the further insight that not unlike the icon, God changes with our changing and yet remains unchanged. Indeed, it is God's unchanging regard that sustains the changes in creatures. "Just as Your Face does not desert the truth of my face, so also it does not follow the changing of the changeable image" (c.15 h 69). God's face and gaze sustain my changing face and viewing while remaining unchanged. Without God's reality my face and sight come to nothing. This reflection on what we might discover were we to view God's face should prevent our constricting Divinity to what we find of ourselves in God. We look through the icon toward God's face with the realization that there mirror image, original, and even mirror are each and all identical in the eternal One who is ultimate Origin and true Source of what gets reflected in both painted portrait and its living human viewer.

At this point toward the end of chapter 15, Cusanus remarks how what he has said manifests God's love and goodness in drawing us to himself. His prayerful remarks now stress the affective side of both God's attracting and human responding:

And in You, O God, being created coincides with creating. For the likeness which seems to be created by me is the Truth which creates me, so that in this way, at least, I apprehend how closely I ought to be bound to You, since, in You, being loved coincides with loving. For if in You who are my likeness I ought to love myself, then I am exceedingly bound to do so when I see that You love me as Your creature and image. How can a father not love a son who is son in such way that he is a father? . . . For You are love that enfolds both filial and paternal love. (h 70)

This passage is typical of much that follows in the second half of *De visione Dei*. Nicholas will first move to the revealed mystery of the Trinity and dwell at greater length on the Incarnation. While this turn marks a change from the more abstruse considerations that have just preceded, it is more than appropriate. No human words or concepts or analogies enable us to touch or grasp or understand even partially what God is—

both icon and wall symbols let us see the impotence of reason and the cognitive impasse for the human mind in search of a God who abides always beyond. But Nicholas is also aware that God has provided help for our frustrated minds and yearning hearts by revealing the Trinity of loving divine Persons and manifesting in Jesus what is beyond our ken. Here we may find a Mediator who can help us "see" and be united with the loving God we desire but cannot fathom.

8. LOVE DIVINE: TRINITY AND INCARNATION

What is problematic for the person who is seeking God is that human knowledge and desire always outrun their putative temporal and limited fulfillments. Cusanus writes:

> My desire, wherein You shine forth, leads me to You, because it casts aside all finite and comprehensible things. For in these things it cannot find rest; for it is led unto You by You Yourself. But You are Beginning without a beginning and End without an end. Therefore, my desire is led by the Eternal Beginning—from which it has the fact that it is desire—unto the End without an end. And this End is infinite. (c.16 h 73)

For Nicholas, the paradoxical fact is that God is the known unknown, known to be infinite and thereby beyond our intellectual grasp. God gifts us with God's own self, yet we never comprehend what we are privileged to possess—"led by the Eternal Beginning—from which it has the fact that it is desire—unto the End without an end." As infinite and thus without limit, God is a fitting End for our unlimited desire to know. This is true even though, as Nicholas puts it, "only that which it understands by not understanding" (c.16 h 74) will fully satisfy the human intellect. The reason is that "the intellect can be fully satisfied only by an intelligible object which it knows to be so intelligible that this object can never fully be understood" (c.16 h 74).

In this light, the mystery of God as one and three confirms and extends what "can never be fully understood." In chapters 17 and 18 Nicholas takes up what faith knows is to be seen beyond the wall and recalls that authentic human fulfillment *(felicitas)* will consist in knowing and loving the God who is three in one. Borrowing from Augustine's *De Trinitate* and against the background of his own earlier *De docta ignorantia*, Cusanus construes the divine Trinity as lover, lovable, and the bond or union between them.[26] *Posse amare, posse amari, amoris nexus* and *amor*

---

26. Augustine, *De Trinitate* 8.14.10; cf. *De doctrina Christiana* 1.5.12; *De docta ignorantia* 1.7–10 (h 18–29). I am also indebted to an unpublished paper by B. McGinn, "Unitrinum seu Triunum: Nicholas of Cusa and Medieval Trinitarian Mysticism"; see 24–25 and notes 96–103.

amans, amor amabilis, amoris amantis et amabilis nexus—this is the language in which we attempt to see the threeness in the one infinite Love who is God. All limits fall away and lover, lovable, and their union are one and the same divine Essence. But seeing here remains not-seeing in any sense we find familiar, just as God's love goes beyond our ordinary experience of love, at best a pale semblance of divine Love.

Nicholas returns at this point to the wall and the garden metaphors. He also invokes Jesus' remark (Mt 13.44) about the kingdom of heaven being a hidden treasure, as he attempts to describe triune love without falsifying it:

> For when I see that the Loving is not the Lovable and that the Union is neither the Loving nor the Lovable, then it is not in the following manner that I see the Loving not to be the Lovable: viz., as if the Loving were one thing and the Lovable another thing. Rather, I see that the distinction between the Loving and the Lovable occurs on the inner side of the wall of the coincidence of oneness and otherness. Hence, this distinction—which is inside the wall of coincidence, where the distinct and the indistinct coincide—precedes all comprehensible otherness and diversity. For the wall is the limit of the power of every intellect, although the eye looks beyond the wall into Paradise. But that which the eye sees, it can neither speak of nor understand. For it is the eye's secret love and hidden treasure, which, having been found, remains hidden. For it is found on the inner side of the wall of the coincidence of the hidden and the manifest. (c.17 h 78)

"Secret love" and "hidden treasure" remind us again that God's reality as triune transcends numbers and counting, lovers and loving, indeed, "all comprehensible otherness and diversity." What lies beyond the wall remains incomprehensible in human terms of any sort. Yet Cusanus places these reminders between chapters on human desire (c.16) and human happiness (c.18). Our unlimited desires can only be satisfied by the infinite Trinity. That same triune God is our fulfilling happiness just because God draws us to God's self as triune Love. The human effort to know or see God and to love God is borne, on our side, by the desires to know and love that nothing finite can satisfy. Only in the infinite triune Love who has first loved us will those desires be fulfilled and happiness be attained.

Cusanus' attempt to briefly describe God as Trinity in chapter 17 is thus related directly to human seeking for the vision of God in chapter 18. The triune God is not just loving and lovable and the bond between them, but also understanding intellect, understandable intellect, and the union of both. That is why human minds and wills can reach happiness in vision and union with God.[27] "For he who receives You, who are God and are rational, receivable Light, can arrive at such a close union

---

27. McGinn, in "Unitrinum seu Trinium," notes 98, 102, points out that chapter 17 stresses various sorts of "seeing," while chapter 18 turns to union (the equivalent of

with You that he will be united to You as a son to his father" (c.18 h 82). Here Cusanus returns to the theme of *filiatio*, to which he had in 1445 devoted a whole treatise *(De filiatione Dei)*. There Nicholas had first articulated one of the senses of "seeing God" as sonship or "deification" *(deificatio)*.[28] Now he explains how *deificatio* or *theosis* beyond this life amounts to the ultimate vision and union with God and represents the fulfillment of the sonship that begins on earth with religious faith.[29] *De filiatione Dei* stressed the point with which he now ends chapter 18: it is only through the perfect sonship of God the Son that every other human being can attain sonship or union with God.

The final six chapters of *De visione Dei* continue this focus on the place of Jesus Christ, God the Son, as enfolding all that is created and as mediating human vision and union with the triune God.[30] It is plausible to imagine Nicholas praying, reflecting, and writing these chapters in front of an all-seeing image of Jesus, perhaps the one he sent to the Tegernsee monks. Because these final chapters are written as personal prayer, they breathe with Nicholas' own response in faith and love to the wonder of the person who is both God and man. Jesus' place as "absolute medium" or "absolute mediator" marks the divine response to our passion for the infinite, transcendent God who remains always beyond, always frustrating to human reason.

In chapter 19 Nicholas returns to ideas he first articulated in Book 3 of *De docta ignorantia* about the Incarnation and Jesus Christ as the mediator. Here he couches his view in the Gospel terms of "son of man" and "son of God." These are the two ways in which God the Son is mediator. As divine Logos, the Word or Concept of the Father, the Son enfolds all created things, and thus mediates between the Trinity and creation (= son of God). In assuming human nature in Jesus, God the Son unites humanity to the Trinity (= son of man). As Nicholas puts it,

I see then, my God, that Your Son is the uniting Medium of all things, so that all things may find rest in You by the medium of Your Son. And I see that Blessed

---

filiatio) and adopts the traditional motif of the soul as God's betrothed, a motif infrequent in Cusanus' works.

28. See Hopkins, *Dialectical Mysticism*, 25–28.

29. In *De filiatione Dei* 1 h 54, Nicholas writes:

Therefore, when we are free from this world, we will have been freed also from these bedarkening modes [restrictions on human knowing]. As a result, our intellect, having been freed from these restricting modes, will obtain (by means of its intellectual light) the divine life as its happiness. By means of that life the intellect will be elevated— though without the contracted bedarkening images of the sensible world—unto an intuition of truth. (translation by Hopkins, *Miscellany*, 160–61)

30. For detailed discussion of these chapters, see K. Reinhardt, "Christus, die 'Absolute Mitte' als der Mittler zur Gotteskindschaft," *MFCG* 18 (1989): 196–220.

Jesus, the son of man, was most closely united to Your Son and that only by the mediation of Your Son, who is Absolute Mediator, could the son of man be united to You who are God the Father. (c.19 h 86)

If the Absolute Mediator is God the Son and the human nature of Christ is united to the divine Nature, then the son of God and the son of man are inseparably one and the same Being. For this reason we cannot understand the Father except in and through the Son. Such understanding is equivalent to union with the triune God through the human nature of Christ that is immediately united to the Son, the absolute uniting Medium or Mediator.[31] Nicholas concludes:

Hence, You are rightly called *Son of God and of man*, since in You nothing mediates between son of man and Son of God. In Absolute Sonship, which the Son of God is, all sonship is enfolded; and to Absolute Sonship Your human sonship, O Jesus, is supremely united. Therefore, Your human sonship exists in the divine Sonship not only in an enfolded manner but also as the attracted in the attracting, the united in the uniting, and the substantified in the substantifying [*substantiatum in substantiante*]. Therefore, in you, O Jesus, separation of the son of man from the Son of God is not possible. (c.19 h 87)

Chapter 20 continues to explain in Cusan terms the union of divine and human natures in Jesus. Nicholas distinguishes the hypostatic union from the union between the divine Persons, noting that there is identity of nature in the Trinity, while the union of natures in Jesus does not make Christ's humanity identical with Christ's divinity. Instead, he terms this unity the greatest possible for a finite nature that is "attracted" or drawn into union with the infinite, divine Nature. Nicholas concludes:

In the attracted finite nature I see the attracting infinite nature. In the Absolute Son I see the Absolute Father, for a son cannot be seen as son unless the father is seen. In You, Jesus, I see the Divine Sonship, which is the Truth of all sonship; and, likewise, [I see] the closest human sonship, which is the closest image of Absolute Sonship. (c.20 h 89)

Here again we see the play on vision and image. Nicholas may be looking at the icon, the image of the historical Jesus. But Jesus is also now seen with the eyes of faith and understood by the mind of the believer. And thus Nicholas can move through the human nature as image to the divine Son or exemplar Sonship united to it, thus "viewing" and

---

31. The Latin term *medium* that Cusanus here applies to Christ is more than a synonym for Christ's role as intermediary or mediator. It also refers to the Son's status as middle person of the Trinity (cf. the triad *principium, medium, finis*—used in *De filiatione Dei* 4 h 76–77). *Medium* also suggests the center point of a circle to which all the radii are drawn and thus the way the Son enfolds all of the creation. *Medium* may also refer to the means to an end and thus to Christ's "mediating" role as savior and redeemer. Cf. Reinhardt, "Christus, die 'absolute Mitte,'" 201.

understanding Jesus as both image and truth of all sonship and thus image of the Father as well.[32] The dialectic of vision and understanding invoked early in the treatise to explain "the vision of God" returns at this point to help us "see" anew the union of human and divine in Jesus. Through this same seeing or understanding we are led, from and through Jesus, the most perfect human likeness, to the original, the divine Son, and the mystery in which it exists.

At the end of chapter 20 Nicholas returns to the "wall of Paradise" he had earlier employed. In chapter 11 Nicholas had plausibly identified the door in the wall with the divine Word. Now he recognizes that the incomprehensible union of human and Divine, of image and true Exemplar, implies that Jesus is "on the inner side of the wall of Paradise" and "cannot possibly be seen on this side of the wall." The reason given is that Jesus' "intellect is both truth and image" (c.20 h 91).

While this reason may seem puzzling, in fact Christ's knowledge parallels in its own way the mystery of his being. Just as his human nature is most perfect likeness or image of the Divine in human form, so his human understanding is the perfect human likeness of all things. As his divine nature is the truth of the Divine, so his divine understanding is the Cause or absolute Idea of everything as real and created. And thus the knowledge of both Jesus' divine Mind and Jesus' human mind are united as Truth and image, Cause and reflected image, of all that is knowable. That the *how* of this union of Absolute and contracted, of Truth and image, is beyond our understanding is dramatized concretely by placing the incarnate Son "on the inner side of the wall of Paradise" *(intra murum paradisi).*

Chapter 21 continues the theme of what is behind the wall of Paradise. Even though the wise of this world will not approach a domain so filled with contradiction, in fact it is here that believers will discover true happiness, for they will eat of the fruit of the Tree of Life in Paradise. That Tree of Life is none other than Jesus—Creator and creature, attracting and attracted, infinite and finite—more than a locus or coincidence of contradictions, as it were, because also nourishment for the spirit. And this nourishment leads to the vision marking human fulfillment and happiness. Nicholas says:

Therefore, to see the God the Father and You who are Jesus, His Son, is to be present in Paradise and in everlasting glory. For if any man is situated outside of Paradise, he cannot have such a vision, since neither God the Father nor You, Jesus, dwell outside of Paradise. (c.21 h 93)

32. Reinhardt calls attention to Cusanus' attribution of a twofold sonship to Jesus (based on the Gospel titles "son of man" and "son of God"); see "Christus, die 'absolute Mitte,'" 209–10.

How does this intellectual vision lead to union? As the Father draws the Son to himself in the infinite unity of the Trinity, so the divine Son draws the human nature of Jesus into the hypostatic union, and so the humanity of Jesus draws all human beings into union with himself, our true though paradoxical happiness. Just as the nature of Christ and the nature of his knowledge are paradoxical and contradictory, with the consequence that we must think them dialectically, so too Cusanus is proposing that true happiness for human beings is paradoxical, a lesser "coincidence of opposites." We must acknowledge that human happiness brings together finite and Infinite, for once blessed we are privileged to see the invisible God, to apprehend the incomprehensible, and to be united to the deathless One who is inaccessible and "ununitable" *(inunibilis)*. All this is ours because we are united in Jesus to the infinite God.

Cusanus opened this chapter by referring to the contradictions in the Incarnation that one sort of wisdom eschews. He closes it by returning again to the contradictions human happiness entails. Whereas contradiction Incarnate kept away the "wise of this world," that same Jesus Christ discloses to those who believe the sole human terms in which to characterize the divine Object of faith and the real Locus and Source of human happiness.

Nicholas then returns to the icon and his central theme of "the vision of God" in order to work out some of its implications in the case of "the vision of Jesus." In chapter 22 the various meanings of human sensory and nonsensory vision visited earlier in *De visione Dei* are invoked once more. Not only did Jesus have perfect human vision when he engaged in visual perception, but he "saw" into the meaning of visible things and perceptible human faces and behavior with a discernment and sensitivity far beyond normal human insight.

During his life on earth, Christ could and did judge the hearts and minds of his contemporaries in an amazing and wondrous way. For Cusanus, this perfect human vision in its various senses was based on the union of Jesus' human capacities of sight with that absolute, infinite Vision characteristic of the divine Word. Absolute Sight, after all, penetrates the substance and quiddity of things as their Creator, while finite seeing has to be content with visible appearances. Jesus' human vision exists in and is encompassed by the absolute Power of seeing that is divine "vision." Moreover, human intellectual "seeing" or understanding depends on images and sensation, that is, on the body.

Nicholas concludes:

Consequently the power of the human intellect is contracted and small and is in need of the aforementioned things. But the divine intellect is Necessity itself and does not depend on or need anything. Instead, all else needs it and cannot exist without it. (c.22 h 97)

The perfection of Jesus' human powers in their hierarchical array from sense through reason to intellect means that the divine Word is received in the highest point of Jesus' perfect human intellect. Even though the human intellect's light illumines all the cognitive powers below it, in this uniting of human and divine natures Jesus' human intellect stands in comparison to his divine intellect as a candle's light joined to the sun's light. Cusanus gives the reason, "for the Word of God illumines the intellect" (c.22 h 99).

Chapter 23 opens with Cusanus "seeing" Jesus on the inner side of the wall once more. Intuitive vision, or *intellectus*, has here gone beyond a straightforward viewing of the icon, for Nicholas recaps his main theses about the union of human and divine natures. First, he points out that this union is not merely a composition, since there is no way of fitting finite to Infinite or vice versa—they are disproportionate in the strictest sense. Second, there is no identity between them such that created nature becomes divine Creator, even in the way that an image is united with its truth. Nor is divine nature changed into human nature since it stands beyond change of any sort. Third, Christ is not the uniting medium who brings together divine and human natures, as if he were some third thing participating in both. Such a view would make Jesus neither divine nor human. Rather Jesus is one Person *"super omnem intellectum"* (beyond all understanding; c.23 h 101). In him there is a particular Cusan coincidence of human and divine, beyond *ratio*, yet available to and transcending intellect.

The key parallel Nicholas uses to attempt some understanding of this union of divine and human natures comes from the way human beings are bodily or sensory natures and thus vulnerable to death, even though human bodiliness is united to and encompassed by human intellectual nature, which is undying. The intellectual nature functions to animate or enliven the sensory powers, no less than the rational and sensory powers of discrimination and attention accompany seeing so that it is human perceiving, not just a passive gaze, that receives but does not register what is seen. The background picture here is rather that of Neoplatonic emanation of lower from higher reality than of Aristotelian composition of form and matter. As a consequence, when Jesus died, the divinity was not withdrawn, even from the body of Jesus; rather Jesus' intellective soul ceased to exercise its power of animating his body until the point when Christ rose from the dead. This was a separation only in a qualified sense.

Reflecting on the nature of Jesus' body and soul leads Nicholas to reflect in chapter 24 on the temporal development of human beings. Speaking biographically and developmentally, human persons move gradually from sensation into reason and intellection, and finally to the full possession of their inner lives and selves without ever forsaking the bodily and sensory-imaginative basis on which human understanding depends.[33] But there is another source of the perfection of intellect apart from the stimulus of the sensible world. This is the influence of the divine Word to which the intellect is subjected by religious faith. And the perfecting one receives from the Word of God leads to a conformity and similarity to that Word as one responds in faith and love to the light and teaching of Christ.

> Through faith the intellect approaches unto the Word; through love it is united therewith. The closer the intellect approaches, the more it is increased in power, and the more it loves [the Word], the more it is fashioned in the Word's light. But the Word of God is within the intellect, which need not search outside itself. For it will find the Word within, and it will be able to approach the Word by faith. (c.24 h 109)

It is only fitting, then, that Cusanus close the chapter thanking and praising Jesus for this teaching.

The final chapter of *De visione Dei* turns to the work of the Holy Spirit in governing and directing and bestowing gifts on created intellectual spirits. While these spirits unfold the likeness of God's infinite power in many different ways, they are surpassed by Jesus, the ultimate likeness of God, to whom they too become likened. Nicholas admonishes himself not to hold back from the God who is drawing him, given that the created world, the Bible, the administering spirits, and, most of all, Jesus are leading him to the knowledge and love of the One who is the infinite Good. "Draw me, O Lord," he prays as he concludes, "because no one can come unto You unless he be drawn by You. [Draw me] so that, being drawn I may be freed from this world and be joined unto You, the Absolute God, in an eternity of glorious life. Amen" (c.25 h 114)

---

33. This is not to deny, as H. L. Bond reminded me in private communication, that adult human knowing may well work in the opposite direction, insofar as intellectual contemplation, in his words, "filters its way down into the rest of a human life."

5

Not Other Than Divine
De li non aliud (1461)

De li non aliud (*On the Not Other;* 1461) is arguably the most original work Nicholas of Cusa composed.[1] In it he proposes "not other" as a symbolic name or description for God, one he calculates will lead us best toward the nameless mystery that transcends all our attempts to name or capture it in discursive thought. Drawn from the Neoplatonic tradition—Pseudo-Dionysius, Eriugena, and especially from reflections on Plato's *Parmenides*[2]—this apparently odd way of characterizing Divinity enables our thinking together God's transcendence and immanence. No less than Cusanus' earlier thought experiments using geometry or

---

1. Nicholas uses *"li"* (= "the") with *"non aliud"* to show that *"non aliud"* is to be taken as a noun expression. See J. Hopkins, *Nicholas of Cusa on God as Not-Other: A Translation and an Appraisal of "De li non aliud,"* 3rd ed. (Minneapolis, Minn.: Banning Press, 1999), 23–25. See also Nikolaus von Kues, *Vom Nichtanderen,* trans. P. Wilpert (Hamburg: Meiner, 1976); G. Schneider, *Gott, das Nichtandere* (Münster: Aschendorff, 1970); and P. Bolberitz, *Philosophischer Gottesbegriff bei Nikolaus Cusanus in seinem Werk: "De non aliud"* (Leipzig: St.-Benno Verlag, 1989). Other relevant essays include J. Stallmach, "Das 'Nichtandere' als Begriff des Absoluten," in *Universitas: Festschrift für Bischof Dr. Albert Stohr,* 2 vols. (Mainz: M. Grünwald, 1960), 1:329–35; D. Pätzold, *Einheit und Andersheit: Die Bedeutung kategorialer Neubildungen in der Philosophie des Nicolaus Cusanus* (Cologne: Pahl-Rugenstein, 1981); R. Scharlemann, "God as Not-Other: Nicholas of Cusa's *De li Non Aliud,*" in *Naming God,* ed. R. Scharlemann (New York: Paragon House, 1985), 116–32; B. Hojsisch, "Die Andersheit Gottes als Koinzidenz, Negation and Nicht-Andersheit bei Nikolaus von Kues: Explikation und Kritik," *Documenti e studi sulla tradizione filosofica medievale* 7 (1996): 437–54; and G. von Bredow, "Gott der Nichtandere—Erwägungen zur Interpretation der cusanischen Philosophie," in *Im Gespräch,* 51–59.

2. E. Wyller's essays have been particularly enlightening on the connection with Plato's *Parmenides:* "Zum Begriff 'Non Aliud' bei Cusanus," in *Nicolò Cusano agli Inizi del Mondo Moderno* (Florence: Sansoni, 1970), 419–43; "Nicolaus Cusanus' *De non aliud* und Platons Dialog *Parmenides*. Ein Beitrag zur Beleuchtung des Renaissanceplatonismus," in *Studia Platonica: Festschrift für Hermann Gundert,* ed. K. Döring and W. Kullmann (Amsterdam: Gruner, 1974), 239–51; and "Henologie als philosophische Diziplin heute," *MFCG* 13 (1978): 422–32. The first two essays are now reprinted with other material on Cusanus in Wyller's *Henologische Perspektiven I/I–II: Platon—Johannes—Cusanus* (Amsterdam: Rodopi B.V., 1995), 489–593.

the all-seeing portrait, once we think through the meaning, presuppositions, and implications of "not other," we are led to discover how this symbolic phrase can explain and explore Cusanus' view of God's transcendence and God's relation to creation. This enigmatic Cusan verbal symbol for God has its own ironic or self-undercutting dimension, because Nicholas continually insists we move beyond whatever understanding we achieve toward the ineffable One who is our mysterious Goal and Source.

Nicholas discusses the Not Other with a series of three interlocutors. Together they engage in a somewhat rambling conversation where what cannot be spelled out entirely may be at least adumbrated or pointed to in speech. Cusanus first discusses with Ferdinand, his personal doctor, how the Not Other makes good sense when applied to Divinity (cc.1–5). Then he turns to reenvision God's relation to created things by exploring how the divine Not Other relates to finite "others" (cc.6–13). Just after he begins the second half of the dialogue, Cusanus presents a list of quotes from Pseudo-Dionysius' works that he believes are relevant to their conversation; then he comments on them (cc.14–17). He and Ferdinand discuss the various ways in which Aristotelian discourse is inadequate to what the Not Other is designed to express (cc.18–19). Then Nicholas takes up Proclus' insights with Peter Balbus (cc.20–21). The dialogue closes with Nicholas and Abbot John Andrea commenting on a series of topics relevant to the Not Other (cc.22–24). An Appendix to the dialogue presents a set of summary propositions about the Not Other.[3]

1. DEFINITION AND NOT OTHER

"What first of all makes us know?" Cusanus asks as the dialogue begins: *"Quid est quod nos apprime facit scire?"* (c.1 h 3).[4] "Definition" is the answer Ferdinand gives and Nicholas approves. If this seems an odd opening question, the opening conversation becomes stranger still. Several interchanges lead to agreement that a definition is a matter of speech or thought *(oratio seu ratio)*. Definition itself is explained circularly ("from defining, because it defines everything"), and then turns out to be self-referential and to include itself as self-defining. Even though questions are posed and answers approved as obvious, so much is elided

---

3. Wilpert, in *Vom Nichtanderen*, xx–xxvii, provides further information about the three interlocutors and their roles representing Aristotelian (Ferdinand) and Neoplatonic (Peter and Abbot John) outlooks. See also Flasch, *Nikolaus von Kues*, 553–58, for a placing of this work in its context both in Nicholas' thought and in Renaissance Rome.
4. All translations from the Latin are my own.

that we well may agree with Ferdinand's puzzlement when he remarks, "I do not see what 'it' is" (c.1 h 3). (That is, "it" as both the particular definition in question and the point of the conversation so far!)

Nor are we really enlightened much when the cardinal repeats what he had already said, "the definition that defines everything is not other than the thing defined," and then calls our attention to the words "not other." Paying attention to the "not other" is supposedly the way to identify just what "it," namely, "the definition that defines everything," is. Then what is the "thing defined"—or the context and purpose for such a "definition"?

In this way Cusanus begins the dialogue by presupposing the epistemic value of definition and by at once extending its meaning so that *definienda* include a concept like "definition" and an expression such as "not other." Cusanus moves quickly to tell us that "not other" is exactly what defines itself and everything else and that "not other" is defined as "not other than not other." Somehow what seemed a comparative verbal expression equivalent to expressions such as "nothing else than" or "the same as" is supposed to lead to our understanding more than words or usage.

What is to be made of all this, indeed, of any of it? It sounds perfectly vague and general, not to mention tautological. Dismissing it as fatuous or specious is a temptation hard to resist at this juncture, but unless we resist this thought Cusanus cannot take us further.[5] There is a serious playfulness here in which "definition" becomes itself enigmatic and its various related meanings call for exploring and explaining. Suppose that there is a context in which such a definition of "not other" might make sense. Suppose further that what seemed like a comparative phrase could also function as a pronoun or even a substantive. Suppose that the tautological definition of "not other" (that is, "not other than not other") is itself paradoxical, a riddle worth entertaining. Then we might proceed as follows: First, recall the ontological presuppositions of the common medieval theory of definitions modeled on Aristotelian definition via genus and specific difference. Second, ask how these presuppositions are at work (or not) in Cusanus' definition of "not other." Finally, see how they must be revised to do justice to the insight, if there

---

5. Thus the appropriateness of the first two words of the fuller title found in the manuscript copy of this dialogue: "*Directio speculantis seu de non aliud.*" See Wilpert, *Vom Nichtanderen,* xviii–xix. In *God as Not-Other,* 4, Hopkins remarks aptly that we should not approach this work in the usual way or we will find that "Nicholas' notion of definition is bizarre. We cannot seriously regard as a definition the sentence 'The sky is not other than the sky' or the sentence 'The earth is not other than the earth.' Moreover, no one could rightly agree with the unqualified claim, advanced in Chapter 1, that 'definition defines everything.'"

is one, in this proposal of a putatively self-defining "not other," even tautologically described as "not other than not other."

In the background stands the epistemological and ontological realism of the medieval Aristotelian view of definition.[6] On that view, human minds can conceive and express the intelligibilities or quiddities of things and their properties, intelligibilities that are not simply mind-dependent. We can capture in thought and language the actual natures of things, spelling out their genera and specific differences. For us as knowers, definition brackets or delimits just what it is we attempt to understand and nothing else.[7] The mind-independent thing-substance or the characteristics that we are attempting to define measure the epistemic correctness of a definition. Such "real" (as opposed to "nominal") definition relies on the intelligible characteristics thing-substances exhibit to perception and thought for understanding what they are and for picking out individuals of a type. In this way the epistemological realism of the definition corresponds to an ontological realism of actual formal features in mind-independent entities.

Moreover, definition presupposes that what is to be defined has a certain ontological unity and identity, a relatively determinate stability that perdures and can be recognized. Yet in order to separate even one kind from another and define it, let alone one individual from a multitude, we have to presuppose a field of many sorts or of multiple individuals against which the one kind or characteristic is to be defined. Unless there were other determinate things (or words or concepts) similar to and different from the determinate *definiendum*, defining (whether real, nominal, or stipulative) would not make much sense. If determinateness makes real definition possible, plurality gives definition its usefulness for theoretical thinking.

In these initial interchanges Cusanus presupposes all this in order to move the sense of definition from delivering the actual natures of things to expressing the meaning of the word *definition*. Then he playfully reverses this movement, beginning with the *verbal expression* "not other," but proceeding to the *reality* he envisions "not other" indicating. "Defining itself" and "defining everything" are thus expressions that do not refer to odd epistemic definitions that are somehow self-performative or

---

6. A helpful survey of Aristotle's view of definition can be found in J. M. LeBlond, "Aristotle on Definition," in *Articles on Aristotle 3: Metaphysics*, ed. J. Barnes, M. Scholfield, and R. Sorabji (New York: Duckworth, 1979), 63–79. Schneider, in *Gott, das Nichtandere*, 109–16, discusses how Nicholas uses definition here.

7. Nicholas writes in *De venatione sapientiae* 14, dealing with the third hunting field, that of *non aliud*: "*Diffinitio enim scire facit. Exprimit enim diffiniti genericam concordantiam et differentiam specificam, quam vocabulum in suo significato complicat. Videtur igitur quaesitum in diffinitione sua eo modo, quo cognosci potest*" (h 39). The whole chapter captures the main themes of *De li non aliud*.

all-inclusive in meaning. Cusanus is pointing us beyond thought and language, to that Reality that ontologically or causally defines everything, that is, to something that delimits and determines the being and nature of a thing, its status in reality. Yet just as epistemic definition mirrors the determinateness of the thing by spelling out its quiddity, and thus separating it from other sorts of things it is not (one sense of the slogan: "every determination is a negation"), so ontological or causal "defining" is responsible for something's being what it is and *not* something else (in a second sense we may give the famous slogan).

Given that real definitions are measured by the things defined, Nicholas is concerned with what the things defined are measured by—what defines them, so to speak? Defining a thing here means *causally* circumscribing or establishing the "definitum" in reality as just what it is. That is why "not other than" is no longer just a comparative phrase or idiomatic expression, but a pronoun or verbal symbol that points to *the* Not Other. In this way "the not other" can become a substantival expression calculated to lead to what is ontologically First and ultimately determinative.[8]

This may make some sense of what seemed an empty formula or tautology defining the not other: "Not other is not other than not other" (*non aliud est non aliud quam non aliud;* c.1 h 4). In this proposition the first and last "not other" may reasonably be taken as substantives, while the middle "not other than" is used comparatively as a predicate adjective. We might paraphrase by saying that the Not Other is not different from (that is, is identical with) the Not Other. But this hardly casts light on how the substantival Not Other defines itself, any more than Nicholas' remark that the sky is not other than sky illuminates his claim that the substantival Not Other defines all other things. At best this seems vague or misleading, at worst merely lame or specious.

On the face of it, the best we can conclude is that the expression "not other than" can be substituted in identity statements where normally we would find such phrases as "identical with" or "nothing but." If the notion of definition can be broadened to include statements of identity, then the expression "not other" may be involved in some or all definitions, but this hardly shows that the Not Other defines all things in an ontological sense.

---

8. W. Beierwaltes puts it as follows in *Der verborgene Gott*, 23: "Von der definition als einer logischen Operation ausgehend, übertragt Cusanus diese auf das absolute Sein Gottes: Sich nur durch sich selbst 'definierend,' sich als un-bestimmbar, un-endlich selbst bestimmend *ist* ER das Nicht-Andere: die absolute Selbstbestimmung oder Grund siener selbst durch sein Nicht-Anders-Sein, dem nichts Anderes 'vorausgeht.'" Nicholas himself clarifies the two sorts of definition later in c.22 h 101: *"Non enim sic ipsum principium quidditativum definit, quasi qui lineis circumpositis triangularem determinat seu definit superficiem, sed quasi superficiem, quae trigonus dicitur, constituat."* See footnote 29 in this chapter.

Yet we might ask what stands as the ontological basis of identity and of definition in a universe of thing-substances. For Nicholas, it is the stable formal nature or essence that keeps something what it is and nothing else. This determinate and separate self-sameness finds expression in identity statements that use "not other," and that same determinate identity measures what gets delineated or circumscribed for thought or utterance in definitions. In this way we may understand how the expression "not other than" in fact may point to the ontological basis for identity, the formal essences of things. Moreover, the universe presents itself as populated by such things, each of which is not any of the others. In this way, each giraffe or maple tree is "not other" than itself. Yet each is different, separate, distinct from all the others. Cusanus' universe can thus be understood as comprising many "others." He believes that each separate "other" is "not other than" itself and "other than" everything else. One might well take this as the Cusan way of framing the classic metaphysical topos of identity and difference.

2. GOD'S TRANSCENDENCE AND THE NOT OTHER

What is still not clear is just how the identity and difference Cusanus takes for granted in the created universe is supposed to cast light on its Creator. How does the expression "the not other" work as a symbolic name for God? Even though the context in his first chapter indicates that Nicholas expects attentiveness to "the secret of not other" to lead us to God, only in the second does Ferdinand state explicitly that all the limited things we encounter are created *(principiata)*. As originated they have all that they are from their Origin and can thus be said to be defined (ontologically) by that Origin: caused to be what they are (*"principium est ratio essendi eius seu definitio"; c.2 h 6*).

Further, since the First Principle or Origin is itself unoriginated and independent of all that depends on it, the First cannot be defined (ontologically) by anything else. As uncaused and independent, the First may be said to "define itself," though hardly in the way it is said to define others. When applied to God, then, "defining itself" is strictly metaphorical, for it does not mean that God is cause of Godself. (A bit later Cusanus will apply this metaphor to God's triune life.) Rather God's self-sufficiency is uncaused or causally independent. Moreover, God is not limited or demarcated the way everything else must be, but unlimited and infinite.

Nicholas' goal is to achieve some insight into this transcendent Infinite. If God is beyond our grasp and our language, we have to look for the least unlikely and least unsuitable verbal expression that will refer us to God and whose sense might disclose something of the divine Principle or Origin. And this returns us to that enigmatic expression, "the not other." Every other way we might characterize the divine Mystery will designate at the same time some feature or aspect we also find among creatures, those things that are "other" than one another, not to mention "other" than their Creator. At best, these names or attributes can take us to God only indirectly; at worst, their ordinary meanings block our moving beyond the realm of what is limited and finite.

Ferdinand returns to the point that every originated other presupposes its origin just to remain what it is qua other. In this way every creature, every other, presupposes the divine Not Other. This ontological dependence is signaled when we assert "Other is *not other* than other." The "not other" in this statement thus does double duty, so to speak. It is first of all the predicate adjectival, comparative use of the expression in an identity statement, as explained earlier. But taken as symbolic, it can also point to the divine Not Other, given the present context where Cusanus is proposing "not other" in a substantival sense as an appropriate name for God. If "not other" used in identity statements is based on the self-identity of something said to be not other than itself, and if we add the presuppositions about creation and ontological dependence already outlined, the essence and identity of any creature or limited "not other" cannot be fully accounted for without the ultimate "Not Other," the God who defines everything. In this way the presuppositions of being not other than one is can point to God. Nicholas writes, *"Nam cum omne, quod quidem est, sit not aliud quam idipsum, hoc utique non habet aliunde; a non alio igitur habet"* (Now, since everything that exists is not other than itself, it does not possess this [self-identity] from another, therefore it possesses it from the Not Other; c.3 h 10).

Since every creature requires God in order to be itself and other than every other creature, the identity or restricted "not otherness" (so to speak) that it exhibits and exercises can be interpreted as symbolic of the ultimate divine Not Other. Cusanus ends the second chapter by formally proposing "not other" as the best of human characterizations or namings of God. (He also believes that God has a proper name that is ineffable for us, just as God's nature is unknowable.) "Not other" is supposed to serve as a way to the source, as a figure or symbol of God's own unspeakable name, a symbol that will disclose God to those who seek the Divine. Nicholas' point here is not one of establishing the reality of God, but given God's reality, of attempting to comprehend to some extent the transcendent divine Mystery in relation to all that is not divine.

Presupposed for the existence and intelligibility of all else that in any way exists or is understood, "not other" is particularly apt as naming God's unique ontological priority and transcendence. Nicholas recalls what in earlier works he had symbolized through the coincidence of opposites: a logical space beyond and thus prior to contraries and contradictories, and an ontological realm prior to positing or removing and therefore prior to being or nonbeing. It is there he believes that we are directed even more readily by thinking "not other."

3. THINKING NOT OTHER

How does such thinking work? Nicholas points out that while any created one is not other than one, it *is* other than what is not one, the many. To repeat the earlier point, the determinate identity of a thing or thought stands in opposition to the other things or thoughts from which it is distinct. Yet the divine Not Other cannot be distinct in the same way since it cannot be other than one or not one. In Nicholas' words, the First Principle "cannot be other either than an other or than nothing and likewise is not opposed to anything" (c.4 h 13). If we generalize this as a kind of rule, what results is the following: For any given nondivine X, X is not other than X, and X is other than not X. What is unique about the divine Not Other is precisely that it is not other than either X or not X ("cannot be other than"—"is not opposed to anything"). The transcendent Not Other thus undercuts both the principles of noncontradiction and of the excluded middle. How, then, can we think the Not Other?

Rational thought, following both those principles, tends to think of the relation of God and creatures as an opposition like that between different created things. In Nicholas' language here, God is thought as opposed to creatures just the way any given other is to a second other or group of others. The reason thinking of God as not other can be so illuminating is that such thinking may reveal how God is not just another other, as it were, since God is the Not Other. Nicholas puts it this way: "But God is Not Other because God is not other than other, even though not other and other seem opposed. But other is not opposed to God from whom it has that it is other" (c.6 h 21).

This opposition is of a different type entirely because, while creatures are dependent functions of God and may be functions one of another, God is not a dependent function of creatures. One way to see this is to recall that God is precisely not any of the others and so is not other in the way creatures are other. God is not just one more other. Here we discover a further meaning for "not other," namely, *not* a finite other. Thus we have two kinds of differentiation or otherness, the opposition between distinct creatures and the opposition between creatures and God. The "not" in "not other" distinguishes God from creatures but not does exclude the divine Not Other since the Not Other defines them. Thinking the divine Not Other requires a characteristic Cusan dialectical thinking, not simply affirming or denying. It means we attempt to recognize and acknowledge in thought that the divine Not Other is *both* not one of the others *and* at once not other than any or all of them.[9]

Putting this somewhat more formally, the difference or opposition between created things or others is both symmetrical and transitive—for the domain of finite things, X is other than Y and likewise Y is other than X. The basis for their distinction from one another is their identity; their symmetrical otherness is the result of their substantial not otherness, so to speak. But the distinction between the divine Not Other and the created others is *a*symmetrical and *in*transitive.[10] True, the Not Other is *not* one of the others—but altogether differently than the way any one of the others is not the Not Other! Look again to the identities of each, so to speak. What it is for an other to be not other than itself is determinate limitation; what it is for the Not Other to be not other than Not Other is (paradoxically) determinate nonlimitation. This means the difference between divine Not Other and created not other marks the gulf between Infinite and finite.[11]

Cusanus gives this important difference expression when he says that the divine Not Other is *not other* than any created other. One side of this is indeed negative, for the Not Other is not finite as the others are. One side, however, is positive, for the reflexivity characteristic of a limited thing's *self-identity* also characterizes the Not Other's relation with it. That is why Cusanus writes of such a thing both that any other is *not oth-*

---

9. E. Wyller summarizes as follows to distinguish Cusan from Hegelian dialectical thinking (*Henologische Perspektiven*, 523–24):

> Was die cusanische *Realisation* betrifft, ist es einleuchtend, dass im Werke *De non aliud* nirgends das *non aliud* selbst—oder irgend etwas anders—als mit ihm selbst oder mit irgend etwas anderem "identisch" betrachtet wird. Das Nicht-Andere, sowohl als alles andere, ist *nicht anders* als es selbst—und nichts anders. Das Prinzip der Nicht-Andersheit hat bei Cusanus—sowohl seiner Intention also auch Realisation nach—das dialektische Prinzip der Identität (Hegel) *ersetzt*.

Cf. Pätzold, *Einheit und Andersheit*, 49–57.

10. Wyller proposes a similar analysis, in *Henologische Perspektiven*, 521–23.

11. Wyller connects *non aliud* with the *infinitum* (*Henologische Perspektiven*, 531): "Das ganze cusanische Denkbemühen nach der Erleuchtung auf der Ruckreise von Byzanz steht *sub specie infinitatis*. Alle Gottesbenennungen bei ihm, so auch die des *non aliud* lässt sich daher zur Frage nach dem Sinn des *in* des spezifisch platonisch-cusanischen *infinitum* übertragen. Das *non* des *non aliud* und das *in* des *infinitum* sind ihrer Begrifflichkeit nach auswechselbar."

er than other (= itself) and that the Not Other is not other than any other. What Cusanus attempts to designate with the expression "the Not Other" both is and is not every other as well.[12]

The basis for Nicholas' assertion that the divine Not Other is not other than any finite other lies in the fact that created others or opposites possess their very status as others, their otherness or oppositeness, from and through God. Nicholas writes, "In this way, then, the Not Other is seen prior to these things and the others, in that they do not exist after it but through it" (c.4 h 14). No finite other is required for the being and intelligibility of other finite things in the way each of them requires God. As Ferdinand puts it in the dialogue, "Were the Not Other removed nothing would remain, nothing would be known" (c.5 h 15). The Not Other *(li non aliud)* thus symbolizes how God is the ground *(ratio)*, differentiation *(discretio)*, and measure *(mensura)* of everything. God is causally responsible for things existing as separate and self-identical others. While *they* measure—at least in part—our knowledge, God measures (that is, defines) *their* reality and intelligibility.

4. "NOT OTHER IN OTHER"

Chapters 6 to 13 of *De non aliud* move Nicholas' discussion from God to creatures.[13] Ferdinand asks him to show "not other in other," that is to say, how this verbal expression may help us construe God's immanence, the divine connection with everything that is not divine. Here Nicholas' own words deserve a careful reading:

12. The requirement that this verbal symbol express both the transcendence and the immanence of the infinite God is underlined by Wyller (*Henologische Perspektiven*, 499–500): "Der gesuchte Begriff fur Gott muss sowohl sich selbst als auch alles *(se ipsum et omnia)* ausdrucken können." Pätzold explains further (*Einheit und Andersheit*, 49): "Das non aliud trägt folglich zwei Bestimmungen: Erstens wird ausgesagt, dass das non aliud nur es selbst ist, und zweitens, dass es gegenüber Anderem nichts anderes ist, da das Andere in ihm nichts anderes als eben dieses ist."

13. K. Flasch proposes the following summary of these chapters (*Nikolaus von Kues*, 567–68):

Cusanus vertieft sie, indem er die Anwesenheit des Nichtanderen in jedem Anderen zeigt (c.6), indem er die Art seiner Voraussetzungs-Forschung (*hypothesis*-Verfahren) erläutert (c.7), indem er das Konzept der Wesenheit *(quiditas)* im Lichte des Nichtanderen klärt (c.8), indem er den Begriff des Universums untersucht und ineins damit das Konzept des Willens Gottes und damit der Allmacht von voluntaristischen Konnotationen befreit (c.9). Er untersucht das Konzept der Tielhabe, *participatio*, was dringlich war, da Proklos von Einen gesagt hatte, man könne an ihm nicht teilnehmen (c.10)—ein Problem, das Cusanus schon in *De coniecturis* beschäftigt hat. Dann illustriert Cusanus an einem anschaulichen Beispiel—dem Rubin, der von sich aus leuchtet—das Sichzeigen als Grundzug der Realität; er unterscheidet verscheidene Bedeutungen im Konzept der Substanz, h.h., er sythetisiert die platonische und die aristotelische Version des Universalienproblems (c.11–13).

Not other is not an other, nor is it other than any other, nor is it other in an other—for no other reason than because it is Not Other and cannot in any way be other, as if something were lacking to it, as to an other. For an other which is other than something lacks that than which it is other. Not Other, however, because it is not other than anything, does not lack anything nor can anything be outside it.(c.6 h 20)

How should we understand Nicholas' contrast between what is lacking to such others, the different things of the created universe, and what is not lacking to the divine Not Other? For Nicholas, each thing that is different from or other than each other thing, by being determinate and *not* the other things, is also lacking or without what the other things are and have. The Not Other, by contrast, is not any one of the things ("others") so differentiated. It is not just one among others, not even *primus inter pares*. The Not Other, then, cannot be opposed to all the separate things nor can it be present to them as they may be opposed (as "other than any other" [*ab alio aliud*]) or present to one another (as "other in an other" [*in alio aliud*]). Rather, because the Not Other is causally prior to created things it is also "not other than anything" and thus is present to each in a distinctive, unlimited way ("does not lack anything"). Moreover, the Not Other also encompasses the whole realm of the created others ("nor can anything be outside it"). The way God is different from, and yet identical with, created things is *toto caelo* different from the ways different limited things are related to one another.

Nicholas thereupon makes the same point more concretely, using the example of the sky. If we take the sky to be something distinct from other created things, it is an other. That means that God, who is not other, while not the sky, is in fact *not other* than the sky just because God is not an other like other things in this domain. To quote Cusanus' cryptic Latin: *"nec in ipso [caelo] sit aliud, nec ab ipso aliud"* ([the Not Other] is neither other in it [the sky] nor other than it; c.6 h 20). Just because God transcends the realm of created others and is none of them, God is identical with each and encompasses them all. "In it all things are antecedently it, and in all things it is all things" (c.6 h 22). Here the verbal suitability of "not other" as symbolizing the Divine is disclosed. As not other, God is exactly not other than (= identical with) the created things to which the Divine is ordinarily thought to be opposed. When he again mentions the sky, Nicholas points out that the sky is antecedently in the Not Other as not other. Not other is thus the Source of what the sky is. Sky is constituted sky through the Not Other as just what it is and nothing else. Even though it is prior to the sky and to every limited thing or name, the Not Other can still be named "sky."[14]

---

14. For the difficulties with and the distinction between the two expressions *"non aliud*

In chapter 7 Nicholas spells out the implications of the idea that the divine Not Other, while inseparable from every other, stands prior to every other reality and antecedent to every name and concept. Ferdinand proposes that Nicholas show how the Not Other is prior even to nothing *(nihil)*. Nicholas replies by taking the concrete example of water and asking about what is prior to it or any given actual item. His answer is that it be possible, hence it follows that not being is also possible for water or any actual thing. For the realm of finite things, the widest possibility is that each thing either be or not be, that is, be something or be nothing. Since God is ontologically prior to the whole finite realm and its possibilities, the possibility of something not being (= being nothing) also is posterior to the divine First. Since not being at all or "nothing" is an intelligible possibility, that means even not being "must obey Omnipotence" (c.7 h 23). If the Not Other were to cease, however, so would possibility, and hence the possibility of being nothing, that is, of not being.[15]

Nicholas then asks Ferdinand to explain whether the divine Not Other they have discovered in other things must be seen in them. The answer is not a matter of perception only. The existence and intelligibility of any and every other cannot be separated from its divine Source. As Ferdinand puts it, "when an other is seen, that other and the Not Other are seen" (c.7 h 25). This is finally to say that the other cannot exist or be seen for what it is as though it were separated from the divine Not Other, even though in God each other is nothing but God in the infinite Oneness of the divine Not Other.

This interchange recalls Nicholas' earlier comparison of the Not Other to light (in chapter 3). Just as when visual perception takes in the visible field of colored objects the viewer does not see light as such but only what light illuminates, so the Not Other is required for there to be something intelligible at all. We are to discover, recognize, and acknowledge the presence of the Not Other in others much the way we discover, recognize, and acknowledge that light is present when we see color. For thought, the Not Other is a kind of "unthinkable thinkable," a necessary condition or presupposition, just as light is a necessary condition, a kind of "invisible visible," for perception. As light is identified with each visible item but not limited to that item, so God is inseparable from each of the things whose constitution depends on God's transcending them.

Nicholas and Ferdinand explore a series of topics in the next several

---

quam" and *"non aliud a"* which come into play in c.6, see Hopkins, *God as Not-Other,* 17–18, 168, 172.

15. See Pátzold, *Einheit und Andersheit,* 50–55, for further discussion of these points in relation to Cusanus' notion of possibility in *De li non aliud.*

chapters in order to explain more fully just how the Not Other is both not other than the limited others and at the same time transcends them all. Quiddity, ground *(ratio)*, form, participation, essence—all these commonly used "terms of art" enable Cusanus and Ferdinand to explore a universe encompassed by the divine Not Other. Each involves using Aristotelian conceptions and reworking them in Neoplatonic terms so that an order of image and original, of dependent and independent entities (some conceptual, some not), can be used to symbolize and give some inkling of just how the Not Other is to be discovered and thought in other.

4.1. Quiddity (c.8)

What is the relation of any finite quiddity to the divine Not Other? For Cusanus, the answer is an application of what has already been said about the relation of the absolute Not Other to the limited others. God's own quiddity is self-identically not other and, in relation to other quiddities, is exactly *not other* than the quiddity of any given other as the infinite Source that makes each what it is. *"Sed in omni alia quidditate ipsum non aliud est ipsa, non alia"* (but in every other quiddity the Not Other itself is that quiddity, not another; c.8 h 27). Since quiddities are what Aristotelian definitions are designed to capture, Nicholas ends the chapter by asserting again that the Not Other ("the quiddity of quiddities") defines the quiddities of all things and indeed is these others without being itself multiplied.

The quiddities of other things are here envisaged as images, as the reflective shining forth *(splendor)* of the quiddity of the Not Other. In that each limited thing's quiddity is determinate, it can be said to be not other than itself. In this way it is an image or reflection of the divine Not Other. Nicholas explains this by paralleling the way that a created substance's accidents are said to be manifestations of its quiddity or whatness. Here Nicholas reframes the mutually constitutive relation between Aristotelian substance and accidents in a finite thing (here, an other) in more Neoplatonic terms, so that the quiddity or whatness of the thing becomes the source from which the accidents flow and to which they return, reflecting all the while their quidditative source. This dependence is imagined concretely as moving from light into shadow and back or, alternately, as the brightness of the quiddity shining forth through and in the accidents that are its image or attenuated reflection.

But quiddities or whatnesses are as much about our knowing of things as about the things themselves. When it comes to our knowledge of quiddity, Cusanus says that we perceive and imagine things as extended or quantified, but penetrate to their true quiddity when we move away from the corporeal world and capture that whatness in purely conceptual terms that defy imagination. This suggests a favorite example,[16] though not of an Aristotelian substance but of an "accident" treated as an abstract substantive, that of magnitude or "greatness." This example illustrates exactly Nicholas' point that we only understand the concept correctly when any imagined or perceived quantity or extension is left aside. "I speak of the magnitude that is seen by the mind beyond imagination before imagined quantity" (c.8 h 29).

The paradox that the meaning of magnitude need not include imagined quantity or extension lets Cusanus differentiate very clearly between what it is that imagination contributes when we think of magnitude and what we grasp of magnitude conceptually by intellect. This in turn lets us see his real motive for turning to magnitude, for Nicholas at once uses it as an opportunity to press beyond the imaginable and the intelligible. As imaginable magnitude is a reflection *(relucentia)* of intelligible magnitude, so intelligible magnitude points to and reflects greatness in a realm beyond: *"supra omnem intellectum . . . , scilicet supra et ante omnem modum cognitivum"* (beyond all understanding . . . , that is, beyond and prior to every way of human knowing; c.8 h 30). Divine greatness—the Not Other itself—shines forth and is known in created reflections and symbols, that is, in created others and in our thought and language about them. Knowing anything at all presupposes that we know the Not Other (since it is not other than any other—real or conceptual—that we might know), but that the Not Other remains *incognitum*—unknown but shining forth in what we know.

4.2. Ground/Ratio *(c.9)*

Cusanus then turns to find in the created universe an ordered unity of natural essences or quiddities, a world of beauty wherein *ratio* is reflected or shines forth. *Ratio* in this context means the intelligent Ground or rational Principle of limited things, plus their resulting intelligibility. Besides, God's will shines forth in the universe no less than the divine Reason *(ratio)* already mentioned, with which it is one. Indeed, God's will creates, determines, causes, orders, makes firm and stable, and conserves the universe in whole and in part. It is even reflected as triune in the human soul. Cusanus asserts that this Principle or divine Ground/*ratio* is nothing else than the Not Other and so is finally beyond comprehension though disclosed in the intelligibility of the individual things and the ordered array of their kinds that compose the universe.

Some things we do not understand because they lack form and the

---

16. Cf. *De docta ignorantia* 1.3–4, *De possest* h 9–10.

definiteness required to be understood—for instance, matter, nothing. Others lack form because they are responsible for form and too intelligible, as it were, for our minds to grasp. This is the case with the divine Not Other responsible for all we do encounter and understand. In both cases we employ language and attempt some understanding, however imprecise. We conceive both what is formless and what transcends form as if they were somehow formal. We bestow an *ersatz* intelligibility and create an understandable structure where none is present: *"per formam videns informatum"* (seeing the unformed through form; c.9 h 33), as Nicholas puts it. In the case of God, Nicholas will often signal this imprecise construction and usage by naming God "Absolute Form of forms" or "Essence of essences."[17] Such expressions attempt to recognize that God is responsible for created forms and essences and is indeed one with them as the divine Not Other, yet God is not form or essence at all, but transcends them as their unitary Source.

4.3. Participation (c.10)

Asked whether creation is a participation in God, the cardinal replies with a paradox. On the one hand, the divine Not Other cannot be named or participated in since it is prior to everything else. On the other hand, every name and every thing is what it is by participation in the Not Other, for the Not Other defines each as its ultimate source and ground. Moreover, there are levels of participation that correspond to the levels of simpleness in essence. For instance, pure intelligences participate more, corporeal things participate less, in the Not Other. To say God is both unable to be participated and *is* nonetheless participated rephrases in the language of participation the point of this treatise: God is both the Not Other prior to everything else and the one who is not other than every other thing.

Although the subject seems to change with Ferdinand's question about the indestructibility of essences, Cusanus' interpretation of this Scholastic dictum enables him to repeat his point about participation in a slightly different way. Because the divine Not Other determines or defines in causal terms the essences of other things and in this sense is in or inseparable from them, they share or participate in the indestructibility of the Not Other. In Nicholas' words, "The Not Other, indeed, is not an essence, but because it is essence in things having essences, it is said to be the Essence of essences" (c.10 h 37). In contrast, perceptible and corporeal things that have essence are destructible, since in them the essence is, so to speak, "othered." There "you see the essence as oth-

---

17. See below, c.10 h 37; *De dato Patris luminum* 2 h 98; *De docta ignorantia* 1.16 h 45; and *Apologia* h 26. See Hopkins, *Metaphysic of Contraction*, 103–6, for commentary.

er in an other" (*ipsam in alio aliam vides;* c.10 h 37), but essence can also be considered in its Source, the Not Other, where it is indestructibly one with the divine Simpleness.

The basic reason for the paradox with which Cusanus begins this chapter gets further elucidation when he completes it by denying that there is any intermediate realm of quasi-Platonic Forms. Rather, there is only the divine Not Other and all the created others. In themselves the essences of things cannot be destroyed, it is true, but this is not due to their subsisting in and by themselves, as in the well-known medieval doctrine of *universalia ante res*.[18] Nicholas accounts for the variety of essences in corporeal things by appealing directly to the divine Not Other, the Form of forms or Essence of essences. As for the variety of abstract essences we grasp in thought apart from the perceptible world, these are matters of our own reason's functioning and its ability to grasp universal ideas in thought. Things have essences which human thought can grasp, though not precisely or completely, but outside the created things there exists only the Creator responsible for those essences as the Essence of essences.

That is why things both do and do not participate in the divine Not Other. They do not participate, because it is not true that finite things *as finite* are not other than God. This is no more the case than that the particular things or features that are images of or participate in Platonic Forms were thought to be identical with them. When particular things are not other than God they are the Not Other itself *as absolute.* In God imparticipable all things are God. Yet in one sense limited things do participate in not other because it is God who is not other than they. In all things God "participated" is all things. As limited others, created things are not the Not Other; as the unlimited Not Other, they are not other than the Not Other itself. We have to think both God imparticipable and God participated together to do justice to Cusan ideas about *li non aliud*.

4.4. Essence/Accidents (cc. 11–13)

The next several chapters of *De li non aliud* return to the theme first discussed in chapter 8 and explain at some length just how Cusanus sees the relationship between the essence and accidents. Once again, although the terms are familiar from medieval Scholasticism, the treatment is more Neoplatonic than Aristotelian, for what is more accessible

---

18. For the background in earlier medieval thought, see M. M. Adams, "Universals in the Early Fourteenth Century," in *The Cambridge History of Later Medieval Philosophy,* ed. N. Kretzmann, A. Kenny, and J. Pinborg (Cambridge: Cambridge University Press, 1982), 411–39. For a selection of relevant texts in translation, see *Five Texts on the Mediaeval Problem of Universals,* trans. and ed. P. V. Spade (Indianapolis, Ind.: Hackett, 1994).

to us is seen as reflecting, imaging, or mirroring the original, the principle or source thus made manifest. Divine, intelligible, and perceptible orders are related as prior and posterior—the latter depend on the former, while the former are impossible or difficult to understand in themselves, yet can be seen "invisibly" in their dependent likenesses.

Nicholas begins with the example of a ruby or carbuncle stone. He recalls the common belief that these gem stones contained light inside them and that this explained why the carbuncles glowed in the dark. The more it glowed, the more perfect and precious such a stone was considered. Nicholas considers the glow, the red color, the stone's shape and size all to be accidental, but also to manifest and make perceptible the essence or substance and "substantial light" of the carbuncle stone. That putative essence is prior to and not other than the perceptible features of the stone, but invisible and internal—it shines forth *(relucet)* in the reddish glow of the stone. It is what makes the carbuncle "not other" than what it is and different from other substances.

Different carbuncles have the same essence but are other or distinct, because being in different matter each embodies a different possibility of being a carbuncle. While the intelligible essence or substance is "not other" or identical in each stone, yet this formal principle is separate (as understood) from the enmattered substance of any perceptible ruby stone. This substantial principle or "absolute" form of every carbuncle is responsible for bestowing actual being on the possibility of existing or matter of any given carbuncle stone. What is seen by the mind as intelligible and abstract can now be recognized in a concrete, perceptible gemstone. In a parallel way, the divine Not Other is also prior to all substances and created others because "it is not other than what they all are but is all in all, that is, all that which exists in anything" (c.11 h 43; compare c.12 h 47: *"sic ipsum non aliud se habere ad alias et alias intelligibiles substantias"* [in this way the not other is related to other and yet other intelligible substances]). The intelligible essence of a carbuncle is a likeness of the Not Other, just as the actual essence of a carbuncle is a likeness of the intelligible essence and its accidents are likenesses of its concrete essence.

Ferdinand then parallels the carbuncle example to coldness and to ice. The stream that freezes does so because the water can be made to freeze by embodying coldness. Anything frozen exemplifies this intelligible coldness but in some other concrete possibility. Nicholas writes: "Just as a sensible cold thing is not intelligible cold, even though it [intelligible cold] is in no way other than that [cold thing], so intelligible cold is not the first Principle, even though the first Principle which is the Not Other is not other than it" (c.13 h 52).

Nicholas generalizes this distinction between the intelligible and the perceptible realms. The composite nature of perceptible things implies that all individuals of one kind are ontologically subsequent to their intelligible essence, and that essence is not other than each of them while they are other than one another. Beyond and prior to both realms stands the divine Not Other. Cusanus terms everything else *"non aliata,"* those things from which the Not Other is not other. His point is twofold: (1) the divine Not Other, without undergoing change or otherness itself, is causally responsible for the fact that intelligible and perceptible things are not other than they are; (2) while the divine Not Other is beyond our grasp, it is reflected in intelligible essences just as they are manifested and shine forth in concrete, perceptible things. The Not Other is causally responsible for created things and in them it is imperceptibly perceptible.

5. AUTHORITIES AND BEYOND

5.1. Pseudo-Dionysius

Chapter 14 interrupts the discussion of *li non aliud*. In response to Ferdinand's request, the cardinal presents a long list of quotations from the works of Pseudo-Dionysius grouped around various "names" or predicates attributed to God. (For example, God is one, good, substance, cause, light, knowledge, beauty, and so on.) This florilegium enables Nicholas to connect his ideas about the Not Other to an earlier eminent authority, to situate the Not Other in earlier thinking about the First Principle or Ultimate Source, and to clarify relevant differences. Since he will go on to take up Aristotle, *The Theology of Plato,* and Proclus, the quotes from Pseudo-Dionysius provide a background against which the distinctiveness of the object picked out by the expression "not other," and the corresponding particular way of thinking the Not Other requires, can be set out more clearly.[19]

Cusanus begins chapter 15 with a discussion of the Dionysian (or Proclean) One, or *unum*, beyond the existing one. This is a "supersubstantial" One that defines everything and stands beyond any encompassing by anything else.[20] He and Ferdinand agree that this *"unum quod supra unum est"* is prior to everything else and equivalent to what the cardinal has termed the Not Other. This is why Pseudo-Dionysius said that

---

19. Flasch, *Nikolaus von Kues*, 569–70.
20. The quotation referred to in c.15 is fourth from the end of Nicholas' list of quotes and taken from *Divine Names* 13.3.980D. In Cusanus' Latin version it concluded: "Now that supersubstantial One determines both the one that exists and every number" (c.14 h 70). The echoes of Proclus seem obvious.

God has a "before"—not that God is temporal, but that God precedes everything else. Antecedent to all the others the Not Other is all things in all things, but in the Not Other all things are the Not Other.[21]

It is just here that Nicholas begins to remind us of where such thinking is designed to take us. Using "A" as a marker for God or the Not Other, Nicholas asserts that A "is before 'before'" (*ante ipsum ante sit;* c.15 h 74). In fact the logic of the before and the after, of priority and posteriority, keeps us locked into the Not Other's connections with others, somewhat on the model of their connections with one another. As Nicholas points out, "'Before,' however can be said of other, so that there is an other that precedes and an other that follows" (c.15 h 74). Cusanus wants to follow Pseudo-Dionysius in attempting to map a new space for thinking and discourse beyond such connections. So Nicholas will say that God is "most eminently that 'before'" (*eminentissime ipsum ante;* c.15 h 74) in the hope that we will understand that our sentences employing "God" and even "the Not Other" and "A" tend to reify what they designate as if their referents were just like those others to which we normally refer. In fact we have no sense of how to understand or what to call the one beyond before and after—perhaps "the Not Other" or "A" will keep us aware of its uniqueness.[22]

This may explain the seemingly confused discourse about time in chapter 16. The conversation conflates the notion of time or duration as an unchanging framework and the now or moment or present as the essence/substance of time. This is undoubtedly because Cusanus is using the discussion to review points made in chapters 10–13 about substance/essence and accidents. Giving a coherent account of time is hardly the issue; instead, Cusanus moves from things participating in time to its essence, the present. He then draws a further parallel, as he did in earlier passages, by asserting that the present moment, the essence of time, is not other than temporal items of whatever sort, just as the divine Not Other is not other than the essence of time, the present. Then he can conclude that, just as without the present moment there could be no time at all, so without A (the Not Other), there could not exist the present or anything else.[23]

---

21. This recalls Nicholas' ideas about the *complicatio-explicatio* couplet.

22. The use of "A" as a marker for God goes back to Ramon Lull's *Ars brevis*. See F. A. Yates, *Lull and Bruno* (London: Routledge, 1982), 9–25 and the plate opposite 116.

23. Cusanus often considers time as the *explicatio* of the now or present (or of eternity), usually as one example of such enfolding and unfolding, e.g., in *Idiota de mente* 4 h 74 and 15 h 157–58. Following the tradition that goes back to Plato and Plotinus, he also refers to time as the image of eternity, e.g., in *De ludo globi* 2 h 87, and in *De venatione sapientiae* 9 h 26. See H. G. Senger, "Die Zeit- und Ewigkeitsverständnis bei Nikolaus von Kues im Hinblick auf die Auferstehung der Toten," *MFCG* 23 (1996): 139–63, esp. 139–42, 158–61.

In chapter 17 Cusanus continues along similar lines, pointing out that A is "more intimately and deeply related to everything than the elemental is to what is composed of elements" (c.17 h 80). He repeats again that "in them A is these things even though it is no one of them" (c.17 h 81). Referring back to Pseudo-Dionysius, Ferdinand and the cardinal recall remarks about how thinking one understands God is to understand something else and about how each and all of the things we understand is a something and hence cannot be God. Cusanus explains why. Everything outside God is a something *(aliquid)*. Every *aliquid* in fact amounts to "something other" *(aliquid aliud)*. To identify such an other with God is to miss how the Not Other is prior and not participated—exactly not such an other. Nicholas writes: "But nothing except Not Other can be seen prior to other. Therefore, you grasp that Not Other directs us toward the Source that excels and precedes the intellect and other and something and every intelligible" (c.17 h 82).

Again we find Cusanus referring to a source beyond not other. "Not other" is not God's real name or essence, even though our discourse tends to treat it as such in explaining its force and appropriateness. In fact Cusanus attributes to Pseudo-Dionysius the point that knowledge of the Not Other is really perfect ignorance, since this is "knowledge" beyond the realm of the knowable. True, there is no help for the way the shape of our language and thinking is accustomed to operate. True, every habit of speaking and thinking directs us to turn the Not Other or God into another thing just like every other thing we pick out in speaking or thinking. Cusanus inserts the florilegium and the discussion of Pseudo-Dionysius and the other Platonists into this dialogue not simply from the medieval penchant for appealing to authorities of the past. He takes very seriously the Dionysian stress on the transcendence and unknowability of God.[24] Unless God is something entirely unlike other things and not knowable the way they are, the whole point of using the verbal symbol "not other" is lost. What using "not other" to direct our minds can do is make us realize that our talk and thought about the Divine is in fact metastable—we keep making proposals, qualifying them, then taking them back and trying other proposals.

---

24. K. Flasch underlines Nicholas' difference from Aquinas and Albert regarding Dionysius. While they interpreted *De divinis nominibus* in terms of discursive reason, Cusan *intellectus* is designed to think the Not Other and the coincidence of opposites beyond the oppositions of ordinary thought and discourse. See his *Nikolaus von Kues*, 432, 567–72. For an overview of the distance from Dionysius to Cusanus that underlines *intellectus*, see D. F. Duclow, "Mystical Theology and the Intellect in Nicholas of Cusa," *American Catholic Philosophical Quarterly* 64 (1990): 111–29.

5.2. Aristotle

That is why the discussion of Aristotle in the next two chapters (18–19) seems so appropriate.[25] Not only is Aristotle given credit for the emphasis on definition with which this conversation began, he also is praised for his focus on the substance and quiddity of things. Yet he is comparable to the person who focuses on the visible things and not on the light that makes them visible. Cusanus criticizes Aristotle for not going beyond the determinate identities of limited things and the essences that made them what they were—namely, not other than themselves and other than others. Aristotle must have realized, he believes, that the kinds of knowing limited to the rational could never take him beyond self-identical and separate thing-substances. He was on the correct path, but got no further than focusing on something other, *aliquid aliud*.

The problem is that what can be attained using Aristotelian reason, logic, and definition is limited to the domain where those philosophical tools are useful and valid, "at home," so to speak. What is required instead is to think through the way in which "other" and "not other" are related. They are not exactly the opposites they appear to be. Cusanus would have had him pursue what seems a contradiction, namely, that any thing-substance is both other and not other. Such a thing is other than other (things) and it is not other than other (itself). This resolves the paradox and does it in accord with Aristotle's strictures on rational discourse by distinguishing the different respects in which a given substance can be said to be different and not different.

In fact Cusanus wants to go further. The real contradiction lies in the fact that a given other or created substance is both other than the divine Not Other *and* not other than the Not Other, while the Not Other remains not other than any created substance. It is in thinking through this inescapable contradiction that we will be set on the way to the truth about the Not Other that transcends rational discourse *(supra rationem)*. This way will disclose that "substance of substances" Cusanus believes Aristotle was seeking. But this involves our recognizing and holding together in thought as best we can what is true of Transcendence: the divine Not Other is both substantial and not substantial *and* neither substantial nor not substantial. To approach the absolute status of the transcendent Not Other thus means moving beyond the first principle of discursive reason. God's absolute status transcends the cognitive realm where the principle of contradiction regulates discourse reflecting an ontological domain of limited determinateness.

---

25. See Flasch, *Nikolaus von Kues*, 572–75, where Flasch points out how these chapters sharpen Cusanus' critique of Aristotle in his earlier *De beryllo* (1458).

Here Cusanus is content to point out a further irony. That first principle of rational discourse that Aristotle singles out, the principle of contradiction, could itself provide another lead "for viewing the truth" (c.19 h 89) beyond discursive reason. Just as in the case of the "substance of substances," one could ask about the "contradiction of contradictions." This would be a query about that contradiction prior to particular cases of contradictories, which, Nicholas claims, is itself without contradictory.[26]

Two simultaneous moves take place if we follow Cusanus here. In one, we move in thought from instances of contradictions we identify to the general notion of contradiction itself. One can think of this as merely stating the truism that in some sense we know the abstract idea whose instances we can identify. Now the idea of contradiction is not contradictory, even though its content refers to contradictories. In that first sense, contradiction is "without contradictory." But in his second move, Cusanus gives "contradiction" his own ontological turn. For him, there exists a Contradiction beyond the contradiction instantiated in contradictories. This further Contradiction is employed to pick out the antecedent *cause* of the oppositions and contrariety reason discerns and must respect in the domain of finite things. To follow Cusanus here is to discern or invent a further sense of "contradiction" beyond (though *not* the present instance of contradictories) that stands free of contradiction *(absque contradictione)* because there is nothing able to oppose a Contradiction ontologically prior to any opposites or contrarieties.[27]

This means that the inadequacies of language and thought about God, the instability of our ways of characterizing the divine Mystery, are matched by the breakdown of the basic principle of discursive reason. What makes the Not Other such an apt verbal symbol for leading our minds toward the Divine is that thinking through the Not Other can keep thought and language about God aware of how and why it is inadequate. If we can recognize how the Contradiction of contradictions might be without contradiction, we can use the Not Other to symbolize

---

26. This recalls Nicholas' similar formulation in *De visione Dei* c.13: *"Oppositio oppositorum est oppositio sine oppositione, sicut finis finitorum est finis sine fine"* (h 55); see Chapter 4, this book.

27. This language is patterned after expressions such as "Form of forms" or "Essence of essences" in which the first singular noun points to what is causally responsible for the limited realities picked out by the second plural noun. Cusanus could have as easily added "Form without form" to "Form of forms," just as he adds "Contradiction without contradiction" to "Contradiction of contradictions." In private correspondence, H. L. Bond has remarked on the importance of taking contradiction to be *first* a matter of speech and thought. This is also true of "definition" with which the whole dialogue begins. But Nicholas never hesitates to move beyond words and thoughts to things, just as he does here.

both what we seek and to undercut our best efforts to conceptualize or think it. Our best hope here is to turn to Cusan *intellectus,* intellectual vision.

5.3. Proclus and Seeing the Not Other

In the final five chapters (20–25) two new interlocutors, Peter Balbus and Abbot John, are the cardinal's interlocutors.[28] Some of the final conversation repeats points already made about naming and conceiving, while relating those points to ideas and remarks in Proclus, Pseudo-Dionysius, and the Gospels. Both interlocutors, however, raise questions that lead Nicholas to speak about "seeing" the Not Other. He tells Peter that the divine Not Other is beyond human conception since "every human concept is a concept of some one thing. But the Not Other is prior to [any] concept, because a concept is not other than a concept" (c.20 h 94). This means that the Not Other, as *conceptus absolutus,* is identically whatever else we conceive. At best we may gain some mental sight of the not other *(videtur quidem mente),* but we do not grasp it conceptually *(non concipitur).*

In chapter 21 Nicholas then reassures Peter that the word "than" in the expression "not other than" is not part of what makes it true that, for instance, "the earth is not other than the earth." But "than" is useful, Nicholas says, because it directs our attention to the Not Other whether we assert that some created thing is not other than itself (here the Not Other is the other in any other) or that the Not Other is not other than not other (there the Not Other is prior to all that is other). This is the way the Not Other defines and is the ultimate answer to why something is what it is, for it is the Origin or First Principle of them all. In that Origin or First all things are identically the First, the divine Not Other.

What this implies is that there are three stages or sorts of vision or seeing. In the first, we "see intuitively" all things in their divine Origin where they do not exist as other or different from other things but as prior to otherness in the Not Other: *"in quo quodlibet, quod in alio aliter, in ipso quidem non aliud cernitur"* (in which anything that exists otherwise in an other is seen in the Not Other; c.21 h 98). In that divine Origin earth is not other than not earth even though in the Not Other it is seen more precisely in its real Truth. Second, we may view the sky or earth, for instance, as posterior to their origin in the Not Other. Here we "see intellectually" that the quiddity of each is not that of the other and indeed is other than the quiddities of other things. A third kind of seeing (*"animaliter,"* in the fashion of soul) amounts to simply discriminating one thing and another, whether on the basis of the different

---

28. Flasch, *Nikolaus von Kues,* 570–72.

quiddities or not. Nicholas' terminology may vary, but these ways of seeing correspond to what he usually says about *intellectus, ratio,* and sense perception.

At this point the abbot John enters the conversation with the cardinal. He begins by raising two objections. (1) If the First is prior to what can be named, how can Cusanus name it "not other"? (2) How can the Not Other *not* be other than other things, since as prior to them and as transcendent it must be opposed to other things? Had not even Dionysius called God "other"?

Cusanus' response to the first question clarifies again what he mentioned earlier. "Not other" is exactly *not* the name of the First that is beyond all naming, rather the expression names Cusanus' way of conceiving that first: *"quod quidem a nullo aliud est"* (which indeed is other than no other thing; c.22 h 99). His response to the second is more indirect. Cusanus returns to definition and remarks once more on the gap between human definitions that are taken from and reflect the quiddities of things in knowledge and the defining done by the divine Not Other.[29] God's defining causally constitutes the actual being of what gets defined.

Nicholas' next comment is particularly revealing. God's difference from created things is not the otherness of something separate, such as the otherness of just another created thing—this may reflect but it does not define what is other or separate. Rather, God is other than what God has created the way a friend is an "alter ego"—not separated at all but attached like "another self." In this case the "attachment" or relationship is not emotional and moral only, but ontological, *"ad essentiam."* The result is that there is an ontological basis for claiming that God is "all in all."

In other words, God's defining things means God is not separate at all, but "stuck to" things, as it were *(propter agglutinationem),* without their becoming divine. It is terming God's being the Not Other that precisely describes God's difference from all the rest of the beings who are other. This difference or opposition is the reason that God is said to be "other" by Dionysius, but it is also that opposition already noted, about which Nicholas had written in chapter 19: "Dionysius the theologian saw that God is the opposition of opposites without opposition. For nothing is opposed to the opposition that is prior to opposites" (c.19 h 89).

Abbot John praises the cardinal's teaching about the Not Other because it provides a way of "seeing" that is clear and certain. Then he asks

---

29. Nicholas proposes an apt geometrical comparison (h 101). We can define a triangular surface conceptually or we can define it by constructing such a surface—the latter is a figure of the Not Other's "defining."

Nicholas to square such "vision" with the words attributed to Jesus in the Fourth Gospel: *"Deum nemo vidit umquam"* (No one has ever seen God; Jn 1.18). Nicholas' reply explains the dialectical seeing that is required to move toward the transcendent Not Other. God is prior to what is visible and invisible, so the special sight required here, as Nicholas puts it,

> is not to see the visible, but it is to see the invisible in the visible. Just as when I see that this is true that no one has seen God, then surely I see that beyond every visible thing God is not other than every visible. However, I in no way see as visible that actual Infinity, the Quiddity of all quiddities, that surpasses all vision. For the visible or the object is other than the power of sight, while God, who cannot be other than anything, surpasses every object.(c.22 h 103)

What we are to look for, so to speak, is God's identity with things—only by understanding that God is not other than what we perceive or grasp by reason will we discern intuitively "the invisible in the visible." Since we know that the divine Not Other at the same time "surpasses all vision," whether perceptual or rational or intellectual, we can look to limited visible things in order to glimpse that same divine Not Other beyond all seeing.

We are to see what is not seeable in looking at what we see—the divine Not Other in the other. Now the Not Other can further be envisioned as *visuum visus*—the Vision prior to and constitutive of all other visions. God is thus identically the One who sees, the visible thing, and the seeing itself, just because divine Vision has ontological priority and is the defining vision for all else, visible or not. We usually become conscious that we are seeing in the course of noticing what we are looking at, that is, something visible. God's Sight, by contrast, is at once and unspeakably of Godself and of all else without distinction. Divine Sight, so to speak, is constitutive—the reason all things are not other than what they are. To express Cusanus' point in the language of this treatise is to recognize that God's priority to any other means that to see God in any other is to see what is *not other* than that other.[30]

The explanation of how God's Sight of things is creative or constitutive reminds the abbot of the line in Genesis about God's seeing that created things are good. Cusanus takes up his request to put together goodness with his teaching about the Not Other. Obviously the first good God sees is Godself, the Not Other. This goodness is prior to anything created, whether good or not. The good, then, is not other than

---

30. These passages recall what Nicholas wrote about seeing in *De visione Dei* in that both works aim to move the meaning of sight beyond ordinary perception and rational insight to the intellectual vision or intuition described in *Idiota de mente* 7 h 106 as *"intuitio veritatis absolutae"* (the intuitive vision of absolute truth). The dialectic of seeing being seen seeing in *De visione Dei* is here recast in terms of the not other.

God—the truest sense of the Gospel saying, "No one is good but God alone" (Mt 19.17). Cusanus writes: "All other things, indeed, because they are an other [*aliud*], are able to be in other ways. And so that Good is least of all verified regarding those [created] things because it cannot be in other ways since it is Not Other" (c.23 h 106).

The final chapter plays with the various meanings of the Latin word *"spiritus"* because the abbot refers to the Fourth Gospel's remark that God is spirit. Nicholas first explains that this means God is incorporeal and nonspatial. Moreover, as first constitutive principle and ground, God is simple or incomposite and indivisible, prior to everything that is composite and able to be seen in things that have components and can be divided. But God is not some part of the composite things; rather, the divine Not Other is antecedent to both part and whole and is seen there as the sign is seen in the signified.

Cusanus suggests a further meaning of *"spiritus"* as power. This takes Cusanus back to God's constituting power as the Not Other. He construes the Not Other as a "Spirit" or Power of separating so that God is described as a "not othering Spirit" responsible for all the different things (the others) that exist. But to see this Not Other is the work of mind, a further sense for *"spiritus,"* since it is made to see the divine Truth of which it is the image. God is thus the Spirit of spirits—whether we take "spirit" to mean something noncorporeal and incomposite, or some power or mind, just because God is not other than and prior to all else that can also be described as spirit.

The many references to the Bible in these final chapters, the abbot's final prayer for face-to-face vision, plus the emphasis on intuitive vision of the divine Not Other who is invisibly visible—all these place what Nicholas of Cusa has done in this dialogue squarely in a Christian Neoplatonic framework. Reflection on the verbal-conceptual symbol of the Not Other is valuable finally because of the direction it takes our hearts and minds and because of the possibilities it opens into what the finite and limited others have to disclose. As Nicholas said of the Not Other, "this Truth alone is perfect; to it nothing can be added by a human being. For it directs sight to the Origin so that one contemplating the same Principle may be delighted, and devotedly nourished, and grow" (c.19 h 87). This mental or intellectual sight beyond the realm of discursive reason and limited things is not some intellectual accomplishment for its own sake. Rather, such an intuition is a kind of gift confirming how the human spirit exists not for itself but for the Mystery who is at once our present Intimate and our transcendent Destiny.

6

Possibility and Divine Prey
De venatione sapientiae (1463)

The year before he died Nicholas of Cusa presented a lengthy summary of his lifelong intellectual quest. He titled it *De venatione sapientiae (The Hunt for Wisdom)*.[1] Nicholas organized the entire work around an elaborate metaphor, that of the hunt or chase.[2] In this work he proposes that the various symbols, rubrics, and symbolic names for God—some of which he had explored in his earlier writings—might be likened to ten *campi*, or hunting fields, where Wisdom could be pursued, that is, where God could be sought.

We may best appreciate the wisdom to be gained from such hunting expeditions, no less than the divine Quarry to be pursued, if we understand some important background assumptions, the lay of the land, so to speak, before beginning this *venatio*. Each *campus*, or hunting field, has to be understood as ordered or structured by the conceptual framework ("the three regions of being") that pervades this work. This framework enables us to identify where we may find the divine Prey we pursue in each hunting field. Each of the ten particular fields or domains affords a different perspective or viewpoint for grasping and appreciating both the conceptual framework and its usefulness for attaining the divine Wisdom we seek.

De venatione sapientiae is organized, then, in both temporal and spatial

---

1. Much helpful commentary on this work is to be found in the Heidelberg critical edition, ed. R. Klibansky and H. G. Senger, 1982, esp. in the editors' *Adnotationes*, 147–69. See also Dangelmayr, *Gotteserkenntnis und Gottesbegriff*, 273–82; Schnarr, *Modi essendi*, 68–166; A. Brüntrup, *Können und Sein* (Munich: Pustet, 1973), 63–102; and P. Casarella, "Nicholas of Cusa and the Power of the Possible," *American Catholic Philosophical Quarterly* 64 (1990): 7–34. J. Hopkins translates *De venatione sapientiae* in *Nicholas of Cusa: Metaphysical Speculations*, vol. 1 (Minneapolis, Minn.: Banning Press, 1998), 151–235. His notes to the translation, 297–322, are particularly useful. Flasch, in *Nikolaus von Kues*, 603–22, admirably locates the entire work within the life and thought of Cusanus.

2. The editors of the Heidelberg critical edition, 147–49, cite Plato and Raymond Lull as earlier influences on Nicholas' choice of this metaphor.

terms. We have an introductory session before the hunt (cc.1–10), the actual pursuit of quarry through ten hunting fields (cc.11–32), and an assessment of the hunt's success at its completion (cc.33–39). Perhaps we might picture a large forest or hunting estate divided into ten separate hunting grounds. Each of the ten areas is replete with the same sort of game or prey to be taken. All of them exemplify or at least presuppose what Cusanus terms "the three regions or domains" of being. Working each hunting field lets the hunter understand the hunted, the divine quarry, in a different intellectual situation or in different metaphorical terms or under somewhat different conditions.

Because the treatise is lengthy and laid out in accord with this elaborate spatial conceit, we may be tempted to read it more discursively and less dialectically than we read some of Nicholas' other writings. Thus we could trudge mentally from field to field as if they were really distinct, but this would be to ignore the first several chapters where Nicholas instructs us about such hunting or seeking God. In fact one must superimpose the same categorial framework on each field and recall lessons from the other fields in order to appreciate the multiperspectival pursuit Cusanus is proposing.[3]

This work is intended to engage the reader in a search for wisdom and for the Divine that results from *not* really attaining or securing knowledge of God. The divine Quarry ever slips away but we may acquire a paradoxical wisdom. Nicholas' emphasis is as much on the seeking and hunting as on the ten *campi* or the prey, as his "Prologue" stresses (h 1). Indeed, the rubrics or themes distinguishing each hunting field are to be seen as providing different strategies, varied cognitive means for the *same* quest, not really a different hunt in a different place. As so often in Cusan thought, even the metaphors that order a given treatise are chosen not simply to organize and explain what Nicholas has to say, but also to enable us to employ the metaphor in an exploratory way for our own quest of the Divine.[4]

---

3. *De venatione sapientiae* frequently alludes to and capitalizes on Nicholas' previous writings, in the fashion of a compendium of his favorite ideas, quite unlike his brief work of 1464 entitled *Compendium*, which rounds off his ideas on knowledge and our use of natural and conventional signs. See the text and translation of *Compendium* in Hopkins, *Wisdom and Knowledge*, 374–441.

4. So Cusanus writes at the end of his preface (h 1): *"Deinde volenti philosphari, quod venationem sapientiae voco, regiones et in illis loca quaedam describam in camposque ducam, praedae, quam quaerunt, apprime puto refertos"* (And so, for one who wants to philosophize—which I term the hunt for wisdom—I will describe the regions and certain places in them, and I will lead him to the fields that I believe are especially full of the prey they seek).

1. THE CONCEPTUAL FRAMEWORK OF
DE VENATIONE SAPIENTIAE

A reasonable point to enter *De venatione sapientiae* would be the comments in chapter 2 that recall the Cusan doctrine first set out two decades earlier in *De docta ignorantia*. There Nicholas had insisted that our knowledge must begin from something certain in order to proceed with some security in the attempt to gain knowledge of things divine.[5] Here is how the present passage restates the point:

> Since the unknown cannot be known through the more unknown, I have to grasp something quite certain, something not doubted but presupposed by all hunters [of wisdom], and seek what is unknown in light of that. For the true is in harmony with the true. While my eager mind was attentively seeking this within itself, the assertion of the philosophers came to me—something even Aristotle takes up at the beginning of the *Physics*—namely, what is impossible does not occur. (c.2 h 6)

"What is impossible does not occur" *(quod impossibile fieri non fit)*. Cusanus will use this as a kind of background principle for his explorations or hunting expeditions in this book. It is one form of the counterpositive of the well-known Scholastic dictum *"Ab esse ad posse valet illatio,"* namely, *"A non-posse ad non-esse valet illatio."* What is characteristically Cusan and Neoplatonic is the emphasis on the impossible and the possible over the actual. A central focus of *De venatione sapientiae* turns out to be possibility framed as *posse fieri*. Depending on the context, Nicholas trades on both meanings of the Latin idiom: the possibility of taking place, that is, of occurring/happening *and* the possibility of being made or produced. Usually he stresses the latter since he has God's creating in mind.

In chapter 3 Cusanus first explains the threefold structure of possibility and reality that provides the overall conceptual framework within which he will be working in what follows. The first reality is God, the one absolute and "incontractible" Principle that is the Source of all else. Even this ultimate First can be characterized in terms of possibility, for God eternally *is* in actuality whatever is possible. All the other temporal things God has created make up the second domain of reality captured in the framework. Created things obviously can be described in terms of possibility. Since they are contingent productions or creations that issue from the absolute First Principle they were once merely possible and have been, are, or will be actual.

At this point Cusanus makes the important move in *De venatione sapi-*

---

5. *De docta ignorantia* 1.1 h 2.

entiae. He introduces a third ontological realm, indeed, a whole third "in-between" domain of possibility, that of *posse fieri*, of being possible in the sense of "being able to be made."[6] This third realm of "creatables" mediates between the fully actualized possibility of divine Being and the possible-and-now-actual creatures we are familiar with in time and space. (See Table 6.1.) In this realm of *posse fieri* we may conceive creatures as *possibly* actual. Nicholas says that this in-between realm is itself created, even though it does not exist in time. It is conceived as that from which God creates everything that has been, is, or will be actual. (In some contexts, *fieri posse* sounds like the dyad or *chora* of Plato's *Timaeus*, a kind of material principle; but this manner of speaking is finally superseded in *De venatione sapientiae* in favor of seeing *fieri posse* as an intermediate phase on the way, as it were, to being created.) For Nicholas, the realm of *fieri posse* is based on the consideration that everything that actually occurs or is created can do or be so only because of its prior possibility. In his words, "that which is made is produced from the possibility of being made, because the possibility of being made becomes actually everything that is made" (c.3 h 7).[7]

Cusanus is here taking the Creator's viewpoint, as it were. If we imagine the totality of all things actual and possible issuing from their divine Source, we can envisage one sector of ontological possibilities (those that will be produced or made actual) as if they were reified or hypostatized. This is the domain Nicholas terms *posse fieri*. Nicholas gives *posse fieri* a status in reality, not created in time and space, but "initiated" *(initiata)* outside of time, posterior to and thus not identical with God's eternal reality where all possibility is actual.[8]

Obvious similarities to Plotinian and Proclean intermediaries come

---

6. Hopkins, *Metaphysical Speculations 1*, 298, notes 18–19.

7. Flasch, *Nikolaus von Kues*, 606–7, underlines the hierarchical and cosmological significance of Nicholas' threefold differentiation of possibility in these chapters. Cf. Brüntrup, *Können und Sein*, 72–86, for a discussion of the varied and not entirely compatible aspects of *fieri posse*. In his *Idiota de mente*, c.11 h 130–32, Cusanus uses *posse fieri* and *posse facere* in a different way. There these two terms, together with *nexus*, refer to Father, Son, and Holy Spirit, respectively.

8. In the *epilogatio* (h 116) to *De venatione sapientiae* Nicholas summarizes as follows:

Sed posse fieri est in omnibus quae facta sunt id quod factum est, nam nihil factum est actu nisi id quod fieri potuit; sed alio essendi modo: imperfectiori modo in potentia et perfectiori in actu. Non igitur posse fieri et posse factum in essentia sunt differentia. Sed posse facere, licet non sit aliud, tamen, cum sit causa essentiae, non est essentia. Essentia enim est suum causatum. [But *posse fieri* is that which is made in all things that have been made, for nothing has been actually made except what could be made, though in another mode of being—more imperfect in potentiality and more perfect in actuality. Therefore *posse fiere* and *posse factum* are not different in essence. But *posse facere*, although it is not something other, still, because it is the Cause of essence, is not itself essence, for essence is what it has caused.]

to mind until Cusanus compares *fieri posse* to *caelestia et intelligibilia* (the heavenly bodies and the intelligences, the angels) and assigns *fieri posse* the similar, less-than-eternal but no-less-everlasting, sphere of *aevum*. Once again we are present in the Christian Neoplatonic cosmos—a sublunar reality subject to change but ruled by the heavens and the intelligences, with both of those realms dependent on the Creator. Cusanus aligns *posse fieri*, the realm of producible possibles governed by Providence, with other realities that are created but everlasting. Temporal and sensible things, then, are their changing and deficient earthly imitations. All everlasting realities are all they can be in being themselves, while sensible creatures are not all they can be, but must struggle through time to become more so.

Cusanus succinctly summarizes this threefold ontological framework of possibility presupposed for the hunt for wisdom. He writes toward the end of chapter 3:

When therefore I turn to contemplate the eternal, I see One who is Actuality without qualification, and I mentally intuit all things in that One as enfolded in the absolute Cause. When I look to the everlasting [*aevum*] and perpetual, I see intellectually the possibility of being made [*ipsum fieri posse*], and in it the nature of all and of each, as they should be made in accord with the perfect unfolding of the divine Mind's predestination. When I look to time, I comprehend sensibly that all things are unfolded in succession by imitating the perfection of perpetual things. (c.3 h 8)

Nicholas thus views *posse fieri* as one way of understanding divine creation in terms of what is ontologically prior to temporal, created things. Cusanus' *posse fieri* lets both possibility and producibility come together here, or rather it restricts the kind of possibility in question to what is producible: what has been, is, or will be created. *Posse fieri* therefore does not comprise the totality of what is imaginable or conceptually possible, whether these are taken as states of affairs or possible worlds or inhabitants of either. Neither is *posse fieri* restricted simply to the possible as opposed to the impossible, nor to the contingent as opposed to the necessary.[9] *Posse fieri* comprises everything that is both possible and contingent because creatable.

Nicholas' point is not to discuss the various sorts of possibility and necessity, whether logical, conceptual, or ontological. He is attempting to view that set of possibles which are creatables, but conceived in semidetachment from the divine Source of all. He labels this realm that of *posse fieri*. In typical Proclean Neoplatonic fashion *posse fieri* thus becomes the

---

9. On these two senses of possibility in Aristotle and how they get played out in medieval notions of modality, see *Cambridge History of Later Medieval Philosophy*, 342–57.

TABLE 6.1 Threefold Possibility *(Posse)* in *De venatione sapientiae*

	Ontological domain	Mode of cognitive access	Parallel from logic	Parallel from geometry
Eternal God	*posse facere:* possibility of making, producing	Eternal: intuitive vision *(intellectus)*	Logic	Geometry
Perpetual "possible creatures"	*posse fieri:* possibility of being made, produced	Perpetual: mental vision *(ratio)*	Syllogistic form	Definition
Actual temporal creatures	*posse factum:* possibility made, produced	Temporal: rational, perceptual vision	Any syllogistic argument	Any drawn figure

mediating member of the triad—between the unlimited actuality of all possibility in God and the attenuated and contingent possibilities realized in the created things "unfolded in succession." *Posse fieri* thus gives us purchase in thought for reaching toward both upper and lower limits of possibility. And as mediating the relation between God and all that is not God, *posse fieri* fittingly has its own independent, though derivative, ontological status.[10]

Chapters 4 and 5 present parallels from logic and mathematics to clarify where and how *posse fieri* fits between God and created things. Nicholas' parallels can be displayed in tabular form, as in Table 6.1. The left side of the table presents the three related sorts of possibility, or *posse*, as well as the kind of "temporality" and beings corresponding to them. The three columns on the right present the cognitive, logical, and mathematical parallels to *posse facere*, *posse fieri*, and *posse factum*.

We should expect that Nicholas would pick logic and mathematics as his preferred examples. Both exemplify his conviction that the human mind produces its ideas just as the divine Mind creates the beings that constitute the universe. But Table 6.1 displays how Nicholas places something intermediate between the arts or sciences of logic and mathematics and our actual employment of them in reasoning or in, say, doing a geometrical construction. He sees the valid forms of reasoning

10. Brüntrup, in *Können und Sein*, 79–80, points out three aspects of *posse fieri:* its connection with the realm of becoming or created things, its relation to the Eternal One beyond all becoming, and the fact that *posse fieri* cannot itself be conceived since it has no essence of itself. See also Schnarr, *Modi essendi*, 101–20.

(Aristotle's syllogistic in "Barbara, Celarent, etc.")[11] and geometrical definitions as determining what *can* be produced in logic or mathematics. The reason is that only in accord with them do we use syllogisms correctly or are we able to construct a circle or a triangle. Syllogistic and mathematical definitions are thus comparable to the ontological domain of *posse fieri* generally. All three limit and determine what can be made—whether in logic, in geometrical construction, or in reality.

One Cusan synonym for *posse fieri* in these chapters is *natura*.[12] This recalls earlier medieval doctrines of the divine Ideas or even Plato's Forms, because, as the paradigmatic "natures" of things, the divine Ideas or Platonic Forms set the possibilities that actual things only partially realize. In a parallel way, definitions in mathematics and the valid forms of the syllogism determine what is possible when we think correctly or use mathematics. While the definition of a circle provides the rule and paradigm for what we draw, any given drawing falls short of that definitional norm and does not exhaust its possibilities. In logic, each instance of reasoning applies and makes actual what the rules for syllogisms allow as valid or make possible logically, though it does not fall short so long as it is correct reasoning.

Cusanus also differentiates these three ontological realms in terms of time and eternity, as displayed in Table 6.1. If creation makes up the temporal realm and God's utter infinity is coincident with eternity, the in-between of *posse fieri* is designated *aevum*, "aeviternity" or "aeon," and *perpetua*, "perpetual" or "everlasting," versus eternal and temporal. A distinct sort of knowledge is assigned to each of these realms as well. To God's eternity corresponds a kind of intellective intuition beyond reason; to the perpetuity of *posse fieri* corresponds rational vision or conceptualization; and the temporal realities of experience correspond to sense perception aided by the discriminations of reason.[13]

Even if *posse fieri* is not actually a Plotinian hypostasis or Proclean intermediate, it seems to function much like one in its mediating function

---

11. Aristotle's basic valid forms of the syllogism were captured for medieval student memory in hexameter verses that began "Barbara, Celarent." In this mnemonic scheme, four vowels (A, E, I, O) stood for universal or particular and affirmative or negative propositions in the premises and conclusion of a syllogism. See Hopkins, *Metaphysical Speculations 1*, 299–300, note 25.

12. Schnarr, *Modi essendi*, 120–37, gives a synoptic overview of *natura* in *De venatione sapientiae*.

13. Notice that this sort of intellectual knowing is not the same as conceptualizing, as Nicholas points out in chapter 6: "One who reads this will no doubt be occupied with how to conceptualize *fieri posse*. And this is difficult because there is no limit to *fieri posse* except in its Source. So how could a concept be formed of something that cannot have limits?" (h 14).

between God and creation.[14] In such a metaphysics, all the various levels of being have to be understood as interrelated and thought together to be understood for all they are. Nicholas cites "Plato" with approval on this very point (he had been reading Diogenes Laertius' *Lives*): "Plato ... considered that higher things exist in things lower by participation, while the lower exist more excellently in higher things" (c.8 h 19). But this means that lower and higher must be understood together to do justice to the reality of their connectedness. Just so, human knowing capacities are to be understood as manifesting and depending on the sourcing oneness of the mind as we descend from the mental *intuitus* beyond words and concepts to insight, reason, and sense perception. Just so, the lower extramental realities, be they *perpetua* or *temporalia*, are only understood for all they are in relation to *posse facere* or *possest*, the divine Oneness or Power from which they proceed. Both in the domain of knowing and in that of being we are able to rise or ascend from lower to higher, just as we can descend from higher to lower.

2. "KNOWING" GOD AS *POSSEST* AND *LI NON ALIUD*: FIELDS 1–3

In the long middle section of *De venatione sapientiae* Nicholas explores the ten hunting fields, always in search of the divine Prey.[15] Not surprisingly, the first three fields (cc.11–14) are those of learned ignorance, *possest*, and *non-aliud*.[16] Each of these three metaphorical themes structured a single treatise or dialogue among Nicholas' earlier writings. Here they are recollected in light of *fieri posse*.

Chapter 12 encapsulates the theme of learned ignorance in a succinct sentence: "... just as God's reality is the cause of knowledge of everything that exists, so, because what God is as knowable is not known, the quiddity of each thing, as knowable, is also unknown" (h 31). This statement begins from God's unknowability and moves to the

---

14. In cc.8–10 Nicholas attempts to synthesize his ideas with those of his Platonic predecessors. As I mentioned earlier, most Neoplatonisms can be interpreted as mapping a hierarchy of interrelated and interdependent human knowing powers onto what there is and what can be known. Ontology recapitulates or at least parallels "gnoseology" in such categorial frameworks. These ontologies may be best understood as projective constructions extrapolating the structure of mind onto that of reality, as Nicholas' examples and references here illustrate.

15. Schnarr, in *Modi essendi*, 69–70, gives a synopsis of the ten fields.

16. See Chapters 1 and 4, this book. For *De possest*, see Hopkins' translation and commentary in *Concise Introduction*, and J. Stallmach, "Sein und das Können-selbst bei Nikolaus von Kues," in his *Suche nach dem Einen* (Bonn: Bouvier Verlag H. Grundmann, 1982), 209–22.

unknowability of the essences of created things. This may be the opposite of the direction from which we might expect thought and reflection to proceed, but for Nicholas it is the "God's-eye" view that is fundamental. Learned ignorance entails an appreciation of how little we know and understand even when, and just because, we adopt that viewpoint.

From that viewpoint, we can understand *fieri posse* as the realm of dynamic possibility or creatability that everything in our normal experience imitates and instantiates. For Nicholas, the framework of *posse facere*, *posse fieri*, and *posse factum* dovetails with the doctrine of learned ignorance. He writes:

> For it is impossible [*fieri non potest*] that what is prior to *posse fieri* be known. Therefore, since God is prior, God cannot become comprehensible. And since what *posse fieri* is is not comprehensible, no more than its cause which is prior to it, no thing's quiddity, while its causes are unknown, is actually comprehended insofar as it is knowable. (c.12 h 31)

This means that we have to temper our employment of the very conceptual framework Nicholas uses here lest we think we can penetrate even the essences of creatures, let alone of their Maker or of their possibility as makeable. The framework enables us to order, explore, and rethink the whole of what exists or can exist, but it gives us no purchase on the essence of anything.

Chapter 13 takes us into the second hunting field, this one named after a term Cusanus concocted for God, the Latin neologism *possest*.[17] This combination of *posse* and *est* fits the divine Reality, Nicholas explains, because God abides *"ubi posse est actu"* (where possibility actually exists) or, alternately, *"quia est actu quod esse potest"* (because God *is* in actuality what can be; h 34). To call God *possest* (= *posse facere*), then, is to remark once more that God precedes both *posse fieri* and *posse factum*, what is contingent and created as producible and as produced.

Nicholas proposes two considerations to explain how *possest* may aid our hunting the divine quarry. First, we are to understand from *possest* that God's reality is prior to and other than any distinction or difference we may find in experience or map in thought. God stands beyond and thus "before" differentiation itself, even the most inclusive distinctions, say, those between actuality and possibility, between *posse fieri* and *posse facere*, between being and nonbeing, between identity and difference. We are to seek God beyond distinctions and contrasts where all that is possible is realized as actual in the divine Eternity.

---

17. In his *Compendium* (c.10 h 29–31) and *De apice theoriae* (h 4 ss.), Nicholas uses *posse* and *posse ipsum*, respectively, as names for God that parallel *posse facere* here. In those works he does not place the same emphasis on what can be created (*posse fieri*) and what has been created (*posse factum*).

Second, Cusanus turns to the number 1 and the series of numbers generated from 1 to provide some image of the relation of *possest* and *posse fieri*. Because any token of the number 1 can be repeated, 1 may be said to be potentially the whole number series. Nicholas distinguishes what the 1 is from what it can be, just as he distinguishes *possest*, the single divine Source, from *posse fieri*, the many—as able to be made or created. We are to move from what is actual in the number 1 and what is possible (the other numbers) back to what is prior to both and to all else in the eternal divine *possest*. As identical with the divine Eternity, the 1 or the 2 is actually all the possible instances of oneness or twoness (whether numerical tokens or not) that have come to be or will do so.

Then Cusanus reminds us, "But the proportion of that two which comes after *posse fieri* to the two which is Eternity is like that of the countable to the uncountable or of the finite to the Infinite" (c.13 h 37). That is to say, there is no proportion or common measure between them at all! In other words, we should understand *posse fieri* as marking the boundary that separates God and creatures. And attempting to think *possest* lets us reach toward a God beyond all oppositions, a God we never grasp, "where *posse esse* and *actu esse* do not differ" (c.13 h 38).

Chapter 14 takes up another neologism Nicholas coined for the divine Reality, *li non aliud*, the Not Other. Here Nicholas recapitulates some of the main themes in his dialogue of that name. To the questions requesting definitions, "What is the Not Other?" and "What then is the other?" Nicholas responds with what sound like playful riddles. *"Non aliud est non aliud quam non aliud"* (Not Other is not other than Not Other). *"Ipsum aliud esse non aliud quam aliud"* (The other is not other than other; h 40). While these responses at first seem mere tautologies, Nicholas' point may be seen if we construe "the other" as any created thing and reserve "the Not Other" for God. Then the first "definition" says that God is nothing else than God, the second that any created "other" is nothing else than itself. In Nicholas' example the world is nothing else than or *not other* than the world. But is this just to claim that God, the Not Other, is self-identical, no less than each created thing?

In fact, Cusanus goes much further. He writes, "The intellect discovers, then, that God is not other than the other, because he defines the other itself. For if the Not Other is removed, the other does not remain" (c.14 h 40). He clarifies this by explaining that to say God is not other than creatures is not to say God is the same as they are or to say that God is different from what is created in the way one creature is different from the next. Both prior to and not other than creatures, the divine Not Other is not identical with any one of them *(idem cum aliquo)*. Nicholas has us hunt for the divine Eternity under the rubric of *li non aliud* so that we can understand how God's "otherness" is unique—not opposed to and not the same as the otherness of creatures (the ways one thing is or can be different or other than another thing). Not other than the heavens, for instance, God is likewise not the same as the heavens; the reason is that the divine Not Other defines the identity of each created thing. The Not Other again points us beyond the realm of *posse fieri* to what precedes it, for all that is other is ontologically posterior to *posse fieri*.[18]

3. LIGHT AND PRAISE—RESPONSE AND ITS WHEREWITHAL: FIELDS 4–5

At chapter 15, Nicholas enters a new domain, that of light, the fourth hunting field of his continuing quest. This and the fifth hunting field, praise, are closely connected. What is remarkable about these two chapters is the change of tone in Nicholas' discourse. The great medieval thinkers never proposed speculation about God just for its theoretical interest. They were also responding as religious believers to the mysterious One whom they believed central to human life and destiny. It is not surprising, then, to find Cusanus combining his continuing exposition with prayerful response and contemplative reflection.

Nicholas invokes Scripture to set the tone: "The light of Your countenance, O Lord, is signed upon us" (Ps 4.7). As Augustine had pointed out centuries before, God is light, the Creator of all light, even and especially the light by which the human intellect sees and understands. Knowledge of God *(notitia Dei)* is equivalent to *lumen vultus*, "the light of God's countenance." And the rest of that biblical verse is implicit in Nicholas' attitude throughout: "You have given gladness in my heart." The chapters of *De venatione sapientiae* that deal with light are not just illuminating in the sense that they extend and give further articulation to the insights in the first three *campi*. Rather, they pause for contemplation and reflection, recapitulating the insights achieved as a matter of satisfaction and even of joy.

Chapter 15, for instance, rejoices that the First Principle that defines itself and everything created is reflected throughout the universe in ten perfections identical with or "not other" than itself: goodness, greatness, truth, beauty, wisdom, delight, perfection, clarity, equality, and sufficiency. In each created thing the ten are not the divine Not Other, strictly speaking, yet because the divine Not Other is not other than created things, even the lowliest creature is not without the ten. In Nicholas'

---

18. Flasch remarks that these three chapters encapsulate Cusan teaching on the coincidence of opposites; see *Nikolaus von Kues*, 608–12.

own words, "And because among all things no one thing is lacking in sufficiency, all things have been established most adequately since each has just as much sufficiency as suffices for it" (c.15 h 44).

These ten perfections recall those perfections the earlier medievals saw as characteristic of both God and creatures, qualities or characteristics each of whose core sense excluded all imperfection. The earlier Scholastic thinkers claimed that these predicates transcend (because they are true of) all ten categories of Aristotle. Later Scholastic thinkers termed them "transcendentals" and taught that their meaning is "analogous" and they are "convertible" with "being."[19] The ten listed here recall a similar list of ten *dignitates*, or divine attributes, which one of Nicholas' favorite thinkers, Raymond Lull, used to mediate between God and creatures in his combinatory art.[20]

Nicholas' reaction in chapter 15 is to marvel at and admire God and his creation. He concludes the chapter by recalling that to be struck with awe is precisely to draw closer to God. Our capacity to wonder in turn "inflames" our intellectual capacities with "unspeakable desire" for what we are seeking (Nicholas' language here refers directly to the Song of Songs 1.3). And we are enabled to proceed in good hope in spite of our bodily estate so that we prefer the divine Wisdom to all else.

Indeed, the final part of chapter 15 and all of chapter 16 should be read as a Cusan exposition and response to the verse in Genesis: "And God saw all the things that he had made and they were very good" (1.31). Things other than God are composite, Nicholas continues (c.16 h 46–47), and so their created goodness and other perfections are not absolute but contracted or limited. They are characterized by "variety," while in contrast the divine Not Other is incomposite and characterized by "simpleness." The diversity of creatures means that they "reflect" the divine goodness and greatness and other perfections in a variety of ways more or less distanced from their source.

Chapter 17 continues Nicholas' reflections on the theme of light. He now turns that light motif to knowing in order to invoke a favorite claim: when the intellective soul looks within itself, it sees God and all else reflected there (compare *Idiota de mente* c.5 h 85, c.7 h 106). Cu-

---

19. For a succinct summary of this doctrine in Thomas Aquinas, for instance, see B. Davies, *The Thought of Thomas Aquinas* (Oxford: Oxford University Press, 1992), 70–75; and J. Wippel, "Metaphysics," in *The Cambridge Companion to Aquinas*, ed. N. Kretzmann and E. Stump (Cambridge: Cambridge University Press, 1993), 85–127, esp. 89–93, 116–17.

20. See the prologue and distinction 1 of Lull's *Ars demonstrativa*, in *Selected Works of Ramon Llull*, ed. and trans. A. Bonner (Princeton, N.J.: Princeton University Press, 1985), 1:317–37, where Lull presents sixteen *dignitates*. Cf. his *Ars Brevis*, part 1, part 2.1, in *Selected Works*, 1:580–83, where these are reduced to nine. See also E. Colomer, *Nikolaus von Kues und Raimund Lull* (Berlin: de Gruyter, 1961), 86–88.

sanus avers that the intellect shares goodness and greatness and truth and the rest of the ten perfections mentioned before and so is able to grasp both absolute and contracted (that is, created) goodness and greatness. Moreover, since knowledge is a kind of assimilation or active likening, the mind realizes that it sees all within it in a kind of living reflection: *"in se ipsum respiciens cuncta in se ipso assimilata videt"* (looking into itself it sees everything "assimilated" in itself; c.17 h 50). But as a living image of God the mind looks within only to find the divine Exemplar whose goodness and greatness exceeds what can be conceived or thought. Cusanus writes:

> Now since it is a living intellectual image of God, and God is not other than anything, therefore, when the intellect enters into itself and knows that it is such an image, it sees in itself what sort of Exemplar it has. For without doubt it knows that this is its God whose likeness it is. For by the goodness of its knowing the intellect knows that the goodness of which it is the image is greater than it can conceive or think. (c.17 h 50)

Cusanus moves to the next field, that of praise, only to find that what had been illumined for understanding and appreciation in the previous hunting field of light can now be seen as praising and affording reasons to praise God.[21] The ten perfections are *laudes dei* (c.18 h 51). Being themselves objects of and grounds for praise, the ten perfections are taken together to apply to God and hence to honor the divine Source of creaturely praise.[22] Here Nicholas quotes the Psalms and Pseudo-Dionysius' treatise on the "divine names" to underscore the point that all created things that share the ten perfections praise their divine Source and are themselves recognizably good and worthy of praise in their own right. Nicholas ends chapter 18 (h 53) by indicating how human life and intelligence are "the best composed hymn" for praising God since human praise embodies the recognition that the core of life is to return to God the existence God bestowed.

Cusanus continues his reflections on the domain of praise in the next two chapters, indicating how important praise is as a reflection of human freedom. Human beings can choose whether to recognize or reject their divine Origin and Goal and live accordingly. One such rejection is to be found in blatant idolatry, where worship of some creature is substi-

---

21. Schnarr, in *Modi essendi*, 70, connects the fields of light and praise by explaining that, for Nicholas, God is the creator of all light, even the light of our intellects. Once enlightened, we are able to recognize the world as God's creation and praise both creature and Creator.

22. Hopkins, in *Metaphysical Speculations 1*, 307, note 133, points out that, in the phrase *"laudes dei"* (the praises of God), the genitive *"Dei"* (God) is both objective and subjective, as when Nicholas writes in c.18 h 51: *"Quid laudatur per illa nisi laus illa, quae deus?"* (What is praised through those [ten] if not that praise which is God?).

tuted for worship of God, which Cusanus finds *"insania"* (c.19 h 54). Another more frequent deviation—more subtle idolatry, perhaps—consists in self-love or love of this world, but Nicholas simply contrasts these loves with the way the saints turned their lives into living praise, something he obviously believes more reasonable.

In fact Nicholas goes on to expand a hint in the Psalms into an elaborate conceit: human beings can become living stringed instruments of praise. "Thus is the human person a living harp possessing everything for playing the praise of God that one recognizes in oneself" (c.20 h 56). Indeed, this is exactly our destiny: by being lives of praise we become ever more likened to God. Hunting in the field of praise merely capitalizes on what Nicholas has discovered in his hunt through the previous fields. Yet it can remind us that the final significance of his thought is always religious—he seeks the truth as wisdom and finds it in acknowledging and praising his divine Source and ultimate Goal.

These two hunting fields (cc.15–20) mark a definite change in tone and affect from the more strictly expository and analytic character of the previous three fields and the introductory explanations with which *De venatione sapientiae* began. But it is also fascinating that in these five chapters Cusanus does not explicitly mention *posse fieri*. As so often in his writings, he moves back and forth from what can be found reflected of God in the many created others to what he has already said of God as the uncreated and thus divine Not Other. These two hunting fields take us into what is a more typical Cusan vision of reality—one that discards any Platonic forms or any intermediaries between God and creatures, even *posse fieri*.

On the other hand, let us suppose that the marvelous wisdom one hunts down in these fields amounts to the realization and "certain intuition" (*certissime intuetur;* c.15 h 44) that the ten perfections, or *laudabilia*, are "most truly said" of both God and creatures. Then it may be possible to see the ten perfections, no less than *posse fieri*, as comprising the realm of what is possible or creatable when one thinks back from creatures toward the Creator. Moreover, we should recall that for Raymond Lull the absolute perfections or emanations (parallel to Cusanus' ten) mediate between the divine Trinity and the relative perfections to be found in created things. They mediate both as the combinatory factors of the *ars major lulliana* and as the actual dimensions of what is real and independent of human thought.[23] Then it may be that "good, great, true, beautiful, wisdom-making, delightful, perfect, clear, equal, and suf-

---

23. See Yates, *Lull and Bruno*, 9–77, esp. 20–22, 41–42, for the mediating function of the perfections in Lull's writing. Bonner summarizes Lull's art in a brief essay on Lull's thought in *Selected Works*, 1:53–70.

ficient" simply spell out the possible features of *posse fieri* or what can be created. This is why they reflect in a limited way those same features of the divine Exemplar.

4. TRINITARIAN HUNTING — *UNITAS, AEQUALITAS, NEXUS:* FIELDS 6–8

Chapters 21 and 22 take up the sixth hunting field of *De venatione sapientiae*, oneness, or *unitas*. Cusanus modifies and adapts the Neoplatonic understanding of the One as first principle as he explores the meaning of oneness or unity *(unitas)*. He agrees with the tradition that the first eternal Principle of all is the One and that oneness is prior to all multiplicity.[24] But Nicholas gives these Neoplatonic truisms his own accent, for he points out that the One is near the Not Other which is prior to it, for the One and the Self-Same *(idem)* participate the Not Other more than the others. As eternal and ontologically prior, the One embraces or enfolds both actual beings and those that are potential.

This last point implies that oneness has an extension beyond that of being *(pace* Aristotle and the medieval Aristotelians),[25] for being is understood here to include only what actually exists. He attributes to Plato the argument that actual being leaves out potential being, even though the latter has some reality. Oneness, on the other hand, "is truly predicated of potency and of act: potency is one; act is one" (c.21 h 60). Nicholas' point here confirms from another direction his original template or framework of *posse facere, posse fieri,* and *posse factum,* for oneness, possibility, and actuality correspond and are parallel to the three sorts of possibility. The new hunting field yields a not dissimilar prey.

Nicholas thereupon returns to his favorite language about God's oneness and ontological priority as contrasted with all other created unitary beings as he proceeds:

> Every many and every plurality and each number and whatever can be called one would cease to be were the One removed. . . . Therefore the One cannot be made since it precedes what is made. Nor can it be destroyed or changed or multiplied since it precedes *posse fieri* and *is* everything that can be. (c.21 h 61)

What follows from this for Cusanus is that all the earlier non-Christian Neoplatonic efforts to interpose many gods, the heavens, and the

---

24. Nicholas' references in these chapters to Diogenes Laertius, Proclus, and Pseudo-Dionysius are traced in the Heidelberg edition, 56–65.
25. For instance, Aquinas writes in *Summa theologiae* 1.11.1r: ". . . *unum non addit supra ens rem aliquam, sed tantum negationem divisionis: unum enim nihil aliud significat quam ens indivisum*" (One does not add anything to being, only the negation of division, for one signifies nothing else than undivided being).

intelligences between the first One and the rest of the beings were wasted labor. Proclus, Plato, Aristotle, and Epicurus all need correction on this point, as well as for the notion that this earth is the center and goal of all that exists. Of course, *posse fieri* itself might be understood as the sort of intermediate realm Nicholas here explicitly eschews. Only by understanding creatables "backward" from actual creatures and "forward" from their divine Source can they be both a limited realm of possibles (since the created realm is limited) and have some reality (as intermediate and as identical with God). Nicholas once again has it both ways: he maintains the traditional conception of the universe—in his own version—at the very same time he rejects the independently existing intermediate realms of his predecessors.

Within the field of oneness, Nicholas continues in chapter 22, there is a particular meadow where a unique prize is to be captured. The prize is called "singularness" or "singularity" *(singularitas)*.[26] Nicholas explains:

> since the One is not other than one, it is seen to be singular, because it is undivided in itself and separated from any other. For the singular embraces everything; for all things are singles and no one of them can be repeated. Therefore single things, since all of them cannot be repeated as well, show that there is one greatest of this sort that is the Cause of every singular thing. And what is singular essentially also cannot be repeated. For it *is* what it can be and is the singularness of all singular things. . . . The Singularness of all singular things is essentially [*per se*] singular, and nothing can possibly be more singular than it. So the singularness of the One and the Good is the greatest, since every singular thing is necessarily one and good and thus is enfolded in the Singularness of the One and the Good. (c.22 h 65)

Nicholas underlines this likeness between God and creatures, pointing out that each created thing receives its singularness from the eternal Cause and thus has a core "desire" or natural conatus for the divine Cause as its perfect good.

That there is a plurality and variety of things is not due to their being single/singular, however, but to what is incidental to them and renders them such and such *(tale et tale)* an individual or single thing. Being other and many is a contingent fact about all creatures. Yet their singularness, for Nicholas, means that as single they are both alike (because they are single) and unlike (because "othered singleness" keeps each creature singular) *and* neither alike (as singular) nor unlike (as single). Because created singularness mirrors the divine Singularness, it can para-

---

26. The Heidelberg editors (h 65, 63 notes) trace *singularitas* to Nicholas' marginal note on Albertus Magnus' commentary on Dionysius' *Mystical Theology*. As used by Nicholas, *singularitas* combines the senses of both individuality/particularity and singularity/uniqueness. What is singular is thus neither plural nor a universal. See Hopkins, *Metaphysical Speculations 1*, 310, note 189.

doxically seem to escape the principle of contradiction governing ordinary discursive thought, no less than does the divine Oneness or Singleness Itself.[27]

In chapters 23 and 24 Nicholas turns to the topics of equality and connection. Together with unity or oneness *(unitas)*, equality *(aequalitas)* and connection *(nexus)* form the triad of terms for the divine Trinity Nicholas took over from Thierry of Chartres and Augustine (already mentioned in chapter 21). Using these unpromising, quasi-mathematical, abstract terms Cusanus had sought some understanding of the Trinitarian mystery from his first speculative writing about it in *De docta ignorantia* 1.7–9. In the present treatise the sixth, seventh, and eighth hunting fields are concerned with the divine Unity and Trinity.

Nicholas makes several points about equality.[28] First, he establishes that it is identical with the eternal divine Oneness and thus is ontologically prior to *posse fieri*, since all other equality (in actual created things) is approximate and no collection of created equals are exactly equal. God's is the strictest equality and it is prior to all plurality. But equality is not somehow multiplied or made plural any more than humanity itself is multiplied in many people. Rather, humans all participate unequally in humanity itself (while all are descriptively human by nature, each is more or less lacking in ideal or paradigmatic humanity), and this unequal sharing is what renders them a multitude or plurality.

In the same fashion equality cannot be itself divided or multiplied, only shared in different (more or less equal!) ways. This is why so-called equal things can always become more equal: they are never exactly equal, but only approach that exactitude asymptotically. With a play on words Nicholas' Latin expresses this creaturely capacity to become more equal as *"aequaliora fieri posse"* (c.23 h 70); this enables him to remark that the divine Equality is prior to and determinative of *posse fieri* itself.

Indeed, the divine Equality is not other than each created thing that shares in equality unequally because each is equally self-identical ("neither more nor less and totally not other than that which it is"). Yet transcendent Equality is to be identified with the divine Word of the Father, a Word whose creating is imagined as speaking each thing's essential name and thus defining ontologically every thing that is not God.[29] The

---

27. Two papers of G. von Bredow expand on these passages: "Der Gedanke der singularitas in der Altersphilosophie des Nikolaus von Kues," and "Participatio Singularitatis. Einzigartigkeit als Grundmuster der Weltgestaltung." They have been collected in *Im Gespräch*, 31–39, and 217–31, respectively.

28. T. Leinkauf, "Die Bestimmung des Einzelseienden durch die Begriffe Contractio, Singularitas, und Aequalitas bei Nicolaus Cusanus," *Archiv für Begriffsgeschichte* 37 (1994): 180–211, esp. 200ff.

29. Cusanus refers to the discussion of equality in the Trinity and in created things in

upshot may be expressed paradoxically: all the equals and unequals of our experience are precisely equal insofar as they share in the divine Equality, but because they share it in unequal ways they are unequal, too.

The eighth hunting field is that of connection or union *(nexus)*, Nicholas' third term for the Third Person of the Trinity. Chapters 24 and 25 summarize Nicholas' ideas about *nexus*, while chapter 26 proposes a geometrical thought experiment for reaching in thought beyond *posse fieri* toward the divine Trinity.

The divine *nexus* or Connection proceeds within the Godhead from the divine Oneness and divine Equality as the Bond of love between Father and Son. No less than Oneness and Equality, their loving Union or Connection remains prior in simple, unchangeable, and indivisible Eternity. The three are not other because they are identically the divine Not Other which is ontologically prior to all otherness. The three are distinct, but *nexus* is not separate from *unitas* and/or *aequalitas* as created things are separate—rather, they are Three in One. As Oneness enfolds all else, so does Equality, while their Connection or Union binds up everything into the eternal divine Oneness.

Created things imitate this divine Trinity for Cusanus, being composite images of unity, entity/equality, and their connection. (Entity, or the form of being, is the equality of unity.) Each creature's oneness restricts its tendency to change, and its equality gives form to that constraint, specifying that oneness to be a certain sort of thing. Both are realized as united or connected in the actual thing. Without oneness, a thing would not be capable of beauty or form, nor ordered to an end, yet that very order or constraint calls forth the required form or structure and both are connected in the unified ontological structure that is the thing.

Cusanus reflects in chapter 25 that this means that the divine Spirit of Love penetrates everything and without it nothing could persist. All are kept in existence by the invisible Spirit of Loving Connection, the ultimate basis of conservation for each and for the whole of which they are parts. Because of this Love or *nexus*, souls are one with bodies; because of it the various parts of the world are gathered into a universe.

This is most evident for Nicholas in intellectual natures where the divine Love that unifies not only preserves the minds destined for wisdom but also shapes and fits them for what they love by nature. At this juncture *nexus* becomes the biblical "Spirit of wisdom" present in our intellectual desires, converting and assimilating the desiring human intellect to itself in love. For Nicholas, a thinker's true happiness is to be found

---

his *De aequalitate* (1459). See Hopkins' translation in *Metaphysical Speculations 1*, esp. 105–17, h 33–42.

in this Union or Connection. This is a wisdom unavailable to so many earlier thinkers who overlooked the third person of the Trinity, who is Union or Loving Connection.

Although Cusanus mentions *posse fieri* several times in his discussion of *unitas, aequalitas,* and *nexus,* it does not figure centrally in his treatment of these terms as synonymous with the Persons of the Christian Trinity.[30] After all, all three Persons are ontologically prior to creation and identical with the eternal Not Other, the Godhead. Yet Oneness, Equality, and Connection or union find their created reflections in the finite world, so by implication these trinitarian reflections *can* be made and must be united as possibilities in the ontologically prior intermediate domain of *posse fieri.* Cusanus always guides our thought toward the divine quarry we desire at the most basic level, something he graphically demonstrates in chapter 26.

5. GEOMETRY AND HEAT—AMBIGUITY OF *POSSE FIERI*

Cusanus begins chapter 26 with an object lesson in geometrical construction and extrapolation calculated, he says, to help us see that the Trinity's oneness is actually all it can possibly be while so transcending our understanding that it can only be "comprehended incomprehensibly"[31] (h 74). The lesson begins with the assumption that a right triangle is the basic rectilinear plane figure to which all others are reducible. Cusanus proposes we extend the dimensions of this triangle in imagination and thought so as to approach "a perfect triangle with three perfect sides." He is thus having us attempt in thought a mathematical image or figure of God as first principle.

In the Cusan thought experiment the two equal sides of a right triangle are constructed and the arc of the circle whose radii are formed by the two sides is to be drawn so that the third side of the triangle is the chord corresponding to the arc. Cusanus then proposes that the sides of this triangle be extended indefinitely. This thought exercise should make it clear, Cusanus believes, that at some indefinite point in the expansion, the two sides, the hypotenuse or chord, and even the arc of the circle must become identically one and the same infinite straight line. At that extrapolated juncture the triangle's three angles are equal (each is 180 degrees), and all three sides have become the same line extended without limit.

---

30. For a summary overview of the Trinity in Nicholas' thought, see Haubst, *Streifzüge,* 255–324; and McGinn, "Unitrinum seu Triunum."

31. This Cusan "slogan" goes back to *De docta ignorantia* and usually signals the coincidence of opposites (God's transcendence) and our learned ignorance (knowledge of God) based on intellectual vision beyond the rational domain (human transcending).

Once again, the context is one of constructing or drawing the figure. One may imagine oneself standing at the center of the circle, as it were, and watching the radii extended further and further. This thought experiment thus embodies an imagined perspective and overlooks the definitional point that a circle is always circular, whatever the size of its radii. Cusanus is using the fact that perception is always perspectival to undercut the conceptual lack of perspective in mathematics so that he can extrapolate to the asymptote and thus undercut both ordinary perception and the conceptual implications of discursive reason. This exercise lets us see how to transcend ordinary reason to "comprehend incomprehensibly" in intellective vision or intuition.

Such a geometrical extrapolation (to infinity, as it were) may be impossible to draw or even imagine—Cusanus says it's a matter of mental or intellectual vision (*mente intueor;* c.26 h 76). Yet he understands this possibility beyond imagining and conceiving as the "enfolding" or ultimate principle of all geometrical figures we can construct or represent in imagination and thought. This figure is as well their resolution or goal and most exact measure (*"omnium figurarum figurabilium complicatio, ut principium, et resolutio, ut finis, atque mensura praecississima";* h 76). The transformation of the finite sides or radii into the enfolded, if extended, oneness of the infinite straight line as the sides are extended in imagination and thought until they cannot be further extended is both ineluctable and available to mental insight.[32]

This "geometrical" exercise can thereby offer an image of perfecting—"extending," as it were—the possibility of being made (*posse fieri*) toward that divine Oneness. There all creatable possibilities, because they are necessarily and eternally realized as Godself, are transformed into the actuality of divine Possibility itself (*posse facere* or *possest*). For Cusanus, the necessity entailed here is incomparably more true and certain than that captured by the geometrical example. *Possest* is prior to any corporeal extension, antecedent in fact to everything finite, whether perceptible or intelligible. Finite things, unlike the infinite God, are available to human conception and comprehension, but in them, as Cusanus says to confirm his point, no threeness is found that is identically oneness nor is oneness found that is identically threeness.

Nicholas next proceeds to a different sort of example that remains in the physical realm of finite beings. He differentiates *possest* and *posse fieri* in finite things by using a quasi-Aristotelian example of burning wood. A piece of wood can become hotter and hotter only to burst into flame at its ignition point. What is in potency and thus able to be heated is thereby parallel to *posse fieri*. When it comes to be fire (heat in act) it parallels

---

32. See Chapter 1, this book, for parallel considerations in *De docta ignorantia* 1.12ff.

possest. What was mentally extrapolated "to the limit" in the previous example here is imagined as undergoing physical change until it becomes itself an active "changer."

Cusanus is presenting a vivid picture, not a scientific example. In this picture, before wood catches fire it is *calefactibile*, able to be heated. Once it is aflame, the burning wood is *calefaciens*, actually heating. It has moved from being a potential heat source to being fire, an actual source of heat. The wood and the fire are not of the same nature, even though the fire is imagined here as potentially in the wood in a different mode of being (potential instead of actual).[33]

For Nicholas, this recalls the meaning of the rule of learned ignorance first discussed in the early chapters of *De docta ignorantia* over twenty years earlier (though not there termed a rule).[34] The rule says that in limited things that allow for degrees of more or less (say, of heat) one never reaches what is strictly speaking the maximum or minimum possible, though one may reach an actual, de facto maximum or minimum—all one can achieve. Were one able to reach the *maximum simpliciter* of hotness (Cusanus is thinking of fire), one would find it not something heatable but something that causes heat—for what causes heat marks the highest degree of what can be heated. He then generalizes the point: "in nature generally what produces [*faciens*] is the highest degree of the producible [*maximum factibilis*]. The capacity to be produced [*factibilitas*] is not the producing capacity, but producing lies in potency in the very capacity to be produced" (c.26 h 79).

Whatever the scientific validity of these medieval ideas about heat and fire, Cusanus clearly is imagining the actual as a limit-goal *(terminus)* of the potential that builds or tends toward it. He then turns to human sensing and understanding and invokes the Aristotelian-Scholastic dictum that the "understandable in act is the understanding in act" (or "what is understandable becomes actual when it is understood").[35] The limit-goal of things able to be sensed or understood is reached when

---

33. This use of heating and fire as an example should be compared with a somewhat different use of fire and heat in chapter 39 of *De venatione sapientiae*. Here Cusanus compares degrees of more and less heat to their cause or maximum, fire, as an image of *posse fieri* vs. *possest;* later he will differentiate *posse facere, posse fieri*, and *posse factum* using the example of fire. See Schnarr, *Modi essendi*, 71–81, for extended paraphrase, commentary, and differentiation of the two uses.

34. *De docta ignorantia* 1.3, 5, 8, 12. For further references and commentary on this "rule," see editorial note 26 in the Heidelberg edition of *De coniecturis*, 208–9. See also Flasch, *Nikolaus von Kues*, 611–12.

35. See Aquinas' *Summa theologiae* 1.14.2.c: *"Unde dicitur in libro De An., quod sensibile in actu est sensus in actu, et intelligibile in actu est intellectus in actu"* (And so it is said in the *De anima* that the sensory in act is the sense in act and the understandable in act is the understanding in act). Cf. Aristotle, *De anima* 3.2.426a15; 3.4.430a3.

they are in fact sensed or understood. In a parallel way, at the limit of what can be illuminated we find light shining and at the limit of what can be created we find the Creator creating.[36]

What is not so obvious from these examples is exactly how they are parallel or consistent. Cusanus slides over the ambiguity in the notion of possibility/potentiality as it applies to existing creatures (the realm of *posse factum*) without noting the Aristotelian differentiation of passive and active *potentia* in the realm of natural things. The first type of potentiality (compare the example of wood and fire) is some thing's capacity to undergo, be affected, and thereby become or be brought into act. Active *potentia*, however, is a thing's native capacity or ability to act or cause or perform (as in the examples of sensing, understanding, illuminating). Cusanus' examples move from the first sense of potentiality to the second without differentiating carefully enough the changes that take place in an Aristotelian *patiens* but are brought on from without from those changes that are brought about by and in an Aristotelian agent from within.[37]

Yet for Cusanus, we are to focus on that point where the wood catches fire or someone understands the point after some effort. In each case what was possible has become actual, and the goal or limit of possibility has been realized. What the rule of learned ignorance reminds us is that even at the point of actuality among created things, we are still dealing with matters of more or less—actual fire, actual light, actual understanding are themselves limited.[38] But the movement from possibility to actuality in finite things provides a pattern for our thinking and imagining. We follow that pattern when we move in thought from *posse fieri*, the realm of possibility antecedent to and encompassing what has been or will be created, toward *posse facere* or *possest*, the realm where divine Actuality is identical with and must exhaust all possibility. Here we search beyond the possibilities that encompass creation to that Term, Goal, or Limit where all possibilities are realized at once in the divine Actuality—the Maximum without qualification, the Limit without limits.

---

36. Nicholas' examples at the end of c.26 provide an easy transition to the topic of the ninth field, limit; this may lead him to elide or pass somewhat quickly over some other distinctions, even in his own teaching about *fieri posse*.

37. Cusanus is paralleling the exemplified changes from possible to actual within the realm of *posse factum* to the movement of our thought toward God: from *posse fieri* (possible) to *possest* or *posse facere* (actual). For the two sorts of actuality/potentiality between and within natural things (which later Scholastics differentiated as transient and immanent action), see Aristotle, *Metaphysics* 9.8.1050a23ff.; and Aquinas, *Summa theologiae* 1.54.2.c.

38. Schnarr, *Modi essendi*, 79.

6. *TERMINUS:* FIELD 9

It is not surprising that Nicholas names the ninth hunting field that follows *"terminus,"* "limit or boundary or end" (cc.27–29).[39] What seemed a bypath in the field of connection or union in fact was the way to this present domain, one "very apt for the hunt and full of the most desirable prey" (c.27 h 80). God, after all, is precisely the greatest Prize for the human heart and mind. For Nicholas, God is without beginning as well as endless (in-finite). That is, all beginnings and all ends, as well as all middles, are comprised in the Godhead where all things created are enfolded and unfolded. Cusanus emphasizes the contrasts. Just because God is unlimited, boundless/infinite, and ontologically prior to all that is possible and creatable, God sets—because God is—the limits, boundaries, and goal for all that is and for all knowledge. God's status is thus prior even and especially to *posse fieri* itself.

Suppose we were to imagine God's free creation in human terms, looking beyond *posse fieri*—as if there were a juncture in God's eternity "before" the decision to create was taken. God could have created a universe totally different in kind from the one we are familiar with. We have no clue to what such created things might have been (*de quibus nullum possumus conceptum facere;* c.27 h 81). But what the created domain of *posse fieri* helps us see, according to *De venatione sapientiae,* is God's determination that the created universe would be the sort of creation we are familiar with: *"mundus iste et non aliud"* (this world and not another; c.27 h 82). This creation is the product of God's free decision. We find the created and attenuated image of the divine Decision in our own minds and decisions—in its own way each human decision is also *"terminus interminus"* (an unlimited limit).

How is the human mind/will, no less than God's, a limit without limits? God's mind creatively determines or limits all that is not God. Human knowing supposedly parallels this by setting limits to its concepts—here Nicholas seems to envisage the construction of definitions as paradigmatic human mental activity. God limits created things as originating Cause of their definite essences and their limited reality; God is their *terminus* both as their Goal and their all-encompassing Source. Yet God remains without limits in at least two senses: nothing else determines or limits God; the limits God sets for created things do not exhaust the divine Omnipotence. That is why Nicholas refers to God as *possest,* the actuality of *all* possibilities, even those not realized in creation.

The oxymoron of "unlimited limit" cannot apply in the same way to

---

39. Hopkins' remarks about the meaning of *terminus* are relevant (*Metaphysical Speculations 1,* 312, note 232): "The Latin word *'terminus'* used through *VS*, conveys many over-

human minds. Our understanding is not simultaneous as is God's, but progressive and discursive. When we manage to understand, we do so gradually, with difficulty, and only in terms we construct for ourselves. Even our best synthetic understandings—overviews, global visions, or *Weltanschauungen*—afford us range at the expense of detail. Such understandings provide maps or outlines or categorial frameworks without necessarily affording an understanding of the particulars they order, organize, and unify.

If these limitations of scope, depth, detail, and temporal succession are obvious, how is it meaningful to say the human mind and its knowing is also unlimited? For Cusanus, no single act of understanding, no content understood, exhausts our knowing capacities (*Nec cuncta quae facit ipsam terminant, quin plura facere possit;* c.27 h 82). We can always understand more or penetrate more deeply what we do know and we can turn to knowing something else. We are not blinded mentally by what our minds envision or see, even though, when compared to God's knowing, as knowers we work at best in less than a kind of mental half-light.

Chapters 28 and 29 take the theme of limit *(terminus)* in two directions: toward the things we know and then toward the human mind. In chapter 28 Cusanus first focuses on the limits God has set in fashioning *kinds* of created things, whose definite limits as types allow the creative, measuring divine Mind to be manifest and shine forth. Their essential definitions *(rationes)* are only imperfectly reflected in particular created specimens of the type, but can be found in their perfection as one with divine Essence. In God the exemplars of created things are one with all their perfected possibilities.[40]

Posse fieri thus has a twofold relation to the exemplars of things enfolded in the divine Oneness. Nicholas puts it as follows (c.28 h 85): "And so the species, since it is a specific determining of *posse fieri* itself, shows that those things are of the same species whose *posse fieri* would be limited [*terminaretur*] in the same [exemplar species], were it possible." First of all, this assumes that, when the intermediate realm of *posse fieri* is conceived as equivalent to all the possibilities to be realized in creation, this realm comprises the various determinate possibilities of natural kinds or species realized when any specimen of a type or kind is created. In this way *posse fieri* as an ontological realm is imagined as divided and defined or limited. Second, the perfection of a given kind or species can be viewed as itself constituting another domain of "specific" possibilities, a second sense for *fieri posse*.

---

lapping conceptualizations: limitation, delimitation, limit, boundary, end, goal, termination, end-point and so on. Nicholas tends to use it interchangeably with '*finis*.'"

40. Schnarr, *Modi essendi,* 88–91.

For instance, each individual human being and each token of a circle instantiates in a limited way the determinate possibilities of its kind. Were either one person or one circle to realize fully its essential possibilities and become all it could be qua human or circular, it would be thereby identical with its species, that definition or limiting essence that is already and eternally one with God's own defining but unlimited perfection. As in one reading of Plato's Forms, only by participating in its exemplar is the actual item the kind of thing it is. Any given actual instance of something finds both the limits and the perfection of its possibilities of becoming (= *fieri posse*) in its exemplar. Cusanus, however, differs from Plato and non-Christian Neoplatonic thinkers because he posits no intermediate realm of Forms or of Nous. Rather all the forms or exemplars are identical with God.

These reflections on *terminus,* or limit, take Cusanus in a second direction in chapter 29. This chapter epitomizes Cusan themes about human knowing first made thematic in his earlier *De coniecturis* and *Idiota de mente.*[41] For Cusanus, the start and finish of the matter of human knowing lies in the fact that human reason cannot grasp in conceptual form the true essences of created things. The reason is that the essences of finite things are identical with God's essence and the divine Essence is beyond our grasp.

The human mind fashions its own concepts that are at best likenesses or assimilations of things—conjectures, to use the quasi-technical term Nicholas mentions here (as he did in the *prologus* to *De venatione sapientiae*). This implies that our intellects are in the same situation regarding the essence of the human mind as well. Just as vision cannot catch a glimpse of its own seeing, so understanding cannot penetrate to its own intelligible core, but employs conjectures to get some idea of what the mind is. Since we exercise understanding without any prior grasp of the essence of the mind, Cusanus argues that the power and capacity to understand are not identical with that essence. Nor does a particular person's limited knowledge exhaust all the possibilities available for human

41. See Chapters 2 and 3, this book. Hopkins' notes on this chapter in *Metaphysical Speculations 1,* 313–14, notes 250–62, propose an alternative interpretation of Nicholas' views on knowledge by emphasizing abstraction of the intelligible *species* whereby the intellect knows things. (See also 316–20, note 303, for his judicious remarks refusing to cast Nicholas as a proto-Kantian.) I would not give as much import to the traditional language which, although present here and in other Cusan texts, is never fleshed out in the full fashion of medieval Aristotelian views on human cognition. Moreover, it seems unclear how to integrate Cusan *intellectus* with the traditional Aristotelian account found, e.g., in Thomas Aquinas. Flasch emphasizes the independence and autonomy of *mens* as intellectus. He recalls how some Cusan texts seem to have *mens* finding its own conceptual measures prior to experience, yet admits that *De venatione sapientiae* puts more emphasis on experience, *assimilatio,* and on the human mind as foundational image of all concepts, not of all things (*Nicholas von Kues,* 612–17).

knowing. Human beings are thus curious composites of finite and infinite, limited and unlimited. On the one hand, the essence of the intellective soul or mind is something determinate and finite—a kind of limit. On the other hand, the possibilities for human knowing are without such limits—never exhausted by any given person's mind.

7. ORDER: FIELD 10

Nicholas begins the tenth and final hunting field, that of order, with a lengthy quote from Pseudo-Dionysius' treatise on divine names. Taken from the section on wisdom in chapter 8 of *The Divine Names*, the point of the quote is that God is both known and unknown in and through created things.[42] In this text creation is viewed as hierarchically arranged from the lower to the higher creatures, an order we can know that points beyond itself to the Cause of all the order and harmony in the universe, the Creator who eludes human knowledge. Cusanus concurs with this Dionysian judgment, adding that God, the Author of the created order, is to be found at the limit of ordered finite things.

In the rest of chapter 30, still following Pseudo-Dionysius, Cusanus comments how the variety of the ordered universe displays a beauty that, as a harmonious whole, reflects the supreme beauty of the Creator. Cusanus alludes to Albert the Great's definition of beauty as the *resplendentia formae* in Albert's commentary on Pseudo-Dionysius' *De divinis nominibus:* intrinsic form is the ontological basis for the shining forth of the Creator's dazzling beauty in the ordered variety and hierarchy of limited created things.[43] Cusanus judges that each thing, however high or low, "is content" with its assigned place in creation since each is required there and nowhere else in order to contribute to the proportioned beauty of the whole. "For it is that harmony [*proportio*] without which the single interrelated condition of the whole, and of the parts to the whole, would in no way appear beautiful and orderly" (c.30 h 91).

In chapter 31 Nicholas elucidates the originating threefold eternal

---

42. For an English version of the passage, see *Complete Works*, 108–9. Cusanus himself owned Latin translations of *De divinis nominibus* by Ambrogio Traversari and Robert Grosseteste. These are codices 43 and 44, respectively, in Nicholas' library at Kues.

43. This work has also been known as *De pulchro et bono* and was long attributed to Aquinas because of a manuscript in Aquinas' handwriting, copied when he was Albert's student. See Albertus Magnus, *Super Dionysium de divinis nominibus I*, ed. P. Simon (Münster: Aschendorff, 1972), 182: *"Ratio pulchri in universali consistit in resplendentia formae super partes materiae porportionatas vel super diversas vires vel actiones."* In *Art and Beauty in the Middle Ages*, trans. H. Bedin (New Haven, Conn.: Yale University Press, 1986), 25, U. Eco comments on Albert's view as follows: "Beauty exists in a thing as the splendor of its form, the form which orders the matter according to canons of proportion, and which in shining forth reveals the ordering activity."

order to be found in God (h 92): *principium sine principio, principium de principio, principium ab utroque procedens* (Beginning [= Origin, Principle] without beginning; Beginning or Principle from or out of [that first] Beginning; Beginning proceeding from both [those Beginnings]). In the same way, the beginning, middle, and end Cusanus believes essential to any order are to be found in the triune divine Origin or uncreated First Principle and thus modeled for everything else that manifests beauty and order. Created things share this threefold divine Order. Each creature comprises an essence *(essentia)* that is the source of its capacities or powers *(virtus);* these two together are the origins of creaturely activity *(operatio).*

Along with this harmony or order internal to each thing, there is also another threefold hierarchical arrangement: things with intellect, things without intellect but possessing life, and things without life or intellect that merely exist. Because thinking things also live and exist, Nicholas proposes that "in the first [intellectual nature] the subsequent things are enfolded" (c.31 h 93). To see the full implications of Nicholas' explanation here, it is helpful to recall the Aristotelian Scholastic dictum, *"Vivere viventibus est esse"* (For living things existing amounts to living, or Living is the being of living things).[44] Here Cusanus proposes that for intellectual things understanding is their being and life. For living things without mind, living is their being and takes the place of understanding. And for merely existing things just to be stands in place of living and understanding.

The universal order (which shares in the eternal divine order of the Trinity) is to be found in the angelic and ecclesiastical hierarchy, in the order of the heavens and their movements, as well as in all the orders that are creations of human beings.[45] All the achievements of the human spirit—moral virtue, practical arts, social and political systems, theoretical knowledge—display order, too. Nicholas closes chapter 31 by remarking that only by proceeding in an orderly way can anyone pursuing an inquiry or keeping things in memory make useful progress. He cites the slave-boy episode from Plato's *Meno* as one example of such orderly question and response. Order underlies intelligibility, whether it is a matter of coming to understanding oneself or being understood by others. It is in the clarity and beauty of order that the light of wisdom shines forth: *est enim relucentia sapientiae ordo* (c.31 h 94).

God put order—the first and most exact image of the eternal Wis-

---

44. Aquinas, for instance, quotes this dictum in his commentary on Aristotle's *De anima* 1, lectio xiv, #210.

45. Nicholas mentions Dionysius explicitly in this passage. The Heidelberg edition refers to both his *Celestial Hierarchy* and *Ecclesiastical Hierarchy*, but without specifying particular passages.

dom—into the created universe to better manifest that divine Wisdom, Nicholas continues in chapter 32. Human beings stand as microcosms of the whole creation—beautifully placed to provide the connecting link between temporal and transtemporal creatures—since humankind marks the summit of sensate, corporeal beings and the lowest rank of intellectual beings.[46] We experience ourselves as belonging to both orders, joined to the lower animals, yet sharing an intellectual nature. We die no less than other bodily creatures, yet we live on because we share a spirit joined to the everlasting intelligences, the angels.

Yet even our bodies have a destiny beyond death, Cusanus adds, for we can be joined through faith and love to Christ Jesus. Here is a mediator who connects far more than lower and higher creatures. Rather, he joins us with the eternal Creator in an order of regeneration, of a second creation wherein we are destined to rise with him. This is not simply another hunting field in our quest for wisdom. Indeed, this is Incarnate Wisdom showing us by example the way through death to resurrection. This is the true wisdom that transforms the necessity of dying into the security and certain possession of immortality.[47]

8. INTERLUDE: INTERPRETING THE LANGUAGE OF THE HUNT

Cusanus entitles chapter 33 "The Meaning (Force) of a Word" (*De vi vocabuli*). In this chapter he proposes how we are to understand the language we must use in our pursuit or hunt for divine Wisdom. As his discussion proceeds, we discover that the sense of *vis vocabuli* is rather broader and more flexible, though hardly a full-blown semantic theory. Nicholas' general ideas about language here tend to reflect his practice: they caution us not to expect exactness or precision in either our naming or our knowing of either creatures or their Creator.[48]

Cusanus identifies true naming with definitional knowledge of the real essence of anything so named. For Platonists the essences of things always are prior ontologically to their created instances, and a fortiori to humanly fashioned definitions and humanly imposed names. We use different words based on varying conceptions to refer to the same things. "But if anyone knew the name of the definition [of the real essence], he would call all things by their proper names and possess the most perfect

---

46. This passage recalls Nicholas' doctrine at the end of Book 2 of *De coniecturis*; see Chapter 2, this book.

47. Compare *De docta ignorantia* 3; see Chapter 1, this book. The whole of *MFCG* 23 is devoted to the themes of immortality and eschatology in Cusanus; see in particular there the essay by Meinhardt, "Das Geheimnis des Todes," 71–82.

48. Flasch, *Nikolaus von Kues*, 618–20.

knowledge of everything" (c.33 h 97).⁴⁹ Since human conceptual knowledge and the language that corresponds to it is our own creation, we find it particularly gratifying. Unfortunately, when it comes to matters divine we have to deny that our human language will apply to God in the way we use it for other things. "Life" may extend to all living things, but it does not describe or characterize the divine Cause of all life.

Urging that we use distinctions quite carefully, Cusanus quotes Aquinas' distinction between the meaning of "this man," "man," and "human nature" to illustrate how useful careful distinctions may be.⁵⁰ Ironically, he places St. Thomas' distinctions within his own framework, a perspective that begins from God where "human nature" is ontologically prior to "man" and "this man." (In Aquinas, as in other medieval Aristotelian thinkers, "man" and "human nature" have the derivative ontological status of ideas and depend on "this man," which alone is thought-independent.)

From another perspective, however, Nicholas wants to eschew all such language and its distinctions, for he proposes that the hunt or search for God is really seeking a wisdom that is literally ineffable. Such wisdom is identical with the divine Oneness that stands prior to all use of language and everything else that can be named. Hence it is to be found rather "in silence and vision rather than in much speaking and hearing" (h 100). *De venatione sapientiae* uses human language, but Cusanus always assumes he cannot be precise about matters divine. Since human words signify created temporal things, they are employed here merely to symbolize *(figurare)* the Cause of such things, a Cause that is eternal.

What Cusanus has done in this chapter is take a lead from Pseudo-Dionysius. In *De divinis nominibus* Pseudo-Dionysius contrasted the ordinary use and meaning of words *(vim vocabuli)* with the way they are extended *(intentionem vocabuli)* to apply to God.⁵¹ This provides no little insight into how to take Cusan language throughout this treatise. Human language is used flexibly and symbolically in each hunting field to help us examine another way of seeking the divine Wisdom. The implication is that the ten hunting fields themselves—Learned Ignorance, Actualized Possibility, the Not Other, Light, Praise, Oneness, Equality, Connection, Limit, and Order—are all calculated to lead our thought *per figuras*, or symbolically, from the realm of *posse factum*, or actual cre-

---

49. Nicholas writes in a similar vein in *Idiota de mente* c.3 h 69: "In this way, if the exact name of one thing were known, then the names of all things would also be known, because outside of God there is no exactness."

50. The reference is to Aquinas' commentary: *In librum Beati Dionysii de divinis nominibus expositio* 5.1, #626.

51. *De divinis nominibus* 4.11.708B–C.

ation, to *posse fieri*, or possible creation, to *posse facere*, or the Creator. This chapter reminds us of what we can and cannot expect of Cusan language (and why) as we follow Nicholas' hunt for wisdom.

9. FINALE: CAPTURED PREY

Cusanus now turns, at the end of his treatise, to recollect and consider the main ideas of *De venatione sapientiae* under the guise of collecting the prize or prey gained in the hunt.[52] He recalls his main purpose: "I have accomplished a great hunt, indeed, so that I might carry off a great prize. For I was not content with just any great prey that could be greater; I sought out the very Cause of greatness, since there could be no greater" (c.34 h 101). This "Cause of greatness" precedes *posse fieri* because it *is* all that can be and thereby all else that is made. Nicholas explicitly calls the Cause of greatness "greatness," even though his previous chapter reminded us that "greatness" cannot really be a fitting appellation since the cause in question is not a limited form, but the absolute Cause of forms and all else. "From everything that can be named, therefore, no name fits that [reality] that remains unnameable, even though its name is not other than every name that can be named and it is named in every name" (c.34 h 103).

But "greatness" suggests three further connections. The first is that of abstract size in geometrical contexts, so Cusanus proposes that eternal greatness can be glimpsed when a geometrical line's magnitude is increased by extending it in imagination and thought until it is so long that no line could be greater. At this point we reach infinite, eternal greatness—all dimensional greatness could amount to—and have left behind lines, length, and dimensions. Moreover, we are reminded of the rule of learned ignorance earlier expounded in chapter 26: what can be made greater or smaller is ontologically posterior to *fieri posse* and never all it can be. Using "greatness" is a favorite way for Nicholas to remind us that we must think God's immanence and transcendence together: In each thing great or small as the Cause of each, God—eternal greatness—is at once none of these things. Because eternal Greatness is prior to *fieri posse*, it is not "greater or smaller than any great or any small thing but the efficient, formal, and final Cause of everything great and small—and their utterly adequate Measure" (c.34 h 102).

A third connection is made if we recall the fifth hunting field, that of praise, where Nicholas had indicated that *magnitudo*, or qualitative

---

52. In a private communication H. L. Bond has noted that the irony of this hunt is that the human hunter turns out to be the "prey" of the One he has been hunting.

greatness, is one of the ten pervasive features to be found throughout all that exists, in God and in creatures. This leads to the main points of chapter 35 where Cusanus draws the further implication that what has been said about *possest* and *posse fieri* as great can be also said about both as good, beautiful, and true. Because *possest* or God is the Cause of all and is all it can be, *possest* is also the Cause of those general features or characteristics that all things display and manifest: goodness, greatness, beauty, truth, wisdom, delight, perfection, clarity, equality, and sufficiency. Press each of these perfections to the limit and you discover God as the term of what each can be. In each case, the *posse fieri* or possibility of more or better goodness or greatness in creatures may lead the mind back to *possest* where nothing can be greater or better.

These praiseworthy features in things also lead the mind and heart to praise the Creator as most praiseworthy. Nicholas reads the book of Exodus as calling God himself praise. He summarizes:

This, then, is what I have captured in my hunt: my God is the one who is praiseworthy by everything worthy of praise, not as participating in praise, but as that absolute Praise, praiseworthy of itself and the Cause of everything praiseworthy, and thus prior to and greater than every praiseworthy thing, because he is the Limit of all things that can be praised and is Actualized Possibility [*possest*]. And all the works of God are praiseworthy because they are constituted by participation in what is praiseworthy, through which God is praised as Cause and each praiseworthy thing as caused. And I know that my God is greater than all praise and cannot be praised as he is worthy to be praised by any praiseworthy thing. (c.35 h 105)

In chapter 36 Cusanus' reflections on what he sought and captured turn to another of the ten *laudabilia*, that of truth. He first proposes that truth be divided in a threefold way between the eternal, the perpetual, and the temporal realms. To them correspond truth *(veritas)*, the true *(verum)*, and the likeness of the true *(verisimile)*. To understand this, we need to realize that Cusanus is talking about ontological truth or objective intelligibility, not just true human knowledge. The three realms are related by likeness or participation in typical Proclean triadic fashion, with the eternal divine *Veritas* absolute and responsible for the intelligibility or truth of the lower realms—images dependent on their higher exemplars.

But Nicholas does not omit speaking of the truth of human knowledge, here importing the medieval Aristotelian view that we gain true understanding of things when what we know does their intelligibility justice. In this ideal case, we arrive at such understanding by purifying the content of our ideas from all that is extraneous (= through abstraction). Our understanding is true when it is identical with the intelligible or formal features of the thing understood. However, all these Aristotelian truisms are framed and thus contextually modified by Nicholas' other remarks and main point. First, the topic itself arose because Nicholas is stressing that the intellect itself shares or participates in (ontological) truth because it participates in the ten praiseworthy features that run through all of creation. Second, he moves from the incorporeal nature of the intellect's ideas to assert that the human intellect is itself incorporeal and thus immortal or perpetual. The reason is that, in understanding, the intellect transforms the changeable and temporal into what is incorporeal and immaterial. This leads to his final remark, with a reference to Proclus' commentary on Plato's *Parmenides*,[53] that some realities and principles are intelligible in and of themselves and thus directly in conformity with intellect. As ever, Cusanus moves back and forth from higher ontological causes to lower ones that are what they are by participation in the higher.[54]

Chapter 37 explicitly clarifies this hierarchical dependence by pointing out that we may move two directions in thought from *posse fieri*: toward created things or toward their Creator. In Cusan language, *posse fieri* has two limits: *possest* is its absolute, unqualified Limit, while each created thing is an actual, contingent limit or term that cannot be replicated. Here Cusanus observes that among things created—de facto limits on *posse fieri*—we differentiate perpetual and temporal beings on the basis of their either being ontologically first or imitating the first by participation. Among the created things that are initiated or created but not subject to time or destruction are angelic intelligences and the heavenly bodies: sun and moon and stars. Other creatures are temporal and changeable and thus imperfect imitations of their intelligible exemplars.

These half-dozen closing chapters of *De venatione sapientiae* do not introduce ideas that Cusanus has not already explicated. Instead, in each chapter Cusanus takes the threefold scheme of possibility and turns it first one way and then another in a kind of recapitulation that reviews what he has already examined and explained. In each he proposes various examples and applications to elucidate the previous analyses and achieve clearer formulations of the threefold structure of possibility. Careful thought about possibility means all three parts of the conceptual scheme have to be thought together, as it were, to do justice to Cusanus' insight.

---

53. Cf. *Proclus' Commentary on Plato's "Parmenides,"* trans. G. R. Morrow and J. M. Dillon (Princeton, NJ: Princeton University Press, 1987), Bk.6.1047, 406.
54. Hopkins uses this passage as an occasion to reject any notion that Nicholas is proto-Kantian in his epistemology. See his lengthy note 303, 316–20, in *Metaphysical Speculations* 1. (See above, note 41 in this chapter.) For a proposal that the present passage is hardly about "das Erkenntnisproblem," see Flasch, *Nikolaus von Kues*, 617.

The last two chapters of *De venatione sapientiae* are no different. Chapter 38 stresses once more the priority of *posse facere* within the threefold structure of possibility, emphasizing again that God's eternity is beyond sense and understanding, representation or metaphor.[55] The distance of God from other things is stressed when Nicholas writes that even though every creature's life bears the image of the divine Life, the life we know is even less like God's than is a picture of fire like real flames! Each section of this summarizing chapter opens with *video* or *conspicio*. Toward its end Cusanus declares that what he "sees" intellectually "cannot be spoken or written as I see it" (c.38 h 113). So he proposes a brief sentence to restate his main insight: the limit of the possibility of all that is made or created is the possibility of making or creating them all (*terminus posse fieri omnia est posse facere omnia;* c.38 h 113). Cusanus concludes the chapter by stressing again that even *posse fieri* is itself made or created.

The last chapter of the treatise is entitled by Nicholas *"Epilogatio,"* or "Epilogue." He presents a dense, striking summary of how the three kinds of possibility are related:

> Since nothing is made that was not able to be made, and since nothing can make itself, it follows that possibility [*posse*] is threefold: namely, possibility-of-making [*posse facere*], possibility-of-being-made [*posse fieri*], and possibility-made [*posse factum*]. Possibility-of-being-made is prior to possibility-made; possibility-of-making is prior to possibility-of-being-made. Possibility-of-making is the principle and limit of possibility-of-being-made. Possibility-made is produced by possibility-of-making from possibility-of-being made. (c.39 h 115)

Because that summary and its accompanying remarks are rather abstruse, Cusanus finishes the treatise by turning again to the sensible image of heat, now as a "contracted" parallel or figure of the "absolute" structure of ontological possibility.[56] The three possibilities in this image are those of heating, of becoming hot, and of being heated or hot. Anything that is hot had to be able to be heated, so the possibility of becoming hot is prior to that of being hot. But the possibility of becoming hot never makes anything hot. So prior to that stands the possibility of heating and it is heating that is the cause of things becoming and being hot. It is not that new insights are revealed by the example. What is noteworthy is that even here Cusanus turns to an image or metaphor to help us understand his point.

The threefold differentiation of *posse,* or possibility, that Nicholas em-

---

55. Brüntrup, in *Können und Sein,* 86–88, points out that *posse facere* is not one of Nicholas' terms for God on a par with *possest* or *non aliud.* Rather it is used dialectically in contrast to *posse fieri,* for which it is both ontological ground and limit.

56. Schnarr bases his exposition of the three different modes of being in *De venatione sapientiae* on an extended explication of this example; see *Modi essendi,* 71–79, and note 33 in this chapter. Cf. Brüntrup, *Können und Sein,* 97–99.

ploys and exploits in *De venatione sapientiae* is what he would call a *coniectura:* a proposal or conceptualization that at best approaches the truth in a provisional way.[57] The doctrine of *posse fieri* is particularly remarkable because Cusan Neoplatonism is distinctive in that the separate realm of Platonic Forms is discarded, indeed, radicalized, in favor of each creature directly participating and reflecting in a contracted, limited, or attenuated way the divine Oneness. Although creature and Creator are related as image and original, there is no intermediate ontological realm—the true essences of things are enfolded in the eternity of God's oneness and not distinguished from it. Even the divine ideas (which Augustine transplanted from Plotinian Nous to the divine Mind) are downplayed in most of Cusanus' writings. Yet in *De venatione sapientiae posse fieri* does play some sort of role as a created intermediate realm.[58]

I propose two different perspectives from which we might understand this. If we take up the perspective of human knowers attempting to think through to what the existence of actual limited things presupposes, we come to understand that the contingency of creatures means they need not exist but are merely able to do so.[59] That they in fact do so is not due to them but to God. But now, if we attempt to think through what this might mean from God's perspective, we see that what has been or will be created is hardly exhaustive of God's power or of the possibilities actualized in God's being. So if we understand or schematize the possibilities actualized or to be actualized in time as that sector of divine Power or possibility connected with creation, we can term such possibilities *posse fieri:* the producibles or creatables. We move from all possibility actual in God to the possibilities that are creatable to the possibilities actually created and extant in the actual universe. What is clear in Cusanus is that we are to think in both directions—at once if we can manage it, but at least alternately if we want to get his ideas straight.

---

57. This way of framing possibility should recall the influential teaching of Ibn Sina who centuries earlier distinguished necessary from possible on the grounds that the latter requires a cause in order to be actual. Ibn Sina's necessary/possible/actual differentiation parallels Cusanus' distinction of *posse facere/posse fieri/posse factum.* See *The Metaphysica of Avicenna (ibn Sina),* trans. P. Morewedge (New York: Columbia University Press, 1973), sections 38–40, 76–80. What might be called Duns Scotus' "phenomenology of divine consciousness" differentiated (1) divine being from (2) the creature's intelligible and hence possible or creatable being in the divine Intellect and this again from (3) the creature actually produced and existing in time. Cf. his *QQ in Meta.* 9.2.6 (Vivès 7:534), and A. Wolter, "Scotus on the Divine Origin of Possibility," *American Catholic Philosophical Quarterly* 67 (1993): 95–107.

58. So it is not surprising to see Cusanus point toward the divine Mind in c.38 h 110: *"Patet posse fieri mundum se referre ad mundum archetypum in aeterna mente dei"* (It is clear that the world's possibility of being made refers to the archetypal world in God's eternal mind).

59. Dangelmayr makes a similar point in *Gotteserkenntnis und Gottesbegriff,* 278, where he characterizes *fieri posse* as "der konzentrierte Ausdruck der Kontingenz der Kontingenten."

Cusanus is willing to risk reifying an intermediate realm between God as infinite actual possibility and creatures as finite actualized possibility so that we can understand creatures as producible possibility and see once more how the divine Creator exceeds and transcends the creature. His threefold schema of possibility itself underlines one continuing impossibility: that we will penetrate the nature or meaning of God's infinite power in that eternal realm where all possibility is actual. In *De venatione sapientiae* Nicholas of Cusa is willing to propose *posse fieri*—the possibility of being produced or created—as having its own kind of reality just to foreclose our thinking we can get very far beyond any possibility except those realized contingently in creatures.

Reprise and Conclusions

Reading these six important works of Nicholas of Cusa reveals his familiarity with earlier thinkers in the Neoplatonic tradition, especially Proclus, Dionysius, Eriugena, Thierry of Chartres, Lull, and Eckhart. But these writings also demonstrate his ability to shape that tradition in his own way. A reader has to admire the ways in which each work following *De docta ignorantia* remains faithful to its basic vision, even when it develops, recasts, or emphasizes one or another theme from Nicholas' masterwork. Perhaps one might propose that Nicholas' later writings stand to *De docta ignorantia* much in the way the whole body of Cusan thought stands to the prior tradition of Christian Neoplatonic thinking. In any case, analyzing and following Nicholas' ideas through this series of treatises and dialogues enables the reader to find some shape and point particular to each work and its details. The drawback is that detailed, careful reading may prevent one from gaining an overall perspective on Nicholas' thought and its main themes and proposals. For that reason, it may be helpful to close these readings by recalling and reviewing in a shorter space the main ideas and proposals of each work studied here.

There is a kind of dialectical thinking already spelled out in *De docta ignorantia*, Book 1. The first book begins with proportional thinking or measuring as the sort of thinking characteristic of the human estate, only to assert as it continues that there are no adequate (or inadequate) proportions or measures when finite minds approach the infinite God. What this means is that no analogy or image or metaphor taken from the finite realm can provide reliable access to knowing what it is to be Divine. As Nicholas states in his final remarks in *De docta ignorantia* 1.26,

Now according to the theology of negation, there is not found in God anything other than infinity. Therefore, according to this theology he is not knowable either in this world or in the world to come (for in this respect every created thing is darkness, which cannot comprehend Infinite Light), but is known only to himself. (h 88)

This conclusion did not prevent Cusanus from proposing various mathematical metaphors in earlier chapters to open up some conceptual space where we might see what is involved in reaching for the Infinite and failing to attain it. His creative extrapolations have his readers move from finite to putative infinite geometrical figures. In so doing we press our language, imagination, and thought to a point where we can extrapolate to certain conclusions or outcomes where we recognize what the conclusions should amount to, yet experience that we have not grasped them (or their full implications) in a positive way. They provide an insight whose content is so qualified that it must be beyond our grasp.

Cusanus asks us to imagine a circle, for instance, whose circumference and radii are increased or decreased until they collapse into one straight line at the infinite or into a point at the infinitesimal. Were they to reach this imagined infinite, he points out, curved line and straight line would no longer be opposed, but would collapse into a single infinite "line" or infinitesimal "point." Exactly here Nicholas brings in *transsumptio*, a metaphorical or symbolic transferal. This transferal or "translation" is also a transformation of the thought exercise or object lesson from geometrical expansion or reduction. It is to be transposed to Cusanus' metaphysics of the Infinite and the finite, where all finite oppositions in reality or in thought "collapse" in the divine infinite Oneness—the coincidence of opposites. Here we enter Nicholas' ontology of the ontological maximum-minimum or Infinite—as contrasted with finite realities that can be ever greater or smaller.

When we reflect further, we also recognize that the geometrical exercise we attempted is itself metastable. By definition, circles do not become less circular when their radii are lengthened or shortened, however large or small we imagine the radii. At the point of imagined or conceptually projected infinity, circles are no longer circles at all, let alone straight lines. And yet this "mathematical" exercise in imagination and thought is profitable if we understand the thought experiment as analogous to the kind of thinking required in Cusan metaphysics. Nicholas' real purpose is to clear away what we normally can and do think about in order to acknowledge the metaphysical Infinite, God—"known," in his words, "only to himself."

All of Nicholas' mathematical exercises in *De docta ignorantia* 1 are metaphorical performances—dances toward the Infinite. They let us see what is involved in reaching toward an ontological Infinite that comprises in its Oneness everything we count as opposites in the finite realm. Nicholas' well-known proposal for a coincidence of opposites in, yet transcended by, God represents a further symbol for thinking toward God's infinite oneness. Recall his reflections on the infinite circle and sphere as symbolic of God's infinity; as circumference, center, and diameter coincide in such a projected infinite figure, so God encompasses, originates, penetrates, and measures everything that is not God. The great opposing categories that go back to Plato are united in God's infinite oneness: time and eternity, motion and rest, sameness and otherness, being and becoming. They are eternally identical in God's oneness and simpleness. So, too, all the contrariety and plurality manifested by created things, just because one finite thing is not another, are coincident in God.

Cusanus does not say created things coincide *with* God, but rather that they coincide *in* God. The reason is that God encompasses and sustains their reality in accord with the kinds of things they are. Such things are not God, yet God is "in" them where "in" loses or surpasses any ordinary sense of location. In this way we can read the "coincidence of opposites" as symbolizing *both* the utter identity of all in God's eternity *and* God's immediate mysterious presence to all temporal things, a presence that is simultaneously absence.

Cusanus extends further a metaphorical couple he inherited from Thierry of Chartres for thinking God and creatures: "enfolding/unfolding" *(complicatio/explicatio)*. While our easiest access to this metaphor is undoubtedly through God's unfolding in and of creatures, it is important to recall that both are identical in God, or better, that God is identically both in his infinite Oneness. In his later *De visione Dei*, Nicholas gives unfolding and enfolding a dynamic, Christological reading. There the divine Word is imagined as a gate or door in the wall marking the limit between Infinite and finite. At that point the one seeking God is both entering and leaving the door at once—going in and going out are compared directly to simultaneous enfolding and unfolding.

Both the coincidence of opposites and the enfolding/unfolding couple are designed to help us understand the infinite God's ontological sustaining of the diversity and oppositions among finite created things. Both are quasi-technical metaphors designed to let us think finite and Infinite together in a way that does justice to their ontological connectedness. At the same time, God is *oppositio oppositionum*, and so God remains beyond those limited oppositions and thus "opposed" to them in a way we cannot fathom using ordinary discursive reason. Thinking with Cusanus here takes us through a dialectical movement that can advance us to a threshold where we attain or touch God—Cusanus says we "comprehend incomprehensibly." In the works that follow *De docta ignorantia*, Nicholas will term this stage *intellectus*, intellectual vision or intuition.

Another noteworthy feature of our attempts to understand the coincidence of opposites and enfolding/unfolding is their ironic or self-undercutting features. God truly is transcendent; that is, God is and is not the coincidence of opposites. God truly is immanent; that is, God is and is not the enfolding and unfolding of everything that is not God. Built into coincidence and enfolding/unfolding as metaphors is the experience of our own ignorance, however learned, when we confront God, at once immanent and transcendent. We cannot know *how* things coincide in God's utter oneness or *how,* enfolded there, they are at once unfolded. Our ignorance is a fitting match for God's transcendence, while the two metaphors help us reach a point where we must finally discard them to acknowledge a reality beyond our grasp. Thinking through coincidence and enfolding/unfolding helps us to reach a kind of threshold at the far edge of ordinary rationality (symbolized for Christian faith as the door that is God's divine Word)—what lies beyond remains transcendent.

In Book 2 of *De docta ignorantia,* Nicholas combines the notion that God's unfolding marks his presence to creatures with the traditional doctrine that creatures are limited reflections or images of their enfolding divine Source. In this way he can signal the dependence of the created realm even if any likeness to the Infinite remains concealed. And the universe itself as the totality of created things becomes an unlikely or dissimilar image or likeness of God, where likeness stands for no more (and no less) than dependence on the divine Source of all. The universe is a "contracted maximum" whose unlimited extent reflects as best it can (as a lack of physical boundaries) the actual infinity of its encompassing Creator.

Toward the end of Book 2, Cusanus "tips" the medieval view of the cosmos by returning to the image of the infinite sphere from Book 1. Now God becomes center and circumference of the created universe and "the world machine will have its center everywhere and its circumference nowhere, so to speak" (2.12 h 162). The cosmological outcome is that the Cusan universe, unlike the typical view of the medieval cosmos, can have no exact physical center or boundaries because our thinking them depends on the standpoint we imagine ourselves taking—whether on earth or at the antipodes.

For Nicholas, this metaphor also lets us approach the divine Mystery via the cosmos. We need to think God's *undique et nullubi* (everywhere and nowhere) together, to see them as dialectical, though not sublatable, poles both in reality and for our limited thought. If the favorite metaphorical conceptions and examples of Book 1 have an ironic or self-canceling character, those of Book 2 emphasize the dialectical way in which we must hold together in thought God and creatures. No image without Exemplar, no unfolding without enfolding—God is *both* center *and* circumference, *both* everywhere *and* nowhere. Cusanus attributes to Anaxagoras what becomes his slogan for the interrelatedness of both universe and things: *"quodlibet in quolibet"* (each thing in each thing). No less is this an image we require for God and all that is not God if we want to do justice to the dynamic relatedness that is the reality of the whole.

Book 3 of *De docta ignorantia* turns to Jesus, the ultimate symbol of the relationship between God and creatures. Yet for Nicholas, as for all Christians, this is a symbol that is also reality, the historical reality of the God-man, Jesus Christ. To make clear how Jesus fits with the coincidence of opposites and learned ignorance, Cusanus reemploys his basic metaphors of absolute and contracted, exemplar and image, unfolding and enfolding.

Cusanus attempts to capture how the absolute Maximum that is God and the contracted maximum that is the created universe are finally united in a third maximum: a maximum at once absolute and contracted. Drawing on the traditional commonplace that saw human beings as microcosms of the universe, Cusanus adds to this one final traditional term, *medium*. That is, when contracted human nature is taken up in a hypostatic union with the divine Absolute, we discover that Christ is midpoint, mediator, and measure. Apart from the traditional soteriological and ethical meanings for mediator and measure, Nicholas' focus is on the ontology of the connection between God and creatures.

In the first two books, we came to understand that there is no proportion between creatures and God, between contracted image and absolute Exemplar. This understanding rendered our lack of knowledge of God precisely learned ignorance. Yet we know from faith that there has lived one human being who mediates between finite and Infinite and who stands as the historic proportion between creatures and God. Jesus is the man-God who enfolds the fullness of all things once the divine Equality or Word has taken up human nature, preserving and transforming it to its perfection as a microcosm of all creation. Even if learned ignorance forces us to recognize that we cannot fathom the "how" of what we traditionally designate as "hypostatic union," we may at least acknowledge that here is a reality, indeed a symbol-sacrament, of the connection between creatures and Creator. We also recognize that the Incarnation must be thought dialectically since Jesus comprises both absolute Maximum and contracted maximum. Our purpose is once again, in this unique case, to attempt "in oneness" to conceive "diversity and in diversity oneness" (3.2 h 194). Christ unites Absolute and contracted, Infinite and finite, God and creation. And just as the other Cusan symbols must be thought dialectically to render us both learned and ignorant at once, so thinking the Incarnation dialectically lets us contact a kind of final measure and security for the validity and import of learned ignorance.

De coniecturis extends the lessons of learned ignorance in three directions. First, the dialectic of Oneness and otherness (or God and creation) is conjecturally and symbolically mapped both numerically (by the decad) and geometrically (by the Figures P and U) onto the whole of the created realm, showing it to be the domain of oneness-in-otherness. Second, the dialectical thinking implicit in the image/original and unfolding/enfolding metaphors is now applied directly to the conjecturing human mind as the image of divine Mind and its creating. Here for the first time Cusanus explicitly introduces *intellectus*, or intellectual vision, as the unitary source of all human cognition and thus equal to mind, as well as a further kind of knowing beyond *ratio*. Third, "conjecture" is both defined and extensively illustrated inasmuch as the book presents and explains some conjectures about the created universe and some of its parts and thus exemplifies how the cognitive universe is one of conjectures.

The crucial moment in conjecturing as human cognitive functioning is underlined in its definition: our conjecturing participates in the truth as it is, but in *otherness*. Human mentality and human understanding and human judgment are conjectural; our knowing captures in attenuated ways the truth or intelligibility to be found in God and God's creating. But this cognitive conjecturing inevitably falls short (when it does not suffer distortion) because of the ineluctable "otherness" of our human conceptual measures and human language, the contracted or "othered" status of everything created we attempt to measure, not to mention the unlimited nature of the Creator. "Otherness" in this case means that the intelligibility in all the things we attempt to know is not matched by the intelligibility of the conceptual measures whereby we know them. Yet the fact that our world and our knowledge of it remain conjectural does not mean that we are left with mere guesswork, only that we cannot penetrate fully finite things as they are any more than we can fathom their Creator.

De coniecturis makes explicit one of Cusanus' original proposals about human knowledge. Continued in his *Idiota de mente*, it marks an important intervention in the history of thought in the West—breaking with past idioms for knowledge and portending those to come. Nicholas is entirely positive about our knowledge being valid if imperfect. Yet he undercuts the medieval Aristotelian *adaequatio rei et intellectus* even when he repeats it, for he proposes that what we come to grasp in perception and thought falls short of all that a given thing or situation offers for understanding. In thrall, as Nicholas believes we are, to "otherness," we will not attain identity, the ideal oneness, with what is intelligible in the mind-independent things we attempt to grasp. Such a complete oneness is impossible for the human mind, even though it unfolds a conceptual universe parallel to God's creative "unfolding" of the real universe.

What we unfold in conjectural understandings and judgments witnesses to the dynamic character of our innate power of judgment, but it retains a perspectival character in both perception and conception. This means that Figure P and Figure U in *De conjecturis* represent conceptual frameworks that highlight how everything can be framed as sharing oneness-in-otherness, but that also leave to one side much else that could be said or known about them. Nicholas will view respectable human knowledge as always perspectival and incomplete, yet he is optimistic about its prospects because it is securely anchored in the divine Oneness it reflects as its own sort of enfolding and unfolding at the various levels of *intellectus*, reason, and sense perception.

What *De coniecturis* contributes to our understanding of Nicholas' use of dialectical metaphor is an opportunity to investigate whether Cusan metaphorical thinking is either primarily exploratory or primarily explanatory. What becomes clear in this treatise is that the human mind can provide fascinating explorations of the created world in both whole and part by using arithmetical schemata and geometrical diagrams. Of course, such explorations provide no more than a first-order provisional explanation, a conjectural perspective on the whole and the part examined. Yet such conjecturing also has second-order implications because of what it exemplifies. If the best truth we can attain is truth in otherness, the appropriateness of metaphorical thinking becomes obvious, even apart from the light such metaphors cast on the things we wish to explore.

Nicholas' self-undercutting metaphors in *De docta ignorantia* and his diagrammatic images of conceptual frameworks in *De coniecturis* thus make sense as conjectural proposals for attaining some understanding of what lies beyond us, whether it be God or God's universe and all it comprises. What Cusanus attempts to do in every case is to propose metaphors, thought experiments, symbolic diagrams of cognitive frameworks that both embody his understanding that our cognition is perspectival and capitalize on perspectivism by forcing us to move back and forth between perspectives, concepts, or frameworks so that our knowing is always learning and our learning is constantly aware of what it does not know and cannot capture.

Thus Figure P must be seen as dynamic, interpenetrating, three-dimensional pyramids if it is to be perceived aright; then what it stands for or symbolizes or diagrams has to be thought through dialectically to really understand how oneness and otherness characterize the created universe. No less, that our cognition shares or participates in or has a share of truth or oneness, but always in otherness, means it too has to be understood as dynamic. Knowers are always making new proposals and constructing different conceptual and verbal metaphors and symbols as they engage the created and uncreated realities they yearn to know. Nicholas' best metaphors, whether for God or the universe, involve thinking moving through and beyond varying perspectives while remaining aware that our progress and any resulting understanding are provisional. The theoretical world Nicholas constructs, especially in philosophical theology, is thus always conjectural, always metaphorical, always dialectical. This is where his genius cannot be gainsaid.

Metaphors and symbols are designedly "other" than the things "for which they stand," yet they open up new perspectives on those "things" just insofar as they are other and thus differ from our ordinary ways of seeing and talking about the same items. If the tried and true "image of God" metaphor is reframed by Cusanus so that our minds stand as "othered" images of God's mind, we come to learn more about both. God's sustaining the world takes on new resonance as we come to experience and realize how our minds sustain our conjectural ideas. In Nicholas' words, "the oneness of the human mind is the being of its conjectures" (1.1 h 5).

Moreover, this understanding of our own mental life turns us to God, for "the more deeply we enter our own mind, of which God is the single living center, the more closely we raise ourselves to becoming like the divine Mind" (1.1 h 5). Even though this sentiment echoes Augustine, Eriugena, Bonaventura, and Eckhart, Nicholas radicalizes the move "within and then beyond," plus the traditional idea that human beings are microcosms of the whole, by claiming that humans are truly "second gods." Such metaphorical self-knowledge is to lead us to the divine Mind, where human minds may discover what they truly are. All these metaphors provide conjectural or provisional explanations. Remarkably, the explanations prove to be explorations as well of the things we know and of ourselves as knowers.

The *Idiota de mente* dialogue recapitulates as its root metaphor the central proposal of *De coniecturis*, namely, that human minds are images of the divine Mind. Our minds create the conceptual world, no less than God does the actual world of existing things. The mind is itself a dynamic oneness, active in likening itself to the things it knows and creative in the conceptual measures it fashions to capture conjecturally the world, God, and itself. The dialogue demonstrates human mental creativity, for

Nicholas' layman proposes telling metaphors and vivid illustrations of the mind's workings. Cusanus extends the *complicatio/explicatio* metaphor beyond the conceptual content of what we know: the world of mental realities. Now it also includes the varied mental capacities of sensation, imagination, conception, and intellectual intuition. All of these are unfoldings of the mind's oneness and enfolded in its unitary power of judgment. This adds to the content of what we know a dramatic portrait of mind and its powers.

But as the layman generates so many images and examples and relates his own conjectures about mind to traditional doctrines and terminology, we come to realize that the dialogue continually modifies its own teachings, calling attention to their metaphorical and inexact character. Measuring and assimilating—the basic metaphors for human creation of a conceptual world parallel in its own way to God's creation of the universe—are flexible enough in Nicholas' practice to both provide some explanation of the human mind and to enable us to explore its limits and its possibilities.

Nicholas of Cusa follows the long tradition begun by Plato when he takes visual perception to be paradigmatic of human cognitive functioning. His explicit work on mystical theology, *De visione Dei*, nonetheless does more than simply repeat the traditional teaching that the Christian faith will be fulfilled in the beatific vision of heaven. Nicholas' real focus is on the divine hidden (mystical) Object of human seeking and seeing. The all-seeing icon he sends the monks at Tegernsee is intended to provide an object lesson in the ambiguity of *"visio Dei."* Nicholas insists that any human sighting of God is anticipated, sustained, and ultimately identically one with God's all-knowing vision of those who seek to see. Our seeing through the icon is identically our being seen and thus one with divine seeing.

Two sorts of dialectic are at work in this treatise. One is the typical Christian Neoplatonic dialectic of presence and absence, rendered here as God's seeing preceding (ontologically) my seeing God and my seeing myself, should I sight God, as no different than my divine Original or Exemplar. The other is the dialectical movement of the book itself, as it leads the reader from the exercise with the icon through the reflection on how seeing God is more like not seeing while being seen. Here the back-and-forth between ordinary and extraordinary meanings of "seeing" leads human reason to the impasse of most Cusan writings: the God sought is not sighted because God is beyond the ordinary ways we see using sensory perception and reason.

But this aporia of reason leads Nicholas to propose the symbolism of the wall—beyond it lies the divine Mystery. We have seen that reason must leave behind its ordinary ways of thinking in order to move to some possible intellectual intuition of what is beyond the finite. As a result, reason fumbles and stammers in attempting to speak "beyond" the principles of identity and contradiction. Nicholas symbolizes how this sort of quest to see God ends in a kind of darkness at the wall. While reason can recognize that the infinite Mystery lies beyond its grasp in utter simpleness, any intellectual intuition that could "see" something of the infinite Oneness will be at best provisional, occasional, and certainly a divine gift. The divine Word stands as the door in the wall and we are to realize that our enfolding or going in is at once our unfolding or going out. Here is the basis for our connection with God and any vision of the divine Mystery.

But *complicatio* and *explicatio* return us to the asymmetries of Cusan Neoplatonic dialectic. Nicholas presses beyond the wall metaphor to verbal paradox. Because of God's distinctive opposedness or transcendence, God is already at the same time the oppositions between the limited things we know and distinguish: God is immanent. Nicholas can term God "opposition of oppositions" and "limit without limit" (*finis sine fine*). Along with the icon and the wall, these verbal oxymorons attempt to articulate through odd and self-undercutting linguistic expressions the absent presence of the Infinite to the finite.

Nicholas spends the final chapters of *De visione Dei* in a prayerful meditation on and with Jesus. If the all-seeing icon that began the book was a depiction of Jesus' suffering as captured on Veronica's veil, we must return to the Christ there portrayed as image and truth. In scriptural terms, "he who sees me sees the Father," and the Christ becomes symbolic of, because mediating reality for, God's presence and self-disclosure in human terms and in human history. It is not less dialectical, finally, but it is through union with Jesus, Nicholas proposes, that we may see and be seen as Jesus sees and is seen. We are taken up into God unitrine no less than Jesus' own human nature is assumed into the hypostatic union with the divine Word of the Father.

In *De li non aliud* Nicholas puts into play an even more original version of the same dialectic between God and creatures. He proposes "Not Other" as an original verbal symbol, another enigmatic predicative expression or "name" for God. This seemingly odd way of characterizing God is designed to help us think together God's transcendence and immanence. But Not Other retains its own ironic edge since Nicholas always insists we move beyond whatever understanding we achieve toward the One beyond who is both our mysterious Source and our ultimate Goal. "Not other is not other than Not Other," Nicholas writes playfully in attempting to "define" Not Other. He begins with this almost nonsensical definition, yet reminds his interlocutors that definition is "what first of all make us know." He then proceeds to move "not other" from linguistic to epistemic to ontological contexts until Not Other can designate the reality that is ontologically both self-defining and defining of everything else. God's causal circumscription lets each thing in the universe stand as what it is and nothing else, that is, as not any of the others the universe also comprises. In this way each thing is not other than itself but is other than anything and everything else. But to be thus self-identical and distinct is to point beyond oneself, for any typical created thing "does not possess this from another, therefore, it possesses it from the Not Other."

The divine Not Other cannot be distinct from any created thing the way ordinary things are different from one another, for it is not other than anything nor is it opposed to anything. God is not just another other precisely because God is the Not Other. While creatures are wholly dependent on God (and on one another in necessary but more limited ways), God is not dependent on any of them. Dialectical thinking here requires that we acknowledge that the divine Not Other is at once not one of the created others and yet not other than any or all of them. Nicholas puts it paradoxically by asserting that any (created) other is not other than other (itself), while the divine Not Other is other (because not other) than any other. The divine Not Other both is and is not every other as well. "Not Other" thus signals how utterly unique is God's immanence and transcendence or God's difference from and identity with created things, when compared with limited things' relations with one another.

The rest of *De li non aliud* involves applications and extensions of these central insights. Nicholas reworks several Aristotelian terms of art in Neoplatonic fashion to show how Not Other is to be discovered and thought in the many others. He appeals to the authority of Dionysius with a selection of quotations, then proceeds to substitute Ramon Lull's "A" for "not other" so that he may assert the divine priority beyond any symbol or favorite name we choose to gain some idea of God. He returns to Aristotle, only to assert that the truth about Not Other must surpass the rational discourse of which Aristotle was master. In a final set of interchanges Nicholas avers that at most "not other" names the best human way of conceiving God. "Not other" is by no means *the* name of the God who is beyond all naming.

De venatione sapientiae is a rather long compendium of Cusan ideas organized around the elaborate spatial metaphor of ten hunting fields. Each of the fields represents a different conceptual and metaphorical domain where we are to seek and find God. Not surprisingly, the fields reprise in brief compass many of the themes to which Nicholas had earlier devoted whole treatises: learned ignorance, *possest*, the not other, the Trinity as oneness-equality-connection. Several fields are distinctive in this work, for they let us see how important are such general notions as praise, light, limit, and order in our pursuit of the Divine. The conjunction of praise and light help us recall that this quest is religious as much as intellectual, that our hunting for the One beyond the limited things of the universe should not blind us or stop our responding to the beauties that have issued from the First we seek.

Cusanus introduces a new conception for our consideration in this work, *posse fieri*, that is, "the possibility of being made," as another way of leading us to think creatures and Creator together. *Posse fieri* refers to a quasi-real realm that Nicholas invents to help us think "backward" from actual creatures to their prior possibility, and in ontological, not merely conceptual, terms. At the same time we may, as it were, think "forward" from the eternal totality of possibility in God (termed *posse facere*, "the possibility of making," in contrast to *posse fieri*) to that sector of creatables designed to be realized in time. Things on the way to being created but not yet real, so to speak, make up the putative realm of *posse fieri*. Once created, actual things make up a realm of "possibility made" (*posse factum*). All three, *posse facere*, *posse fieri*, and *posse factum*, should be thought inseparably, even if distinguished for purposes of clarity and analysis.

Generally Nicholas follows his Christian Neoplatonic predecessors and excludes any ontological intermediaries between God and creatures in the manner of Proclus. But here Nicholas has reintroduced an intermediate realm of quasi-things, the creatables. Because of this we can see once more the distance between actual creatures and the Creator, whose infinite Oneness realizes all possibilities, not just the more familiar creatures that occur in time. *Fieri posse* provides a conceptual, almost imaginable, prop that Nicholas claims is more, a reification of creatables. The underlying metaphor is taken from medieval commonplaces about the *factibilia*, or possibilities in the mind of a human artist or craftsman. Whether *posse fieri* is ultimately questionable or not, it reminds Nicholas' readers not to limit God's absolute reality to what God sustains in the contracted universe and not to imagine we penetrate more than the surface of infinite Possibility itself.

In these readings of Cusan texts, I have provisionally characterized Nicholas' metaphors and neologisms as both explanatory and exploratory, with one or the other of these purposes dominating at any given point in Cusanus' writings. Explanatory metaphors, such as the "image-exemplar" couple in *Idiota de mente* or the "unfolding-enfolding" couple used in both ontological and epistemic contexts through *De docta ignorantia*, *De conjecturis*, and *Idiota de mente*, may provide a basic framework for a whole work or recur frequently to establish parallels in different domains and to spell out likenesses and differences. Such metaphors are crucial to the plausibility and coherence of Nicholas' expositions. Exploratory metaphors include many striking examples: the infinite sphere and the coincidence of opposites in *De docta ignorantia*, the icon and the wall in *De visione Dei*, the conceit of the ten hunting fields in *De venatione sapientiae*, the interpenetrating pyramids of light and darkness in *De conjecturis*, and the various neologisms for God such as "not other." These are Cusan inventions that witness to his varied attempts to capture in original ways the insights about God and creation he considered most significant. Add to this his adoption and extension of ordinary terms such as "contraction" and "conjecture" so that they become "terms of art" employed to exhibit his own speculative insights, and it is clear that the most striking ideas in Cusanus are metaphorical.

It seems fair, then, to raise a question Nicholas himself does not entertain directly about the relation between literal and metaphorical in Nicholas' conjectural universe. Without pretending that either literal or metaphorical language and thought have priority or make sense apart from each other, I take the literal domain to include the concepts and language we use when we are attempting to say "what's what" as plainly and accurately as possible. Following the spirit of Nicholas' conjectures, I propose that Nicholas takes the realm of discursive reason, for all its limitations, to be importantly literal. (In the same way, he depends on the principle of contradiction governing ordinary discourse so that he can demarcate what attempts to transcend such thought and talk.) We may not penetrate completely what is knowable about each thing's essence, even apart from God, but what we do assimilate and measure is literally if provisionally true of that thing, as far as it goes. Nonetheless, the basic measures or conceptions we employ to capture the world as a whole and reach for its Creator ironically are themselves often metaphorical and always conjectural constructions.

Yet even when he speaks of the wonders of created things, as in *De coniecturis*, Nicholas often frames what he says in metaphorical terms. His metaphors are not chosen in place of literal language and conceptions, but as the best tools at hand if we want to reach some literal understanding of reality. This means that we have no literal language or concepts available for understanding "what's what" in some domains, and particularly in philosophical theology. Cusanus' results when he turns to God are fascinating, for his "enigmatic" symbols and striking expressions turn out to be both literal and metaphorical. They let us reach for what Nicholas believed is literally most real, but they do so using the ways of metaphor.

The reason, then, that the differentiation between exploratory and explanatory metaphors must remain provisional is that the metaphors that exemplify explanation also explore, while those labeled exploratory also explain. Original proposals abound in Cusan writings, for Nicholas never hesitates to press our imaginations and to undercut previous ways of understanding and doing philosophical theology in order to help us seek and find the *Unum Necessarium* and to think it less reductively and one-sidedly. Just because human thinking and speaking about God and human beings is always tied to a standpoint, Nicholas' practice is to move us beyond any one viewpoint and to have us entertain multiple perspectives on the same matter. He understands the all-too-human tendency, even in theology and philosophy, to construe God in terms of limited creatures, so he insists on combining a further perspective (imagined as God's) with the usual viewpoints familiar to us. Throughout I have called this the dialectical dimension of his thinking about God and creatures, the attempt not to think in the merely linear terms codified so brilliantly for discursive reason in Aristotle's logic, but to think beyond them, or better, to put them together with what lies beyond.

These readings emphasize as well that Nicholas of Cusa stands squarely in the Neoplatonic Christian tradition that stretches from Dionysius through Eckhart. In that tradition the part is always related to the whole, each inferior is connected with a superior, every creature is incompletely understood unless it is connected to its Creator. One moves most easily in such a Christian outlook via correspondences or analogies, where what is discovered or analyzed in one sector turns out to be applicable once more in another. The most general categories of Platonism—being and becoming, one and other, participated and participant, image and original—are useful in coming to understand any more specific domain and the realities in it. So, too, the whole of reality is seen as issuing from and simultaneously returning to the first or original Source. Thinking about any part of the whole means a dialectical holding together of opposed and related terms. This dialectical thinking is not one that moves to resolution or that sublates other and earlier moments of the dialectic in some ultimate synthesis. Rather, it is a dialectic that holds parts together simultaneously within a whole, a dialectic that has to be constantly sustained to do justice to difference-in-likeness. This kind of thinking moves back and forth in the attempt to join alternative perspectives and to keep *relata* connected. Nicholas directs us, as it were, to what stands as the horizon of human theory and careful thinking about created beings, to what counts as ground to the usual figures that rivet our theoretical and speculative attention, to what counts as the light whereby we view the ideas and realities illuminated for typical philosophical theology. Yet we cannot simply exchange horizon for observer's viewpoint, ground for figure, light for illuminated. That would be to understand them as equals whose functions are coordinate and interchangeable one for the other. But horizon is not viewpoint, context is not what it situates, ground is not figure, light is not something illumined. Given together, they need to be thought together in ways that recognize what each contributes that is different from the other and what each makes possible that otherwise would go unrecognized. Cusanus' metaphors move beyond his theoretical inheritance and work to let us put together unlimited and limited in a dialectic of presence and absence, of other and not other, of absolute and contracted, of unfolding and enfolding. His conjectures for thinking God are ironic because no one of them can satisfy him or us, because no one of them can capture more than an inkling of what he is attempting to think together as his ignorance becomes ever more learned.

Select Bibliography

PRIMARY SOURCES

Latin Texts

Nicolai de Cusa Opera omnia iussu et auctoritate Academiae Litterarum Heidelbergensis. Leipzig-Hamburg: Meiner, 1932–.
Vol. 1. *De docta ignorantia,* ed. E. Hoffman and R. Klibansky, 1932.
Vol. 3. *De coniecturis,* ed. J. Koch, K. Bormann, and H. G. Senger, 1972.
Vol. 4. *Opuscula I: De Deo abscondito, De quaerendo Deum, De filiatione Dei, De dato Patris luminum, Coniectura de ultimis diebus, De genesi,* ed. P. Wilpert, 1959.
Vol. 5. *Idiota. De sapientia, De mente, De staticis experimentis,* ed. R. Steiger and L. Baur, 1983.
Vol. 6. *De visione Dei,* ed. A. D. Riemann, 2000.
Vol. 12. *De venatione sapientiae, De apice theoriae,* ed. R. Klibansky and H. G. Senger, 1982.
Vol. 13. *Directio speculantis seu de non aliud,* ed. L. Baur and P. Wilpert, 1950.
Schriften des Nikolaus von Kues in deutscher Übersetzung im Auftrag der Heidelberger Akademie der Wissenschaften. Philosophische Bibliothek. Leipzig-Hamburg: Meiner, 1936–.

Latin Texts with German Translations

De docta ignorantia I, Philosophische Bibliothek, Vol. 264a, ed. and trans. P. Wilpert and H. G. Senger, 1994.
De docta ignorantia II, Philosophische Bibliothek, Vol. 264b, ed. and trans. P. Wilpert and H. G. Senger, 1999.
De docta ignorantia III, Philosophische Bibliothek, Vol. 264c, ed. R. Klibansky, trans. H. G. Senger, 1999.
De coniecturis, Philosophische Bibliothek, Vol. 268, ed. and trans. J. Koch and W. Happ, 1988.
Idiota de mente, Philosophische Bibliothek, Vol. 432, ed. and trans. R. Steiger, 1995.

German Translations

De Deo abscondito, in *Drei Schriften vom verborgenen Gott,* Vol. 218, ed. and trans. E. Bohnenstaedt, 1967.
De li non aliud, Vol. 232, ed. and trans. P. Wilpert, 1976.

English Translations

Bond, H. L., trans. *Nicholas of Cusa: Selected Spiritual Writings.* New York: Paulist Press, 1997. [Translations of *De docta ignorantia, De Deo abscondito,* and *De visione Dei.*]
Hopkins, J. *Nicholas of Cusa on Learned Ignorance. A Translation and Appraisal of De docta ignorantia.* 2nd ed. Minneapolis, Minn.: Banning Press, 1985.

―――. *Nicholas of Cusa on God as Not-Other.* 3rd ed. Minneapolis, Minn.: Banning Press, 1999.
―――. *Nicholas of Cusa's Dialectical Mysticism: Text, Translation, and Interpretive Study of "De visione Dei."* 2nd ed. Minneapolis, Minn.: Banning Press, 1988.
―――. *A Miscellany on Nicholas of Cusa.* Minneapolis, Minn.: Banning Press, 1994. [Translation of *De Deo abscondito.*]
―――. *Nicholas of Cusa on Wisdom and Knowledge.* Minneapolis, Minn.: Banning Press, 1996. [Text and Translation of *Idiota de mente.*]
―――. *Nicholas of Cusa: Metaphysical Speculations.* Vol. 1. Minneapolis, Minn.: Banning Press, 1998. [Translation of *De venatione sapientiae.*]
―――. *Nicholas of Cusa: Metaphysical Speculations.* Vol. 2. Minneapolis, Minn.: Banning Press, 2000. [Translation of *De coniecturis.*]
Lull, Ramon. *Ars demonstrativa,* in *Selected Works of Ramon Llull,* vol. 1. Edited and translated by A. Bonner. Princeton: Princeton University Press, 1985.
Miller, C. L., trans. *Nicholas de Cusa. "Idiota de mente": "The Layman: About Mind."* New York: Abaris Books, 1979.

SECONDARY SOURCES

Adams, M. M. "Universals in the Early Fourteenth Century." In *The Cambridge History of Later Medieval Philosophy,* ed. N. Kretzmann, A. Kenny, and J. Pinborg, 411–39. Cambridge: Cambridge University Press, 1982.
―――. *William Ockham.* 2 vols. South Bend, Ind.: University of Notre Dame Press, 1987.
Albertus Magnus. *Super Dionysium de Divinis Nominibus.* Edited by P. Simon. Münster: Aschendorff, 1972.
Apel, K. "Die Idee der Sprache bei Nicolaus von Cues." *Archiv für Begriffsgeschichte* 1 (1955): 200–221.
Augustine. *On Christian Doctrine.* Translated by D. W. Robertson Jr. Indianapolis, Ind.: Bobbs-Merrill, 1958.
Avicenna. *The Metaphysica of Avicenna (ibn Sina).* Translated by P. Morewedge. New York: Columbia University Press, 1973.
Beierwaltes, W. "Deus Oppositio Oppositorum (Nicolaus Cusanus *De visione Dei* XIII)." *Salzburger Jahrbuch für Philosophie* 8 (1964): 175–85.
―――. "Identität und Differenz: Zum Prinzip cusanischen Denkens." In *Rheinisch-Westfälische Akademie der Wissenschaften.* Opladen: Westdeutscher Verlag, 1977.
―――. "Visio Absoluta: Reflexion als Grundzug des göttlichen Prinzips bei Nicolaus Cusanus." *Sitzungsberichte der Heidelberger Akademie der Wissenschaften* (1978): 5–33.
―――. *Denken des Einen.* Frankfurt am Main: V. Klostermann, 1985.
―――. *Visio Facialis—Sehen ins Angesicht.* Munich: Verlag der Bayerische Akademie der Wissenschaften, 1988.
―――. "Visio Facialis: Sehen ins Angesicht." *MFCG* 18 (1989): 91–118.
―――. *"Der verborgene Gott: Cusanus und Dionysius,"* Trierer Cusanus Lecture 4 (Trier: Paulinus-Verlag, 1997.
Blumenberg, H. *The Legitimacy of the Modern Age.* Translated by R. Wallace. Cambridge, Mass.: MIT Press, 1983.
Bolberitz, P. *Philosophischer Gottesbegriff bei Nikolaus Cusanus in seinem Werk: "De non aliud."* Leipzig: St.-Benno Verlag, 1989.

Bond, H. L. "Nicholas of Cusa and the Reconstruction of Christology: The Centrality of Christology in the Coincidence of Opposites." In *Contemporary Reflections on the Medieval Christian Tradition*, ed. G. H. Shriver, 81–94. Durham, N.C.: Duke University Press, 1974.

———. "Nicholas of Cusa from Constantinople to 'Learned Ignorance': The Historical Matrix for the Formation of the *De docta ignorantia*." In *Nicholas of Cusa on Christ and the Church*, ed. G. Christianson and T. M. Izbicki, 135–63. Leiden: Brill, 1996.

Bormann, K. "Zur Lehre des Nikolaus von Kues von der 'Andersheit' und deren Quellen." *MFCG* 10 (1973): 130–37.

———. "'Übereinstimmung und Verschiedenheit der Menschen' (*De Coni.* II,15)." *MFCG* 13 (1978): 88–104.

Brand, D. J., trans. *The Book of Causes*. Niagara, N.Y.: Niagara University Press, 1981.

Brient, E. "Transitions to a Modern Cosmology: Meister Eckhart and Nicholas of Cusa on the Intensive Infinite." *Journal of the History of Philosophy* 37 (1999): 575–600.

Brüntrup, A. *Können und Sein*. Munich: Pustet, 1973.

Burrell, D. *Knowing the Unknowable God: Ibn Sina, Maimonides, Aquinas*. South Bend, Ind.: University of Notre Dame Press, 1986.

———. "Aquinas and Jewish and Islamic Thinkers." In *The Cambridge Companion to Aquinas*, ed. N. Kretzmann and E. Stump, 60–84. Cambridge: Cambridge University Press, 1993.

Carlson, T. A. *Indiscretion*. Chicago: University of Chicago Press, 1999.

Casarella, P. "Nicholas of Cusa and the Power of the Possible." *American Catholic Philosophical Quarterly* 64 (1990): 7–34.

———. "Neues zu den Quellen der cusanischen Mauersymbolik." *MFCG* 19 (1991): 273–86.

———. "His Name Is Jesus: Negative Theology and Christology in Two Writings of Nicholas of Cusa from 1440." In *Nicholas of Cusa on Christ and the Church*, ed. G. Christianson and T. Izbicki, 281–307. Leiden: Brill, 1996.

Cassirer, E. *Das Erkenntnisproblem in der Philosophie und Wissenschaft der neueren Zeit*. Berlin: B. Cassirer, 1906.

———. *The Individual and the Cosmos in Renaissance Philosophy*. Translated by M. Domandi. Oxford: Blackwell, 1963.

Chenu, M.-D. *Toward Understanding St. Thomas*. Translated by A. M. Landry and D. Hughes. Chicago: Henry Regnery, 1964.

Christianson, G., and T. Izbicki, eds. *Nicholas of Cusa: In Search of God and Wisdom*. Leiden: Brill, 1991.

———, eds. *Nicholas of Cusa on Christ and the Church*. Leiden: Brill, 1996.

Colomer, E. *Nikolaus von Kues und Raimund Lull*. Berlin: de Gruyter, 1961.

Copenhaver, B., and C. Schmitt. *Renaissance Philosophy*. Oxford: Oxford University Press, 1992.

Cranz, F. E. "The Transmutation of Platonism in the Development of Nicolaus Cusanus and of Martin Luther." In *Nicolò Cusano agli Inizi del Mondo Moderno*, 73–102. Florence: Sansoni, 1970.

Dangelmayr, S. *Gotteserkenntnis und Gottesbegriff in den philosophischen Schriften des Nikolaus von Kues*. Meisenheim: Hain, 1969.

Das Sehen Gottes nach Nikolaus von Kues (= *MFCG* 18). Trier: Paulinus Verlag, 1989.

Davies, B. *The Thought of Thomas Aquinas*. Oxford: Oxford University Press, 1992.

de Certeau, M. "The Gaze—Nicholas of Cusa." *Diacritics* 17 (1987): 2–38.
de Gandillac, M. *Nikolaus von Cues.* Düsseldorf: Schwann, 1953.
———. "Nikolaus von Kues zwischen Platon und Hegel." *MFCG* 11 (1975): 21–38.
Duclow, D. "The Analogy of the Word: Nicholas of Cusa's Theory of Language." *Bijdragen* 38 (1977): 282–99.
———. "Anselm's Proslogion and Nicholas of Cusa's Wall of Paradise." *Downside Review* 100 (1982): 22–30.
———. "Mystical Theology and the Intellect in Nicholas of Cusa." *American Catholic Philosophical Quarterly* 64 (1990): 111–29.
Dupré, L. "Nature and Grace in Nicholas of Cusa's Mystical Theology." *American Catholic Philosophical Quarterly* 64 (1990): 153–70.
———. *Passage to Modernity: An Essay in the Hermeneutics of Nature and Culture.* New Haven, Conn.: Yale University Press, 1993.
———. "The Mystical Theology of Cusanus' *De visione Dei.*" In *Nicholas of Cusa on Christ and the Church,* ed. G. Christianson and T. M. Izbicki, 205–20. Leiden: Brill, 1996.
Dupré, W. "Der Mensch als Mikrokosmos im Denken des Nikolaus von Kues." *MFCG* 13 (1978): 68–87.
Eco, U. *Art and Beauty in the Middle Ages.* Translated by H. Bedin. New Haven, Conn.: Yale University Press, 1986.
Fine, G. "Separation." *Oxford Studies in Ancient Philosophy* 2 (1984): 31–87.
Flasch, K. "Der Mensch als Mass Gottes." In *Gott Heute: Fünfzehn Beiträge zur Gottesfrage,* ed. N. Kutschki, 20–30. Mainz: Matthias-Grünewald, 1967.
———. *Die Metaphysik des Einen bei Nikolaus von Kues.* Leiden: Brill, 1973.
———. "*Procedere ut Imago:* Das Hervogehen des Intellekts aus seinem göttlichen Grund bei Meister Dietrich, Meister Eckhart und Berthold von Moosburg." In *Abendländische Mystik im Mittelalter,* ed. K. Ruh, 125–34. Stuttgart: Metzlersche Verlagsbuchhandlung, 1986.
———. *Nikolaus von Kues: Geschichte einer Entwicklung.* Frankfurt am Main: V. Klostermann, 1998.
Fräntzki, E. *Nikolaus von Kues und das Problem der absolute Subjecktivität.* Meisenheim am Glan: A. Hein, 1972.
Gerhardt V., and N. Herold, eds. *Wahrheit und Begründung.* Würzburg: Konigshausen und Neumann, 1985.
Haas, A. M. *Deum mistice videre . . . in caligine coincidencie: Zum Verhältnis Nikolaus von Kues zur Mystik.* Basel: Helbing und Lichtenhahn, 1989.
Håring, N. M., ed. *Commentaries on Boethius by Thierry of Chartres and His School.* Toronto: Pontifical Institute of Mediaeval Studies, 1971.
Harries, K. "The Infinite Sphere: Comments on the History of a Metaphor." *Journal of the History of Philosophy* 13 (1975): 5–15.
———. "Problems of the Infinite: Cusanus and Descartes." *American Catholic Philosophical Quarterly* 64 (1990): 89–110.
———. *Infinity and Perspective.* Cambridge, Mass.: MIT Press, 2001.
Haubst, R. *Die Christologie des Nikolaus von Kues.* Freiburg: Herder, 1956.
———. "Nicolaus von Kues und die heutige Christologie." In *Universitas. Dienst an Wahrheit und Leben,* 2 vols., ed. L. Lenhart, 1:165–75. Mainz: Matthias-Grünewald, 1960.
———. "Die Wege der christologischen manuductio." *MFCG* 16 (1984): 164–83.

———. "Die erkenntnistheoretische und mystische Bedeutung der 'Mauer der Koinzidenz.'" *MFCG* 18 (1989): 167–95.
———. "Nachwort der Herausgebers." *MFCG* 18 (1989): 68.
———. *Streifzüge in die cusanische Theologie.* Münster: Aschendorff, 1991.
Haug, W. "Die Mauer des Paradieses. Zur mystica theologia des Nicolaus Cusanus in *De visione Dei.*" *Theologische Zeitschrift* 45 (1989): 216–30.
Helander, B. H. *Die visio intellectualis als Erkenntnisweg und -ziel bei Nikolaus Cusanus.* Stockholm: Almqvist & Wiksell, 1988.
Hennigfeld, J. *Geschichte der Sprachphilosophie. Antike und Mittelalter.* New York: de Gruyter, 1994.
Herold, N. "Bild der Wahrheit—Wahrheit des Bildes: Zur Deutung des Blicks aus dem Bild in der Cusanische Schrift *De visione dei.*" In *Wahrheit und Begründung,* ed. V. Gerhardt and N. Herold, 71–98. Würzburg: Konigshausen und Neumann, 1985.
Hirt, P. "Vom Wesen der konjekturalen Logik bei Nikolaus von Kues." *MFCG* 8 (1970): 179–91.
Hojsisch, B. "Die Andersheit Gottes als Koinzidenz, Negation and Nicht-Andersheit bei Nikolaus von Kues: Explikation und Kritik." *Documenti e studi sulla tradizione filosofica medievale* 7 (1996): 437–54.
Hopkins, J. *Nicholas of Cusa's Metaphysic of Contraction.* Minneapolis, Minn.: Banning Press, 1983.
———. *Nicholas of Cusa on Learned Ignorance.* 2nd ed. Minneapolis, Minn.: Banning Press, 1985.
———. *A Concise Introduction to the Philosophy of Nicholas of Cusa.* 3rd ed. Minneapolis, Minn.: Banning Press, 1986.
———. *A New, Interpretive Translation of St. Anselm's "Monologion" and "Proslogion."* Minneapolis, Minn.: Banning Press, 1986.
———. *Nicholas of Cusa on God as Not-Other.* 3rd ed. Minneapolis, Minn.: Banning Press, 1999.
———. *Nicholas of Cusa's Dialectical Mysticism.* 2nd ed. Minneapolis, Minn.: Banning Press, 1988.
———. *A Miscellany on Nicholas of Cusa.* Minneapolis, Minn.: Banning Press, 1994.
———. "Glaube und Vernunft im Denken des Nikolaus von Kues." *Trier Cusanus Lecture* 3. Trier: Paulinus Verlag, 1996.
———. *Nicholas of Cusa on Wisdom and Knowledge.* Minneapolis, Minn.: Banning Press, 1996.
———. *Nicholas of Cusa: Metaphysical Speculations.* Vol. 1. Minneapolis, Minn.: Banning Press, 1998.
———. *Nicholas of Cusa: Metaphysical Speculations.* Vol. 2. Minneapolis, Minn.: Banning Press, 2000.
Hösle, V. "Platonism and Anti-Platonism in Nicholas of Cusa's Philosophy of Mathematics." *Graduate Faculty Philosophy Journal* 13 (1990): 79–112.
Iamblichus. *The Theology of Arithmetic.* Translated by R. Waterfield. Grand Rapids, Mich.: Phanes Press, 1988.
Izbicki, T. "The Church in the Light of Learned Ignorance." *Medieval Philosophy and Theology* 3 (1993): 186–214.
Jacobi, K. *Die Methode der cusanischen Philosophie.* Munich: Alber, 1969.
———, ed. *Nikolaus von Kues: Einführung in sein philosophisches Denken.* Munich: Alber, 1979.

Kessler, E., C. B. Schmitt, and Q. Skinner, eds. *The Cambridge History of Renaissance Philosophy*. Cambridge: Cambridge University Press, 1988.

Klein, J. *A Commentary on Plato's "Meno."* Chapel Hill: University of North Carolina Press, 1965.

Koch, J. *Die ars coniecturalis des Nikolaus von Kues*. Cologne: Westdeutscher Verlag, 1956.

Kraut, R. "Introduction to the Study of Plato." In *The Cambridge Companion to Plato*, ed. R. Kraut, 1–51. Cambridge: Cambridge University Press, 1992.

Kremer, K. "Erkennen bei Nikolaus von Kues. Apriorismus-Assimilation-Abstraktion." *MFCG* 13 (1978): 23–57.

———. "Gott—in allem alles, in nichts nichts." *MFCG* 17 (1986): 188–219.

———. "Gottes Vorsehung and die Menschliche Freiheit ('Sis tu tuus, et Ego ero tuus')." *MFCG* 18 (1989): 227–52.

———. "Philosophische Überlegungen des Cusanus zur Unsterblichkeit der menschlichen Geistseele." *MFCG* 23 (1996): 21–70.

———. "Das kognitive und affektive Apriori bei der Erfassung des Sittlichen." *MFCG* 26 (2000): 101–44.

Kretzmann, N., A. Kenny, and J. Pinborg, eds. *The Cambridge History of Later Medieval Philosophy*. Cambridge: Cambridge University Press, 1982.

Kuntz, M. L., and P. G. Kuntz, eds. *Jacob's Ladder and the Tree of Life: Concepts of Hierarchy and the Great Chain of Being*. New York: Peter Lang, 1987.

Lai, T. "Nicholas of Cusa and the Finite Universe." *Journal of the History of Philosophy* 11 (1973): 161–67.

LeBlond, J. M. "Aristotle on Definition." In *Articles on Aristotle 3: Metaphysics*, ed. J. Barnes, M. Scholfield, and R. Sorabji, 63–79. New York: Duckworth, 1979.

Leinkauf, T. "Die Bestimmung des Einzelseienden durch die Begriffe Contractio, Singularitas, und Aequalitas bei Nicolaus Cusanus." *Archiv für Begriffsgeschichte* 37 (1994): 180–211.

Lonergan, B. *Verbum: Word and Idea in Aquinas*. Edited by D. B. Burrell. South Bend, Ind.: University of Notre Dame Press, 1967.

Mahoney, E. P. "Metaphysical Foundations of the Hierarchy of Being According to Some Late-Medieval and Renaissance Philosophers." In *Philosophies of Existence Ancient and Medieval*, ed. P. Morewedge, 165–257. New York: Fordham University Press, 1982.

Marsh, D. *The Quattrocentro Dialogue: Classical Tradition and Humanist Innovation*. Cambridge, Mass.: Harvard University Press, 1980.

McDermott, T., trans. *Thomas Aquinas: Selected Philosophical Writings*. Oxford: Oxford University Press, 1993.

McGinn, B. "Unitrinum seu Triunum: Nicholas of Cusa and Medieval Trinitarian Mysticism." Unpublished paper, Divinity School, University of Chicago.

McTighe, T. P. "The Meaning of the Couple 'Complicatio-Explicatio' in the Philosophy of Nicholas of Cusa." *Proceedings of the American Catholic Philosophical Association* 32 (1958): 206–14.

———. "Eternity and Time in Boethius: His *Complicatio-Explicatio* Method." In *History of Philosophy in the Making*, ed. L. J. Thro, 35–62. Washington, D.C.: University Press of America, 1982.

———. "*Contingentia* and *Alteritas* in Cusa's Metaphysics." *American Catholic Philosophical Quarterly* 64 (1990): 55–71.

Meinhardt, H. "Exaktheit und Mutmassungscharakter der Erkenntnis." In *Nikolaus von Kues: Einführung in sein philosophisches Denken*, ed. K. Jacobi, 101–20. Munich: Alber, 1979.

———. "Das Geheimnis des Todes und der Auferstehung Jesu Christi nach Cusanus, ineins damit sein Verständnis der Auferstehung der Toten." *MFCG* 23 (1996): 71–82.
Meuthen, E. *Nikolaus von Kues (1401–1464). Skizze einer Biographie.* 7th ed. Münster: Aschendorff, 1992.
Miller, C. L. "Aristotelian *Natura* and Nicholas of Cusa." *Downside Review* 96 (1978): 13–20.
———. "Nicholas of Cusa and Philosophic Knowledge." *Proceedings of the American Catholic Philosophical Association* 54 (1980): 155–63.
———. "Metaphor and Simile in Nicolas of Cusa's *Idiota de mente*." *Acta* 8 (1981): 47–59.
———. "Irony and the History of Philosophy." *Poetics Today* 4 (1983): 465–78.
———. "Nicholas of Cusa's *De ludo globi*: Symbolic Roundness and Eccentric Life Paths." *Acta* 10 (1983): 135–48.
———. "A Road Not Taken: Nicholas of Cusa and Today's Intellectual World." *Proceedings of the American Catholic Philosophical Association* 57 (1983): 68–77.
———. "Nicholas of Cusa's *The Vision of God*." In *An Introduction to the Medieval Mystics of Europe*, ed. P. Szarmach, 293–312. Albany: State University of New York Press, 1984.
———. "The Icon and the Wall: *Visio* and *Ratio* in Nicholas of Cusa's *De visione Dei*." *Proceedings of the American Catholic Philosophical Association* 64 (1990): 86–98.
———. "Perception, Conjecture and Dialectic." *American Catholic Philosophical Quarterly* 64 (1990): 35–54.
———. "Nicholas of Cusa's *On Conjectures (De coniecturis)*." In *Nicholas of Cusa: In Search of God and Wisdom*, ed. G. Christianson and T. Izbicki, 119–40. Leiden: Brill, 1991.
———. "God's Presence: Some Cusan Proposals." In *Nicholas of Cusa on Christ and the Church*, ed. G. Christianson and T. Izbicki, 241–49. Leiden: Brill, 1996.
———, trans. *Nicholas de Cusa. "Idiota de mente": "The Layman: About Mind."* New York: Abaris Books, 1979.
Mittellateinisches Wörterbuch. Munich: Beck, 1959.
Neumeyer, A. *Der Blick aus dem Bild.* Berlin: Gebr. Mann, 1964.
Nicolò Cusano agli Inizi del Mondo Moderno. Florence: Sansoni, 1970.
Nikolaus von Kues in der Geschichte des Erkenntnisproblems (= *MFCG* 11). Mainz: Matthias-Grünewald, 1975.
Offermann, U. *Christus—Wahrheit des Denkens.* Münster: Aschendorff, 1991.
Oide, S. "Über die Grundlagen der cusanischen Konjekturenlehre." *MFCG* 8 (1970): 147–78.
Olds, C. "Aspect and Perspective in Renaissance Thought: Nicholas of Cusa and Jan Van Eyck." In *Nicholas of Cusa on Christ and the Church*, ed. G. Christianson and T. Izbicki, 251–64. Leiden: Brill, 1996.
O'Meara, D. J. *Pythagoras Revived.* Oxford: Clarendon Press, 1987.
Patterson, R. *Image and Reality in Plato's Metaphysics.* Indianapolis, Ind.: Hackett, 1985.
Pätzold, D. *Einheit und Andersheit: Die Bedeutung kategorialer Neubildungen in der Philosophie des Nicolaus Cusanus.* Cologne: Pahl-Rugenstein, 1981.
Proclus. *The Elements of Theology.* 2nd ed. Translated by E. R. Dodds. Oxford: Oxford University Press, 1963.
———. *Proclus' Commentary on Plato's "Parmenides."* Translated by G. R. Morrow and J. M. Dillon. Princeton, N.J.: Princeton University Press, 1987.

Pseudo-Dionysius. *Pseudo-Dionysius: The Complete Works*. Translated by C. Luibheid and P. Rorem. New York: Paulist Press, 1987.
Reinhardt, K. "Christus, die 'Absolute Mitte' als der Mittler zur Gotteskindschaft." *MFCG* 18 (1989): 196–220.
———. "Islamische Wurzeln der cusanischen Mauersymbolik? Die 'Mauer des Paradieses' im *Liber scalae Mahometi*." *MFCG* 19 (1991): 287–91.
Santinello, G. "Einleitung" to Nikolaus von Kues, *Idiota de mente*, ed. R. Steiger, 9–28. Hamburg: Meiner, 1995.
Scharlemann, R. "God as Not-Other: Nicholas of Cusa's *De li non aliud*." In *Naming God*, ed. R. Scharlemann, 116–32. New York: Paragon House, 1985.
Schmidt, M. "Nikolaus von Kues im Gespräch mit den Tegernseer Mönchen über Wesen und Sinn der Mystik." *MFCG* 18 (1989): 25–49.
Schnarr, H. *Modi essendi*. Münster: Aschendorff, 1973.
Schneider, G. *Gott, das Nichtandere*. Münster: Aschendorff, 1970.
Schönborn, C. "'De docta ignorantia' als christozentrischer Entwurf." In *Nikolaus von Kues: Einführung in sein philosophisches Denken*, ed. K. Jacobi, 138–56. Munich: Alber, 1979.
Schulze, W. *Zahl, Proportion, Analogie*. Münster: Aschendorff, 1978.
Sells, M. *Mystical Languages of Unsaying*. Chicago: University of Chicago Press, 1994.
Senger, H. G. *Die Philosophie des Nikolaus von Kues vor dem Jahre 1440*. Münster: Aschendorff, 1971.
———. "Die Sprache der Metaphysik." In *Nikolaus von Kues: Einführung in sein philosophisches Denken*, ed. K. Jacobi, 74–100. Munich: Alber, 1979.
———. "Die Zeit- und Ewigskeitsverständnis bei Nikolaus von Kues im Hinblick auf die Auferstehung der Toten." *MFCG* 23 (1996): 139–63.
Simon, P., ed. Albertus Magnus, *Super Dionysium de divinis nominibus I*. Münster: Aschendorff, 1972.
Spade, P. V., trans. and ed. *Five Texts on the Mediaeval Problem of Universals*. Indianapolis, Ind.: Hackett, 1994.
Stachel, G. "Schweigen vor Gott: Bermerkungen zur mystischen Theologie der Schrift *De visione Dei*." *MFCG* 14 (1980): 167–81.
Stadler, M. *Rekonstruction einer Philosophie der Ungegenständlichkeit*. Munich: Fink, 1983.
———. "Zum Begriff der *mensuratio* bei Cusanus. Ein Beitrag zur Ortung der cusanischen Erkenntnislehre." In *Mensura, Mass, Zahl, Zahlensymbolik im Mittelalter*, 2 vols., ed. A. Zimmermann, 1:118–31. New York: de Gruyter, 1983.
Stallmach, J. "Das 'Nichtandere' als Begriff des Absoluten." In *Universitas. Dienst an Wahrheit und Leben*, 2 vols., ed. L. Lenhart, 1:329–35. Mainz: Matthias Grünwald, 1960.
———. "Geist als Einheit und Andersheit." *MFCG* 11 (1975): 86–116.
———. "Der 'Zusammenfall der Gegensätze' und der unendliche Gott." In *Nikolaus von Kues: Einführung in sein philosophisches Denken*, ed. K. Jacobi, 56–73. Munich: Alber, 1979.
———. "Sein und das Können-selbst bei Nikolaus von Kues." In *Suche nach dem Einen*, 209–22. Bonn: Bouvier Verlag H. Grundmann, 1982.
———. *Ineinsfall der Gegensätze und Weisheit des Nichtwissens*. Münster: Aschendorff, 1989.
Stock, A. "Die Rolle der 'icona Dei' in der Spekulation *De visione Dei*." *MFCG* 18 (1989): 50–62.

Thomas, M. "Zur Ursprung der Andersheit (Alteritas)." *MFCG* 22 (1995): 55–67.

———. *Die Teilhabegedanke in den Schriften und Predigten des Nikolaus von Kues (1430–1450)*. Münster: Aschendorff, 1996.

Thro, L. J., ed. *History of Philosophy in the Making*. Washington, D.C.: University Press of America, 1982.

Trinkaus, C. *In Our Image and Likeness: Humanity and Divinity in Italian Humanist Thought*. 2 vols. London: Constable, 1970.

———. "Marsilio Ficino and the Ideal of Human Autonomy." In *Marsilio Ficino e il ritorno di Platone: Studi e documenti*, 2 vols., ed. G. Garfignini, 1:197–210. Florence: L. S. Olschki, 1986.

Turner, D. *The Darkness of God: Negativity in Western Mysticism*. Cambridge: Cambridge University Press, 1995.

Vansteenberghe, E. *Autour de la docte ignorance. Une controverse sur la théologie mystique au XVe siècle. Beiträge zur Geschichte der Philosophie und Theologie des Mittelalters* 14. Münster: Aschendorff, 1915.

Van Velthoven, T. *Gottesschau und menschliche Kreativität*. Leiden: Brill, 1977.

Volkmann-Schluck, K. *Nicolaus Cusanus: Die Philosophie in Übergang vom Mittelalter zur Neuzeit*. Frankfurt: V. Klostermann, 1957.

Von Bredow, G. "Complicatio/explicatio." In *Historisches Wörterbuch der Philosophie*, 6 vols., ed. J. Ritter, 1:1026–28. Basel: Schwabe, 1971.

———. *Im Gespräch mit Nikolaus von Kues: Gesammelte Aufsätze 1948–1993*. Edited by H. Schnarr. Münster: Aschendorff, 1995.

———, ed. *Das Vermächtnis des Nikolaus von Kues*. Cusanus-Texte IV-3. Heidelberg: Winter, 1955.

Watts, P. M. *Nicolaus Cusanus: A Fifteenth-Century Vision of Man*. Leiden: Brill, 1982.

Wippel, J. "Metaphysics." In *The Cambridge Companion to Aquinas*, ed. N. Kretzmann and E. Stump, 85–127. Cambridge: Cambridge University Press, 1993.

Wolter, A. *The Philosophical Theology of John Duns Scotus*, ed. M. M. Adams. Ithaca, N.Y.: Cornell University Press, 1990.

———. "Scotus on the Divine Origin of Possibility." *American Catholic Philosophical Quarterly* 67 (1993): 95–107.

Wyller, E. "Zum Begriff 'Non Aliud' bei Cusanus." In *Nicolò Cusano agli Inizi del Mondo Moderno*, 419–43. Florence: Sansoni, 1970.

———. "Nicolaus Cusanus' *De non aliud* und Platons Dialog *Parmenides*. Ein Beitrag zur Beleuchtung des Renaissanceplatonismus." In *Studia Platonica: Festschrift für Hermann Gundert*, ed. K. Döring and W. Kullmann, 239–51. Amsterdam: Gruner, 1974.

———. "Henologie als philosophische Disziplin heute." *MFCG* 13 (1978): 422–32.

———. *Henologische Perspektiven I/I–II: Platon—Johannes—Cusanus*. Amsterdam: Rodopi B.V., 1995.

Yamaki, K. "Die 'manuductio' von der 'ratio' zur Intuition in *De visione Dei*." *MFCG* 18 (1989): 276–95.

Yates, F. A. *Lull and Bruno*. London: Routledge, 1982.

Zimmermann, A. "'Belehrte Unwissenheit' als Ziel der Naturforschung." In *Nikolaus von Kues: Einführung in sein philosophisches Denken*, ed. K. Jacobi, 129–34. Munich: Alber, 1979.

———, ed. *Mensura, Mass, Zahl, Zahlensymbolik im Mittelalter*. 2 vols. New York: de Gruyter, 1983.

Index

Absolute, 3–4, 6, 18, 33, 40, 45–61, 63–69, 71, 77–78, 87–88, 99, 102, 104, 104n, 105, 107, 110, 117–19, 126, 130n, 134–36, 136n, 139–40, 145, 152–53, 152n, 154n, 155n, 160–62, 164, 166, 168–71, 174–77, 192, 194–96, 204n, 208, 210, 217–19, 236–38, 245, 252, 255; defined, 18; as Maximum, 12, 16–18, 20, 11, 17, 31–33, 39, 40, 43–44, 48; *See also* Contraction.
Actuality, 99, 214, 220, 227; God's, 208, 210–11, 225, 227–28
Adams, M. M., 129n, 195n
Aevum/everlasting, 210–13
Affirmation and negation, 8, 19–23, 21n, 77
Agent intellect, 126n,140
Albergati, N., 127n
Albert the Great, 20n, 104n, 116n, 199n, 221n, 231n
Anaxagoras, 40, 103, 245
Andrea, Abbot John, 181, 202–5
Angels, 58, 121, 210
Anselm, 17, 111,152; proof of God's existence, 156; description of God, 156; and God's presence/absence, 156
Apel, K., 124n
A priori concepts, 124, 137n
Aquinas, 14n, 31n, 93n, 94n, 102n, 115n, 116n, 126n, 129, 129n, 137, 199n, 217n, 220n, 226n, 227n, 230n, 231n, 232n, 234, 234n
Aristotle, 3, 9, 14n, 62, 92, 104n, 111, 115, 116n, 122, 129n, 137, 169, 183n, 197, 200–201, 208, 210n, 212, 212n, 217, 220–21, 226n, 227n, 232n, 251
Aristotelian 52, 74, 112, 113n, 116, 116n, 124–25, 126n, 129, 137, 139–40, 146, 169–70, 178, 181–83, 192–93, 195, 200, 225–27, 230n, 232, 234, 236, 246
Arithmetic, 31–32, 73
Arithmology, 86, 96
Art: conjectural 85, 88, 96–99, 100n, 101; divine, 117, 122, 123, 126–27; human (craft), 32, 43, 100, 113–14, 116n, 117n, 122–24, 126–27, 127n, 131, 141–44; Lull's, 217, 219n
Arterial/bodily spirits, 102, 106, 114, 131–32, 131n
Ascent to God, 72, 72n
Assimilation/likening, 110, 117–19, 121, 121n, 127–35, 133n, 137–38, 144–46, 218, 230, 230n, 248–49, 253; active, 131–33, 218, 248; tension with measuring, 134–35, 137–38
Augustine, 10n, 70n, 72, 109, 111, 115, 116n, 172, 216, 222, 239, 248
Avicenna (Ibn Sina), 239n

Balbus, P., 181, 202
Beierwaltes, W., 24n, 29n, 57n, 80n, 152n, 154n,155n, 157n, 165n, 184n
Being: finite, 2, 6n, 7, 9, 19, 20, 21n, 22, 24, 26–27, 31, 35, 40, 48, 51–52, 58, 50, 63n, 71, 73, 76, 81n, 83, 85, 91, 99, 100, 102, 105, 117, 119–21, 122n, 130, 136n, 155, 157, 169, 170, 184, 187, 189, 191, 196, 203, 214, 220–21, 223, 225–26, 232–33, 237, 239n, 255; conceptual, 118–19, 135, 248; God's, 8, 21n, 26–27, 33, 44, 51, 58, 71, 118–19, 152–53, 155, 168–70, 203, 239, 239n; three regions of, 206–13, 225, 238, 238n, 252
Blumenburg, H., 1n
Body, 12, 42, 58, 82, 130n, 131; and four elements, 92–94; in Jesus, 55, 64, 67, 177–79; as metaphysical unity, 76–78, 105–6; and perception, 81–82; and soul, 6, 100, 110–11, 116n, 139–45, 139n, 177–79, 217, 223, 233
Boethius, 36, 37n, 114, 115n, 130
Bolberitz, P., 180n
Bonaventure, 58n, 115, 125n, 248
Bond, H. L., 4n, 12n, 20n, 24n, 37n, 43n, 50n, 51n, 55n, 57n, 64n, 75n, 84n, 91n, 115n, 134n, 147n, 179n, 201n, 235n
Bonner, A., 219n
Bormann, K., 80n, 104n
Boundaries, of physical universe, 46–48

267

INDEX

Brient, E., 40n
Brüntrup, A., 206n, 209n, 211n, 238n
Burrell, D., 30n

Cardinal Julian (Caesarini), 68–69, 72n, 81, 88, 90, 107–9
Carlson, T. A., 21n
Casarella, P., 51n, 161n, 206n
Cassirer, E., 129, 129n
Causal account of knowledge, 131
Center: and circumference, 26, 46–48, 50, 57, 60, 242, 244; of universe, 46–48, 244; conjectural, 46; God, 46, 60, 71–72, 242–44; Jesus, 63, 65, 67
Chenu, M.-D., 115n
Christianson, G., 12n, 69n
Cicero, 112n
Cognitive access to God, 2, 15–16, 27–28, 31–32, 38, 72, 159, 161, 195, 211; God inaccessible, 50, 127, 146, 156, 161, 177, 241; thinking God, 1, 10; touching God, 1, 9, 17, 19, 20, 102, 167, 171, 243
Cognitive capacities/powers, 89–90, 101–7, 124–25, 130–33; extrapolated, 104–5
Cognitive norms, 134
Coincidence of opposites, 5–6, 12, 16, 18–24, 30–31, 30n, 45, 47, 57, 60, 66, 77n, 83, 87n, 124, 135, 148, 161–66, 171, 173, 187, 199n, 212, 242–44, 253; and contraries/contradictories, 19–20, 22, 161–62; and dialectical thought, 19, 163; and Dionysius, 20–23; and *intellectus*, 77n; and Jesus Christ, 55, 55n, 60, 66, 178; of mathematical figures, 25, 242; and names, 124; and Not Other, 187; and rational thought, 19, 77n; vision of, 164n, 173; at and inside wall, 161–66, 173
Colomer, E., 217n
Color, 6, 9, 108
Comprehend incomprehensibly, 23, 31–33, 224–25, 243
Concepts/conceptual knowledge, 1, 9–10, 13, 15, 17, 22–26, 28–29, 32, 47–48, 53, 70–71, 74–75, 84–85, 99, 103, 118–21, 123–24, 132, 134, 137, 158–61, 167, 202, 230; Absolute, 202
Conjecture *(coniectura)*, 2, 46, 66–67, 68–78, 80–86, 80n, 84n, 88–91, 95, 96–97, 99–101, 110, 115, 123, 131–32, 134, 137–38, 146, 230, 239, 246–48, 253; about God, 81; defined, 81; and learned ignorance, 95; and models, 75, 99; not a guess, hypothesis, 80, 246; and three kinds of possibility, 239

Contingency, 34–37, 39, 45, 55, 68–69, 88, 208, 210, 214, 221, 237, 239
Contraction: of creatures, 4, 6, 22, 32–34, 39–41, 41n, 42–43, 43n, 44–52, 52n, 53–66, 68–69, 76–77, 80–82, 84–87, 91, 91n, 95, 100, 102–5, 107–8, 110, 135, 152–53, 152n, 155, 168–70, 174n, 176–77, 217–18, 238, 244–46, 252–53, 255; degrees of, 43, 52; in Jesus Christ, 50–66, 176–77; meaning of, 41–42; and universals/particulars, 43–44, 52, 91, 91n; universe, 39–45, 66; *See also* Absolute.
Contradiction/contradictory, 7–8, 10n, 19, 24, 26n, 57, 77n, 160–63, 167, 176–77, 187, 200–201, 201n, 222, 250, 253; principle of, 51, 162, 187, 253; as boundary of reason, 161–62; God as contradiction of contradictions, 201
Copenhaver, B., 113n
Counting, 73, 73n, 74, 76, 95, 141
Craft/artisanry, 32, 43, 100, 113–14, 116n, 117n, 122–24, 126–27, 127n, 131, 141–144; *See also* Art.
Creatable *(posse fieri)*, 208–14, 214n, 220–21, 225, 227–29, 235, 238–40, 239n, 252
Creating/Creator, 4–5, 16, 32–38, 45, 48, 51–52, 53n, 54n, 55–57, 59–61, 68, 70–72, 85–86, 97–98, 105, 111, 114, 116, 116n, 117–18, 118n, 120–22, 124, 126–28, 130n, 134, 138, 141–43, 146, 152–53, 155, 155n, 163–64, 164n, 169, 171, 174, 175n, 176, 178, 184–86, 193–95, 197, 203–4, 208–11, 216, 218–19, 218n, 221–22, 227–29, 231–37, 239–40, 243–46, 249, 251, 252–54
Creating/human, 70–72, 86, 103–4, 110, 116n, 117–18, 121–24, 127–28, 134, 136, 138n, 143–46, 234, 246–48
Creatures, 4, 6, 9, 12, 14n, 15–18, 23n, 24, 26–27, 31–36, 36n, 37–39, 41–43, 43n, 44–53, 53n, 54, 54n, 55–63, 63n, 67–72, 76, 79–81, 84–88, 90–91, 96–101, 103, 103n, 104–5, 108, 109n, 110–11, 117, 119–21, 130n, 140–41, 144, 146–47, 150, 155, 157–58, 160, 163–64, 164n, 166–71, 174, 176–78, 181, 185–90, 193–200, 202–4, 208–24, 227–29, 231–34, 236–41, 243–55

Dangelmayr, S., 118n, 206n, 239n
Darkness, 159–61, 163, 165
Davies, B., 217n
Decad, 73, 75–76, 75n, 85–87, 89, 96–100, 246

de Certeau, M., 149n, 154n
Definition, 34, 183n, 228–29; Aristotelian, 182–83; as causing, 184; and determinateness, 183; and Not Other, 181–85, 182n, 202–3, 203n, 251; real vs. nominal, 183; as self-defining, 181–83, 251
de Gandillac, M., 57n, 74n, 113n, 117n
Deification (*theosis*), 174
Deiformitas, 104, 104n, 107–9
Dependence of creatures, 34–35, 51, 71, 186, 244, 251; and unfolding, 37–39; of image on original, 38–39, 51, 244; and not otherness, 186
Descartes, 47n, 124
Desire for God, 71, 172–74, 217
Determination: and limitation, 184, 188; and non-limitation, 188
Dialectic: of oneness and otherness, 69–70, 248; of *visio* and *ratio*, 150–66, 249; of enfolding and unfolding, 164; of God's identity/difference, 158; of God's in and beyond, 160; and metaphor, 147, 244, 247–55; of God's presence/absence, 153, 158, 249; of seeing/being seen, 153, 249
Dialectical thinking, 19, 22, 25–26, 57, 68, 79–80, 147–68, 204, 241–44, 247–51, 254–55; and conjecture, 69, 101, 248; with geometrical figures, 25–26, 28; and Incarnation, 245–46; and Not Other, 188; Neoplatonic, not Hegelian, 57n
Dialogue, as literary form, 111–16, 111n, 112n
Dietrich of Freiburg, 116n, 120n
Diogenes Laertius, 213, 220n
Discursive thought, 2–6, 28, 70, 73n, 74, 77, 122n, 123, 125, 131–32, 158–61, 180, 202–3, 243, 253; *See also Ratio*.
Distinguishing and relating, 6, 73, 73n, 74–75, 78, 131
Divided line: in Plato, 1–6; Cusan, 130n
Duclow, D., 124n, 161n, 199n
Dupré, L., 148n
Dupré, W., 103n
Dürer, A., 157n

Earth in universe, 46–48
Eckhart, 21n, 40n, 65, 70n, 116n, 120n, 125n, 241, 248, 254
Eco, U., 231n
Element/compound, 91–96; in Aristotle, 92; four, 92–94, 93n, 94n
Encompassing/encompassed by God, 6, 6n, 10, 20, 26, 50, 51, 55, 56, 59, 118–19, 127, 152, 152n, 167–69, 190,

192; by Jesus, 65; by mind, 103, 118–19, 130, 132; by soul, 142; by universe, 40
End without end (*finis sine fine*), 166–67, 201n
Enfolding/unfolding (*complicatio/explicatio*), 22, 36–39, 43–44, 47–48, 51, 59–61, 66, 72, 91, 95, 97, 104, 117–21, 124, 163–64, 167–68, 225, 243–44, 250; across domains, 95; in Jesus Christ, 55, 59, 61, 163–64, 243; in human knowledge, 71–73, 102–3, 117–21, 124, 138n, 247, 249; of knowing powers, 78, 249; and names, 124; in number, 74, 95; papal power, 95, 95n
Epicurus, 221
Epistemic account of knowledge, 131
Equality: of God, 18, 46, 59, 104, 104n, 168, 222–24, 252; of divine Word/Jesus, 56, 59, 60, 61, 65, 108, 109, 120, 222–23, 245; of human mind, 59, 109, 120
Eriugena, 29n, 65, 70n, 111, 122, 141n, 180, 241, 248
Essence: and accidents, 192, 194–97; God as Essence of essences, 194
Eternity, 6, 51, 55–56, 63n, 73, 117, 120, 125, 130n, 155, 162, 170–72, 179, 198n, 208, 214–15, 220–25, 228, 230–36, 238–40, 243, 252; vs. everlasting/perpetual, 210–13
Exemplar/paradigm: divine, 41, 70, 117–19, 125, 135–36, 155, 157, 170–71, 218
Exitus-reditus (outflow-return), 63n, 70–72, 78–79, 97–98, 104–5, 213; of knowing powers, 105–6, 213

Face: as qualitative measure, 135–36; Jesus', 147–51, 154–56; God's, 148, 154–57, 159, 170–71; God's a mirror, 170; God's as transcendent, 155, 160; human, 171
Faith, 50, 56, 60–61, 65, 65n, 66–67, 80, 84, 117, 172, 174–75, 177, 179, 233, 244–45, 249
Ferdinand, 181, 182, 185, 186, 189, 191, 192, 194, 196, 197, 199
Ficino, 103n
Figure P (*paradigmatica*), 78–79, 78n, 87–88, 90, 100, 246–47
Figure U (*universalis*), 87–90, 94, 100–101, 104n, 108, 246–47
Fine, G., 18n
Flasch, K., 1n, 12n, 13n, 17n, 20n, 28n, 42n, 45n, 49n, 51n, 58n, 63n, 68n,

Flasch, K. *(continued)*
  69n, 70n, 77n, 78n, 111n, 113n, 114n, 115n, 117n, 120n, 124n, 135n, 137n, 138n, 147n, 149n, 161n, 181n, 189n, 197n, 199n, 200n, 202n, 206n, 209n, 216n, 226n, 230n, 233n, 237n
Form: Aristotelian, 169–70; Boethian, 130; in creatures, 34, 52, 54, 132, 169; gives being, 169; God as Form, 71, 140, 169; God as Form of forms, 169–70, 194; in knowledge, 123; Platonic, 16, 18, 52, 54, 54n, 74, 123, 212, 230; no intermediate realm of Forms, 39, 58, 195, 221, 230, 239–40, 252
Fräntzki, E., 82n

Galen, 131n
Garden of paradise, 164–66, 173
Genera, 43–44, 50, 52, 91, 100, 183
Geometry, 31–32, 47, 73, 74, 85, 93, 180, 203n, 211–12; geometrical figures: and the infinite, 2, 13, 25–26, 26n, 28–29, 47, 66, 223–25, 235, 242; as conjectural schemata, 73, 76, 78, 86–88, 92–93, 96–97, 99, 101, 136n, 246–47
Gift, 23, 44n, 108, 165, 172, 179, 205, 250
God: actually all possibles, 19, 164, 170, 208–9, 214–15, 239–40 *(See also Possest)*; being, 8, 51, 71, 102, 118–19, 130n, 152–53, 169; cause/creator/source/origin, 4–5, 16, 18, 32–37, 40, 50–52, 53, 53n, 55–57, 59–60, 68, 71–72, 74n, 76, 97–98, 111, 117–18, 124, 128–29, 134, 139, 141–43, 164, 164n, 170, 172, 185–86, 194, 202–4, 208, 222, 228, 231–32, 234–36, 248–49, 250; center and circumference, 26, 46–47, 57, 60, 242–44; encompassing all, 6, 6n, 10, 18, 20, 26, 50–51, 55–56, 167–68, 242–43; equality, 18, 46, 168, 222; end/goal, 71–72, 165–67, 172, 227–31; exemplar, 155, 157, 170–71, 217–18; divine mind as exemplar, 70–73, 83, 101, 116–19, 121, 124–26, 128, 134, 136, 144, 146, 247–48; face of God, 135, 148, 154–55, 157, 159, 170–71; immanent, 48, 51n, 167, 180, 189, 189n, 190–91, 235, 243–44, 250–51; incomprehensible/unknowable, 1, 4, 4n, 7, 9–10, 12, 15–16, 18, 26–29, 47, 64, 67, 119, 147, 159–61, 164–65, 186, 199, 207, 213–14, 223–24, 241; ineffable, 7, 9, 10n, 19, 23n, 77, 123, 160, 165, 234; invisible, 9, 153, 158–60, 164–64, 204; language about/names of, 7–9, 16, 19–21, 21n, 22–23, 23n, 28–31, 30n, 160, 165, 186, 197, 199, 201, 233–35; limit/measure, 14n, 48, 50, 121, 135n, 166, 168–69, 184, 186, 189, 203, 227–31, 235, 237; Oneness, 6, 29, 37, 39, 40–41, 50–52, 55, 57, 59, 66, 68–71, 76–80, 84–86, 87n, 88, 92–93, 95, 101, 107–8, 117, 121, 124, 134, 155, 158, 162–64, 167, 180–81, 191, 220–21, 229, 234, 239, 242–44; oppositeness *(oppositio)*, 51, 167, 187–89, 201, 203, 243, 250; ontologically prior, 8, 38, 148, 152–54, 158, 162, 170, 185–87, 189–91, 197–98, 204, 214–15; relation/connection with creatures, 25–26, 28, 33–48, 51, 55–56, 147–51, 154–56, 158, 160, 167, 169, 181, 245, 251; seeing/being seen, 9n, 147–52, 152n, 153–65, 170–71, 173–74, 176–77, 204, 249; simple, 7–9, 27, 29, 77, 97, 117–18, 120, 120n, 123, 126, 138n, 162–63, 194–95, 205, 217, 243, 250; transcendent/beyond, 7–10, 13, 16, 18–19, 23, 24n, 27, 29, 31, 38, 47–48, 51n, 55, 152, 160, 162–65, 167–68, 172, 174, 180, 185–87, 190–91, 199–201, 204, 234, 238, 243–44, 249, 250–51; *See also* Absolute; Coincidence of opposites; Dependence of creatures; Enfolding/unfolding; Infinite; Not Other; Presence.
Good/goodness: of creatures, 34, 204–5, 216–18, 221, 236; of God, 45, 171, 179, 197, 204–5, 216–18, 221, 236; Plato's, 2–3; as transcendental, 122n
Grosseteste, R., 231n
Ground *(ratio)*, 192–94

Haas, A. M., 148n
Happiness, 63, 172–73; as coincidence/paradoxical, 177; as fulfilled desire, 173; as union with Jesus, 177; as vision of, union with God, 176–77
Harmony (concord): and difference, 90–91; of universal order, 231–33 of soul/body, 142–43
Harries, K., 46n, 47n
Haubst, R., 4n, 20n, 30n, 49n, 70n, 78n, 147n, 161n, 224n
Haug, W., 161n
Heat: as image of *posse fieri*, 225–26; image of three kinds of possibility, 238
Hegel, 57n, 115n, 188n
Helander, B. H., 159n
Hennigfeld, J., 124n

Hermes Trismegistus, 124
Herold, N., 149n, 153n
Heymericus de Campo, 20n
Hierarchy, 18, 42, 58, 63n, 76–80; of knowing powers, 78–80, 130
Hirt, P., 70n
Hojsisch, B., 180n
Holy Spirit, 45, 108, 179, 223
Hopkins, J., 4n, 5, 9n, 12n, 13n, 14n, 17n, 25n, 30n, 34n, 36n, 40n, 41n, 44n, 47n, 49n, 64n, 65n, 69n, 74n, 80n, 82n, 83n, 91n, 94n, 113n, 115n, 117n, 118n, 129n, 133n, 136n, 147n, 148n, 149n, 152n, 156n, 174n, 180n, 182n, 191n, 194n, 206n, 207n, 209n, 212n, 213n, 218n, 221n, 223n, 228n, 230n, 237n
Hösle, V., 96n
Human being/nature, 48–49, 101–9; capacities common to all creatures, 58; *capax omnium* as knower, 102–3, 125; destiny of, 111; enfolds/unfolds all things, 102–3; and divine in Jesus Christ, 56, 58, 61–64; human god, 102–3, 103n, 248; image of God's mind, 83, 102, 116–21; as in-between nature, 59, 62–63; maximal 52–55, 65; microcosm, 58–60, 62, 101–4; as contracted oneness, 102–3, 107; perfect, 61, 67
Hunt, 206–7; as search for wisdom, God, 206–7, 251–52
Hunting fields *(campi)*, 206–7, 251–52; as figures leading to God, 234
Hypostases, 18, 39, 209, 212; *See also* Form.
Hypostatic union, 50, 54–55, 61–67, 175, 178, 245, 250
Hypothetical: infinite figure, 25–29; perfect individual, 53, 55

Iamblichus, 86n
Icon, 147–53, 169–70, 177; as connecting levels of reality, 153; and illusion, 149–51; omnivoyant/all-seeing, 148–50, 249; rule for interpreting, 149, 151; symbol of *visio Dei*, 149, 153
Identity: basis of, 185, 251; of absolute with contracted, 51; and difference/otherness, 185; of knower and known, 13–14, 16, 83–84; statements and not other, 184–85
Ignorance, 5–8; about God, 10–11, 15–17, 22, 30, 32–33; and darkness, 159–61, 165; and Not Other, 199; about universe, 45, 47–48; *See also* Learned ignorance.

Image and original, 2–3, 6, 56, 61, 66, 71, 117, 151, 154–55, 157, 170, 175–76, 218; and assimilating/likening in knowledge, 128–33; and dialectic, 151; and Equality in Trinity, 120; icon, 147–51; image as contracted, 34–35, 244; *imago Dei*, 70–71, 84, 101, 116–21, 218, 248; language as image, 83; mind as image/likeness, 70–71, 83, 116–22, 246; mirror image, 35, 170; and Not Other, 192, 199; portrait image, 38, 119–20, 126–27, 127n; universe as image, 52; vs. unfolding, 117n, 120, 120n
Imagination, 17, 47, 62, 83, 85, 102, 105–7, 123, 125, 130–31, 138, 144; and perspective, 47
Immortality, 116n, 141–44
Impossibility for reason, 161–66
Incarnation, 49, 55, 58–60, 66, 171–72, 174–79, 245–46
Independence of God, 55, 185
Individual things, 40–41, 52, 90, 100; as contracted reflections, 41, 52; as limiting and concentrating, 52, 52n; and universals, 43–44, 52, 90–91; specimens of type, 52
Infinite, 7, 10, 17, 25, 27, 29–30, 39–40, 50–51, 65, 123, 160–61, 163–69, 172, 185, 188, 188n, 204, 228, 241–42; privative, 40
Innate ideas, 124, 129, 138n, 139, 139n
Intellect: God's, 107; maximal in Jesus Christ, 62
Intellectus/intellectual vision, 4–6, 8–9, 20, 70, 70n, 72, 76, 133n, 167, 178, 202–3, 205, 225, 230, 248, 250; ascent and descent, 105; and conjecture, 81, 89–90, 92, 96; as gift, 205; God beyond, 161; knowing powers traced to, 102, 105n; and judgment, 124; *ratio* in *intellectus*, 6; tension with *ratio*, 4–6; *See also* Discursive thought; *Ratio*.
Intelligence: as metaphysical unity, 76–80
Izbicki, T., 12n, 69n, 95n

Jacobi, K., 13n, 24n, 31n, 34n
Jesus Christ/Word, 15, 48–67, 69, 120, 126n, 147–51, 153–55, 163, 171–79, 204, 233, 245–46, 250; cosmic, 61; as divine equality and Second Person, 56, 59–61, 120; door to wall of Paradise, 163, 243–44, 250; friend and brother, 65; his human powers, 177–78; icon of-face, 147–51; image of the Father, 150, 176; as knower, 176; mediator, 60–63, 66–67, 172, 174, 245; mysteries

INDEX

Jesus Christ/Word *(continued)*
of life, death, resurrection, 64–64, 178, 233; as norm/measure, 66–67; as Tree of Life, 176; uniqueness, 61; union with humankind, 65, 120; his vision, 177
John Damascene, 102n
John of Salisbury, 131n
Judgment/assertion, 10, 15, 17, 20, 23, 57, 70, 75, 77, 81–84, 124–25, 130, 132, 137n, 146

Kant, 74n, 116n, 122, 136, 138n, 146, 237n; Kantian, 116, 116n, 122, 136–37, 136n, 138n, 230n
Klein, J., 2n, 73n
Knowing God, 5–7, 10, 17, 30
Knowing activities, 130–34
Knowing powers, 89–90, 101–7, 124–25; extrapolated, 104–5
Knowledge, 110–46; active, 71, 110, 115, 116n, 121–27, 132, 138; adult's vs. child's, 138–39; Aristotelian view of, 129, 137, 136n, 146; beyond conceptual, 48; as conjectural, 69–71, 69n, 72–74, 77–78, 80–86, 110, 115, 123, 131–32, 134, 137; constructed, 14, 18, 27, 53, 70–71, 73–74, 77, 84, 86, 99, 136–38; of created nature, 12, 16–17, 31–32; encompasses all things, 102–3; of essence, 5, 16; four-fold analysis of, 131; as image of God's creative knowledge, 70–71, 116–22; and incommensurability, 15–16; Kantian view of, 116, 116n, 122, 136–37, 136n, 138n, 146; as measuring, 12–16, 27, 32, 48, 73n, 110, 115–16, 118, 118n, 121, 127–39, 241; as passive, 129, 129n; productive/creative, 71, 103, 122–28; of quiddity, 192–93; of self, 71
Koch, J., 68n, 69n, 70n, 75n, 76n, 78n, 80n
Kraut, R., 18n,
Kremer, K., 82n, 116n, 121n, 129n, 137n, 157n, 164n
Kristeller, P. O., 112n

Lai, T., 40n
Language, 8–9, 66, 81, 83, 83n, 122–24, 233–35; about God, 16, 19–21, 21n, 23–24, 26, 28–31, 30n, 160, 165, 186, 197, 199, 201, 233–35; analogical, 30; metaphorical, 16; naming God, 23n, 28–31; paradoxical, 166–67; and otherness, 83; religious, 65
Layman/*idiota*, 110–43; as principal speaker, 112

Learned ignorance, 12–13, 15–16, 30, 32–33, 38–39, 45, 47–49, 56, 60, 64–66, 69, 119, 148, 161, 165, 213–14, 244–45, 255; as achievement, 22, 64, 255; as attitude, 115; and conjecture, 95; as Cusan method, 49, 66; embodied in layman, 112–15; and otherness, 14–15; rule of, 31n, 91, 226–27, 226n, 235; sacred, 24, 27; as self-knowledge, 107–9; Socratic ignorance, 16; as wisdom, 112–13
LeBlond, J. L., 183n
Leinkauf, T., 222n
Light, 78–79, 102, 105n, 106, 108, 191; as God, 216–18
Likeness: in knowledge, 116–21, 128; likening/*assimilatio*, 127–33
Limit: as asymptote, 25; God as unlimited limit, 19, 48, 50, 250
Lonergan, B., 129n
Look/glance/gaze, *see* Seeing; Vision.
Love, 109, 171–73, 179; coincidence of loving and lovable, 173; and Incarnation/Trinity, 172–79; Trinity as lover, lovable, bond, 172–73
Lull, R., 20n, 65, 70n, 198n, 206n, 217, 217n, 219, 219n, 241, 251

Mahoney, E. P., 63n
Magnitude, 73, 193
Maimonides, 31n
Mar, G., 25
Marsh, D., 112n
Mathematics, 31–32, 73–76, 86, 132–33, 137, 211–12; as image, 97; as human construction, 73, 86, 97, 133; and knowledge, 12–16, 27; infinite incommensurable, 28; and numerology, 97; Platonic, 97; and precision/exactness, 13, 16, 27, 32, 67, 70, 74, 77, 81, 84–86, 123, 133; and proportion, 13–17
Mathematical symbols, 24–28, 97; constructed, 25; extrapolated, 25, 224–25, 242; and dialectic, 25–26; geometrical, 25, 66; polygon and circle, 13, 15; triangle and circle, 224–25
Maximum: absolute, 12, 16–23, 27, 39–40, 47–49, 53–54, 58–60, 227; God, 16–23; and infinite, 22; and minimum, 17, 21; contracted, 31–49, 53–54, 60, 244–45; at once absolute and contracted, 48–57, 60–61, 245; intensive/extensive, 54
McGinn, B., 21n, 172n, 173n, 224n
McTighe, T. P., 36n, 80n
Measure: Jesus Christ, 65–67; cognitive, 67, 127–39; qualitative, 134–36

Measurement: and knowledge, 12–16, 75, 108, 115–16, 118, 118n, 121, 127–39, 241, 248; analysis of, 14, 134n; first and second-order, 14; of world, 32; and quadrivial arts, 32–33

Measuring/*mensuratio:* and knowing, 110, 115–16, 118, 118n, 121, 127–39; tension with assimilating, 134–35

Mediation: of Jesus Christ, 60–63, 66–67, 172; as enfolding, 61–62; of extremes, 106, 106n

Meinhardt, H., 24n, 54n, 70n, 233n

Miller, C. L., 34n, 46n, 47n, 68n, 111n, 128n, 147n

Memory, 62, 131

Metaphor/*figura,* 16, 66, 86, 107, 110, 144–46, 147, 234, 242; and dialectic, 147, 244, 247–51, 254–55; explanatory/exploratory, 28, 99, 110, 122, 144–46, 207, 247–49, 252–54; foundational, 70n, 121–22; hermetic, 66; ironic, 21n, 181, 243–44; vs. literal, 253; mathematical, 73, 75; for mind, 110–46, 248–49

Microcosm: and macrocosm, 42; and human nature, 58–60, 62, 101–4, 108, 233, 245, 248

Mind, 110–46, 236–37; adaptive, 136; *capax omnium,* 102–3, 125, 229–31; coprimordial with reality, 78, 86; discriminating/relating, 6, 73, 73n, 74–75, 78; defined as limit and measure, 116, 127, 134, 228–29; divine, 76, 86, 105, 117–18, 127, 248; essence unknowable, 230; flexibility of, 132–33; human, as image of divine, 83, 86, 108, 110, 116–22, 139, 218, 246, 248; living substance, 140; living measure, 134; *mens* from *mensurare,* 115; not Hegel's *Geist,* 115n; oneness of, 74, 78, 105–6, 119; ontological priority, 120; revelation of God, 126; as self-subsistent, 139; as soul, 139–41; as substantial form, 140; as unlimited, 229–31

Mirror, 35, 141–42, 170

More or less, 31, 38, 41, 50, 54, 88, 92, 100–101; as rule, 31n, 91, 226, 226n

Motion, 45–47; and rest, 160

Multitude/multiplicity, 73, 168; in knowledge, 119

Mutability: of creatures, 34, 51; and number, 74

Mystical theology, 147–79, 148n, 162

Mystical vision, sight, 148, 153, 158–59; three stages of, 163–65

Names, 122–24, 233–34, 234n; and exactness, 123; God's, 186; Not-other as symbolic name, 180, 203, 250–51

Nature: contracted, 58; human, 48–54, 58–60; human-and-divine, 54; human as intermediate, 59, 62–63; inseparability of human and divine in Christ, 55; as possibility, 212

Necessity: absolute, 88, 99, 130; consequent, 88, 99, 130n

Negative theology, 26–31, 77, 117; cataphatic/apophatic, 22–23, 23n

Neoplatonism/Neoplatonic, 3–4, 18, 29n, 34, 52, 54n, 57n, 65, 70, 72, 77, 82, 86, 91, 96, 98, 101, 104, 106, 110, 138n, 139, 140, 142, 151, 154, 178, 180–81, 192, 195, 205, 208, 210, 213n, 220–21, 230, 239, 241, 249, 250–52, 254

Nexus/connection: as Holy Spirit in Trinity, 45, 59, 104n, 108, 109, 220–24; as the Spirit's loving union, 223–24

Neumeyer, A., 149n

Nicholas of Cusa: works: *Apologia,* 194n; *Compendium,* 83, 207n, 214n; *Complementum theologicum,* 82n; *De apice theoriae,* 214n; *De beryllo,* 81n; *De coniecturis,* 68–109, 110, 115n, 117n, 118, 226n, 230, 233n, 246–48, 253; *De dato patris luminum,* 44n, 194n; *De deo abscondito,* 4–11, 111n; *De docta ignorantia,* 12–67, 68–70, 68n, 72, 73n, 74n, 78n, 82, 84n, 92n, 103, 103n, 110, 117, 118, 120n, 130n, 146, 174, 193n, 194n, 208, 208n, 222, 224n, 225n, 226, 226n, 230, 233n, 241–47, 253; *De filiatione Dei,* 174–75, 174n; *De li non aliud,* 180–205, 213, 215–16, 250–51; *De ludo globi,* 198n; *De possest,* 74n, 199n, 213–15, 213n; *De venatione sapientiae,* 183n, 198n, 206–40, 251–53; *De visione Dei,* 147–79, 201n, 204n, 243, 249–50, 253; *Idiota de mente,* 110–46, 116n, 198n, 204n, 217, 246, 248–49, 252–53; *Idiota de sapientia,* 112n; *Idiota de staticis experimentis,* 94n, 110

Nothingness *(nihil),* 78–79, 191

Not other/*Non aliud,* 180–205, 215–17, 250–51; as "A," 198–99; definition of, 182–83; defines everything, 182, 202–3, 203n, 215, 251; designates transcendence and immanence, 189, 250; and dialectical thinking, 188–89, 251; as essence, 195–97; essence of essences, 194; and infinite, 188, 188n; and intelligibles, 195–97; ironic, 181; and Neo

Not other/*Non aliud (continued)*
    platonic One, 197–99; in other, 189–90; not participated and participated, 194–95; and possibility, 191; presupposed for knowledge, 193; prior to One, 220; priority of, 191, 198, 215–16; and quiddity, 192–93; self-defining, 182–83, 185, 251; not separate from others, 203; source, origin of others, 190, 194, 199, 202; symbolic name for God, 180–81, 185–86, 189, 199, 251; points to God's transcendence, 186, 199, 204; and three sorts of "seeing," 202–3
Numbers, 56, 73–74; not conjectural, 74; non-material number, 141; and *possest*, 215
Numerology, 96–97

Objects of thought (*entia rationis*), 44, 121; *rationalia*, 71, 74n; conjectural, 71
Ockham, 129
Offerman, U., 13n, 33n, 50n, 52n, 61n, 64n, 65n
Oide, S., 70n, 75n, 76n, 78n, 87n
Olds, C., 150n
O'Meara, D. J., 97n
One: Proclean and Dionysian as Not Other, 197–99; Not Other prior, 220; prior to *posse fieri*, 220
One and many: and unfolding, 37; as universe, 39–43
Oneness: of creatures, 34, 39, 41, 52, 68, 78–80, 88, 91, 101; contracted, 90; defined, 80; and difference, 51; in diversity, 57; of elements, 94; and enfolding/*complicatio*, 37, 95; of God, 6, 29, 37, 39, 40–41, 50–52, 55, 57, 59, 66, 68–71, 76–80, 84–86, 87n, 88, 92–93, 95, 101, 107–8, 117, 121, 124, 134, 155, 158, 162–64, 167, 180–81, 191, 220–21, 229, 234, 239, 242–44; Jesus Christ, 50, 54, 56–57, 61–64, 66–67; of human knower, 62; of mind, 74, 78, 107–8; of mind's activities, 106; and numbers, 56, 74n, 76; of truth, 70, 96; of universe, 48, 51–52, 66
Oneness-in-otherness, 68–69, 79, 87n, 89, 95; of cognitive powers, 106
Opposites, 19–20, 22; coincidence of, 16–23, 30, 31, 57, 60, 66, 77n, 148, 161–62; God without opposite, 40, 77, 187; oppositeness of, 167, 203, 243, 250
Opposition: of God and creatures, 187–89, 203; of other and Not Other, 200, 203; two sorts, 188

Order, 231–33; of created whole, 42, 73; systematic, 77; hierarchical, 77–80, 231–33; Trinitarian, 232; and wisdom, 232–33
Origin/source (*principium*), 171, 185, 190, 193–94, 205, 208, 218–19, 232, 250
Otherness/*alteritas*, 68–70, 80–88, 91, 101, 168, 246–47; of God, 152, 203, 216; and conjecture, 70, 81–86, 246–47; defined, 69; of human intellect, 107; and oneness, 71, 78–86
Other/*alius*, 215–16, 251; distinct from Not Other, 181; each distinct from others, 185, 251; encompassed by Not Other, 190

Paradox, 1, 4, 19, 31, 40, 81, 158, 160, 162, 164, 166–67
Participation, 27, 27n, 41, 68n, 69, 78, 80, 86–88, 90, 96, 100, 118n, 192, 213; in mind, 119; and Not Other, 194–95
Pätzold, D., 180n, 188n, 189n, 191n
Patterson, R., 38n
Paul, St., 60, 61, 66, 120
Perception, 81–83, 129, 144, 203, 249; conjectural, 81, 83, 85; not passive, 132; initiates mental life, 129, 138–39
Perfection: of creation, 32, 36, 38, 217; of individual of type, 53–54; ten perfections, 216–19, 236
Perspective/perspectival, 25, 28, 47–48, 81–84, 110, 149–50, 154n, 160, 163, 167, 206–7, 225, 234, 239, 247–48, 254
Peter Lombard, 111
Phenomenological account of knowledge, 131
Philo, 114
Physiology: and knowledge, 131
Pico, 103n
Plato, 2–7, 2n, 9n, 16, 18, 18n, 38, 38n, 54n, 62, 98n, 112, 112n, 113, 115, 122, 129, 130n, 137n, 138n, 180, 180n, 198n, 206n, 209, 212–13, 220–21, 230, 232, 237, 243, 249; *Republic:* divided line, 1–6; mathematics, 97; *See also* Form, Platonic.
Plotinus, 18, 29, 39, 43, 70, 198, 209, 212, 239
Plurality, 34, 76; and definition, 183; of universe, 39–43, 51
Polygon and circle, 13–15, 63
Portrait image, 38, 119, 122n, 145; all-seeing portrait/icon, 147–53, 169–70, 177, 181; self-portrait, 126–27, 127n, 136

Posse fieri/producibility, 208–16, 209n, 211n, 219–25, 226n, 227–29, 227n, 235–40, 238n, 239n, 252; described, 210; and intermediate realm, 220–21, 229–30, 239–40, 252; and learned ignorance, 214

Possest/actual possibility, 214–15, 225–27, 236–37, 252

Possibility, 99, 130n, 170, 191, 208–14; actualized in God, 170, 209, 252; as *posse fieri*, 208–14; three regions of, 208–13, 209n, 237–40, 252

Praise, 218–19, 235–36

Precision/exactness, 13, 16, 27, 32, 67, 70, 74, 77, 81, 84–85, 101, 119, 122–24, 233

Presence: of God, 37–38, 40–41, 47, 147–49, 160–61, 243, 250; God's presence/absence, 152–54, 156–58, 249; of universe, 41; of each thing in each, 40–41

Proclus/Proclean, 18, 24n, 29n, 39, 63n, 70, 70n, 77n, 97n, 105n, 138n, 181, 197, 197n, 202, 202n, 209, 210, 212, 220n, 221, 236–37, 237n, 241, 252

Progression, 75n, 76

Proportion, 13–14; and form, 142; Jesus Christ as, 67; *nulla proportio* 15–17, 32, 50, 60, 66, 84, 117, 146–47, 215, 241, 245

Pseudo-Dionysius, 20–23, 24n, 27, 29n, 63n, 117n, 141, 159, 164n, 180–81, 197–99, 202–3, 218, 220n, 231, 232n, 234, 241, 251, 254

Ptolemy, 46, 104n

Pyramid: and four elements, 93; of light/darkness (Figure P), 78–80

Pythagoras/Pythagorean, 75, 86, 87n, 96, 97, 114

Quadrivium, 31–33; as normative measure, 33

Quiddity, 5, 34, 177, 183, 192–93, 204; and accidents, 192; unknowable, 213–14

Quodlibet in quolibet, 40–41, 52–53, 53n, 57, 91n, 103, 245; and contraction, 41

Ratio/discursive reason, 19–20, 28, 70, 74, 74n, 76–80, 123, 131, 158–62, 164–65, 180, 203, 193, 243, 253; and conjecture, 81, 89–90, 92, 96, 123; and *dianoia*, 2–10; God beyond, 161; in *intellectus*, 6

Realism: Cusan, 83n; not Aristotelian, 116, 137

Reference, 128, 137

Reflection: in human perception, 82; as *resplendentia*, 35–36, 125; of whole in each thing, 41; of all in mind, 217–18

Reinhardt, K., 161n, 174n, 175n, 176n

Relation: among creatures, 42, 49, 52; of God and creatures, 33–48, 55–56, 147–51, 154–56; *See also* Enfolding/unfolding.

Revelation, 50, 56, 58; revealing/concealing, 159

Rorty, R., 2n

Sanchez, R., 95
Santinello, G., 116n
Scharlemann, R., 180n
Schmidt, M., 148n
Schmitt, C., 113n
Schnarr, H., 70n, 206n, 211n–13n, 218n, 226n, 227n, 229n, 238n
Schneider, G., 180n, 183n
Schönborn, C., 49n, 53n, 60n
Schulze, W., 16n
Scotus, 129, 239n

Seeing/sight/being seen, 147–79, 249–50; absolute, 152, 152n, 177; beyond seeing, 173; dialectical, 204; God's causative, 170, 204, 204n; God subject/object of seeing, 153–54, 157, 204, 204n; God's without limits, 151–52; identity of seeing/being seen, 152–53, 249; as metastable, 150; and ordinary perception, 158; priority of God's, 149, 151–54, 154n, 171, 249; seeing invisible in visible, 203; three types of seeing Not Other, 202–3; two-sided, 147–48; uncontracted, 152, 152n

Self, 104–9; be/choose your own (self), 157–58; as identical with God seen, 155–56

Self-knowledge, 71–72, 107–9, 115, 248; and self-possession, 157–58

Self-identity, 80; as not other than self, 185

Sells, M., 21n

Senger, G. H., 28n, 30n, 49n, 58n, 62n, 64n, 74n, 198n, 206n

Sensation, 62, 72, 76–77, 81, 81n, 83, 89, 90, 92, 98, 102–3, 105n, 125, 129–32, 138–39, 144; and conjecture, 81, 89–90, 92, 96

Shapes/*configurationes*: in wax, clay, mind, 132–33

Silence, 159–60

Singularity/*singularitas*, 221–22, 221n

Simpleness/simplicity, 7–9, 27, 29, 77, 97, 117–18, 120, 120n, 123, 126, 138n, 162–63, 194–95, 205, 217, 243, 250

Socrates, 2, 3, 9n, 16, 112, 113, 169
Son of man/Son of God, 174–75
Sonship/*filiatio*, 120, 174–75
Soul, 104–9 and body, 110–11, 139–44, 178; creation of, 141–44; immortal, 140–44; in Jesus, 178; as metaphysical unity, 76
Species: sense impression, 131, 170; abstracted from sense experience, 230n
Species, 44, 52, 91, 100
Spoon carving, 123, 141–42
Stachel, G., 154n
Stadler, M., 14n, 119n
Stallmach, J., 20n, 84n, 107n, 180n, 213n
Stock, A., 149n

Tetraktys/tetrad (fourness), 75, 75n, 86–88, 87n, 96–97; doubly mediated, 106, 106n
Thales, 3
Thierry of Chartres, 29n, 36, 99n, 123n, 138n, 222, 241, 243
Things: as mind-independent measures, 128–30, 130n
Thomas, M., 27n, 34n, 80n
Time: and the present/eternity, 120, 138n, 198, 198n; vs. eternal and perpetual, 210–12, 237
Transformation in Jesus Christ 63, 66
Transcendence and immanence, 7–10, 13, 16, 18–19, 23, 24n, 27, 29, 31, 38, 47–48, 51n, 55, 152, 160,162–65, 167, 172, 174, 180, 187, 189, 189n, 190–91, 199–201, 204, 234–35, 238, 243–44, 249, 250–51
Transcendentals, medieval, 121n, 217
Traversari, A., 231n
Trinity: beyond otherness/diversity, 173; in creatures, 223; in universe, 43, 45; in human nature, 59, 109; and Jesus Christ, 55–56; and love, 172–79; in mind, 73, 104, 108, 108n; as Oneness, Equality, Connection, 45, 59, 104n, 108, 109, 120, 220–24; and triad, 97
Trinkaus, C., 103n
Truth, 236–37; in conjecture, 70, 81–84, 131, 247; and God, 85, 118–19, 124, 170–71, 236; and image, 56; and infinite Oneness, 96, 107; in human mind's unfolding, 119; and truths, 5–8; of type, 52
Turner, D., 21n, 51n, 58n, 72n

Unity: of God, 76; of Jesus Christ, 67, 74; mind as operative, 130; of number, 74; in Trinity, 220–24; of universe, 39, 41–42, 54; *See also* Hypostatic union; Oneness.
Unities: four numerical, 75–76, 79, 86–87, 96; four metaphysical, 76–79, 87
Union: with Jesus, 177; with Trinity, 173–75, 173n, 175n
Universals, 43–44, 52, 90–91, 91n; *universalia ante res*, 195, 195n
Universe, 31–48, 70n; as contracted maximum, 39–43, 49; limited in extent, 40; priority to parts, 42; God as center and circumference of, 46–48; of discourse/thought, 124; relation to God, 47; as whole of interrelated parts, 39–42, 51, 59

Van Eyck, J., 150n
Vansteenberghe, E., 148n
Van Velthoven, T., 16n, 72n, 74n, 82n, 129n
Vision: absolute, 152, 164; as ambiguous, 153, 249; conjectural, 72; and creation, 164; divine and human, 147–79; face-to-face, 205; as gift, 165; of God in paradise, 176; and image, 175; intellectual, 5, 7, 8–9, 9n, 10, 20, 70, 70n, 72, 76, 133n, 167, 178, 202–5, 225, 230n, 250; Jesus' vision, 177; meanings of, 159–60; and *ratio*, 158–61; sensory/perceptual, 9, 249; simultaneity of, 72
Volkmann-Schluck, L., 74n
Von Bredow, G., 18n, 36n, 125n, 180n, 222n

Wall of paradise symbol, 148, 161–66, 173, 176, 178, 249–50
Whole, 73; of parts, 39–42, 51, 68; of ideas, concepts, 119
Wilpert, P., 181n, 182n
Wippel, J., 217n
Wisdom, 49, 110, 112–13, 113n, 125, 232–33
Wolter, A., 129n, 239n
Word, Divine, 55, 59, 61–62, 65, 120, 123–24, 150–51, 163, 174–79, 222, 243–44, 250
World: captured in quadrivium 31–32; conceptual, 71, 103, 121, 125, 129; of a painting, 149; physical, 31–48
World soul, 45, 140

Yates, F. A., 198n, 219n
Yamaki, K., 159n

Zimmerman, A., 45n

www.ingramcontent.com/pod-product-compliance
Lightning Source LLC
Chambersburg PA
CBHW031410290426
44110CB00011B/324